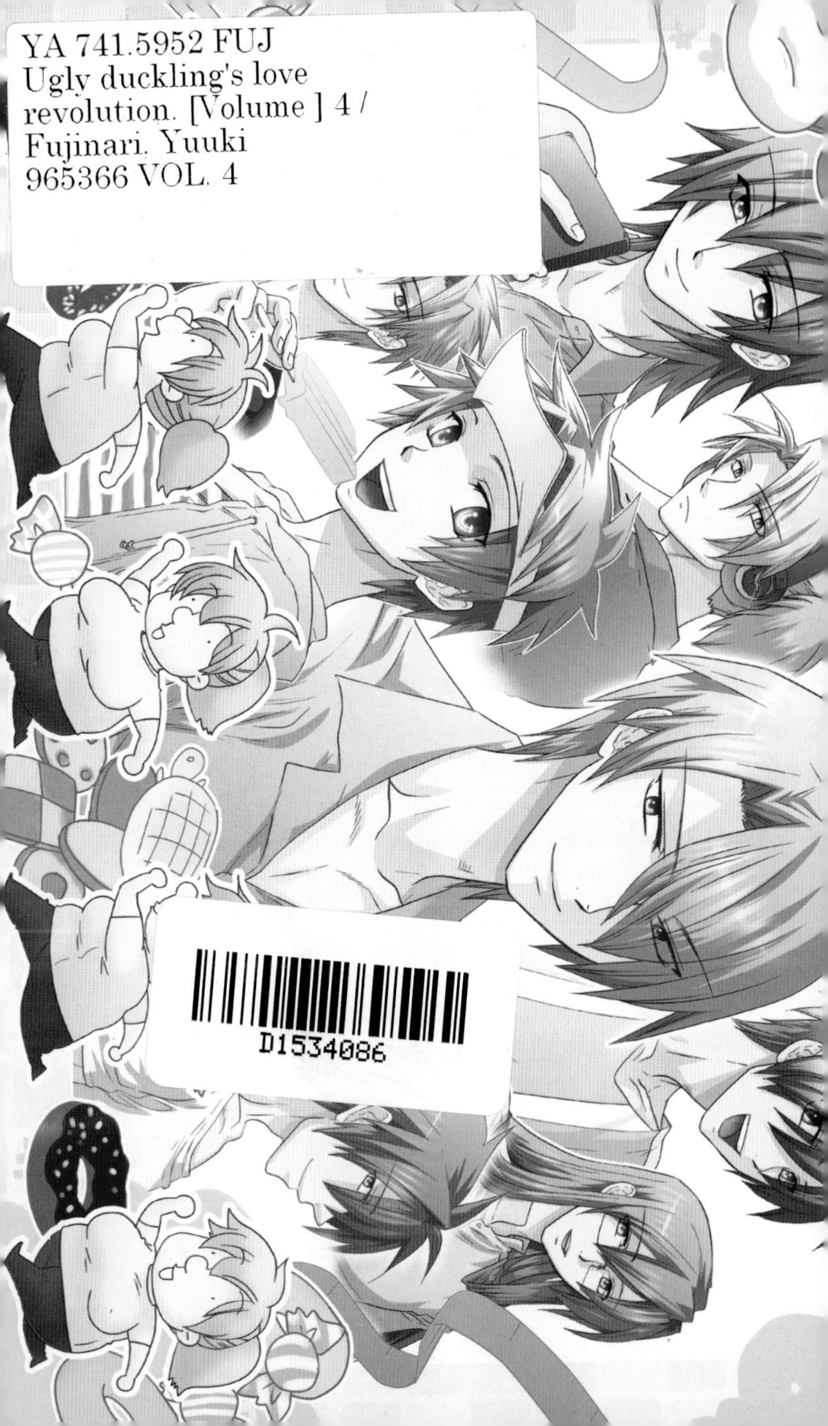

UGLY DUCKLING'S LOVE REVOLUTION

CONTENTS ④

YUUKI
FUJINARI

BASED ON ORIGINAL WORK BY
GungHo Online Entertainment, Inc.

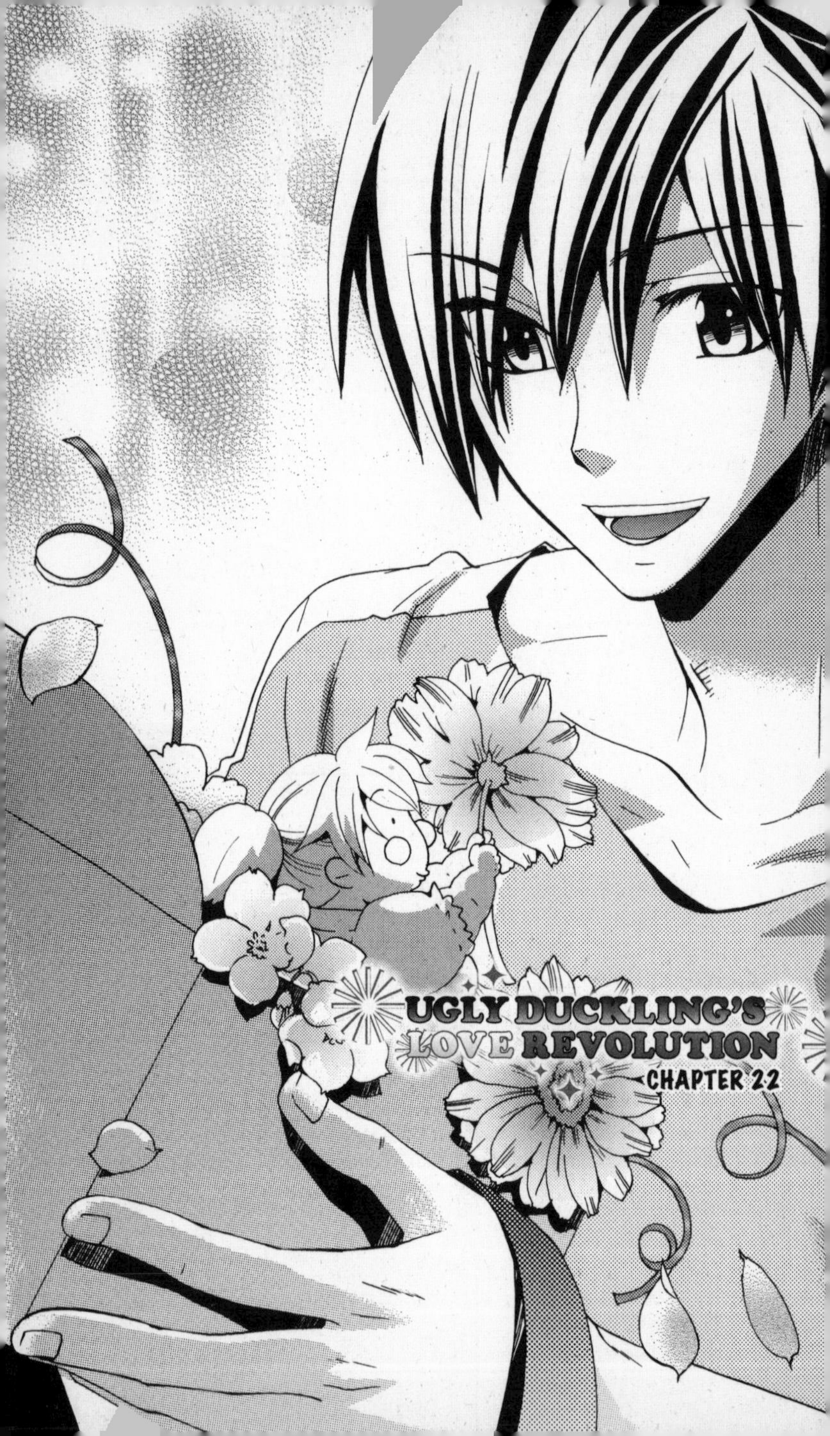
UGLY DUCKLING'S LOVE REVOLUTION
CHAPTER 22

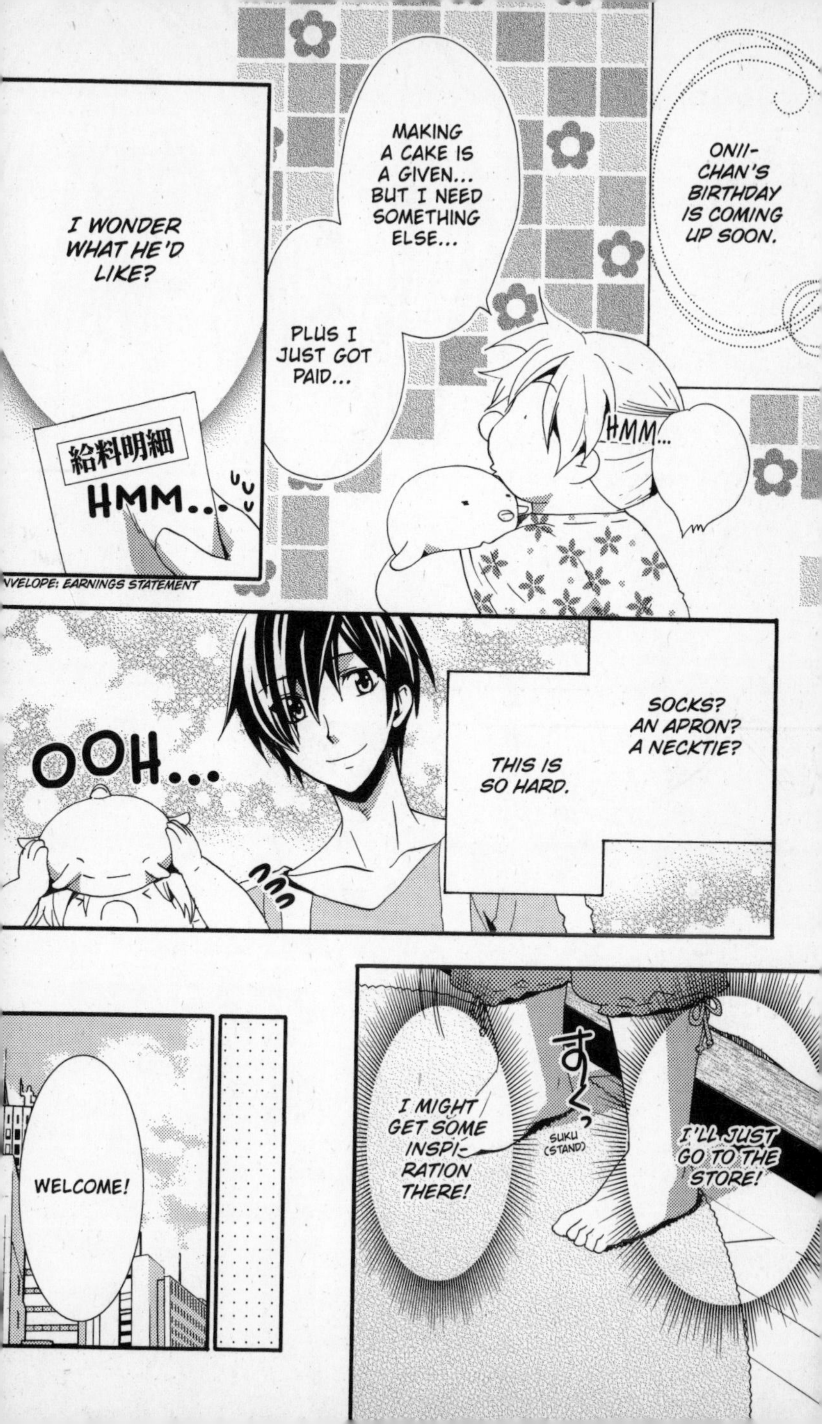
ONII-CHAN'S BIRTHDAY IS COMING UP SOON.
MAKING A CAKE IS A GIVEN... BUT I NEED SOMETHING ELSE...
PLUS I JUST GOT PAID...
HMM...
I WONDER WHAT HE'D LIKE?
給料明細
HMM...
NVELOPE: EARNINGS STATEMENT
SOCKS? AN APRON? A NECKTIE?
THIS IS SO HARD.
OOH...
I'LL JUST GO TO THE STORE!
すくっ
SUKU (STAND)
I MIGHT GET SOME INSPI-RATION THERE!
WELCOME!

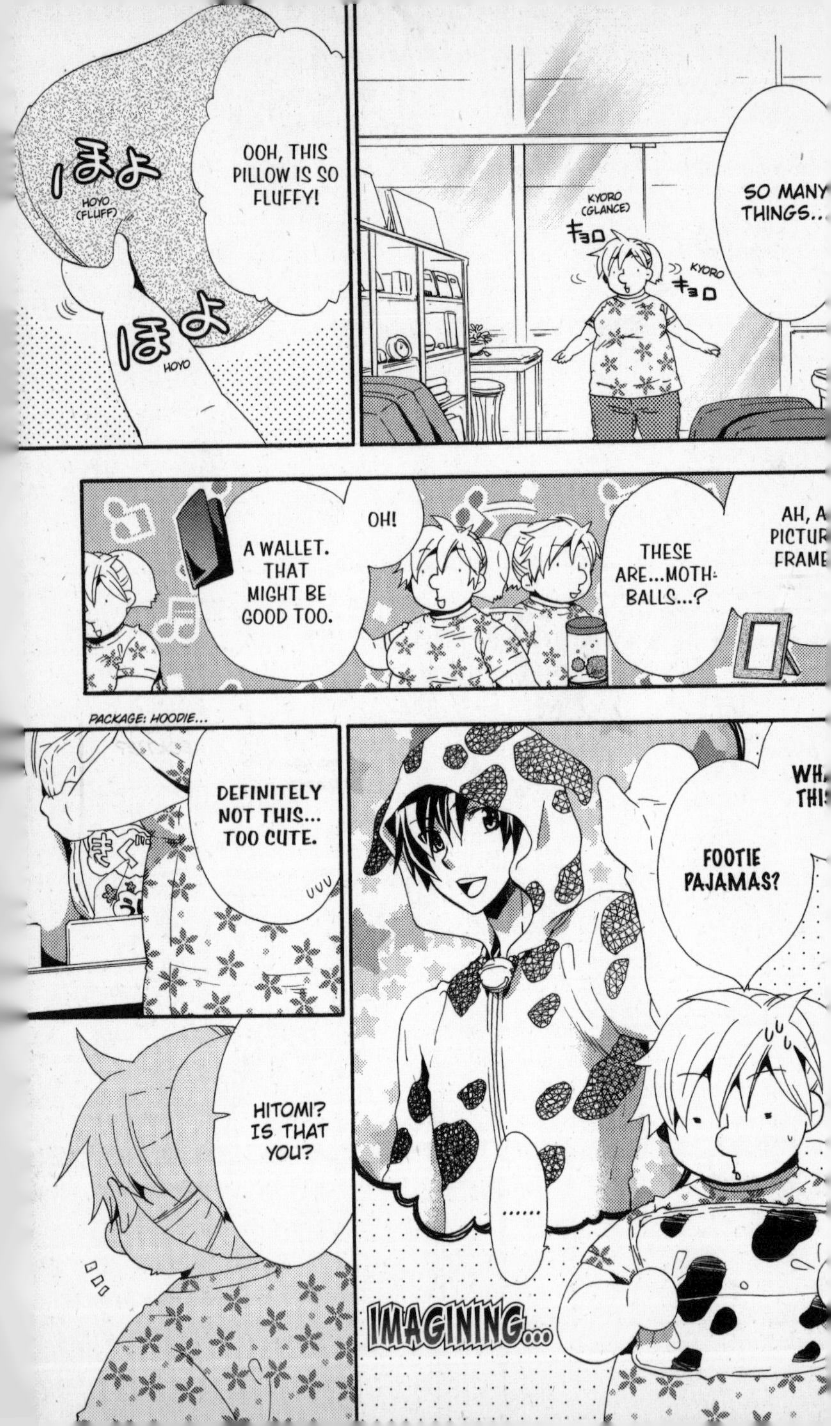
SO MANY THINGS...
KYORO (GLANCE)
キョロ
KYORO
キョロ
OOH, THIS PILLOW IS SO FLUFFY!
ほよ
HOYO (FLUFF)
ほよ
HOYO
AH, A PICTUR FRAME
THESE ARE...MOTH-BALLS...?
OH!
A WALLET. THAT MIGHT BE GOOD TOO.
PACKAGE: HOODIE...
WHA THI
FOOTIE PAJAMAS?
......
IMAGINING...
DEFINITELY NOT THIS... TOO CUTE.
HITOMI? IS THAT YOU?

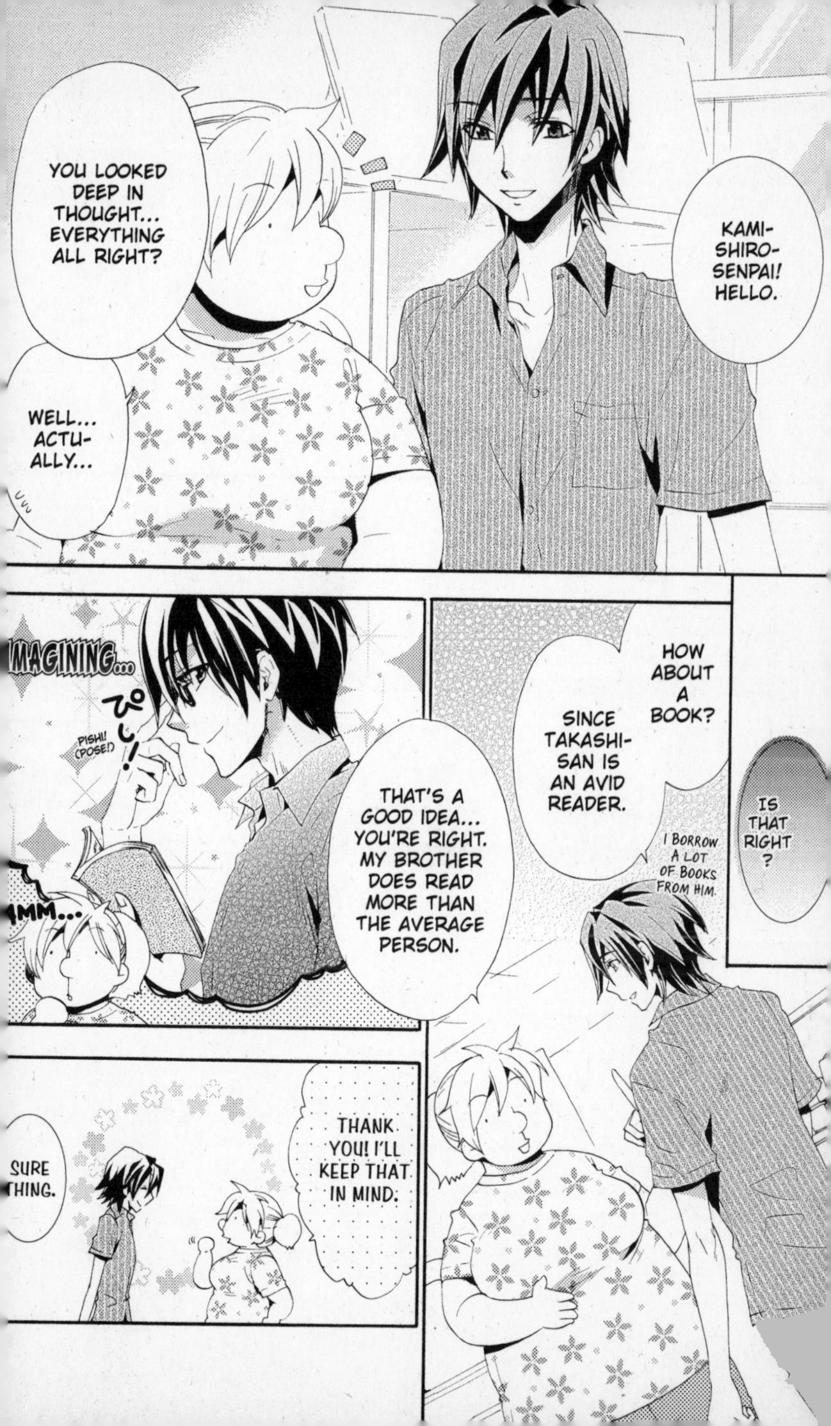
KAMI-SHIRO-SENPAI! HELLO.
YOU LOOKED DEEP IN THOUGHT... EVERYTHING ALL RIGHT?
WELL... ACTU-ALLY...
IS THAT RIGHT?
HOW ABOUT A BOOK?
SINCE TAKASHI-SAN IS AN AVID READER.
I BORROW A LOT OF BOOKS FROM HIM.
THAT'S A GOOD IDEA... YOU'RE RIGHT. MY BROTHER DOES READ MORE THAN THE AVERAGE PERSON.
IMAGINING...
PISHI! (POSE!)
MM...
THANK YOU! I'LL KEEP THAT IN MIND.
SURE THING.

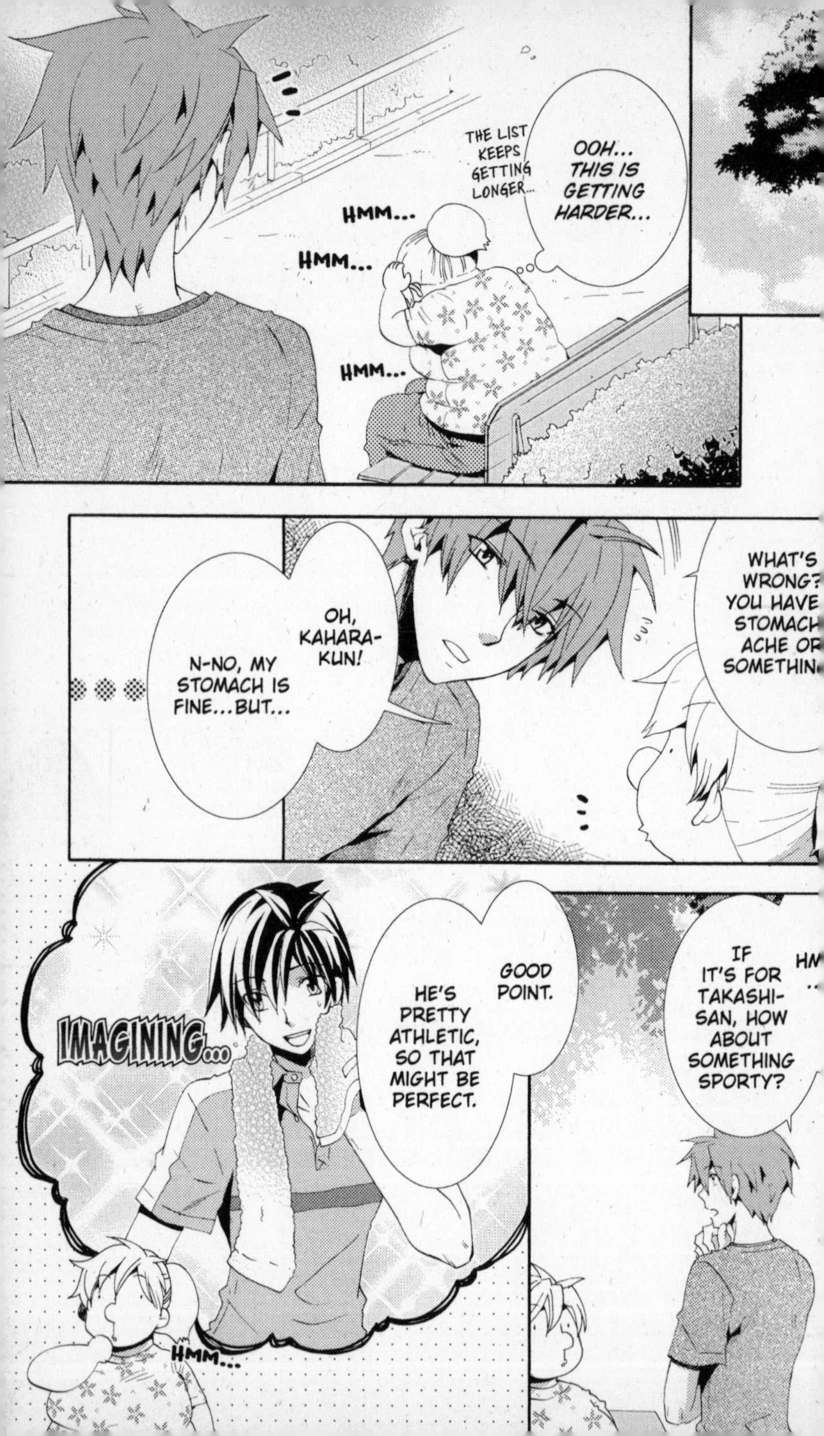
OOH... THIS IS GETTING HARDER...
THE LIST KEEPS GETTING LONGER...
HMM...
HMM...
HMM...
WHAT'S WRONG? YOU HAVE STOMACH ACHE OR SOMETHIN
OH, KAHARA-KUN!
N-NO, MY STOMACH IS FINE...BUT...
HM
IF IT'S FOR TAKASHI-SAN, HOW ABOUT SOMETHING SPORTY?
GOOD POINT.
HE'S PRETTY ATHLETIC, SO THAT MIGHT BE PERFECT.
IMAGINING...
HMM...

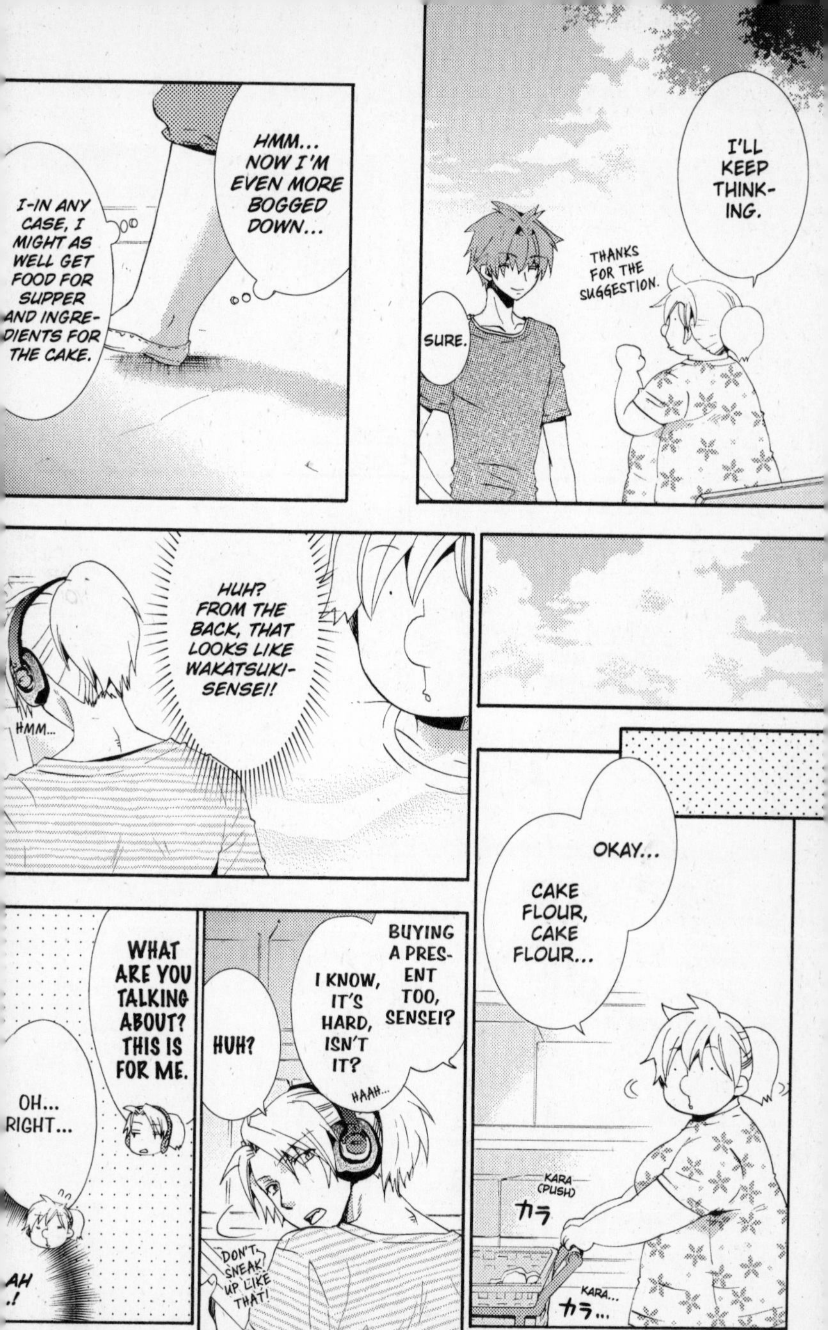
I'LL KEEP THINKING.
THANKS FOR THE SUGGESTION.
SURE.
HMM... NOW I'M EVEN MORE BOGGED DOWN...
I-IN ANY CASE, I MIGHT AS WELL GET FOOD FOR SUPPER AND INGREDIENTS FOR THE CAKE.
OKAY...
CAKE FLOUR, CAKE FLOUR...
KARA (PUSH)
カラ
KARA...
カラ...
HUH? FROM THE BACK, THAT LOOKS LIKE WAKATSUKI-SENSEI!
HMM...
BUYING A PRESENT TOO, SENSEI?
I KNOW, IT'S HARD, ISN'T IT?
HAAH...
HUH?
DON'T SNEAK UP LIKE THAT!
WHAT ARE YOU TALKING ABOUT? THIS IS FOR ME.
OH... RIGHT...
AH .!

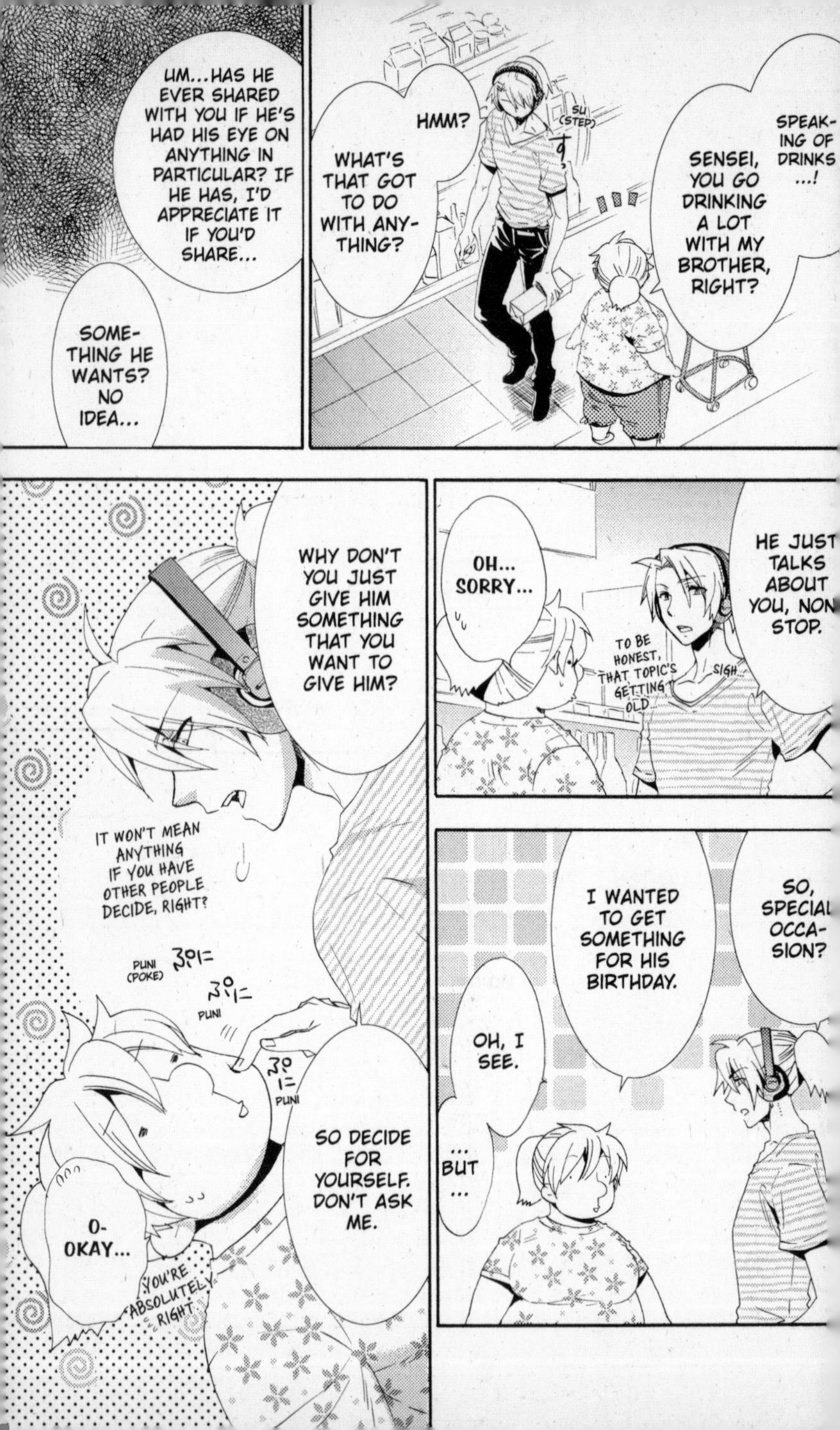
SPEAK-ING OF DRINKS ...!
SENSEI, YOU GO DRINKING A LOT WITH MY BROTHER, RIGHT?
HMM?
SU (STEP)
WHAT'S THAT GOT TO DO WITH ANY-THING?
UM...HAS HE EVER SHARED WITH YOU IF HE'S HAD HIS EYE ON ANYTHING IN PARTICULAR? IF HE HAS, I'D APPRECIATE IT IF YOU'D SHARE...
SOME-THING HE WANTS? NO IDEA...
HE JUST TALKS ABOUT YOU, NON STOP.
TO BE HONEST, THAT TOPIC'S GETTING OLD...
SIGH...
OH... SORRY...
SO, SPECIAL OCCA-SION?
I WANTED TO GET SOMETHING FOR HIS BIRTHDAY.
OH, I SEE.
... BUT ...
WHY DON'T YOU JUST GIVE HIM SOMETHING THAT YOU WANT TO GIVE HIM?
IT WON'T MEAN ANYTHING IF YOU HAVE OTHER PEOPLE DECIDE, RIGHT?
PUNI (POKE)
PUNI
PUNI
SO DECIDE FOR YOURSELF. DON'T ASK ME.
O-OKAY...
YOU'RE ABSOLUTELY RIGHT

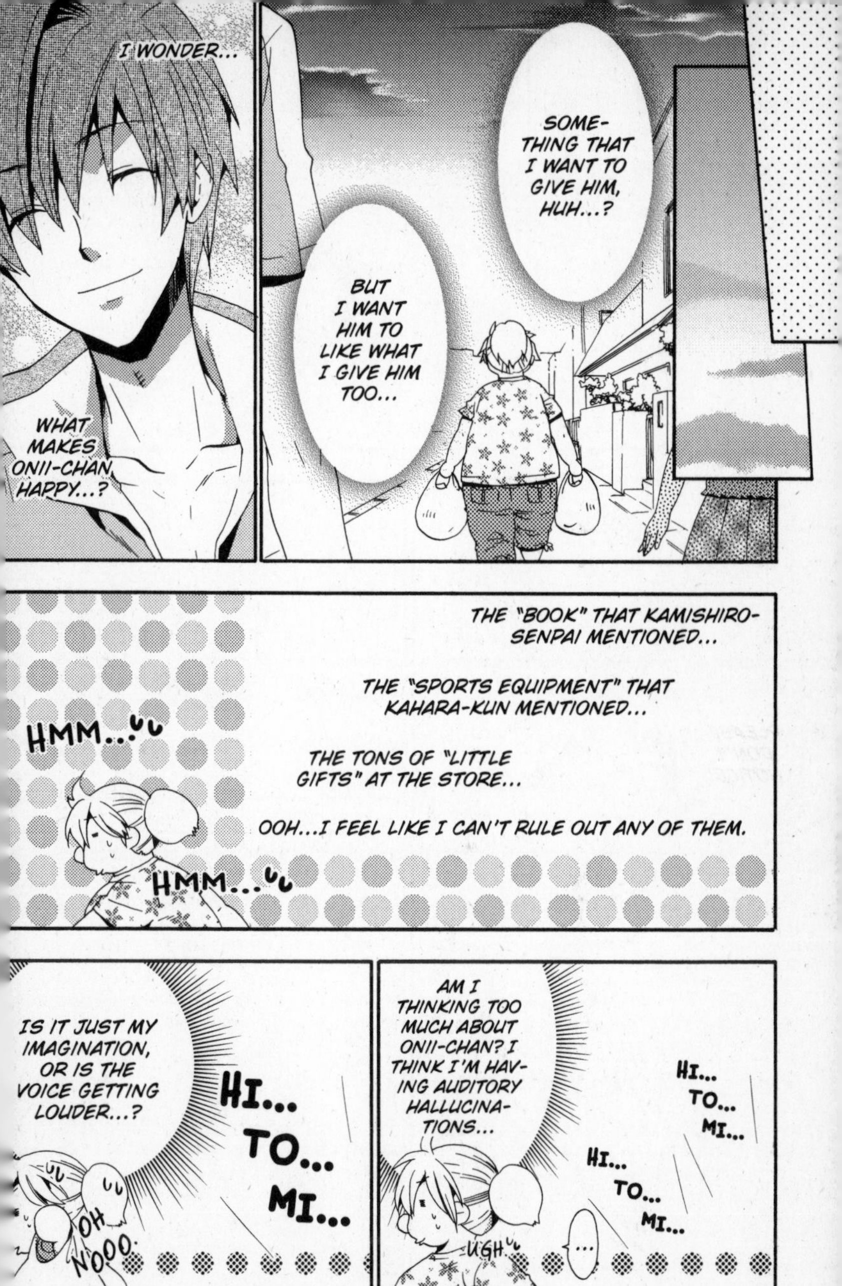
SOMETHING THAT I WANT TO GIVE HIM, HUH...?
BUT I WANT HIM TO LIKE WHAT I GIVE HIM TOO...
I WONDER...
WHAT MAKES ONII-CHAN HAPPY...?
THE "BOOK" THAT KAMISHIRO-SENPAI MENTIONED...
THE "SPORTS EQUIPMENT" THAT KAHARA-KUN MENTIONED...
THE TONS OF "LITTLE GIFTS" AT THE STORE...
OOH...I FEEL LIKE I CAN'T RULE OUT ANY OF THEM.
HMM...
HMM...
AM I THINKING TOO MUCH ABOUT ONII-CHAN? I THINK I'M HAVING AUDITORY HALLUCINATIONS...
HI... TO... MI...
HI... TO... MI...
UGH
...
IS IT JUST MY IMAGINATION, OR IS THE VOICE GETTING LOUDER...?
HI... TO... MI...
OH NOOO

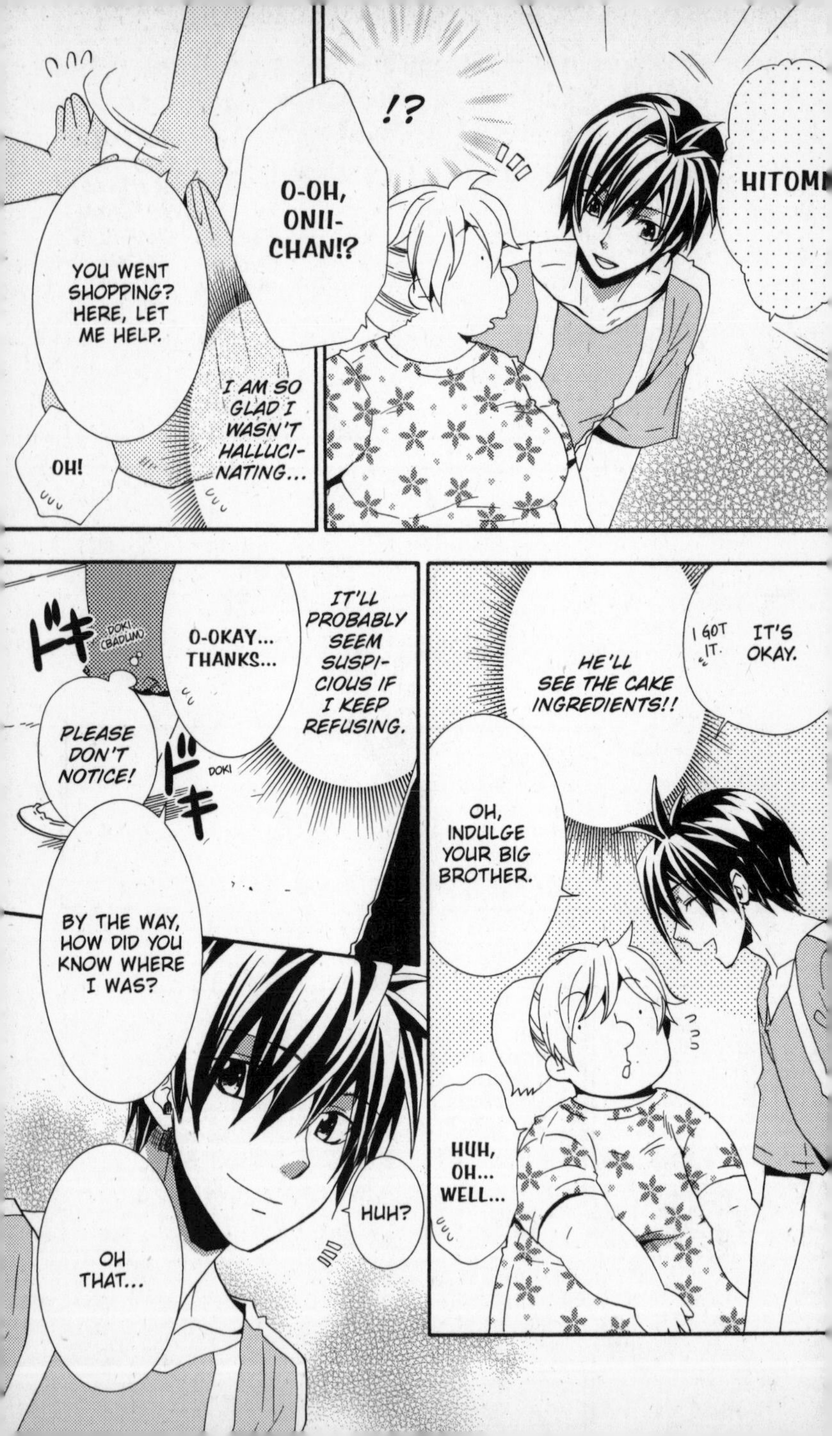
HITOMI
!?
O-OH, ONII-CHAN!?
YOU WENT SHOPPING? HERE, LET ME HELP.
I AM SO GLAD I WASN'T HALLUCINATING...
OH!
IT'S OKAY.
I GOT IT.
HE'LL SEE THE CAKE INGREDIENTS!!
OH, INDULGE YOUR BIG BROTHER.
HUH, OH... WELL...
IT'LL PROBABLY SEEM SUSPICIOUS IF I KEEP REFUSING.
O-OKAY... THANKS...
ドキ
DOKI (BADUM)
PLEASE DON'T NOTICE!
ドキ
DOKI
BY THE WAY, HOW DID YOU KNOW WHERE I WAS?
HUH?
OH THAT...

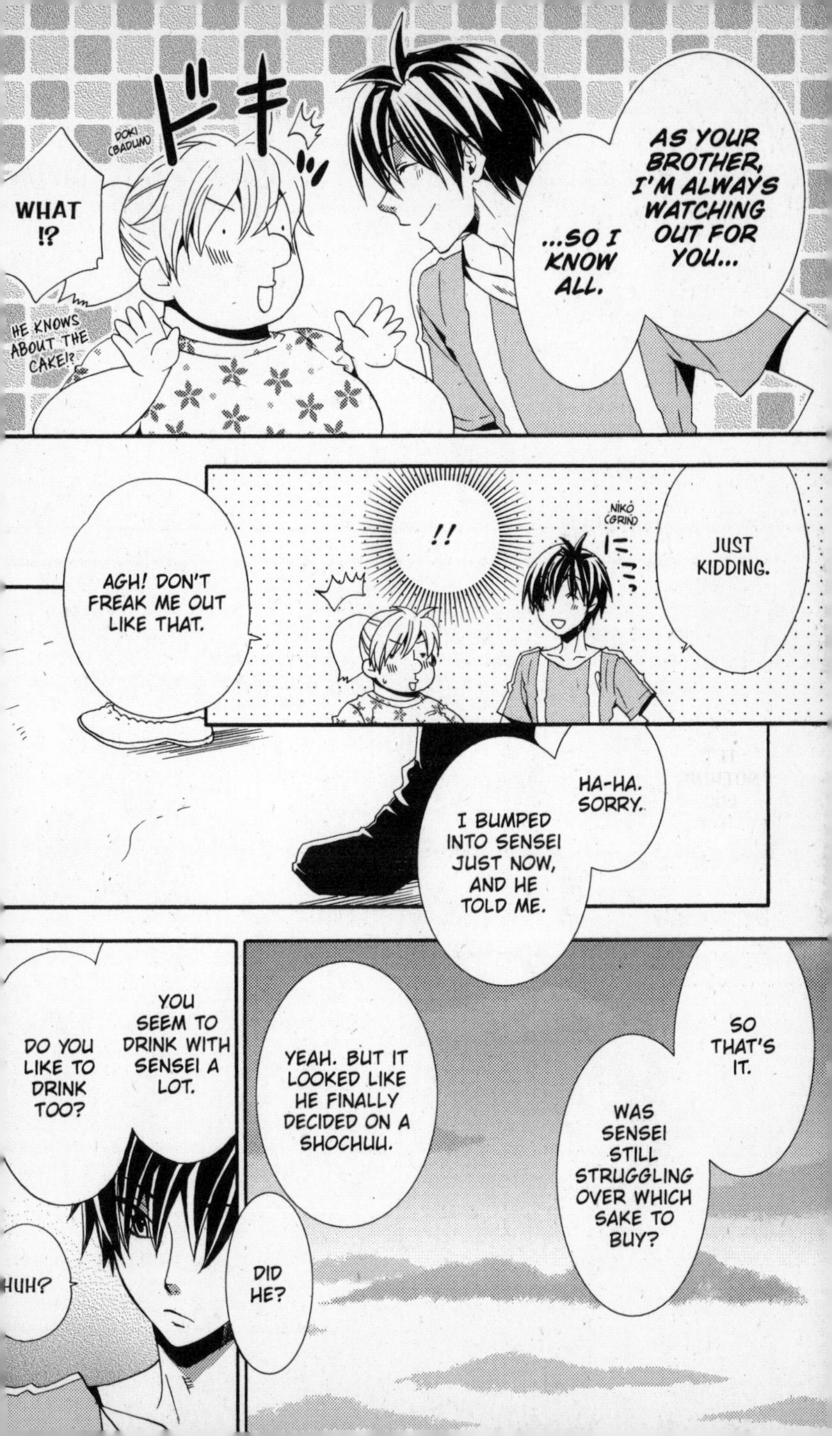
AS YOUR BROTHER, I'M ALWAYS WATCHING OUT FOR YOU...
...SO I KNOW ALL.
DOKI (BADUM)
WHAT!?
HE KNOWS ABOUT THE CAKE!?
NIKO (GRIN)
JUST KIDDING.
!!
AGH! DON'T FREAK ME OUT LIKE THAT.
HA-HA. SORRY.
I BUMPED INTO SENSEI JUST NOW, AND HE TOLD ME.
SO THAT'S IT.
WAS SENSEI STILL STRUGGLING OVER WHICH SAKE TO BUY?
YEAH. BUT IT LOOKED LIKE HE FINALLY DECIDED ON A SHOCHUU.
DID HE?
YOU SEEM TO DRINK WITH SENSEI A LOT.
DO YOU LIKE TO DRINK TOO?
HUH?

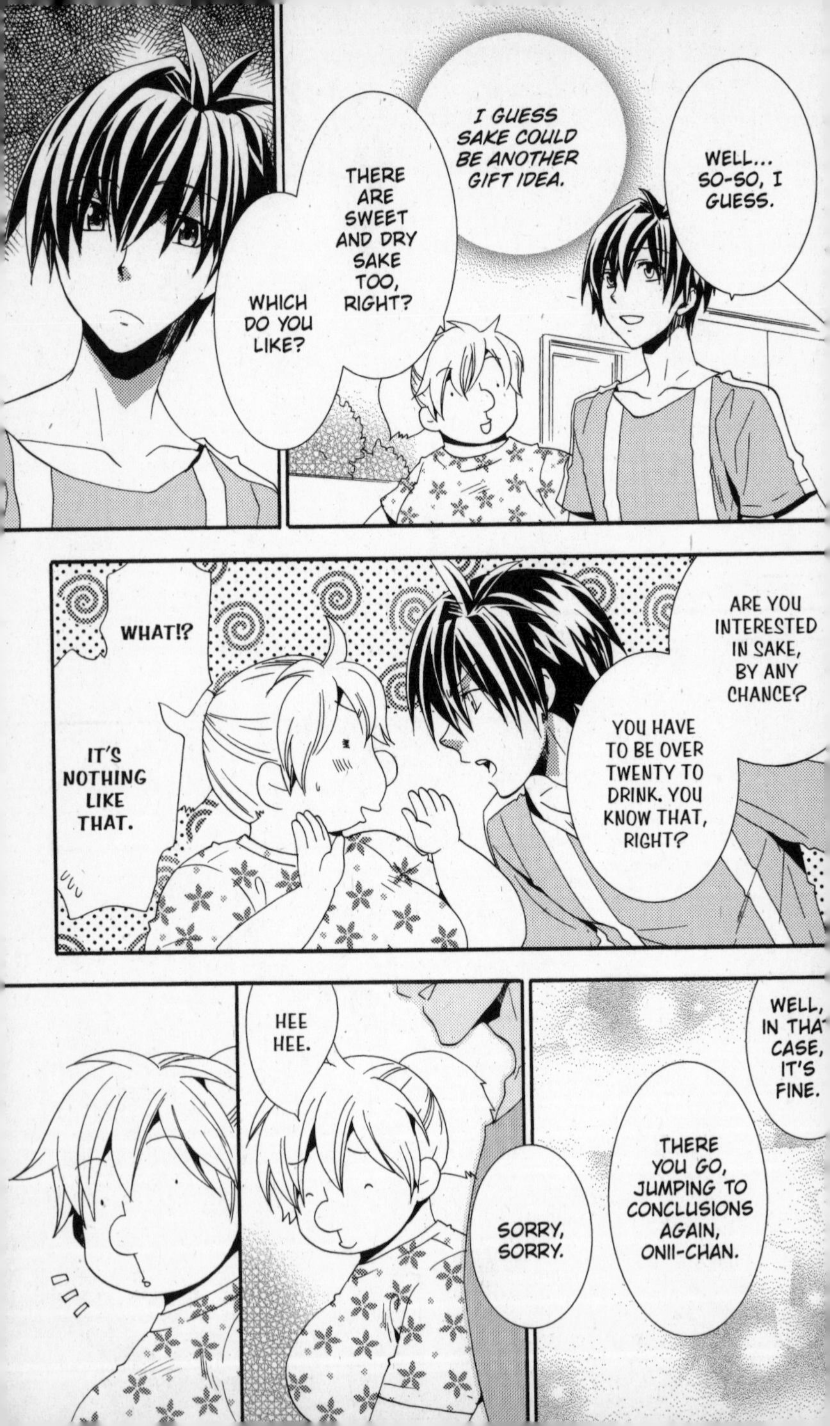
WELL... SO-SO, I GUESS.
I GUESS SAKE COULD BE ANOTHER GIFT IDEA.
THERE ARE SWEET AND DRY SAKE TOO, RIGHT?
WHICH DO YOU LIKE?
ARE YOU INTERESTED IN SAKE, BY ANY CHANCE?
YOU HAVE TO BE OVER TWENTY TO DRINK. YOU KNOW THAT, RIGHT?
WHAT!?
IT'S NOTHING LIKE THAT.
WELL, IN THA CASE, IT'S FINE.
THERE YOU GO, JUMPING TO CONCLUSIONS AGAIN, ONII-CHAN.
SORRY, SORRY.
HEE HEE.

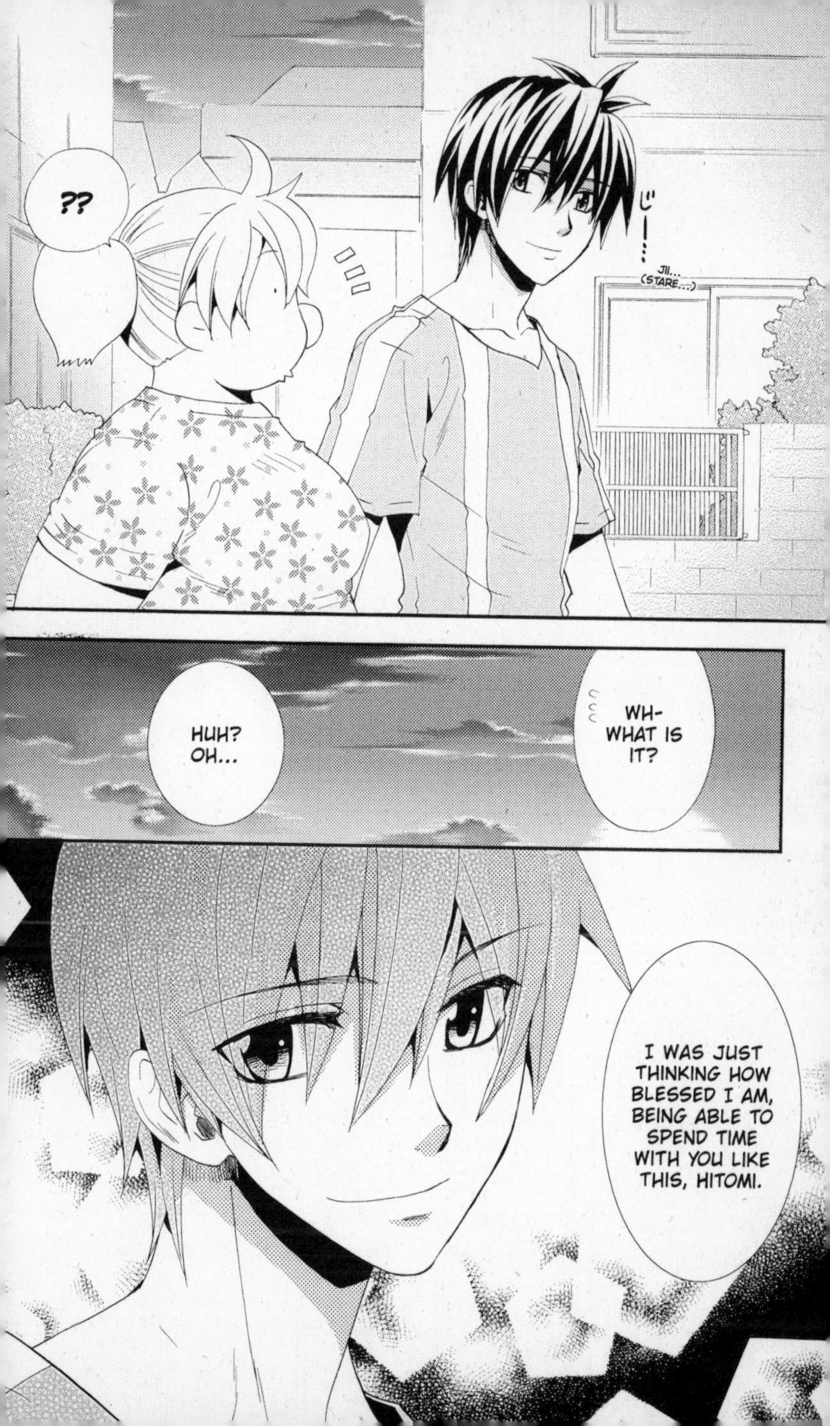
じー…
JII... (STARE...)
??
WH- WHAT IS IT?
HUH? OH...
I WAS JUST THINKING HOW BLESSED I AM, BEING ABLE TO SPEND TIME WITH YOU LIKE THIS, HITOMI.

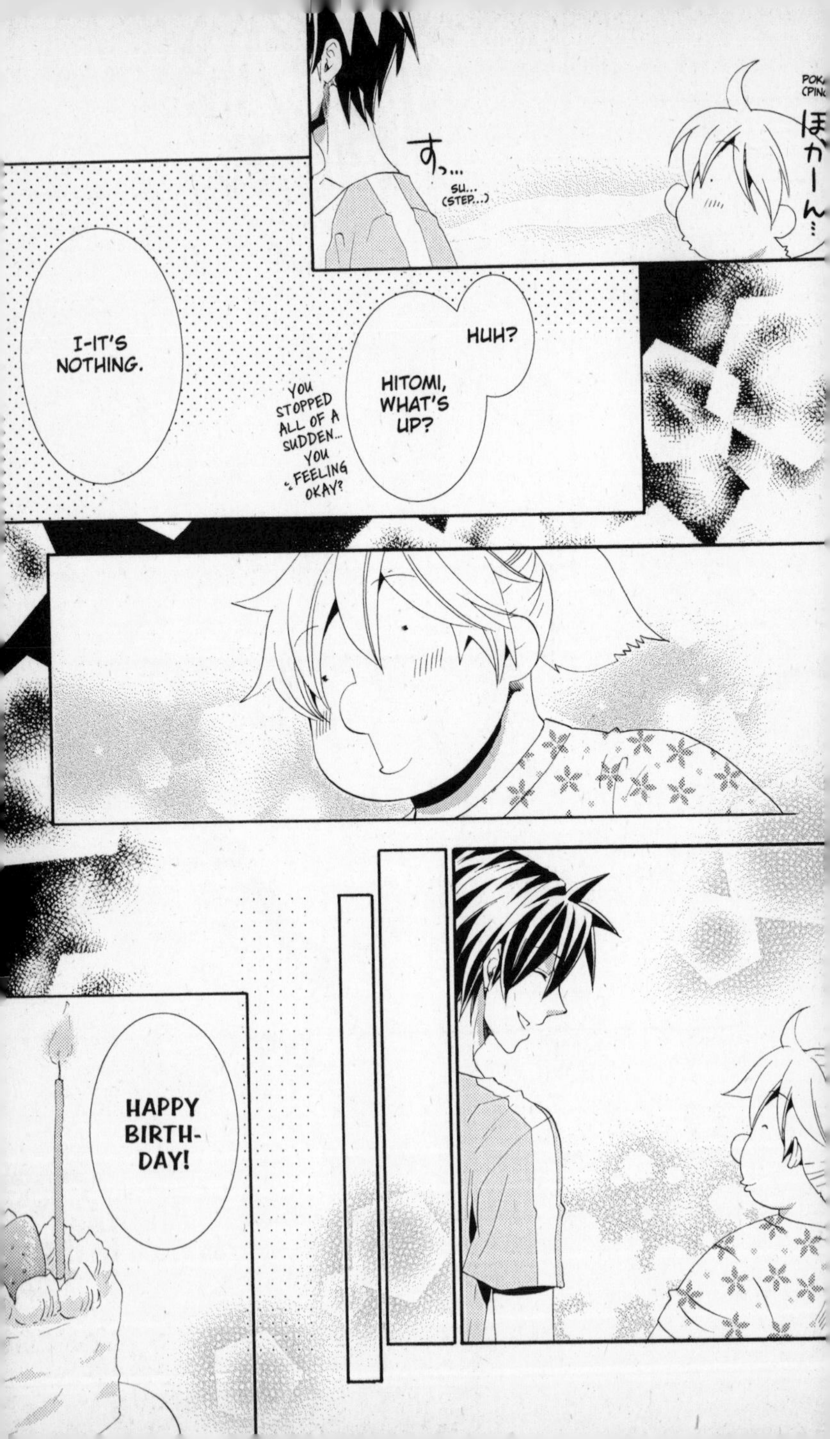

POK
(PIN
ほかーん…
すっ…
SU... (STEP...)
HUH?
HITOMI, WHAT'S UP?
YOU STOPPED ALL OF A SUDDEN... YOU FEELING OKAY?
I-IT'S NOTHING.
HAPPY BIRTH-DAY!

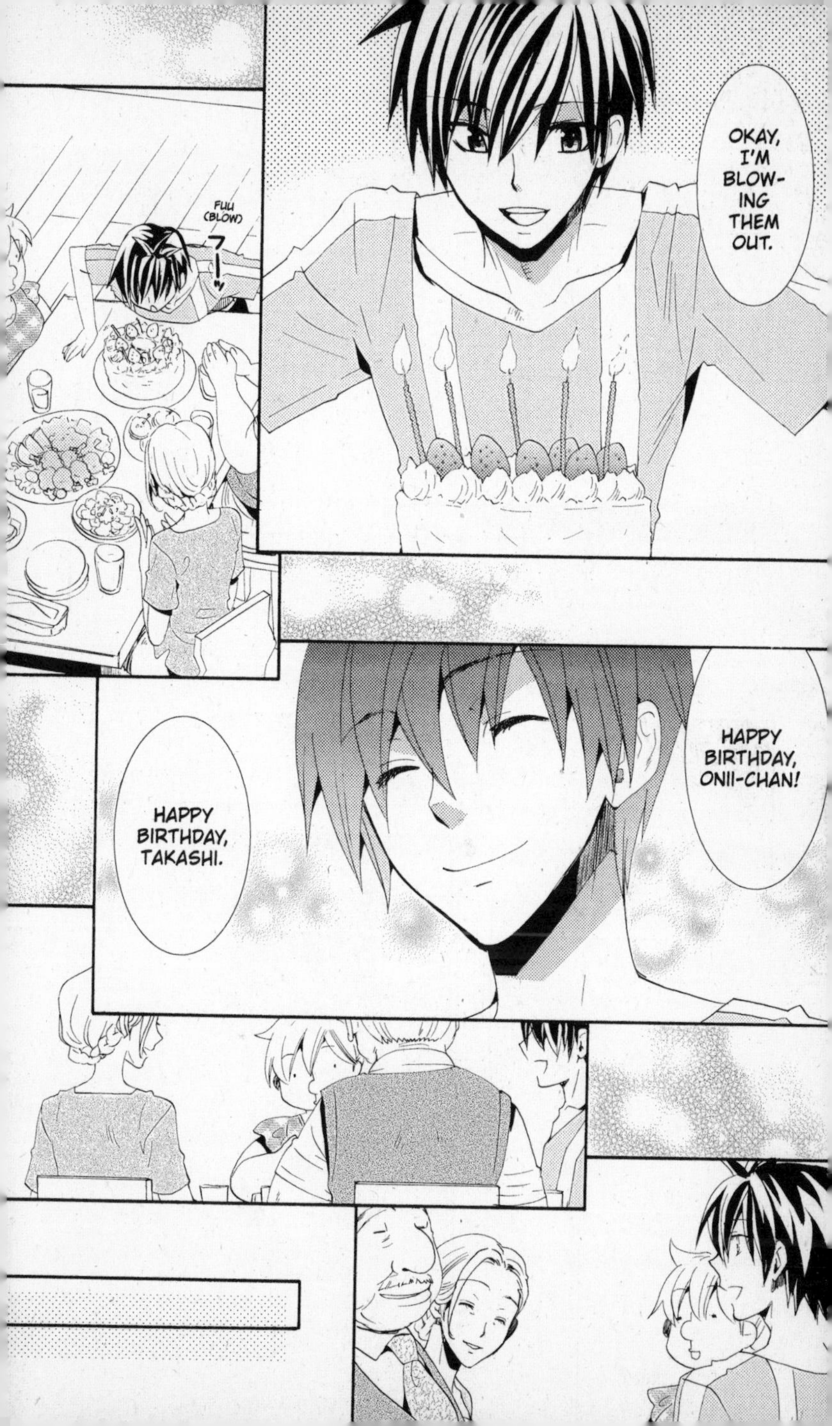
OKAY, I'M BLOWING THEM OUT.
FUU (BLOW)
HAPPY BIRTHDAY, ONII-CHAN!
HAPPY BIRTHDAY, TAKASHI.

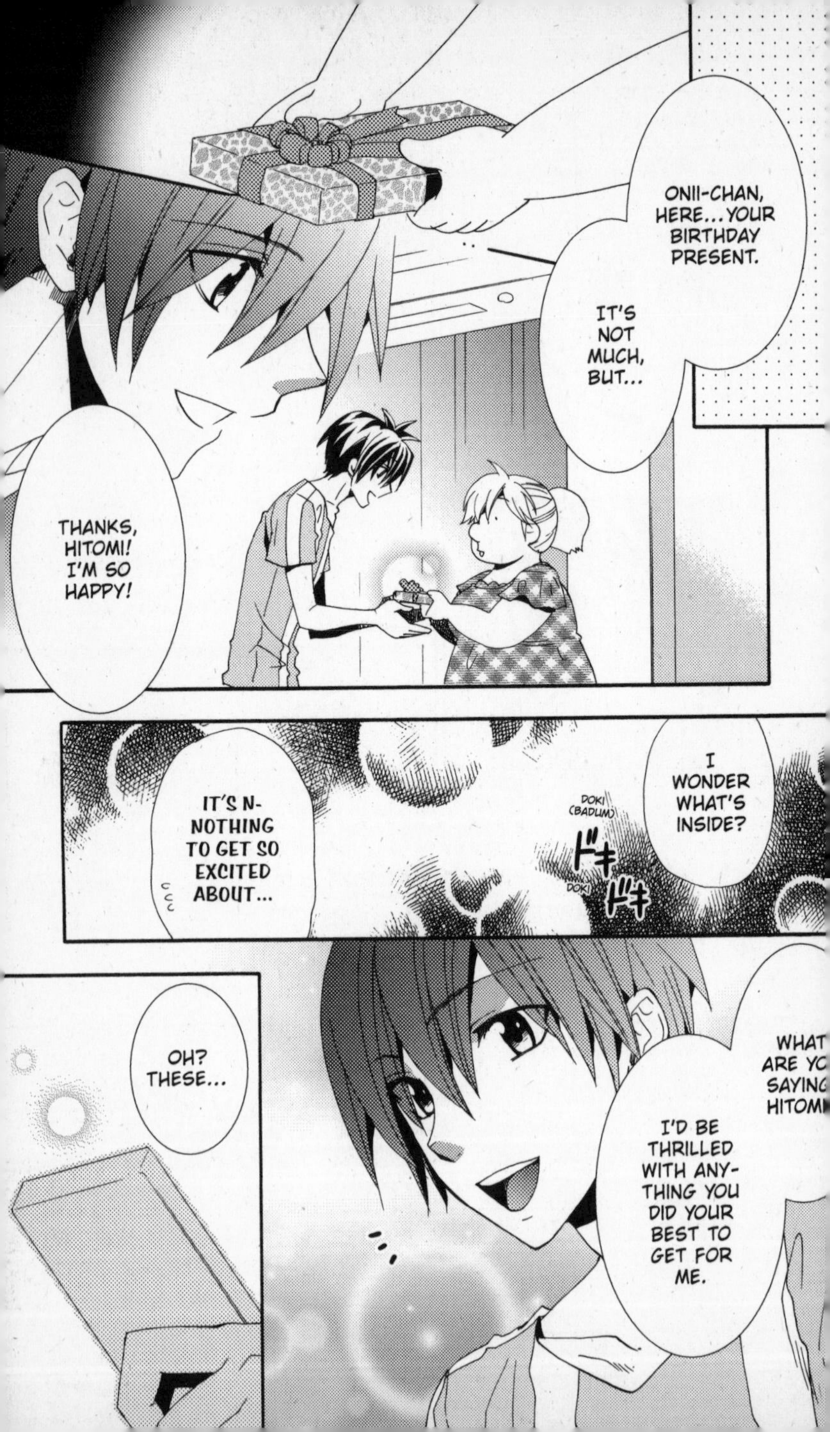
ONII-CHAN, HERE...YOUR BIRTHDAY PRESENT.
IT'S NOT MUCH, BUT...
THANKS, HITOMI! I'M SO HAPPY!
I WONDER WHAT'S INSIDE?
DOKI (BADUM)
ドキ
DOKI
ドキ
IT'S N-NOTHING TO GET SO EXCITED ABOUT...
WHAT ARE YO SAYING HITOM
I'D BE THRILLED WITH ANY-THING YOU DID YOUR BEST TO GET FOR ME.
OH? THESE...

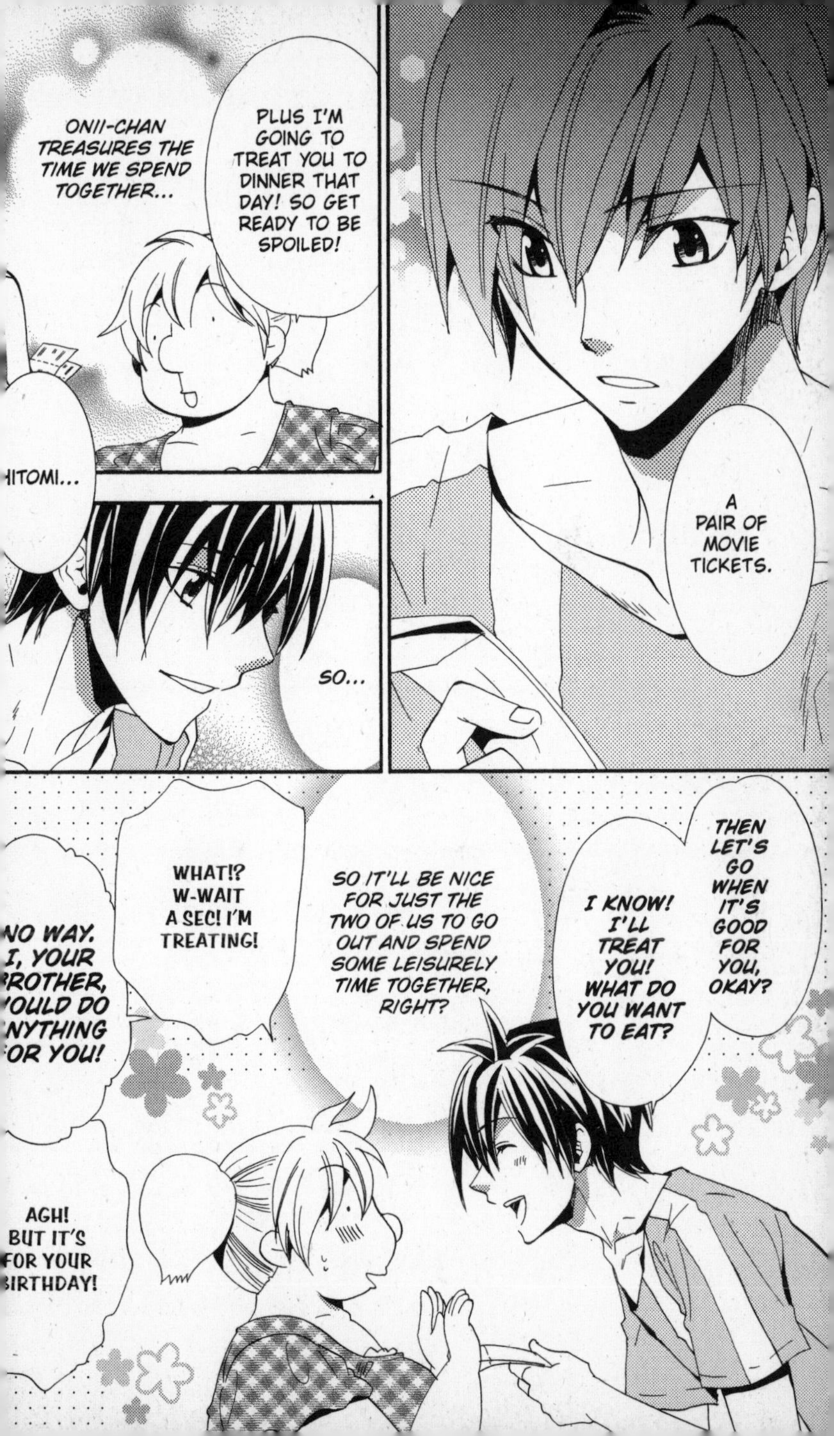
A PAIR OF MOVIE TICKETS.
PLUS I'M GOING TO TREAT YOU TO DINNER THAT DAY! SO GET READY TO BE SPOILED!
ONII-CHAN TREASURES THE TIME WE SPEND TOGETHER...
HITOMI...
SO...
THEN LET'S GO WHEN IT'S GOOD FOR YOU, OKAY?
I KNOW! I'LL TREAT YOU! WHAT DO YOU WANT TO EAT?
SO IT'LL BE NICE FOR JUST THE TWO OF US TO GO OUT AND SPEND SOME LEISURELY TIME TOGETHER, RIGHT?
WHAT!? W-WAIT A SEC! I'M TREATING!
NO WAY. I, YOUR BROTHER, WOULD DO ANYTHING FOR YOU!
AGH! BUT IT'S FOR YOUR BIRTHDAY!

UGLY DUCKLING'S LOVE REVOLUTION

OUR HEROINE IS A 220-POUND HIGH SCHOOL SOPHOMORE. ONE DAY, A GROUP OF THE MOST GORGEOUS GUYS...LIKE THE SCHOOL'S #1 COOL GUY AND THE DOC WITH A REPUTATION AS A LADIES' MAN...MOVES INTO HER FATHER'S APARTMENT COMPLEX!! WHAT NOW...!?

★ STORY CHARACTERS ♥

★ HITOMI SAKURAGAWA

FAMOUS FOR HER BEAUTY WHEN SHE WAS LITTLE, SHE FELL PREY TO THE SEDUCTION OF SWEETS. BEFORE SHE REALIZED IT, SHE HAD SWELLED TO 220 LBS. OPTIMISTIC AND BRIGHT. A HIGH SCHOOL SOPHOMORE WORKING HARD ON HER DIET.

★ HITOMI'S BROTHER

HITOMI'S OLDER BROTHER. THINKS HIS SISTER IS THE CUTEST PERSON IN THE WORLD. AVIDLY CHEERS HER ON WITH HER DIET. WORKING AS THE APARTMENT MANAGER WHERE THE OTHER STORY CHARACTERS LIVE.

UGLY DUCKLING'S LOVE REVOLUTION

♥ STORY CHARACTERS

★ REN ICHINOSE

...ERFECTION PERSONIFIED, THE #1 MOST
...OPULAR GUY IN SCHOOL. WITH A DETACHED,
...OOL PERSONALITY, HE'S ALSO VERY BLUNT
...ITH HIS COMMENTS. JUNIOR.

★ SOUTA FUKAMI

LOVES SPORTS! LOVES SWEETS! QUITE
THE ENERGETIC GUY. FOR SOME REASON,
VERY ATTACHED TO HITOMI! IS IN THE SAME
EXTRACURRICULAR CLUB AS HITOMI AS WELL.
FRESHMAN.

★ ...KENNOSUKE TACHIBANA

...OUGH GUY WITH A BRUSQUE PERSONALITY.
...INCE HIS FATHER IS A YAKUZA BOSS, IS
...ALLED "WAKA" AT HOME. HAS THREE SISTERS.
...FRESHMAN BASKETBALL STAR.

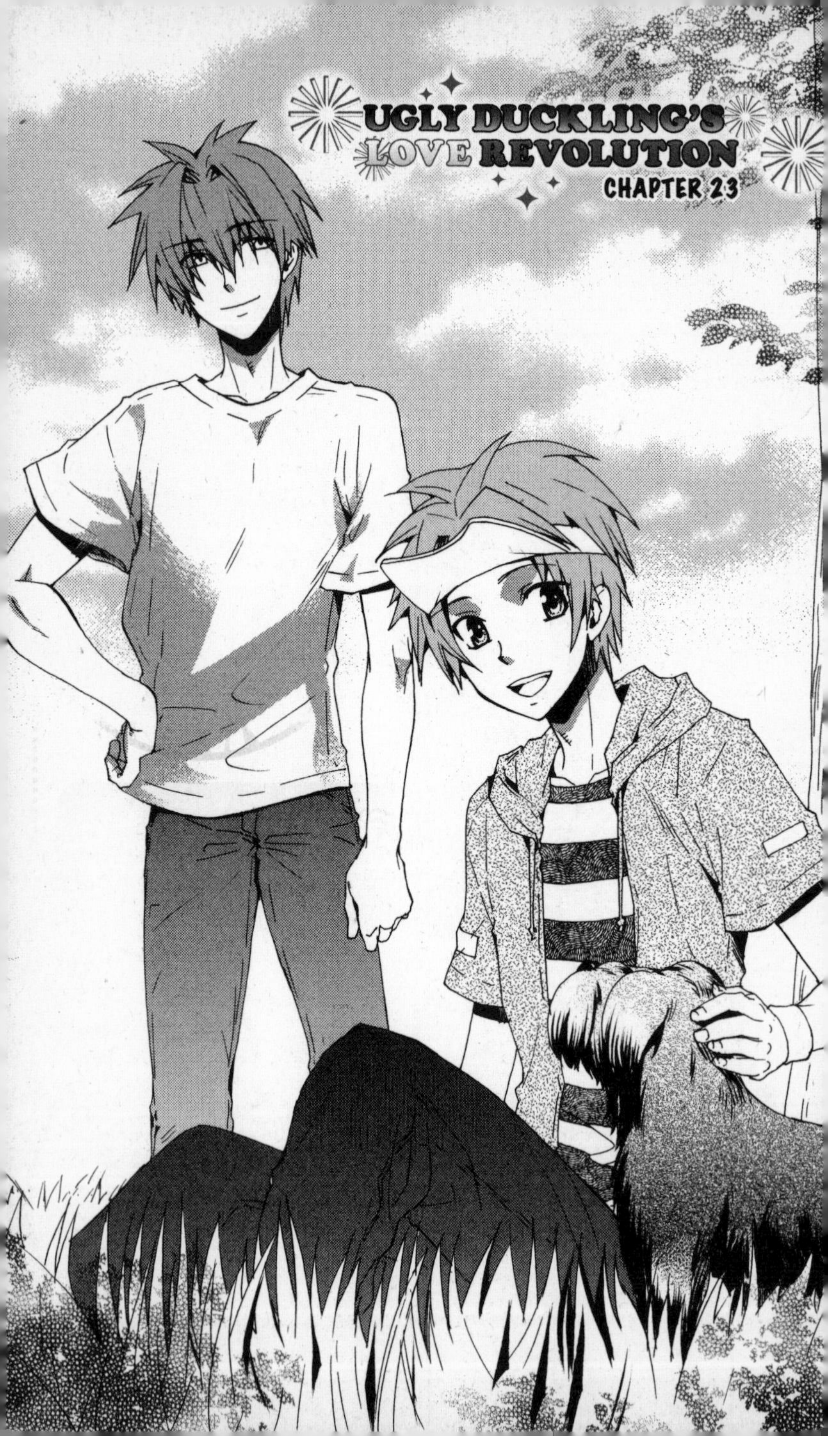
UGLY DUCKLING'S LOVE REVOLUTION
CHAPTER 23

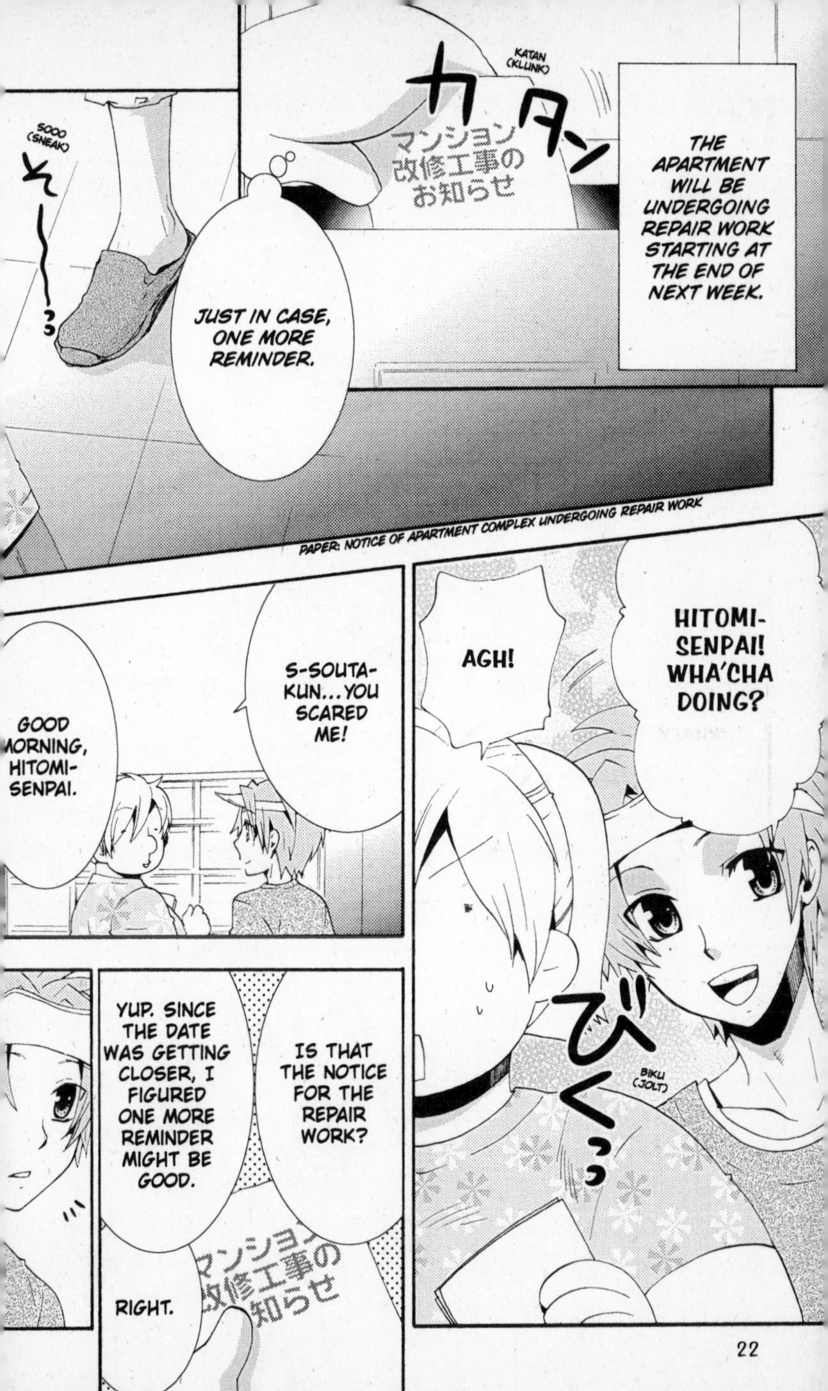
THE APARTMENT WILL BE UNDERGOING REPAIR WORK STARTING AT THE END OF NEXT WEEK.
カタン
KATAN (KLUNK)
マンション改修工事のお知らせ
JUST IN CASE, ONE MORE REMINDER.
そ〜〜っ
SOOO (SNEAK)
PAPER: NOTICE OF APARTMENT COMPLEX UNDERGOING REPAIR WORK
HITOMI-SENPAI! WHA'CHA DOING?
AGH!
びくっ
BIKU (JOLT)
S-SOUTA-KUN...YOU SCARED ME!
GOOD MORNING, HITOMI-SENPAI.
IS THAT THE NOTICE FOR THE REPAIR WORK?
YUP. SINCE THE DATE WAS GETTING CLOSER, I FIGURED ONE MORE REMINDER MIGHT BE GOOD.
マンション改修工事のお知らせ
RIGHT.

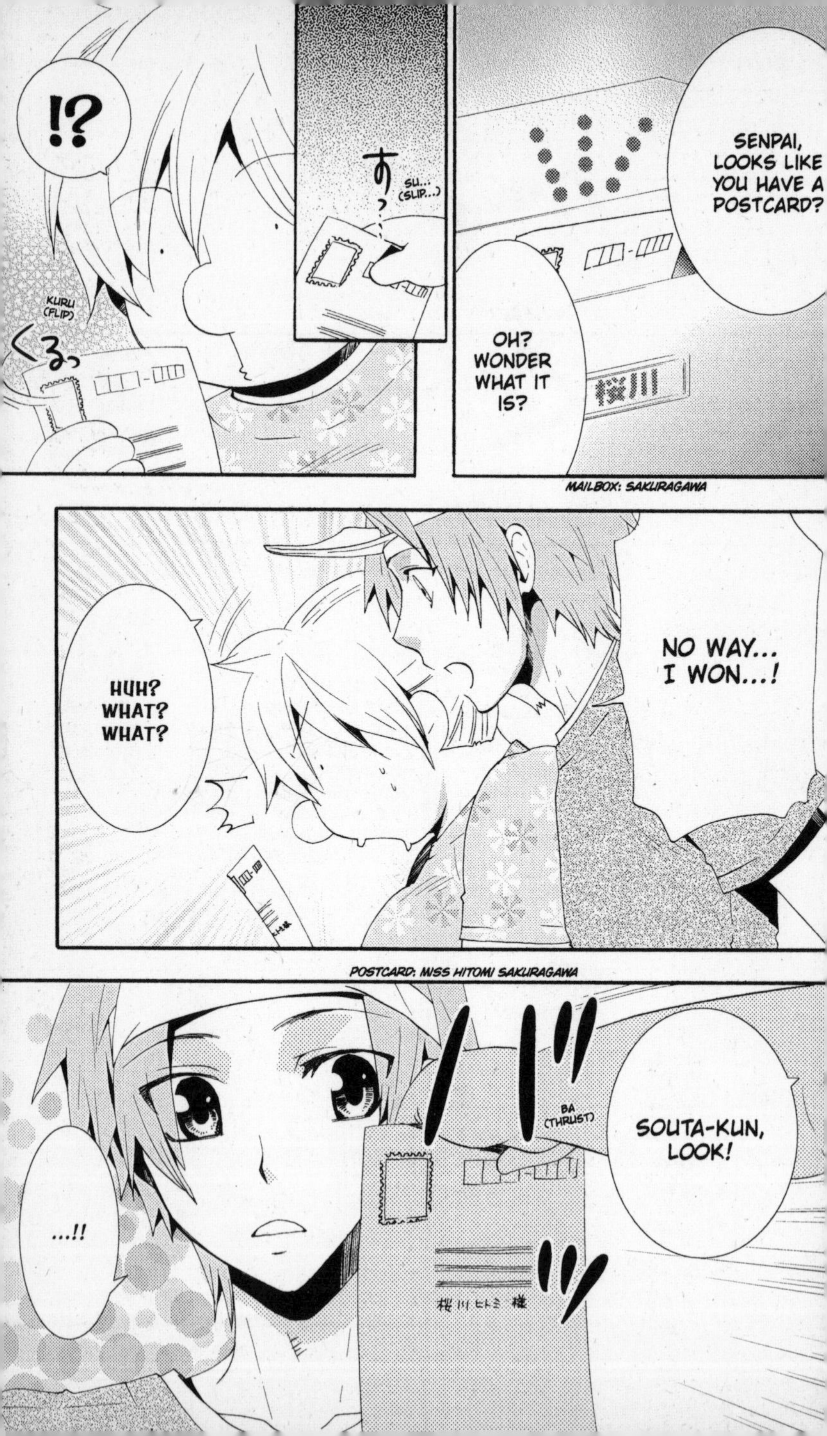

SENPAI, LOOKS LIKE YOU HAVE A POSTCARD?
OH? WONDER WHAT IT IS?
桜川
MAILBOX: SAKURAGAWA
すっ
SU... (SLIP...)
!?
KURU (FLIP)
くるっ
NO WAY... I WON...!
HUH? WHAT? WHAT?
POSTCARD: MISS HITOMI SAKURAGAWA
SOUTA-KUN, LOOK!
BA (THRUST)
...!!
桜川ヒトミ 様

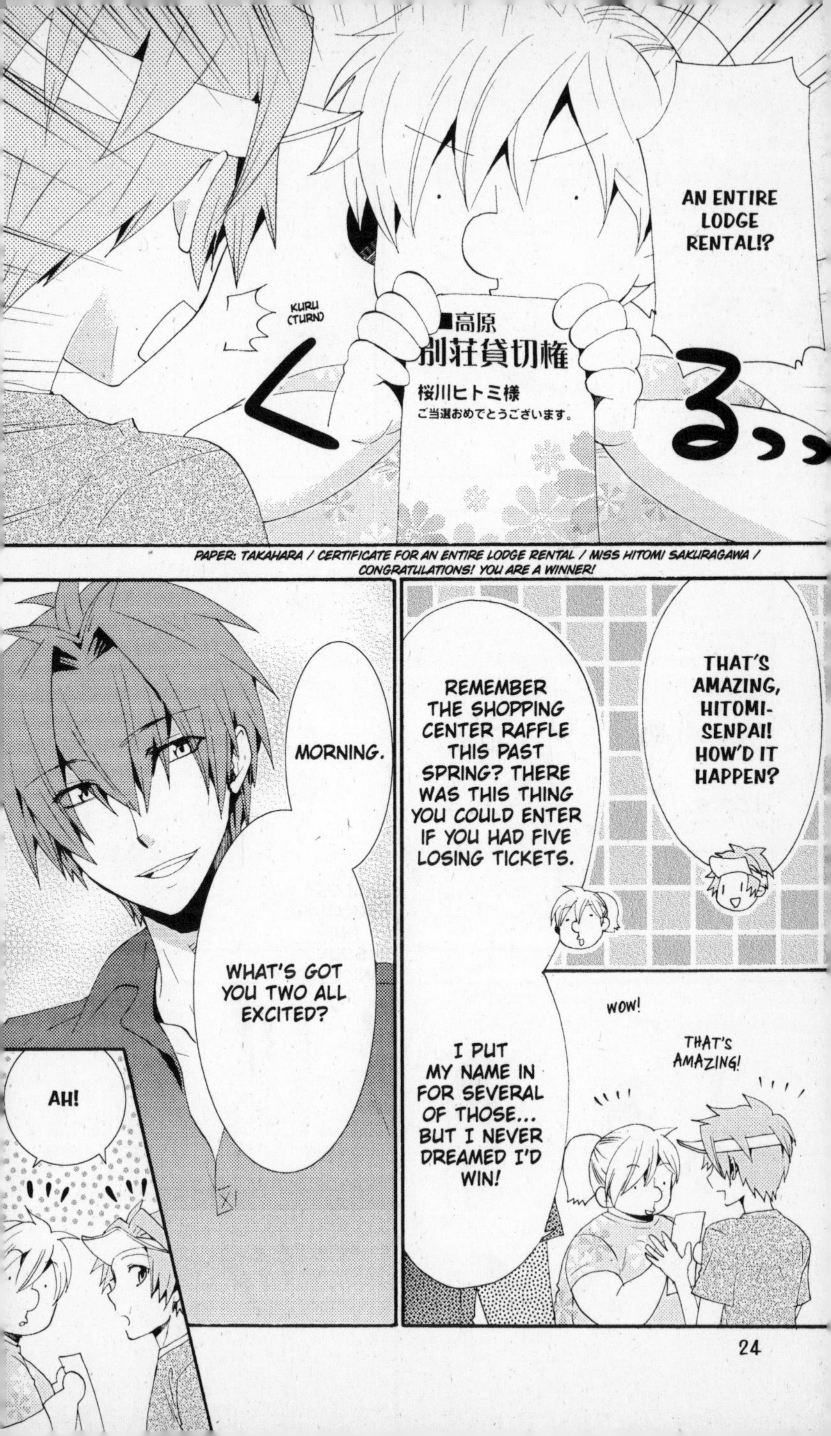
AN ENTIRE LODGE RENTAL!?
■高原
別荘貸切権
桜川ヒトミ様
ご当選おめでとうございます。
くる
KURU (TURN)
PAPER: TAKAHARA / CERTIFICATE FOR AN ENTIRE LODGE RENTAL / MISS HITOMI SAKURAGAWA / CONGRATULATIONS! YOU ARE A WINNER!
THAT'S AMAZING, HITOMI-SENPAI! HOW'D IT HAPPEN?
REMEMBER THE SHOPPING CENTER RAFFLE THIS PAST SPRING? THERE WAS THIS THING YOU COULD ENTER IF YOU HAD FIVE LOSING TICKETS.
THAT'S AMAZING!
WOW!
I PUT MY NAME IN FOR SEVERAL OF THOSE... BUT I NEVER DREAMED I'D WIN!
MORNING.
WHAT'S GOT YOU TWO ALL EXCITED?
AH!

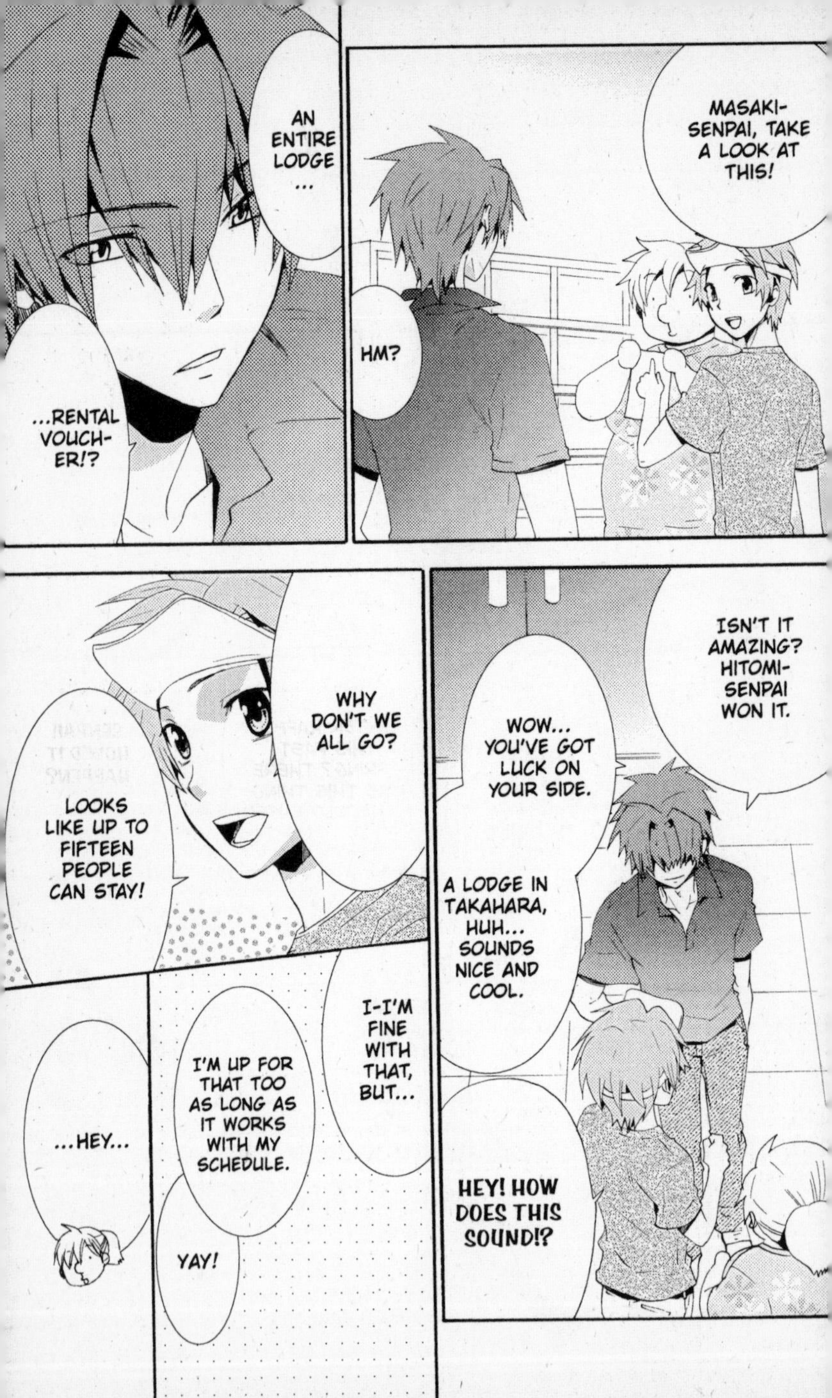
MASAKI-SENPAI, TAKE A LOOK AT THIS!
HM?
AN ENTIRE LODGE ...
...RENTAL VOUCHER!?
ISN'T IT AMAZING? HITOMI-SENPAI WON IT.
WOW... YOU'VE GOT LUCK ON YOUR SIDE.
A LODGE IN TAKAHARA, HUH... SOUNDS NICE AND COOL.
HEY! HOW DOES THIS SOUND!?
WHY DON'T WE ALL GO?
LOOKS LIKE UP TO FIFTEEN PEOPLE CAN STAY!
I-I'M FINE WITH THAT, BUT...
I'M UP FOR THAT TOO AS LONG AS IT WORKS WITH MY SCHEDULE.
YAY!
...HEY...

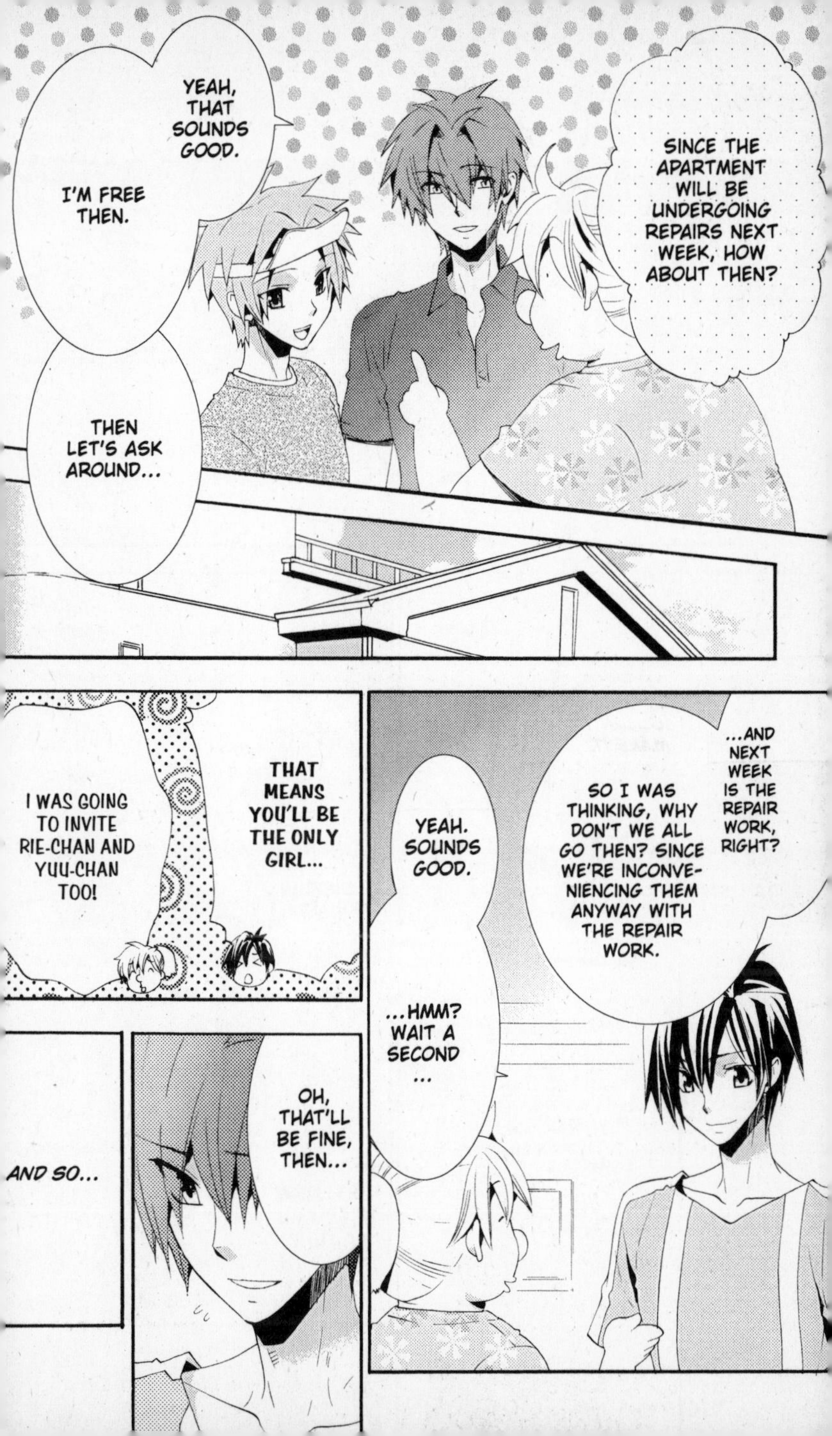
SINCE THE APARTMENT WILL BE UNDERGOING REPAIRS NEXT WEEK, HOW ABOUT THEN?
YEAH, THAT SOUNDS GOOD.
I'M FREE THEN.
THEN LET'S ASK AROUND...
...AND NEXT WEEK IS THE REPAIR WORK, RIGHT?
SO I WAS THINKING, WHY DON'T WE ALL GO THEN? SINCE WE'RE INCONVE-NIENCING THEM ANYWAY WITH THE REPAIR WORK.
YEAH. SOUNDS GOOD.
...HMM? WAIT A SECOND ...
THAT MEANS YOU'LL BE THE ONLY GIRL...
I WAS GOING TO INVITE RIE-CHAN AND YUU-CHAN TOO!
OH, THAT'LL BE FINE, THEN...
AND SO...

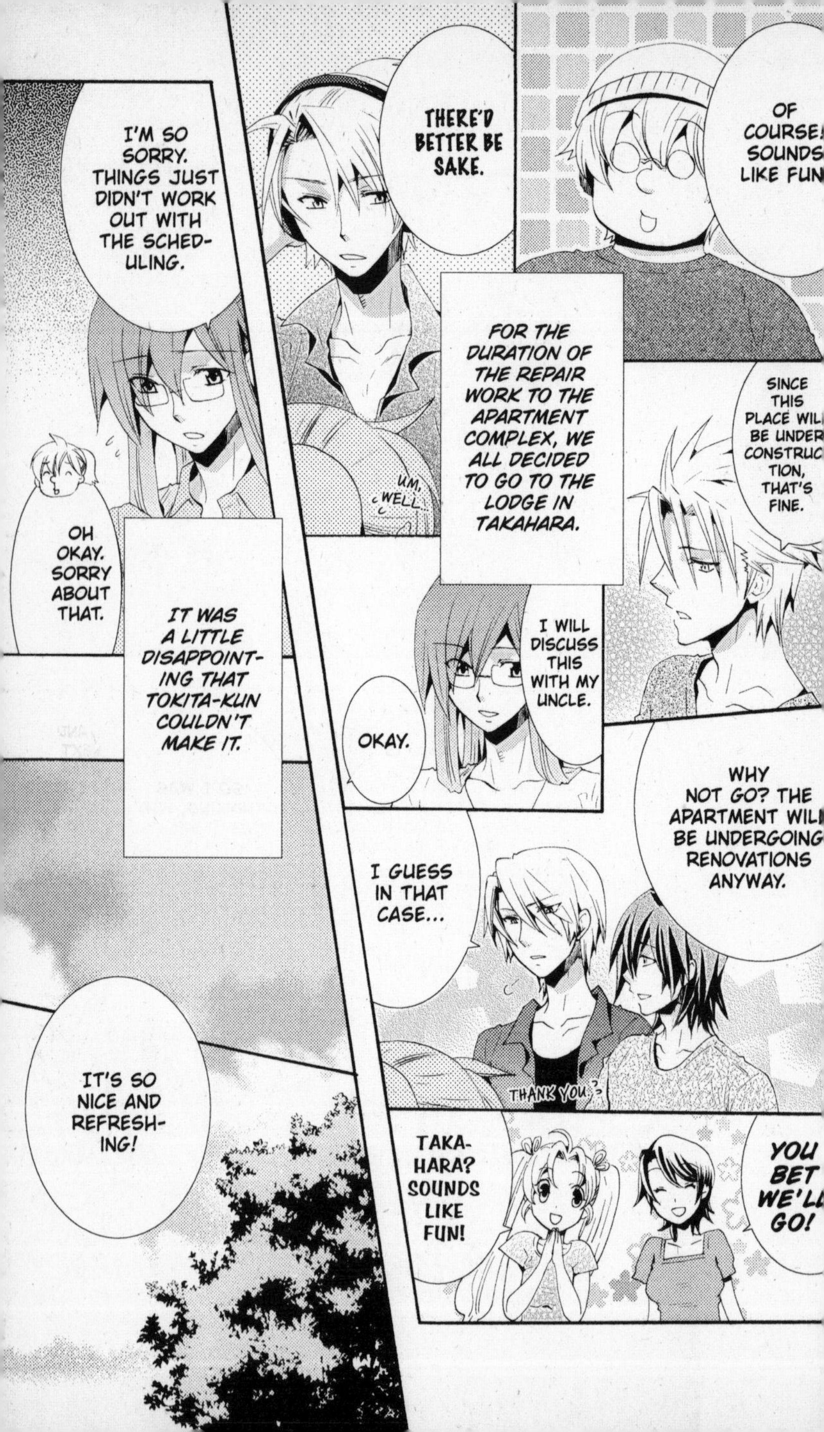

OF COURSE! SOUNDS LIKE FUN
THERE'D BETTER BE SAKE.
FOR THE DURATION OF THE REPAIR WORK TO THE APARTMENT COMPLEX, WE ALL DECIDED TO GO TO THE LODGE IN TAKAHARA.
SINCE THIS PLACE WILL BE UNDER CONSTRUCTION, THAT'S FINE.
I WILL DISCUSS THIS WITH MY UNCLE.
OKAY.
WHY NOT GO? THE APARTMENT WILL BE UNDERGOING RENOVATIONS ANYWAY.
I GUESS IN THAT CASE...
THANK YOU.
YOU BET WE'LL GO!
TAKAHARA? SOUNDS LIKE FUN!
UM, WELL...
I'M SO SORRY. THINGS JUST DIDN'T WORK OUT WITH THE SCHEDULING.
OH OKAY. SORRY ABOUT THAT.
IT WAS A LITTLE DISAPPOINTING THAT TOKITA-KUN COULDN'T MAKE IT.
IT'S SO NICE AND REFRESHING!

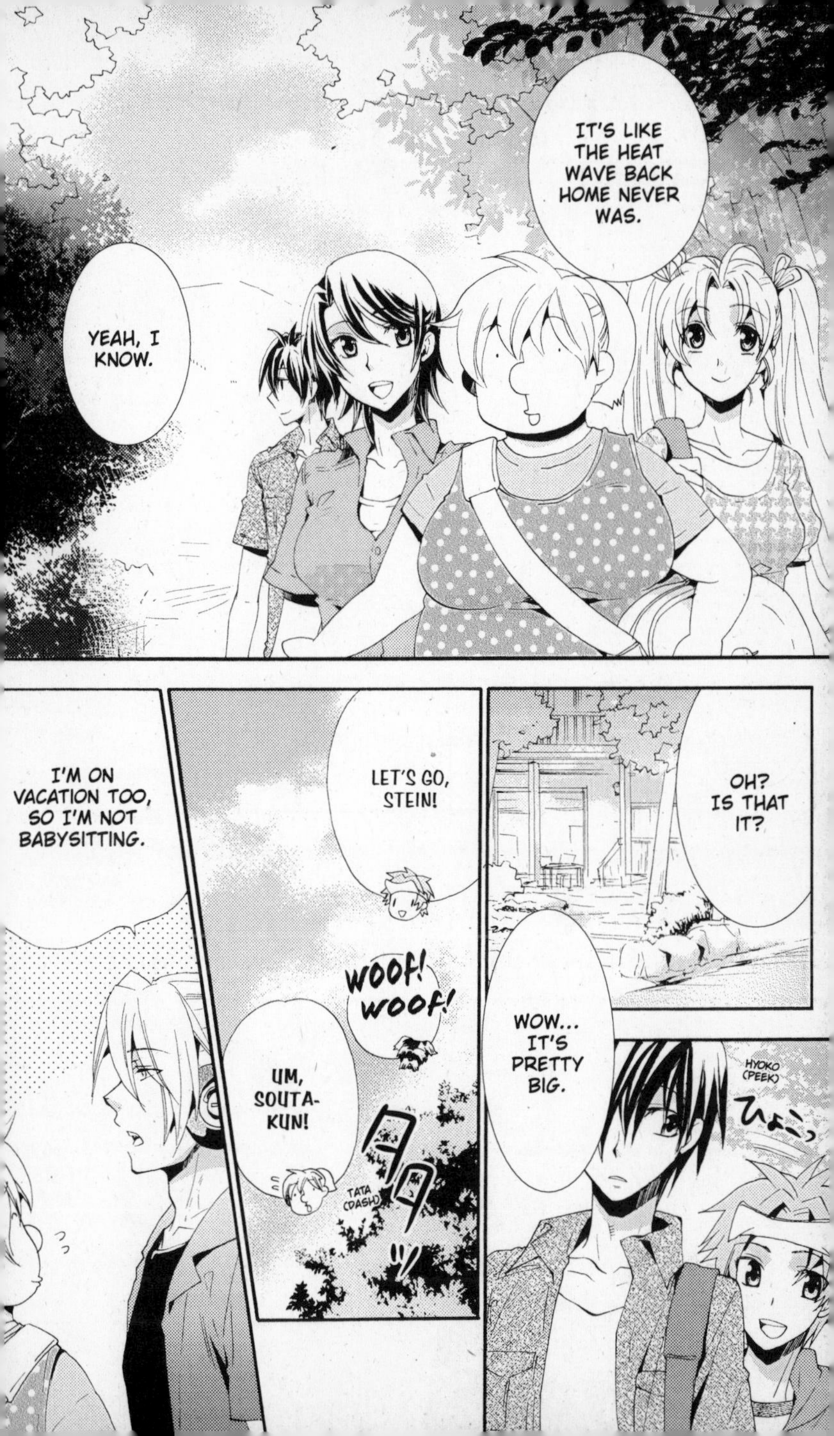
IT'S LIKE THE HEAT WAVE BACK HOME NEVER WAS.
YEAH, I KNOW.
OH? IS THAT IT?
WOW... IT'S PRETTY BIG.
ひょこっ
HYOKO (PEEK)
LET'S GO, STEIN!
WOOF! WOOF!
UM, SOUTA-KUN!
タタッ
TATA (DASH)
I'M ON VACATION TOO, SO I'M NOT BABYSITTING.

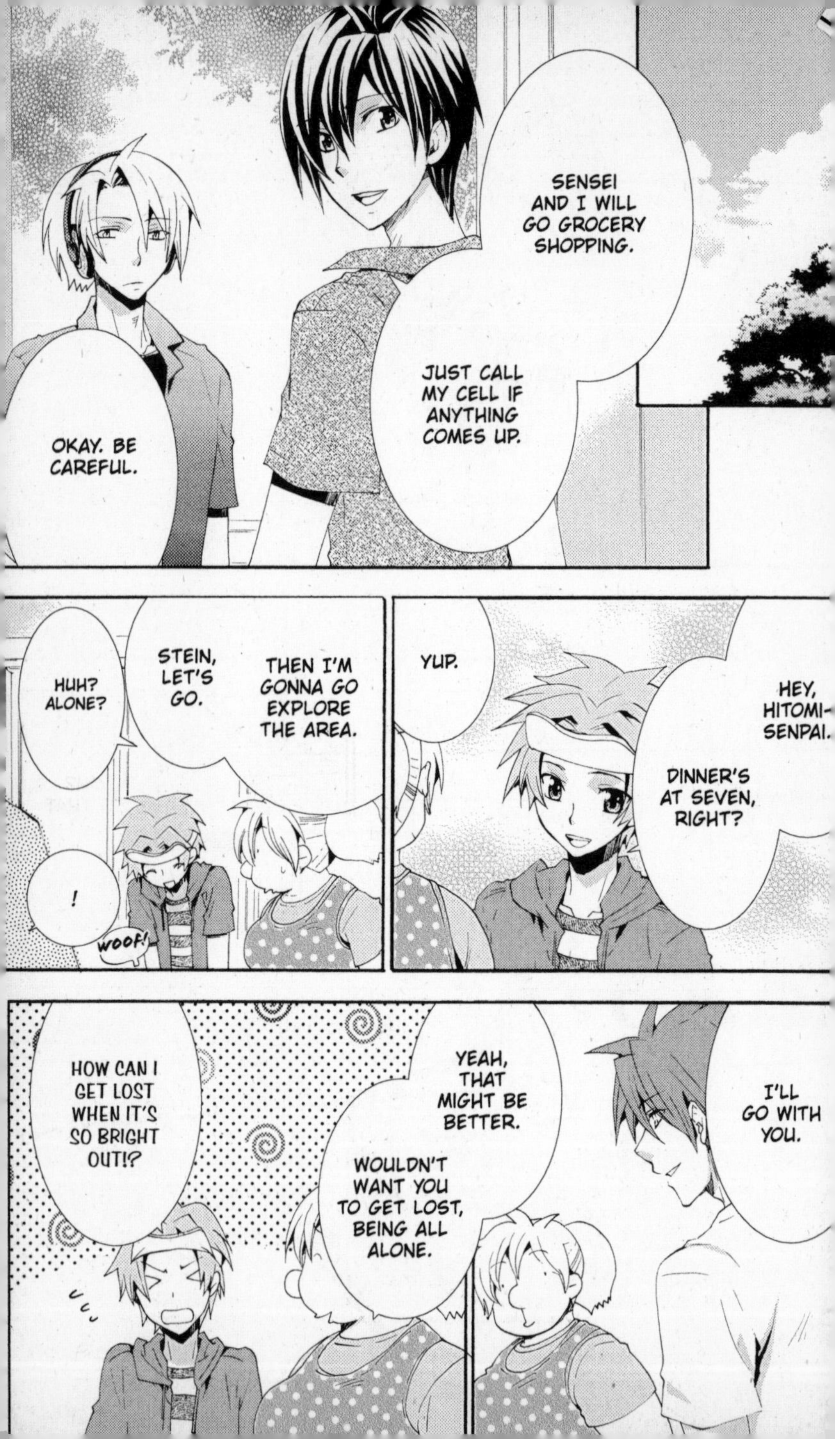
SENSEI AND I WILL GO GROCERY SHOPPING.
JUST CALL MY CELL IF ANYTHING COMES UP.
OKAY. BE CAREFUL.
HEY, HITOMI-SENPAI.
DINNER'S AT SEVEN, RIGHT?
YUP.
THEN I'M GONNA GO EXPLORE THE AREA.
STEIN, LET'S GO.
HUH? ALONE?
!
WOOF!
I'LL GO WITH YOU.
YEAH, THAT MIGHT BE BETTER.
WOULDN'T WANT YOU TO GET LOST, BEING ALL ALONE.
HOW CAN I GET LOST WHEN IT'S SO BRIGHT OUT!?

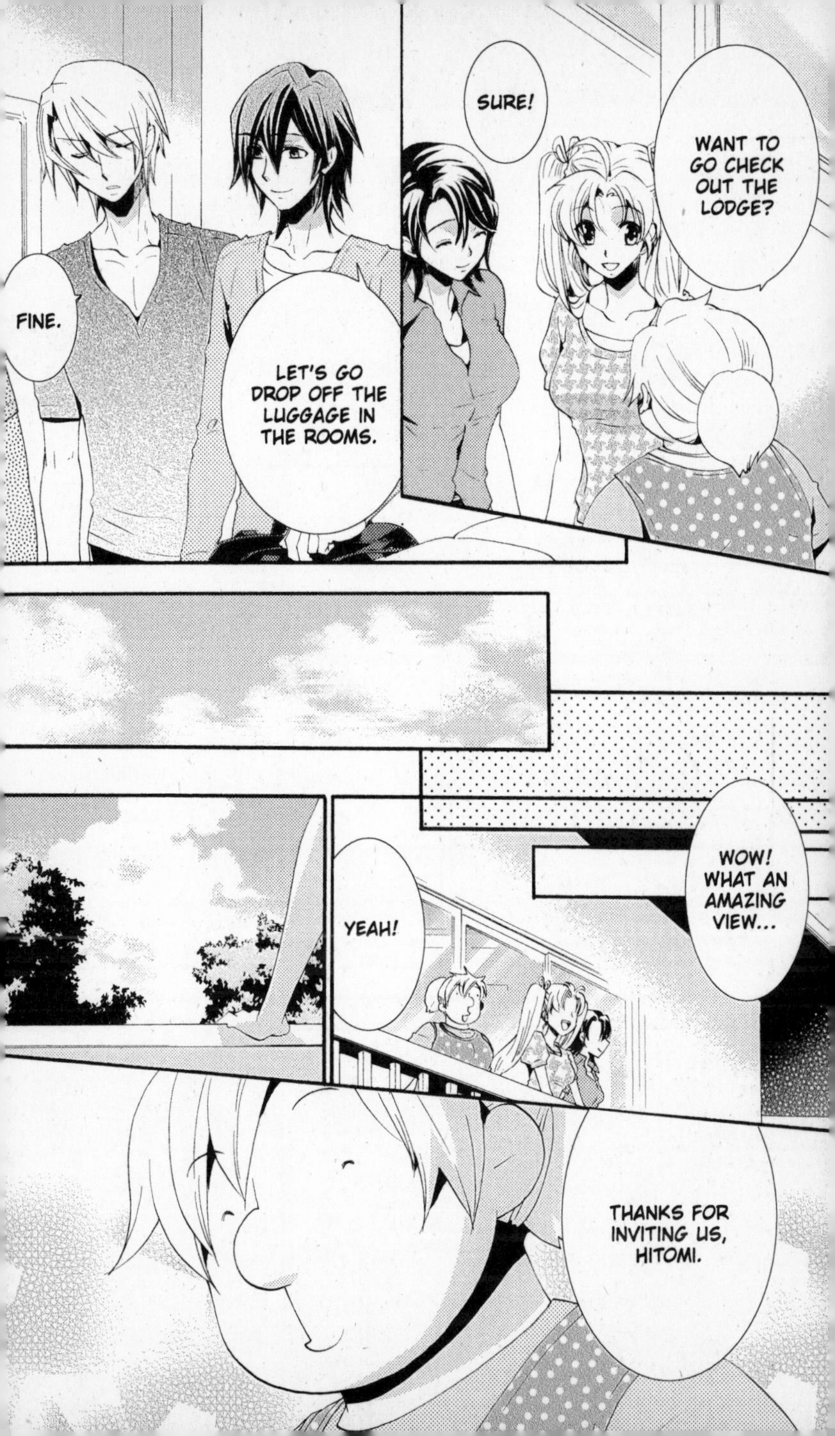
WANT TO GO CHECK OUT THE LODGE?
SURE!
LET'S GO DROP OFF THE LUGGAGE IN THE ROOMS.
FINE.
WOW! WHAT AN AMAZING VIEW...
YEAH!
THANKS FOR INVITING US, HITOMI.

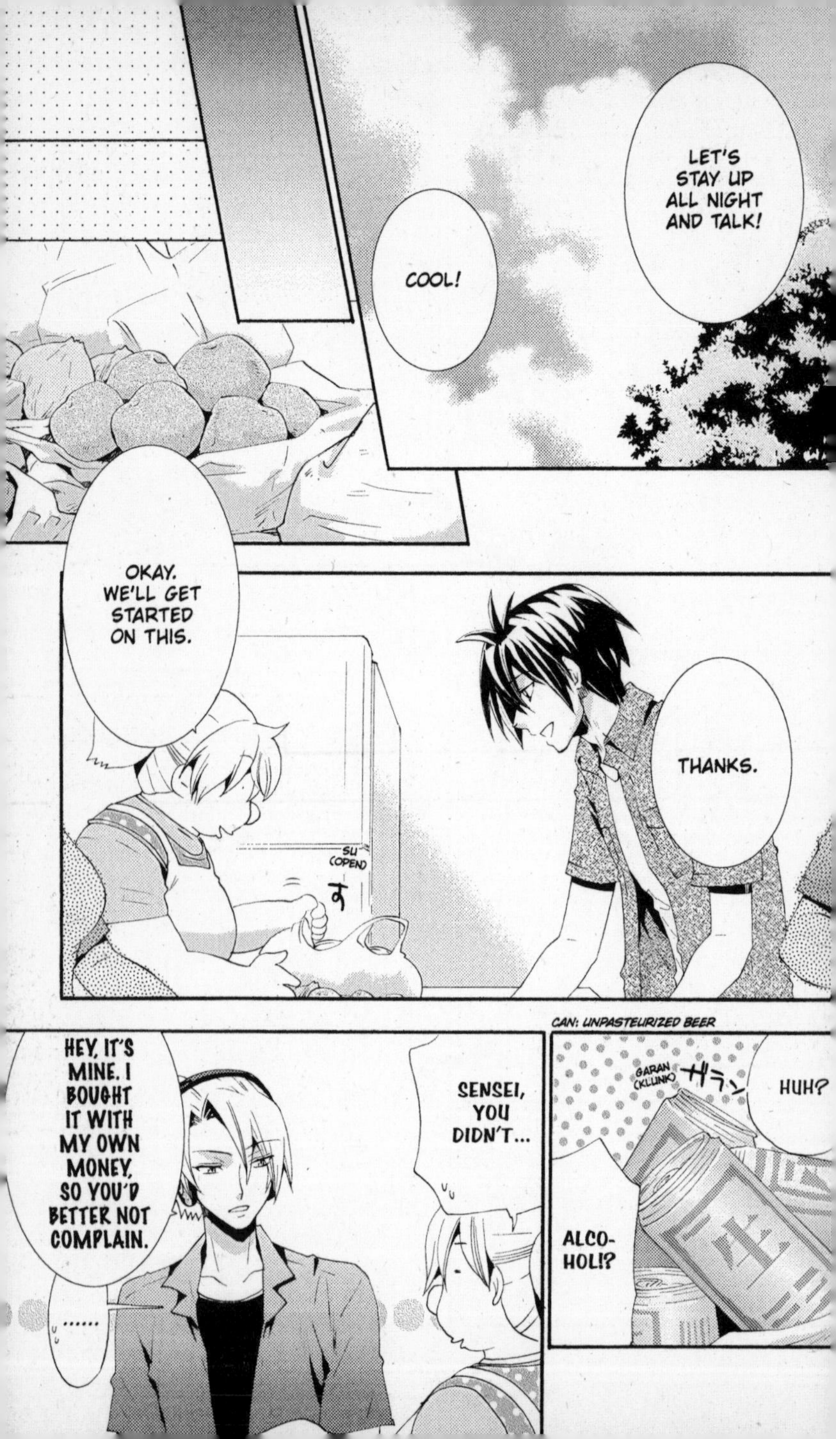
LET'S STAY UP ALL NIGHT AND TALK!
COOL!
OKAY. WE'LL GET STARTED ON THIS.
THANKS.
SU (OPEN)
す
CAN: UNPASTEURIZED BEER
HUH?
GARAN (KLUNK)
ガラン
ALCO-HOL!?
SENSEI, YOU DIDN'T...
HEY, IT'S MINE. I BOUGHT IT WITH MY OWN MONEY, SO YOU'D BETTER NOT COMPLAIN.
......

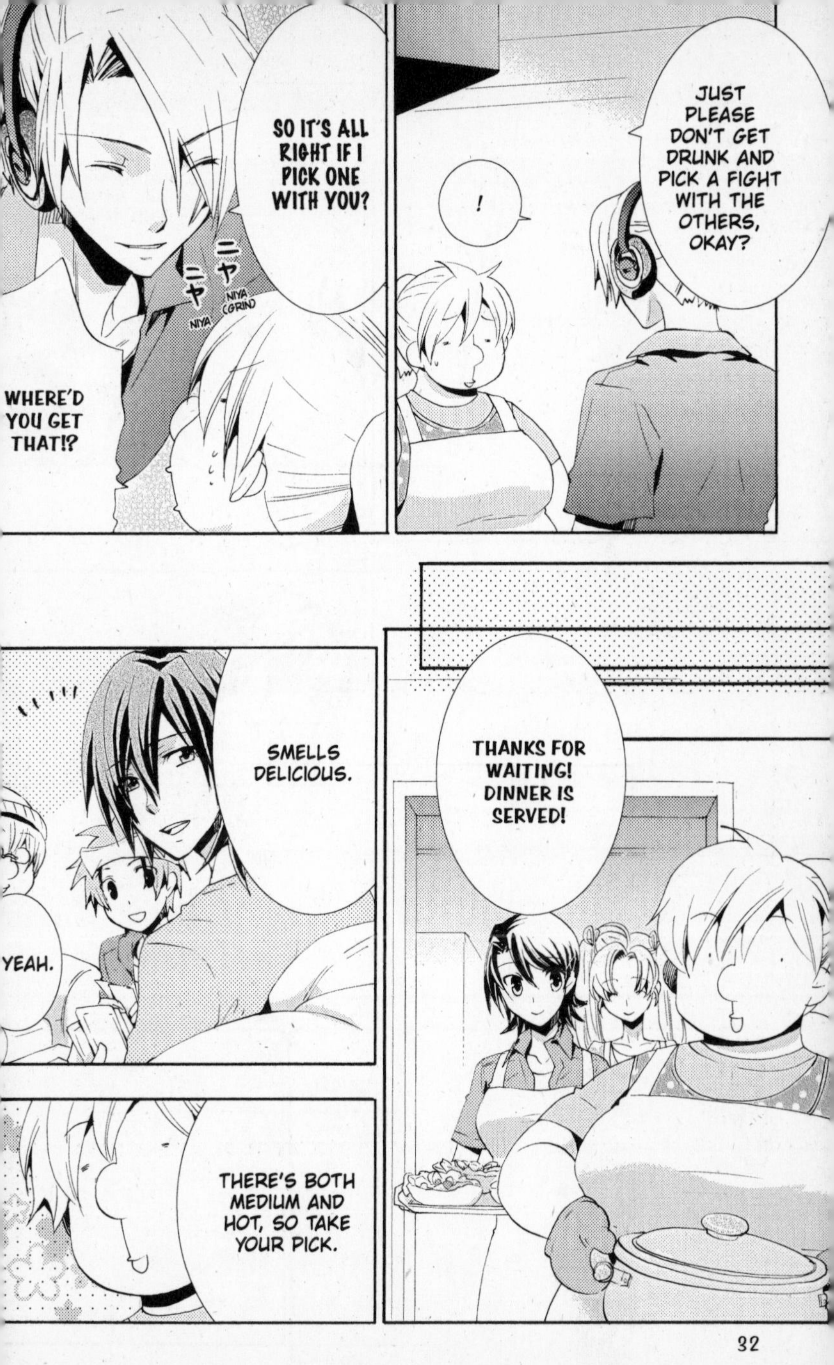
JUST PLEASE DON'T GET DRUNK AND PICK A FIGHT WITH THE OTHERS, OKAY?
!
SO IT'S ALL RIGHT IF I PICK ONE WITH YOU?
ニヤ ニヤ
NIYA NIYA (GRIN)
WHERE'D YOU GET THAT!?
THANKS FOR WAITING! DINNER IS SERVED!
SMELLS DELICIOUS.
YEAH.
THERE'S BOTH MEDIUM AND HOT, SO TAKE YOUR PICK.

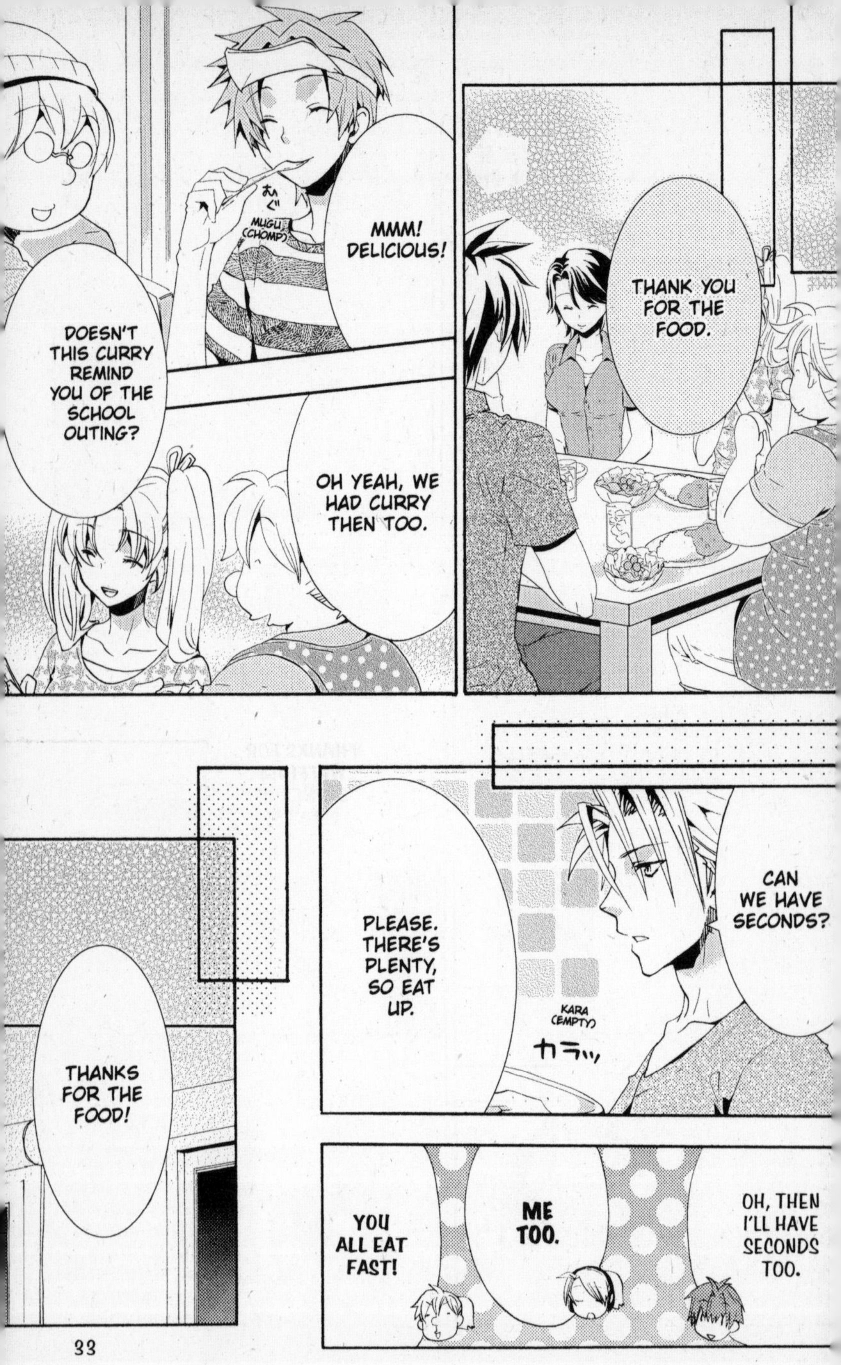
THANK YOU FOR THE FOOD.
MUGU (CHOMP)
MMM! DELICIOUS!
DOESN'T THIS CURRY REMIND YOU OF THE SCHOOL OUTING?
OH YEAH, WE HAD CURRY THEN TOO.
CAN WE HAVE SECONDS?
KARA (EMPTY)
カラッ
PLEASE. THERE'S PLENTY, SO EAT UP.
OH, THEN I'LL HAVE SECONDS TOO.
ME TOO.
YOU ALL EAT FAST!
THANKS FOR THE FOOD!

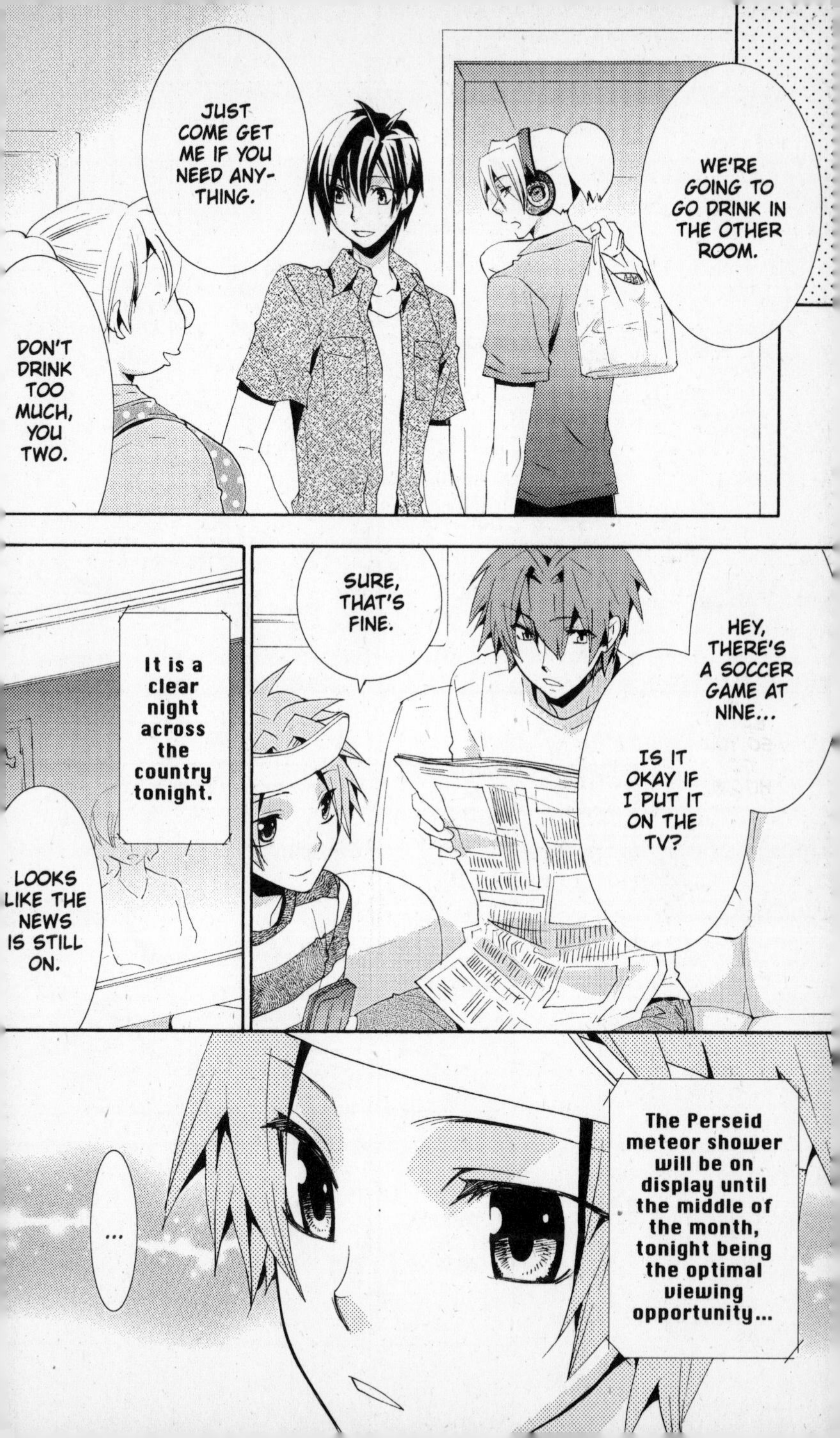
WE'RE GOING TO GO DRINK IN THE OTHER ROOM.
JUST COME GET ME IF YOU NEED ANY-THING.
DON'T DRINK TOO MUCH, YOU TWO.
HEY, THERE'S A SOCCER GAME AT NINE...
IS IT OKAY IF I PUT IT ON THE TV?
SURE, THAT'S FINE.
It is a clear night across the country tonight.
LOOKS LIKE THE NEWS IS STILL ON.
The Perseid meteor shower will be on display until the middle of the month, tonight being the optimal viewing opportunity...
...

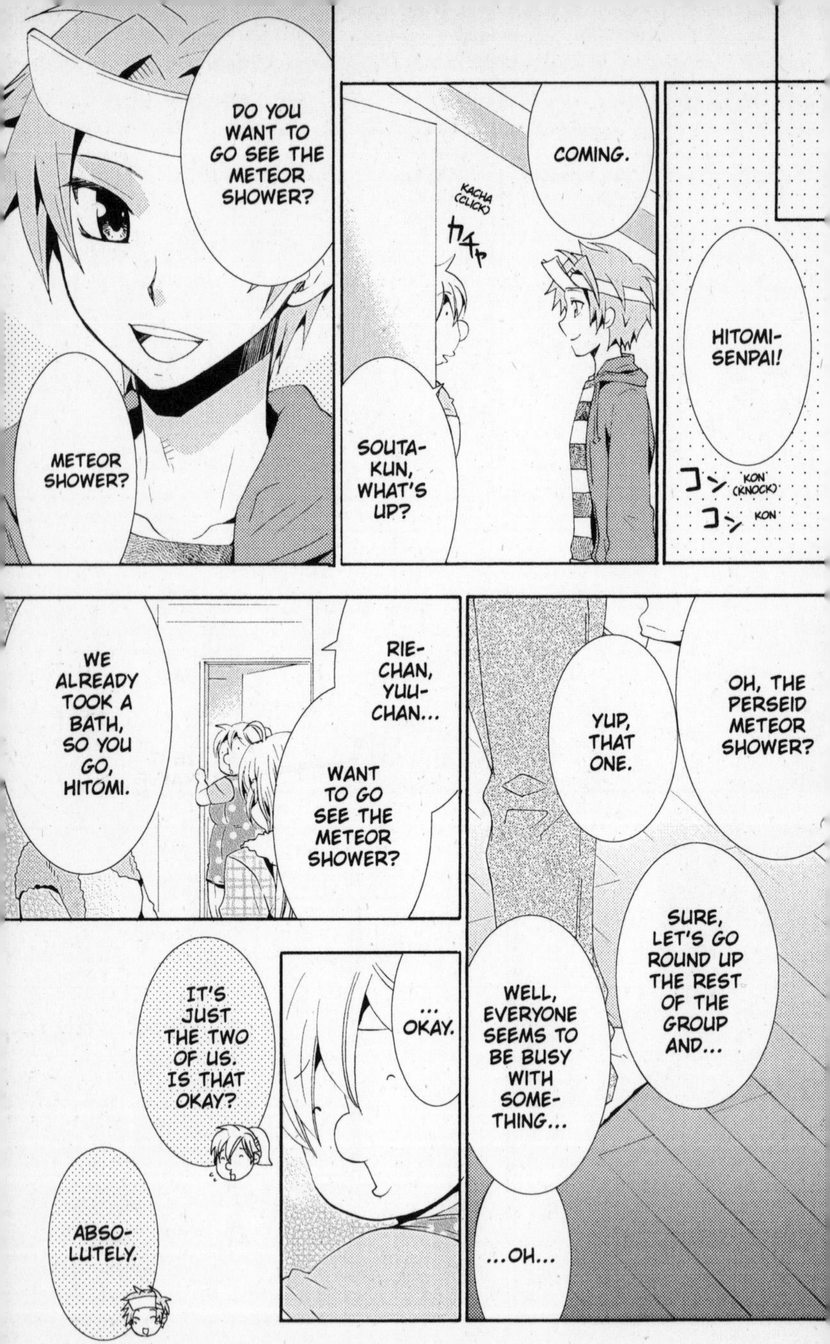
HITOMI-SENPAI!
コン 'KON' (KNOCK)
コン KON
COMING.
カチャ KACHA (CLICK)
SOUTA-KUN, WHAT'S UP?
DO YOU WANT TO GO SEE THE METEOR SHOWER?
METEOR SHOWER?
OH, THE PERSEID METEOR SHOWER?
YUP, THAT ONE.
SURE, LET'S GO ROUND UP THE REST OF THE GROUP AND...
WELL, EVERYONE SEEMS TO BE BUSY WITH SOME-THING...
...OH...
RIE-CHAN, YUU-CHAN...
WANT TO GO SEE THE METEOR SHOWER?
WE ALREADY TOOK A BATH, SO YOU GO, HITOMI.
...OKAY.
IT'S JUST THE TWO OF US. IS THAT OKAY?
ABSO-LUTELY.

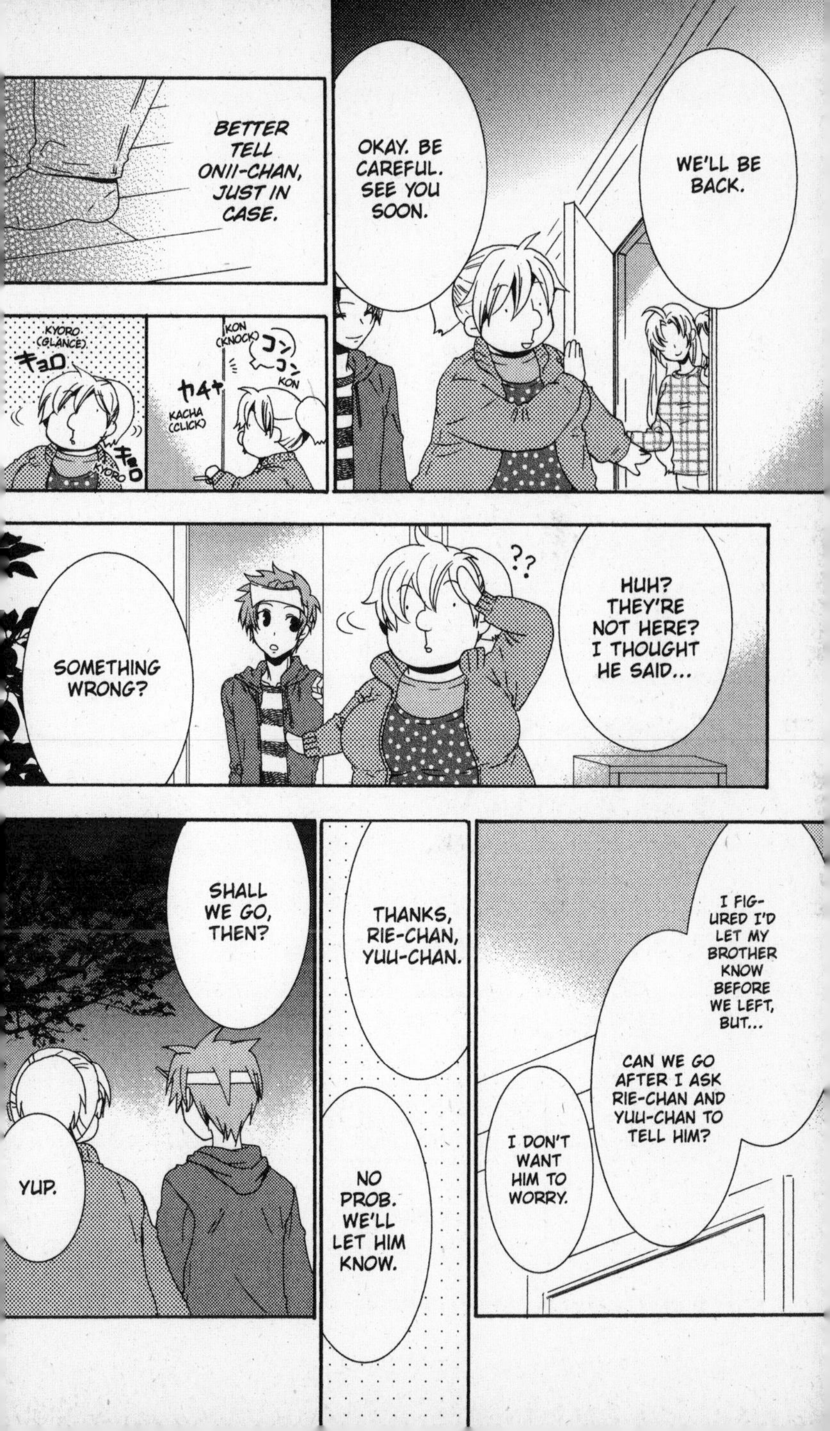
WE'LL BE BACK.
OKAY. BE CAREFUL. SEE YOU SOON.
BETTER TELL ONII-CHAN, JUST IN CASE.
コン コン
KON (KNOCK) KON
カチャ
KACHA (CLICK)
キョロ キョロ
KYORO (GLANCE) KYORO
HUH? THEY'RE NOT HERE? I THOUGHT HE SAID...
SOMETHING WRONG?
I FIG-URED I'D LET MY BROTHER KNOW BEFORE WE LEFT, BUT...
CAN WE GO AFTER I ASK RIE-CHAN AND YUU-CHAN TO TELL HIM?
I DON'T WANT HIM TO WORRY.
THANKS, RIE-CHAN, YUU-CHAN.
NO PROB. WE'LL LET HIM KNOW.
SHALL WE GO, THEN?
YUP.

UGLY DUCKLING'S LOVE REVOLUTION

★ STORY CHARACTERS

MASAKI KAHARA

THE POPULAR LIFE OF THE PARTY IN HITOMI'S CLASS WHO CAN SEEMINGLY DO EVERYTHING. PART OF THE SOCCER TEAM AND A DOG LOVER. PRECIOUS DOG'S NAME IS STEIN.

AYATO KAMISHIRO

WITH HIS QUIET, CONTEMPLATIVE PERSONALITY, HE HAS QUITE THE FEMALE FAN BASE. PHYSICALLY ON THE FRAGILE SIDE, HE OCCASIONALLY HAS FAINTING SPELLS. A JUNIOR.

RYUTAROU WAKATSUKI

HITOMI'S SCHOOL'S HEALTH CLINIC DOC. A DELINQUENT OF A TEACHER, HE IS FREQUENTLY FOUND SMOKING IN THE CLINIC. AGE IS KEPT SECRET.

UGLY DUCKLING'S LOVE REVOLUTION

STORY CHARACTERS

KAEDE TOKITA

THE SLIGHTLY MYSTERIOUS TRANSFER STUDENT WHO IS ALWAYS STUDYING. READS BOOKS MORE OFTEN THAN HE CHATS WITH OTHERS. SOPHOMORE.

TOORU KINOMURA

A CHILDHOOD FRIEND WHOM HITOMI PLAYED WITH OFTEN SINCE THEY WERE LITTLE. INSPIRED BY THE SIGHT OF HITOMI WORKING HARD AT HER DIET, HE STARTED HIS OWN DIET. SOPHOMORE.

YURIKA TOUJOU

HE PRINCESS IN HITOMI'S CLASS. COMPLETELY
'FFERENT PERSONALITY IN FRONT OF GUYS VS.
IRLS. BECAUSE OF HER ENDLESS BITING
OMMENTS, SHE IS HITOMI'S NEMESIS.

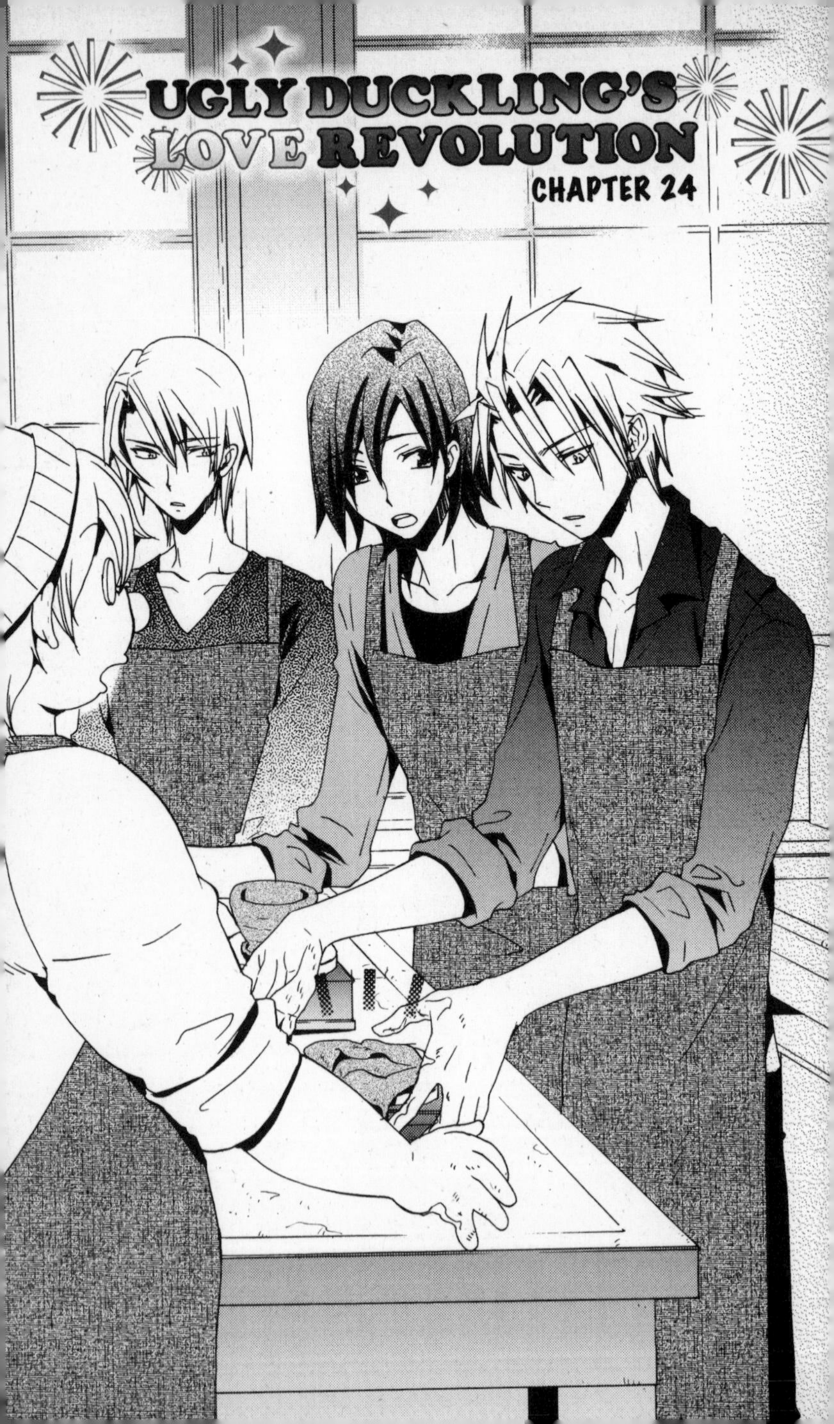
UGLY DUCKLING'S LOVE REVOLUTION
CHAPTER 24

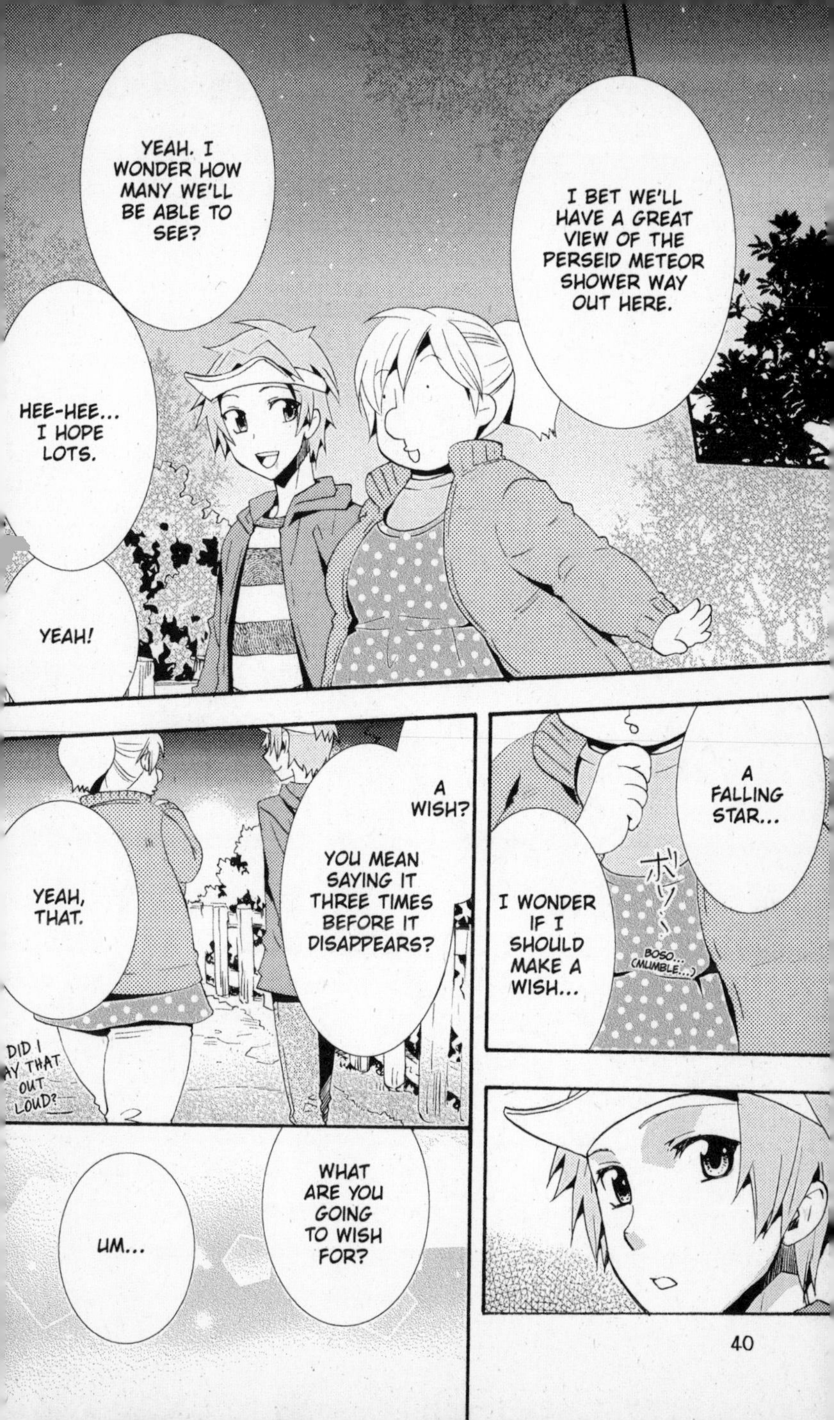

I BET WE'LL HAVE A GREAT VIEW OF THE PERSEID METEOR SHOWER WAY OUT HERE.
YEAH. I WONDER HOW MANY WE'LL BE ABLE TO SEE?
HEE-HEE... I HOPE LOTS.
YEAH!
A FALLING STAR...
ボソ…
BOSO... (MUMBLE...)
I WONDER IF I SHOULD MAKE A WISH...
A WISH?
YOU MEAN SAYING IT THREE TIMES BEFORE IT DISAPPEARS?
YEAH, THAT.
DID I Y THAT OUT LOUD?
WHAT ARE YOU GOING TO WISH FOR?
UM...

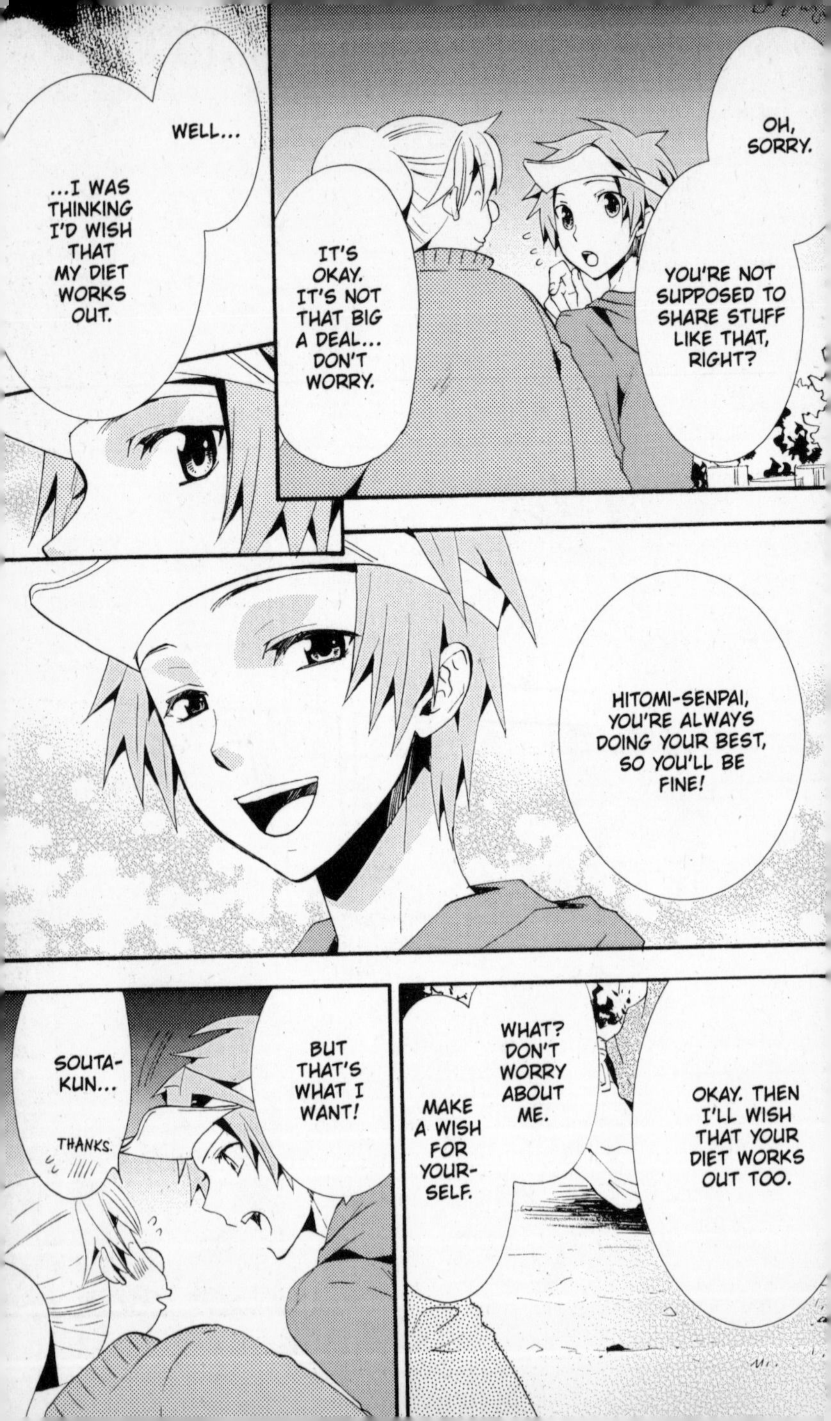
OH, SORRY.
YOU'RE NOT SUPPOSED TO SHARE STUFF LIKE THAT, RIGHT?
IT'S OKAY. IT'S NOT THAT BIG A DEAL... DON'T WORRY.
WELL...
...I WAS THINKING I'D WISH THAT MY DIET WORKS OUT.
HITOMI-SENPAI, YOU'RE ALWAYS DOING YOUR BEST, SO YOU'LL BE FINE!
OKAY. THEN I'LL WISH THAT YOUR DIET WORKS OUT TOO.
WHAT? DON'T WORRY ABOUT ME.
MAKE A WISH FOR YOURSELF.
BUT THAT'S WHAT I WANT!
SOUTA-KUN...
THANKS.

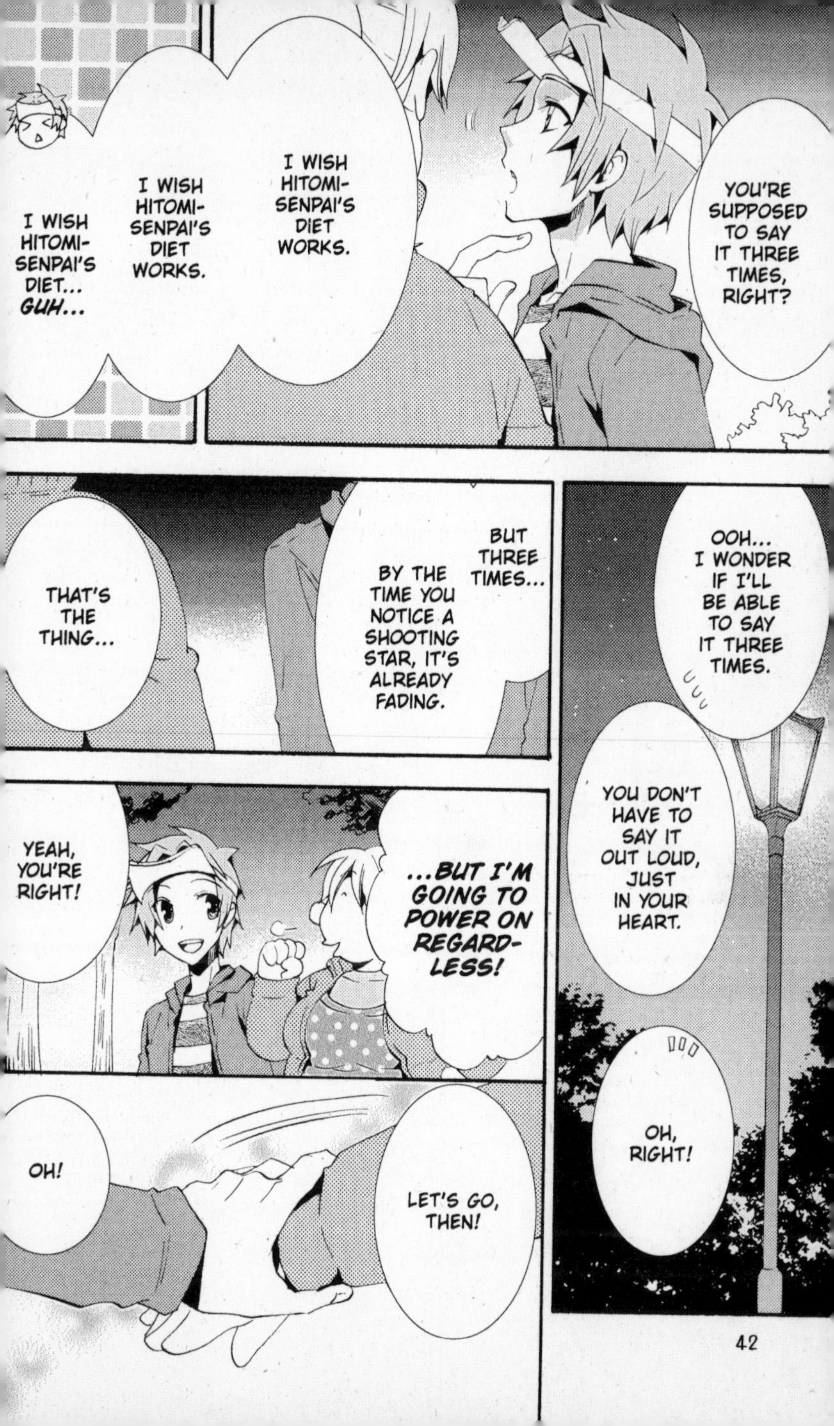

YOU'RE SUPPOSED TO SAY IT THREE TIMES, RIGHT?
I WISH HITOMI-SENPAI'S DIET WORKS.
I WISH HITOMI-SENPAI'S DIET WORKS.
I WISH HITOMI-SENPAI'S DIET... *GUH...*
OOH... I WONDER IF I'LL BE ABLE TO SAY IT THREE TIMES.
YOU DON'T HAVE TO SAY IT OUT LOUD, JUST IN YOUR HEART.
OH, RIGHT!
BUT THREE TIMES...
BY THE TIME YOU NOTICE A SHOOTING STAR, IT'S ALREADY FADING.
THAT'S THE THING...
...BUT I'M GOING TO POWER ON REGARDLESS!
YEAH, YOU'RE RIGHT!
LET'S GO, THEN!
OH!

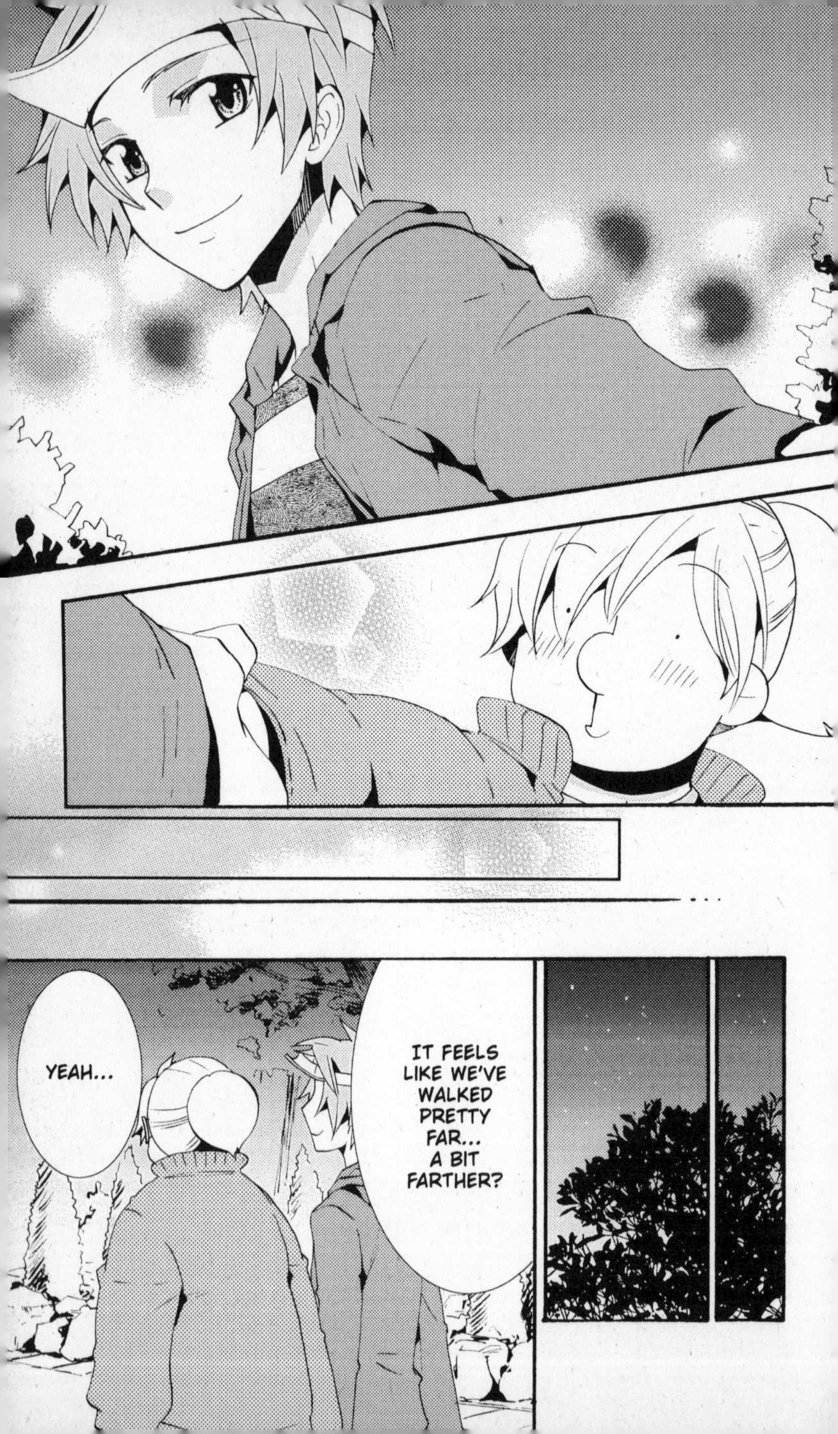
IT FEELS LIKE WE'VE WALKED PRETTY FAR... A BIT FARTHER?
YEAH...

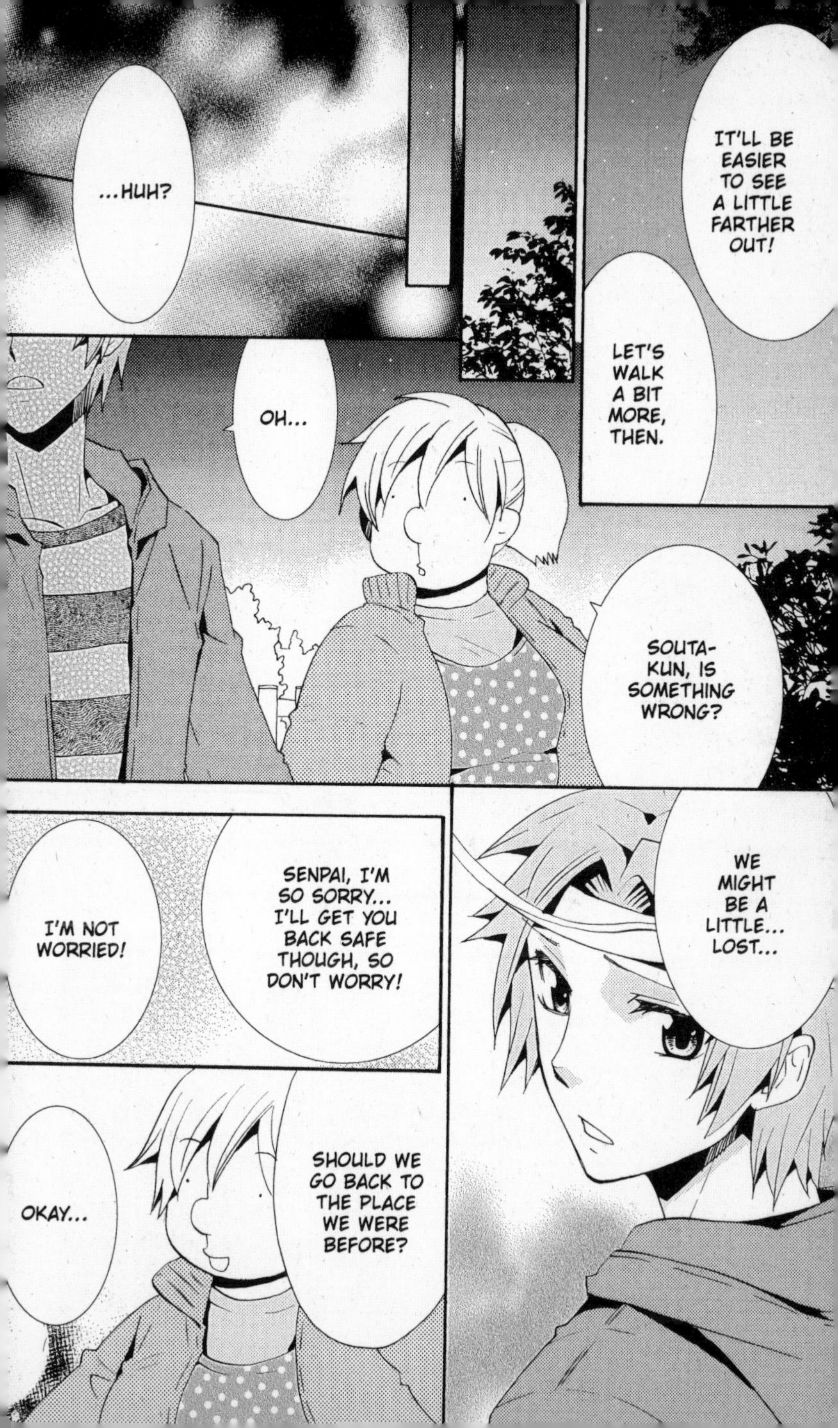
IT'LL BE EASIER TO SEE A LITTLE FARTHER OUT!
LET'S WALK A BIT MORE, THEN.
...HUH?
OH...
SOUTA-KUN, IS SOMETHING WRONG?
WE MIGHT BE A LITTLE... LOST...
SENPAI, I'M SO SORRY... I'LL GET YOU BACK SAFE THOUGH, SO DON'T WORRY!
I'M NOT WORRIED!
SHOULD WE GO BACK TO THE PLACE WE WERE BEFORE?
OKAY...

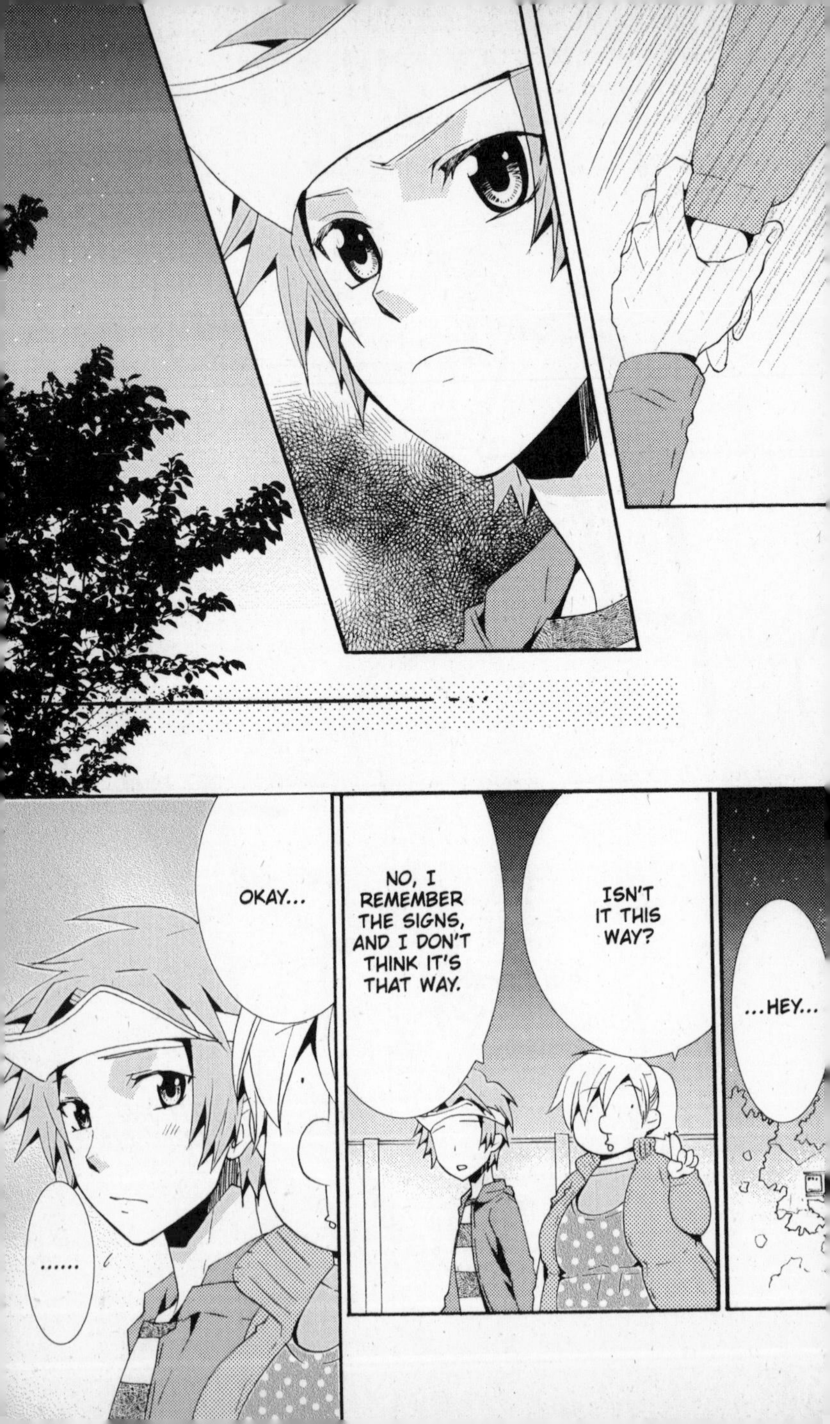
...HEY...
ISN'T IT THIS WAY?
NO, I REMEMBER THE SIGNS, AND I DON'T THINK IT'S THAT WAY.
OKAY...
......

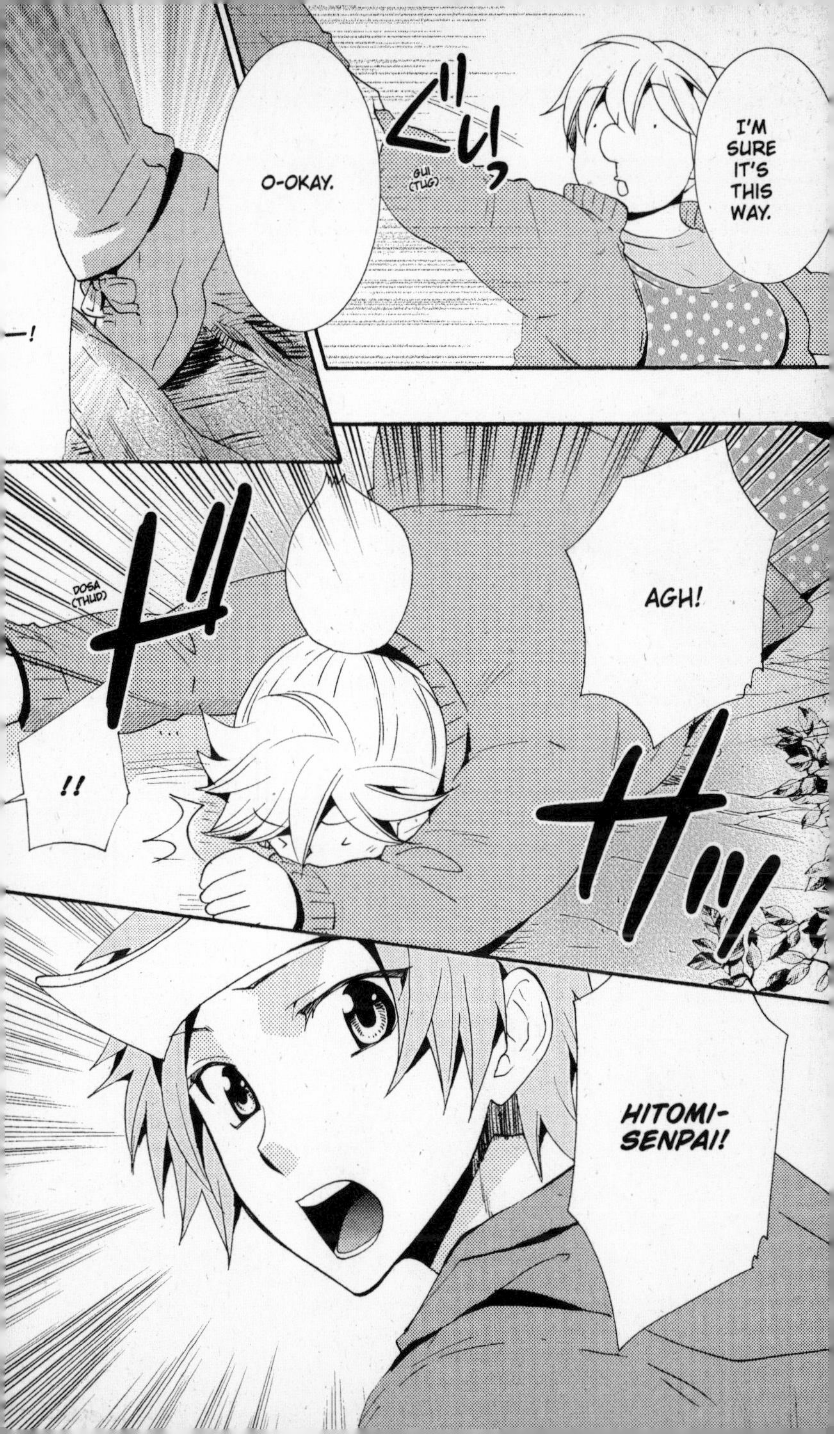
I'M SURE IT'S THIS WAY.
GUI (TUG)
O-OKAY.
—!
AGH!
DOSA (THUD)
!!
HITOMI-SENPAI!

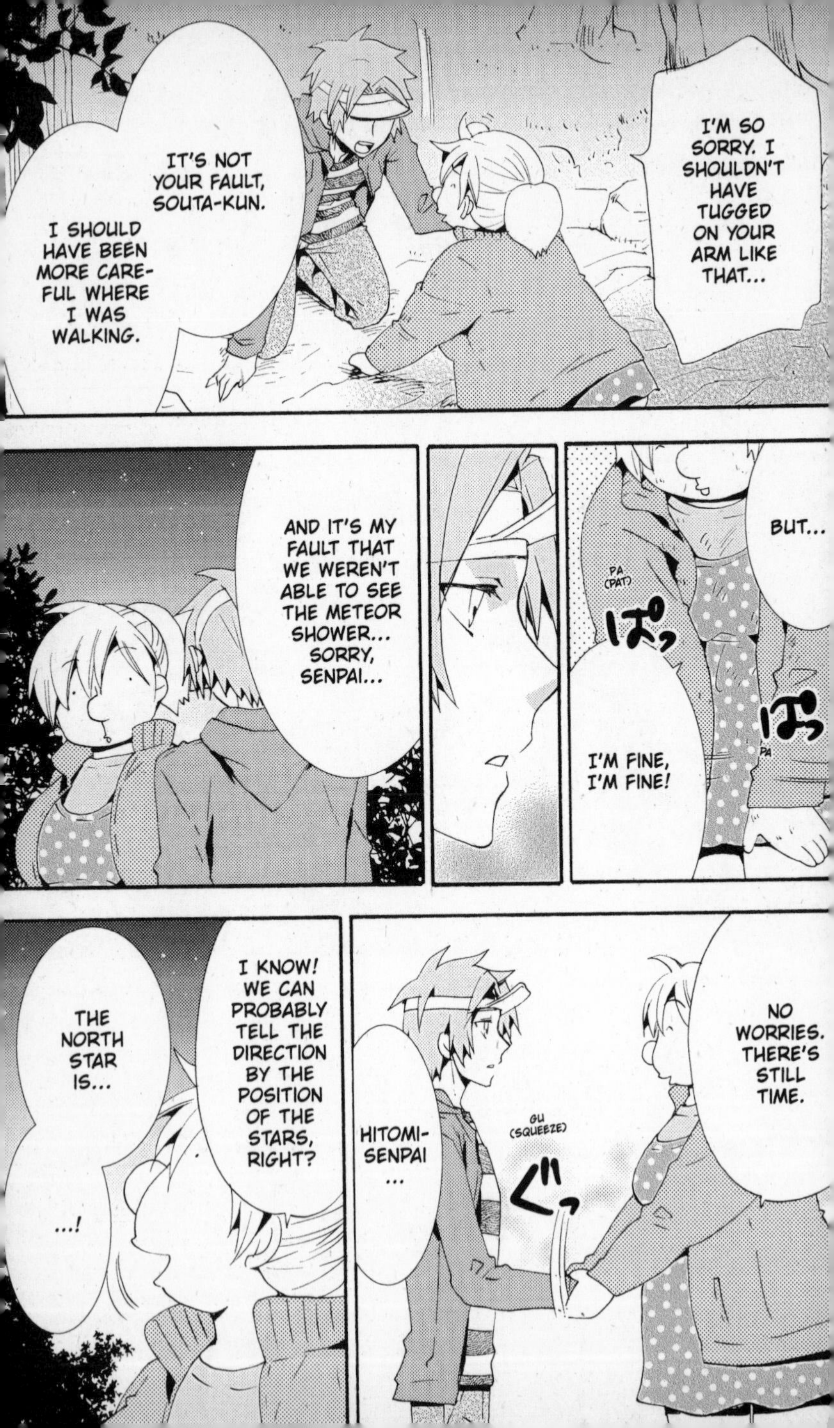
I'M SO SORRY. I SHOULDN'T HAVE TUGGED ON YOUR ARM LIKE THAT...
IT'S NOT YOUR FAULT, SOUTA-KUN.
I SHOULD HAVE BEEN MORE CARE-FUL WHERE I WAS WALKING.
BUT...
PA (PAT)
ぱっ
ぱっ
PA
I'M FINE, I'M FINE!
AND IT'S MY FAULT THAT WE WEREN'T ABLE TO SEE THE METEOR SHOWER... SORRY, SENPAI...
NO WORRIES. THERE'S STILL TIME.
GU (SQUEEZE)
ぐっ
HITOMI-SENPAI...
I KNOW! WE CAN PROBABLY TELL THE DIRECTION BY THE POSITION OF THE STARS, RIGHT?
THE NORTH STAR IS...
...!

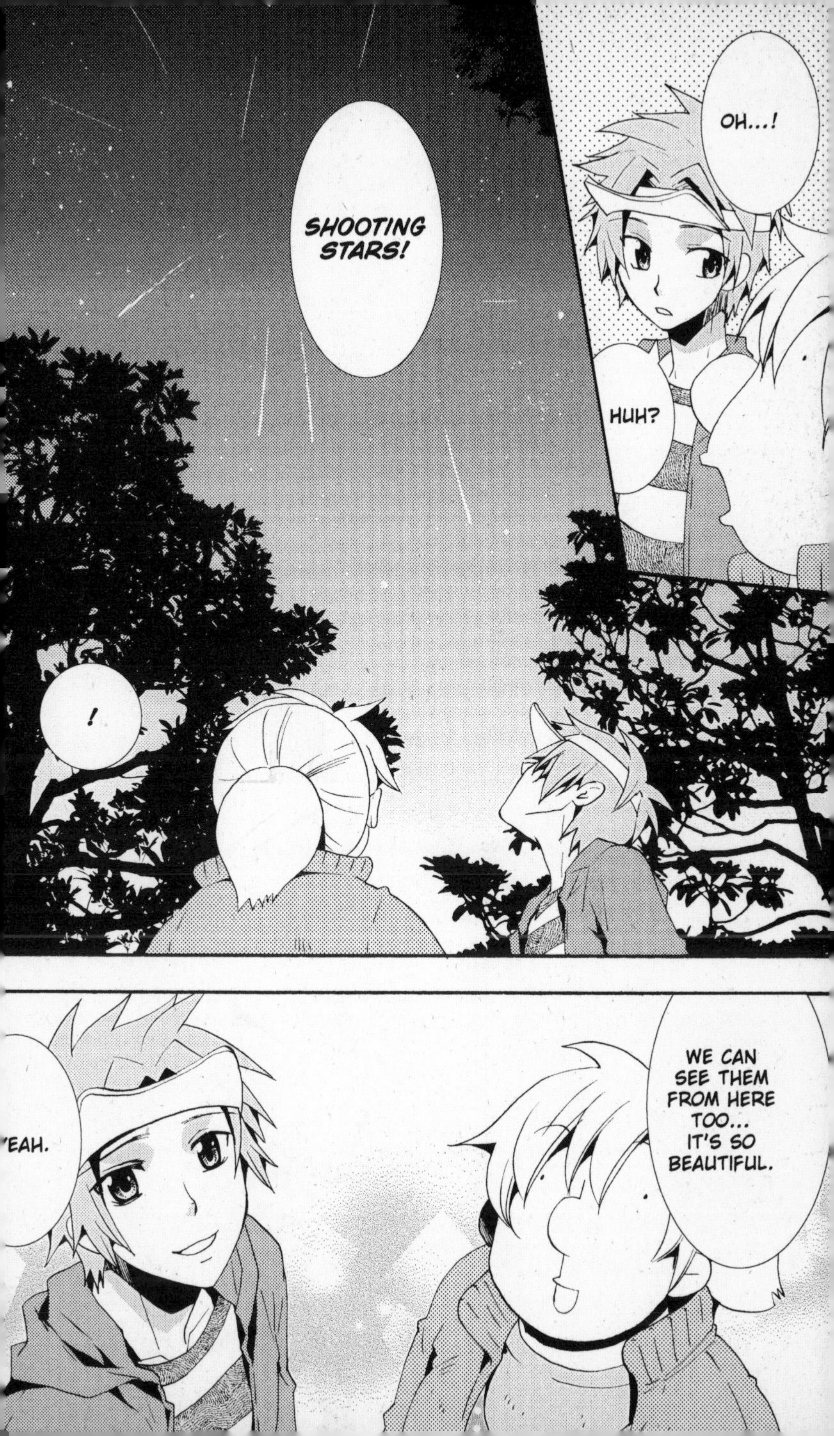
OH...!
HUH?
SHOOTING STARS!
!
WE CAN SEE THEM FROM HERE TOO... IT'S SO BEAUTIFUL.
EAH.

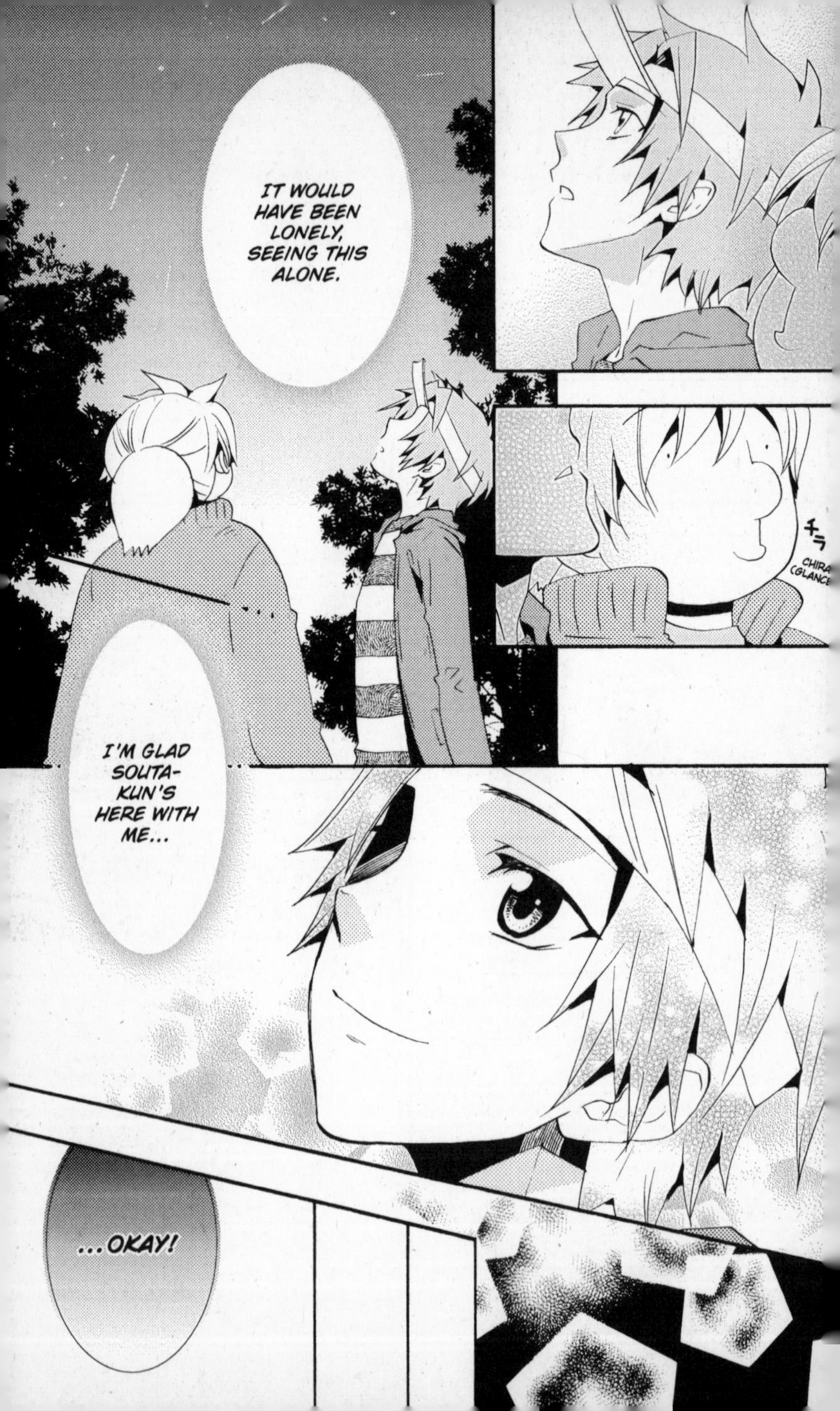
CHIRA (GLANCE
IT WOULD HAVE BEEN LONELY, SEEING THIS ALONE.
I'M GLAD SOUTA-KUN'S HERE WITH ME...
...OKAY!

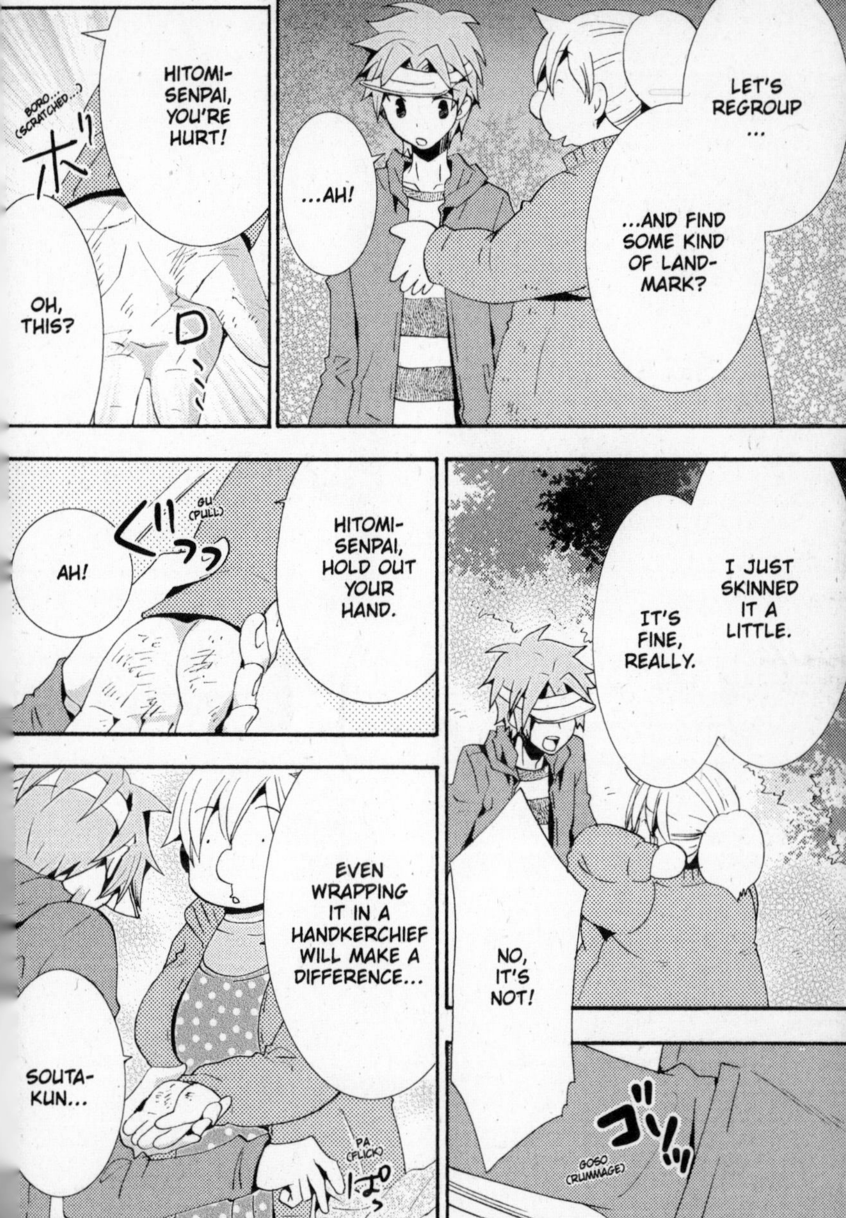
LET'S REGROUP ...
...AND FIND SOME KIND OF LAND-MARK?
...AH!
HITOMI-SENPAI, YOU'RE HURT!
BORO... (SCRATCHED...)
OH, THIS?
I JUST SKINNED IT A LITTLE.
IT'S FINE, REALLY.
NO, IT'S NOT!
GOSO (RUMMAGE)
HITOMI-SENPAI, HOLD OUT YOUR HAND.
GU (PULL)
AH!
EVEN WRAPPING IT IN A HANDKERCHIEF WILL MAKE A DIFFERENCE...
SOUTA-KUN...
PA (FLICK)

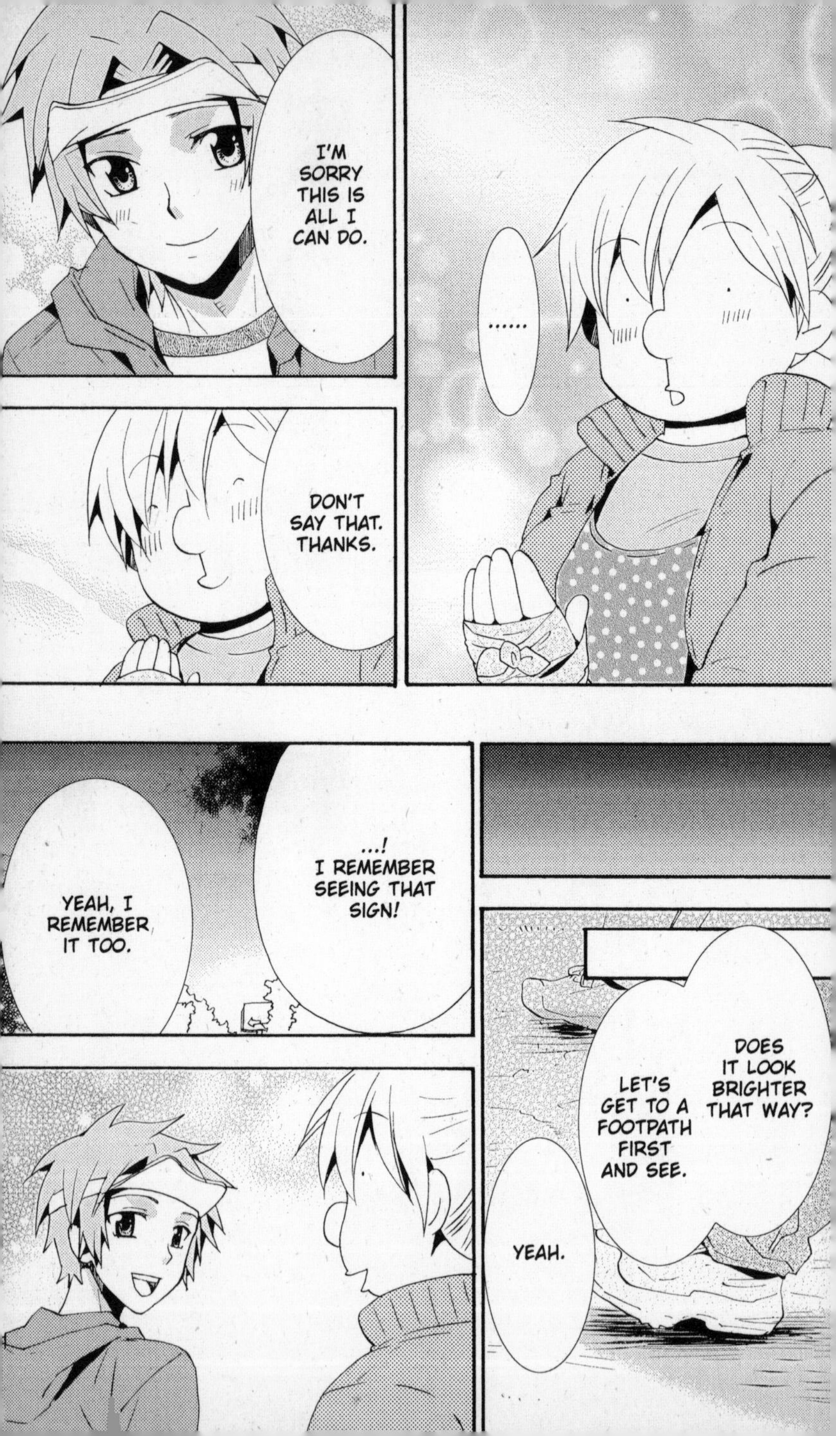
......
I'M SORRY THIS IS ALL I CAN DO.
DON'T SAY THAT. THANKS.
DOES IT LOOK BRIGHTER THAT WAY?
LET'S GET TO A FOOTPATH FIRST AND SEE.
YEAH.
...! I REMEMBER SEEING THAT SIGN!
YEAH, I REMEMBER IT TOO.

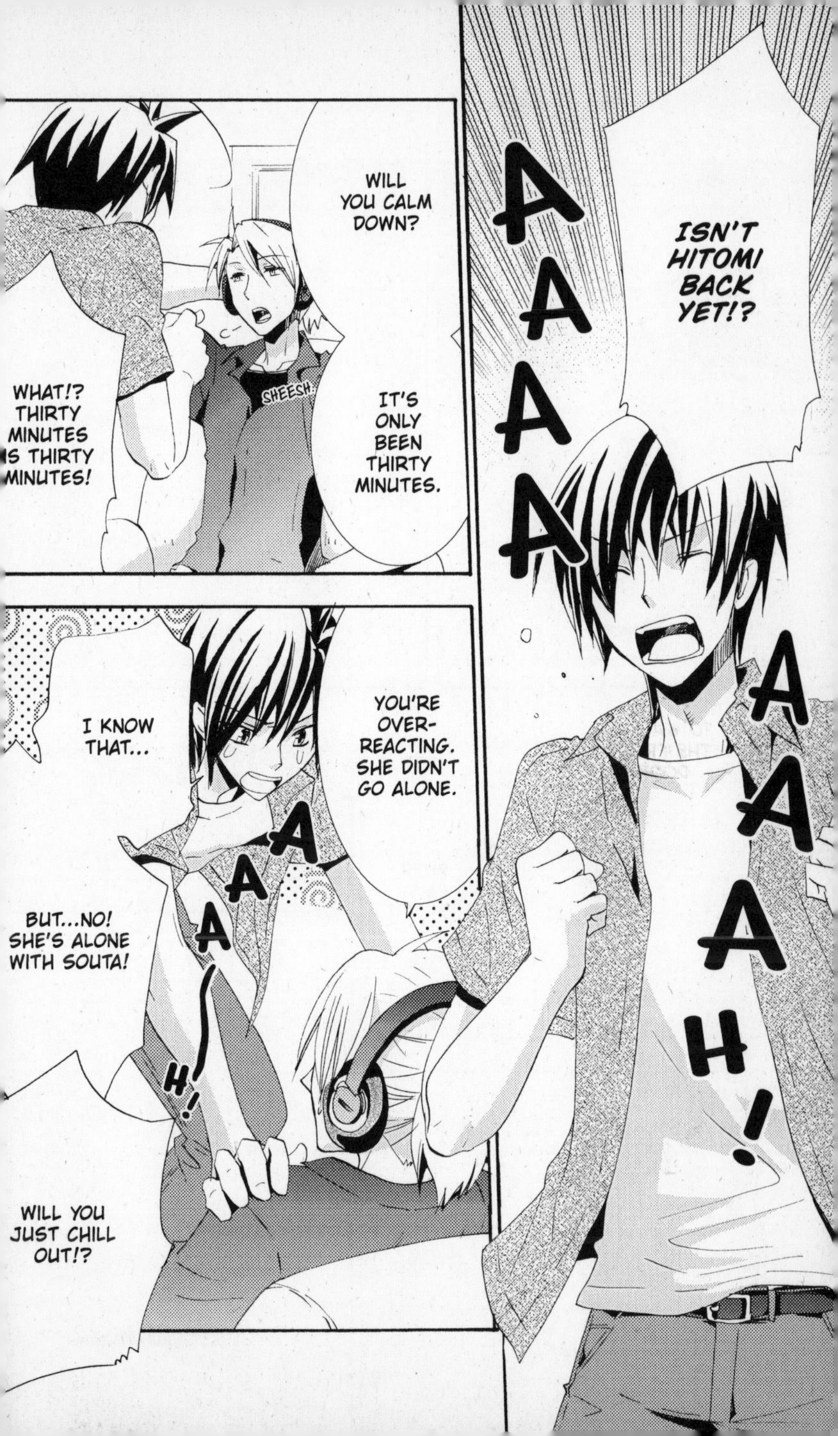
ISN'T HITOMI BACK YET!?
AAAAAAAH!
WILL YOU CALM DOWN?
SHEESH.
IT'S ONLY BEEN THIRTY MINUTES.
WHAT!? THIRTY MINUTES IS THIRTY MINUTES!
YOU'RE OVER-REACTING. SHE DIDN'T GO ALONE.
I KNOW THAT...
BUT...NO! SHE'S ALONE WITH SOUTA!
AAAH!
WILL YOU JUST CHILL OUT!?

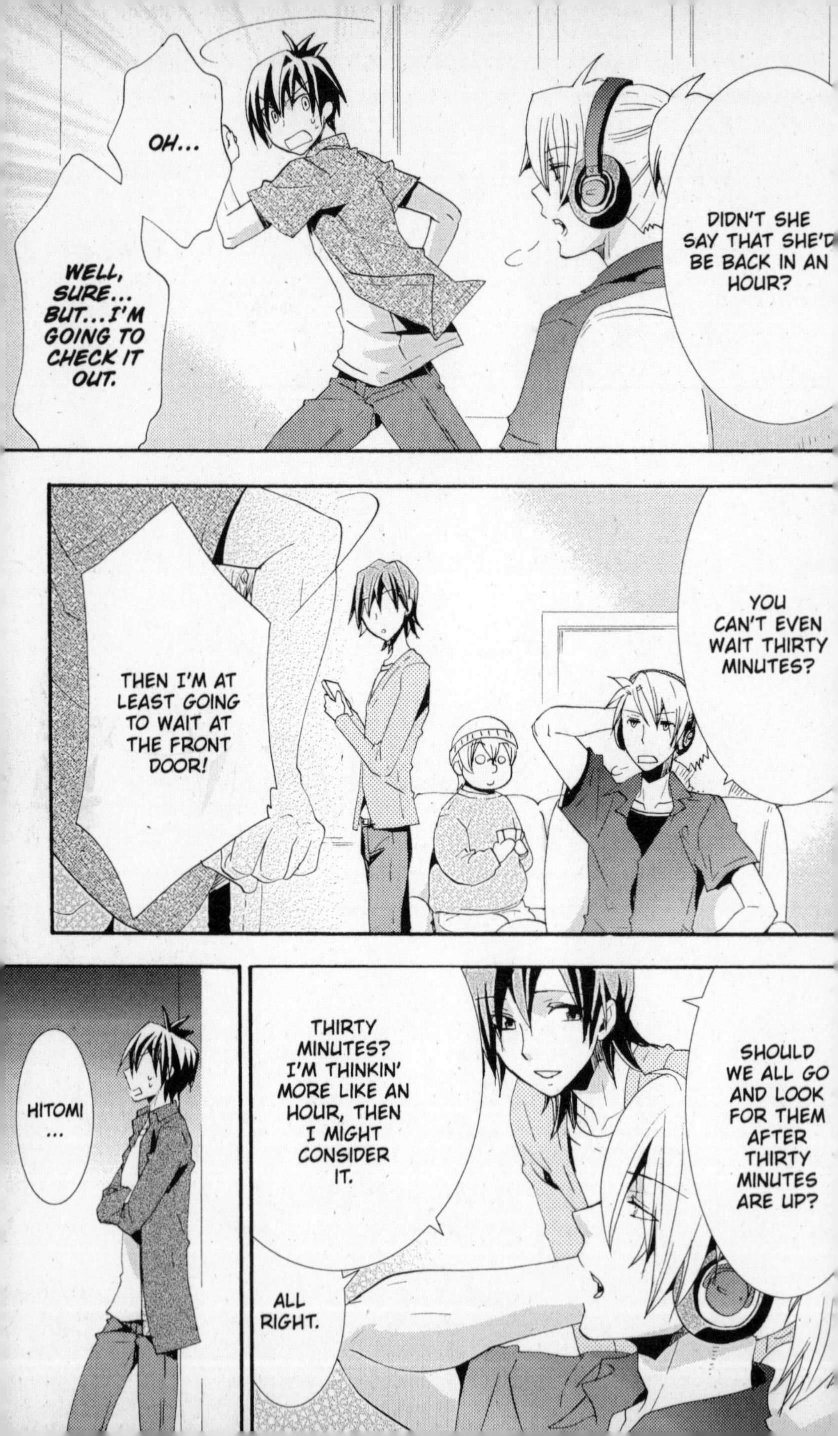
DIDN'T SHE SAY THAT SHE'D BE BACK IN AN HOUR?
OH...
WELL, SURE... BUT...I'M GOING TO CHECK IT OUT.
YOU CAN'T EVEN WAIT THIRTY MINUTES?
THEN I'M AT LEAST GOING TO WAIT AT THE FRONT DOOR!
SHOULD WE ALL GO AND LOOK FOR THEM AFTER THIRTY MINUTES ARE UP?
THIRTY MINUTES? I'M THINKIN' MORE LIKE AN HOUR, THEN I MIGHT CONSIDER IT.
ALL RIGHT.
HITOMI ...

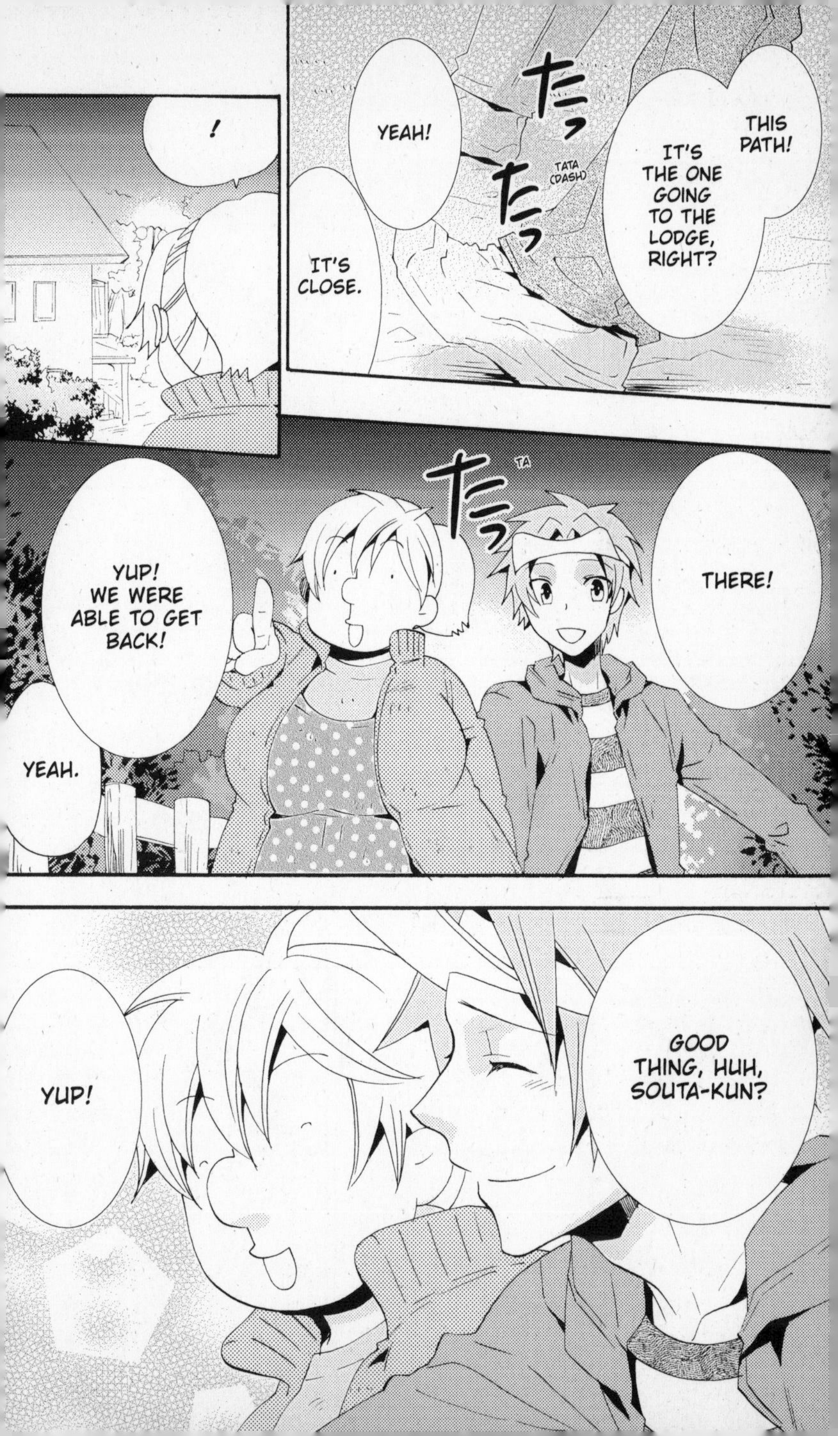
THIS PATH!
IT'S THE ONE GOING TO THE LODGE, RIGHT?
TATA (DASH)
YEAH!
IT'S CLOSE.
!
TA
THERE!
YUP! WE WERE ABLE TO GET BACK!
YEAH.
GOOD THING, HUH, SOUTA-KUN?
YUP!

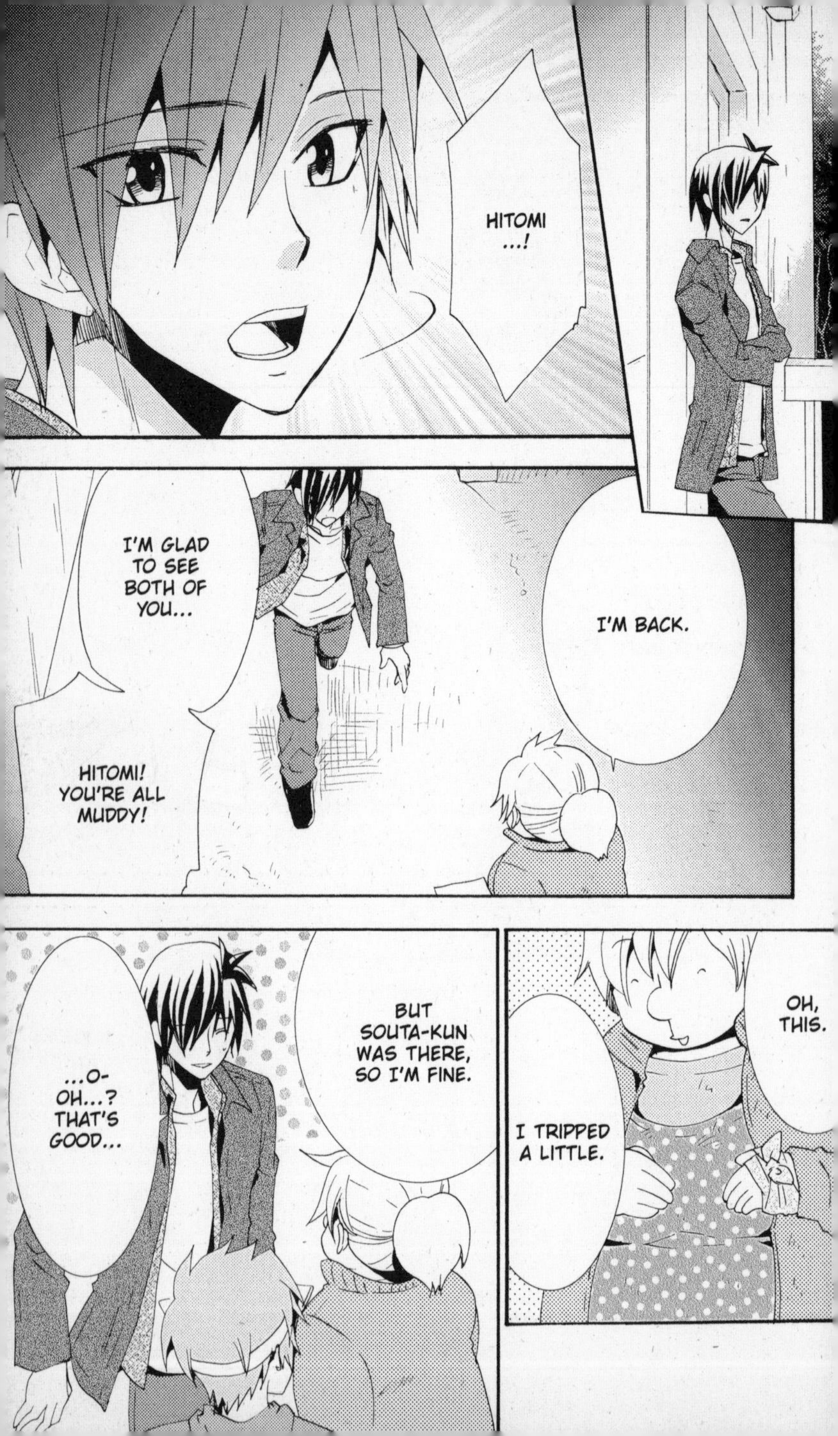
HITOMI ...!
I'M BACK.
I'M GLAD TO SEE BOTH OF YOU...
HITOMI! YOU'RE ALL MUDDY!
OH, THIS.
I TRIPPED A LITTLE.
BUT SOUTA-KUN WAS THERE, SO I'M FINE.
...O-OH...? THAT'S GOOD...

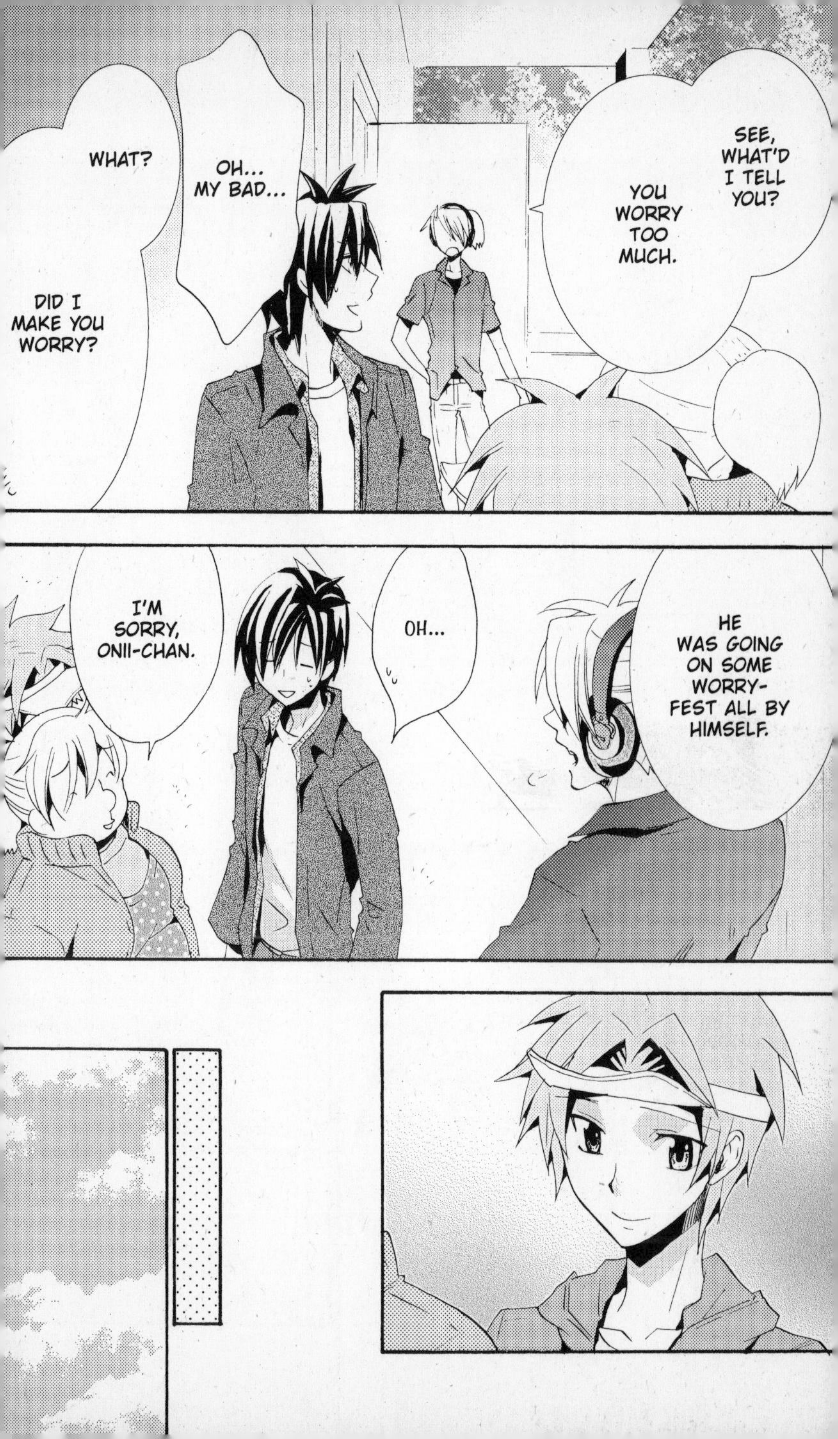
SEE, WHAT'D I TELL YOU?
YOU WORRY TOO MUCH.
OH... MY BAD...
WHAT?
DID I MAKE YOU WORRY?
HE WAS GOING ON SOME WORRY-FEST ALL BY HIMSELF.
OH...
I'M SORRY, ONII-CHAN.

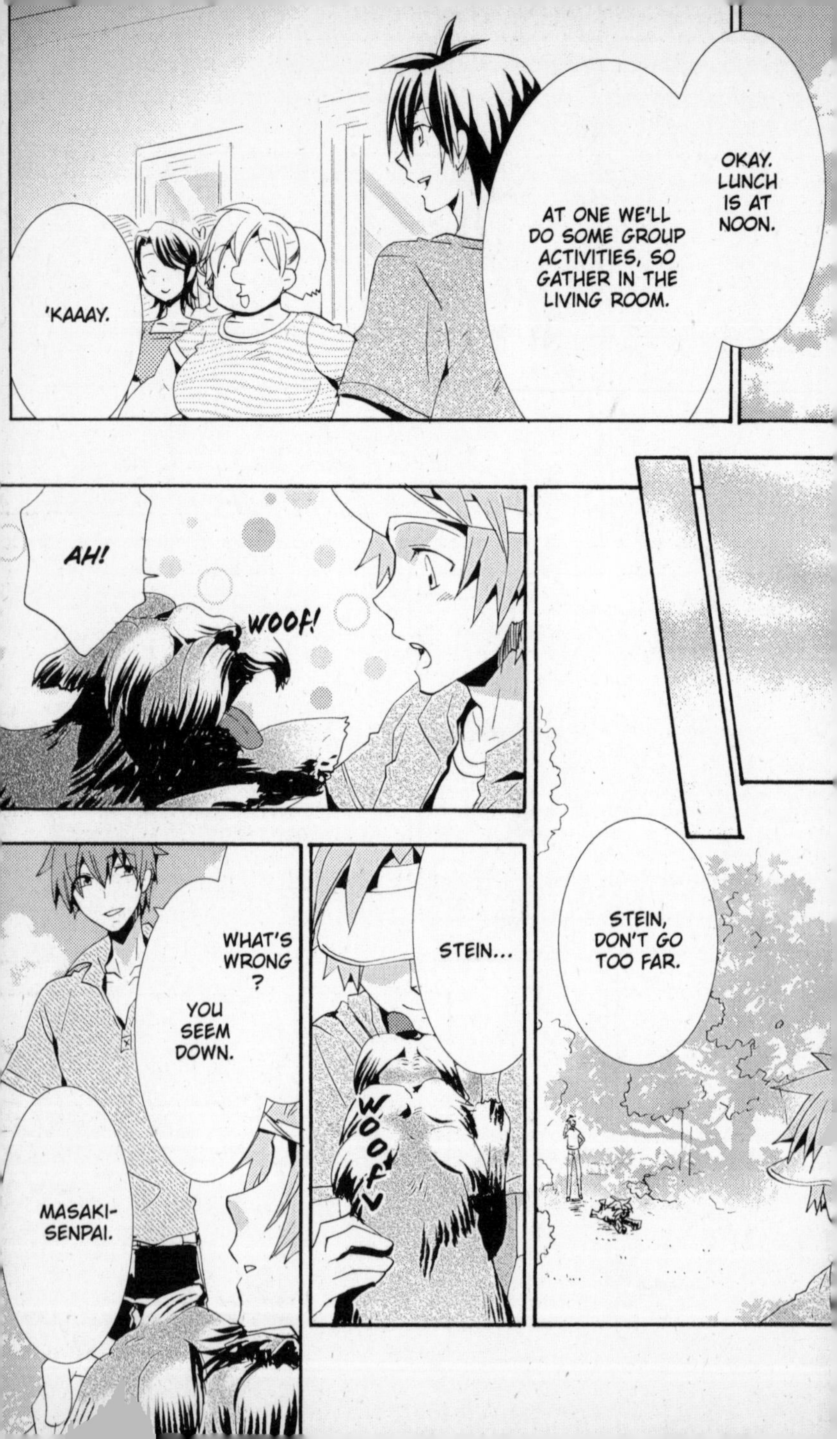
OKAY. LUNCH IS AT NOON.
AT ONE WE'LL DO SOME GROUP ACTIVITIES, SO GATHER IN THE LIVING ROOM.
'KAAAY.
STEIN, DON'T GO TOO FAR.
AH!
WOOF!
STEIN...
WOOF♪
WHAT'S WRONG?
YOU SEEM DOWN.
MASAKI-SENPAI.

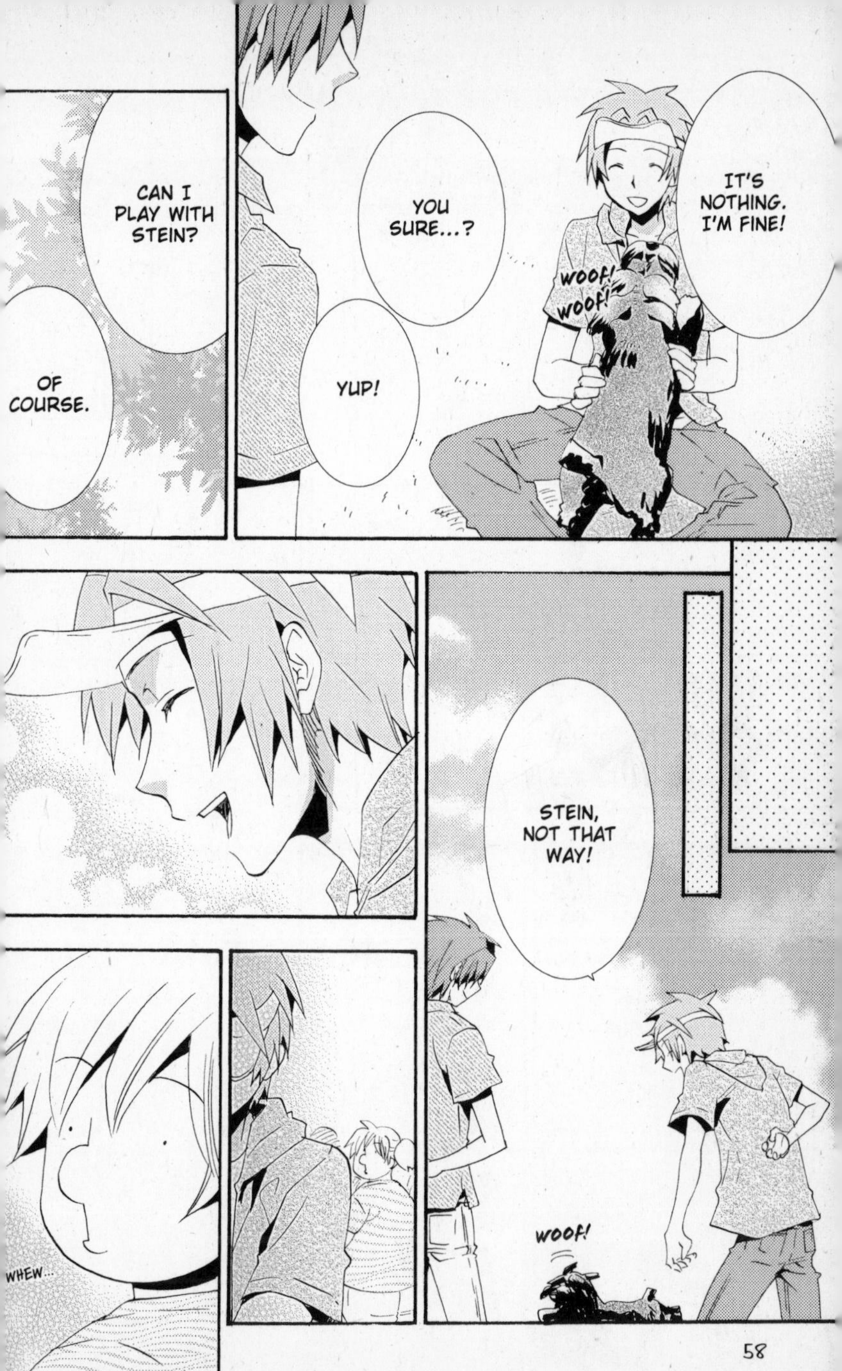
IT'S NOTHING. I'M FINE!
WOOF! WOOF!
YOU SURE...?
YUP!
CAN I PLAY WITH STEIN?
OF COURSE.
STEIN, NOT THAT WAY!
WOOF!
WHEW...

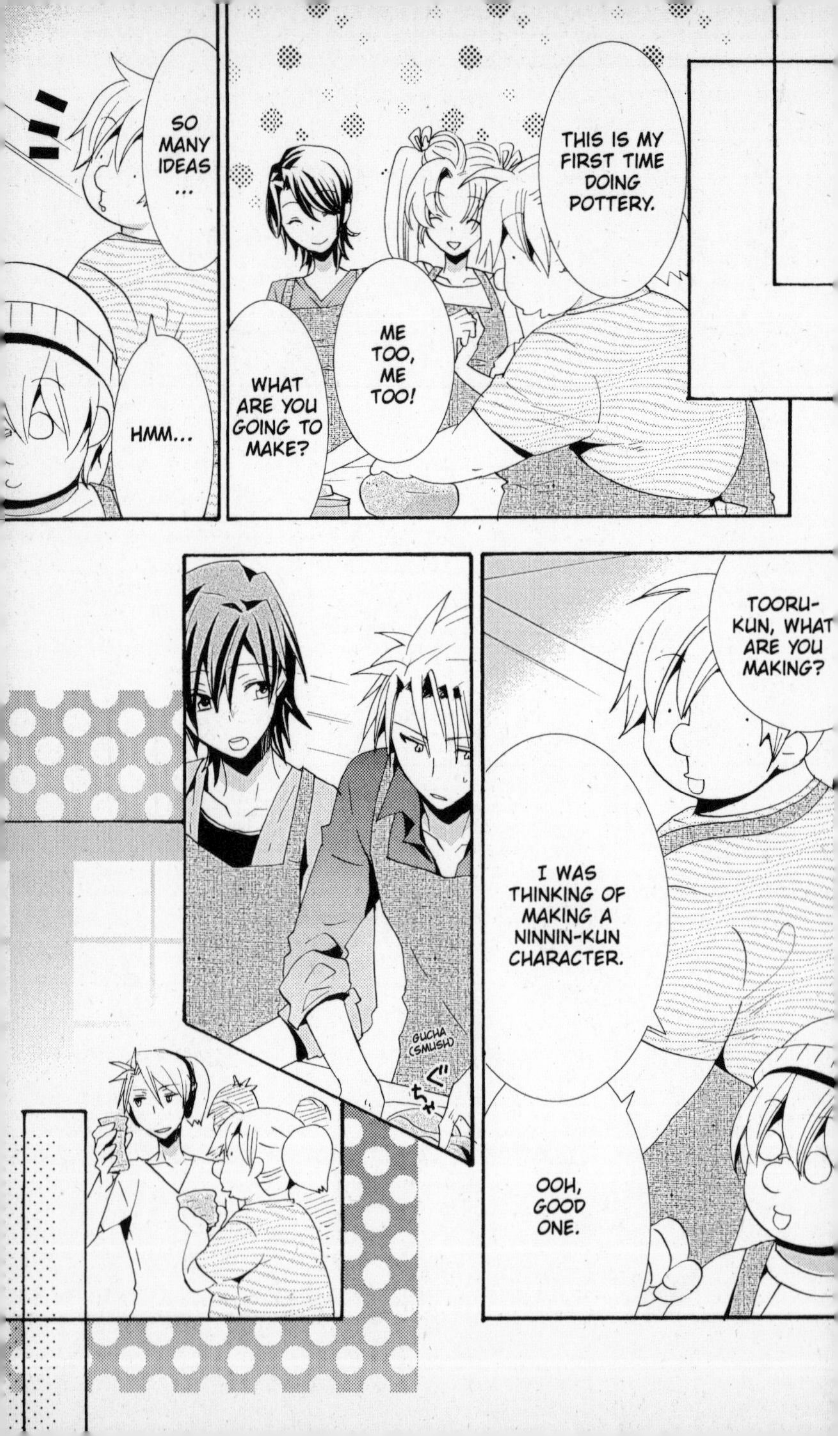
THIS IS MY FIRST TIME DOING POTTERY.
ME TOO, ME TOO!
WHAT ARE YOU GOING TO MAKE?
SO MANY IDEAS...
HMM...
TOORU-KUN, WHAT ARE YOU MAKING?
I WAS THINKING OF MAKING A NINNIN-KUN CHARACTER.
OOH, GOOD ONE.
ぐちゃ
GUCHA (SMUSH)

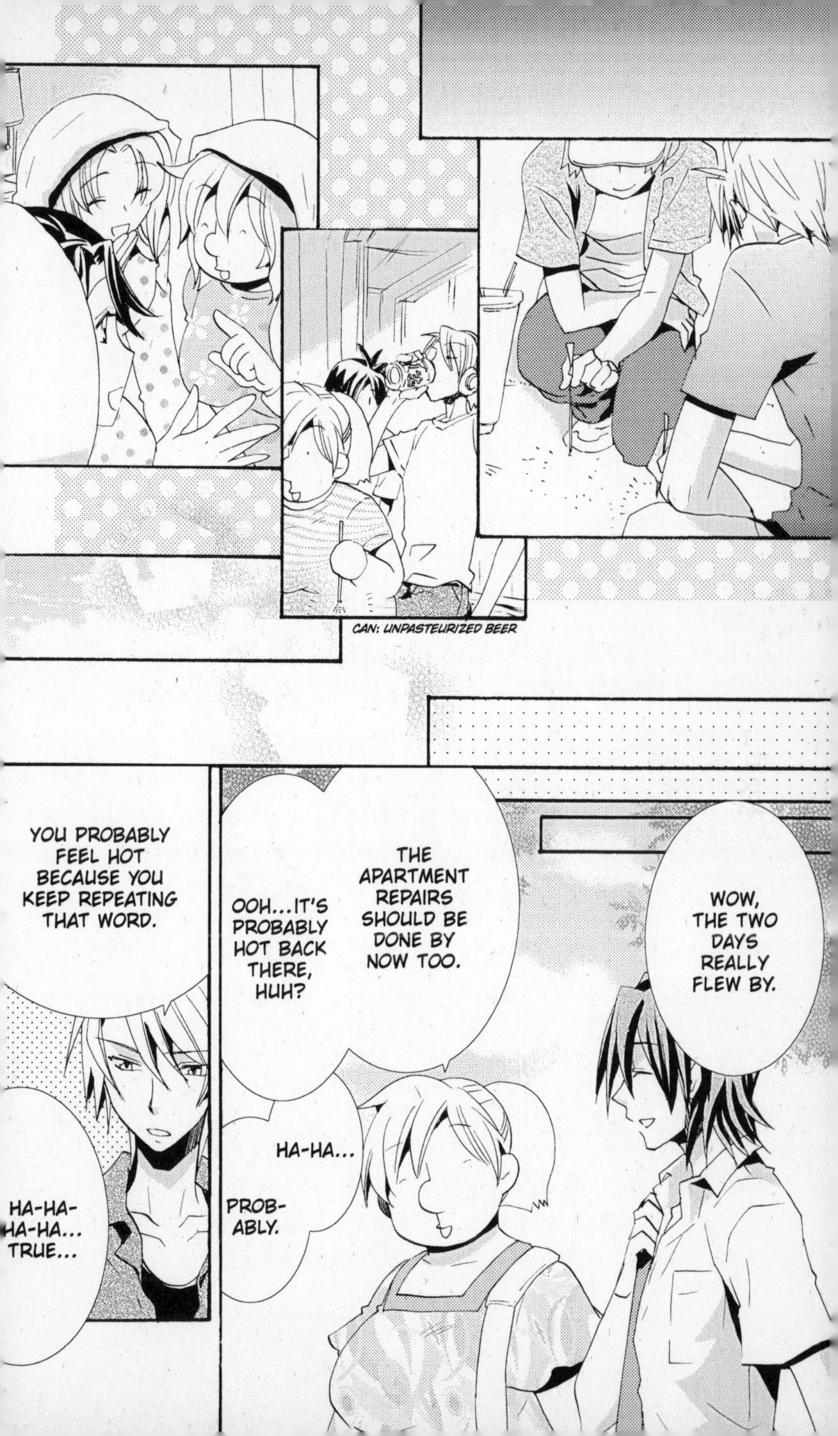
CAN: UNPASTEURIZED BEER
WOW, THE TWO DAYS REALLY FLEW BY.
THE APARTMENT REPAIRS SHOULD BE DONE BY NOW TOO.
OOH...IT'S PROBABLY HOT BACK THERE, HUH?
HA-HA...
PROB-ABLY.
YOU PROBABLY FEEL HOT BECAUSE YOU KEEP REPEATING THAT WORD.
HA-HA-HA-HA... TRUE...

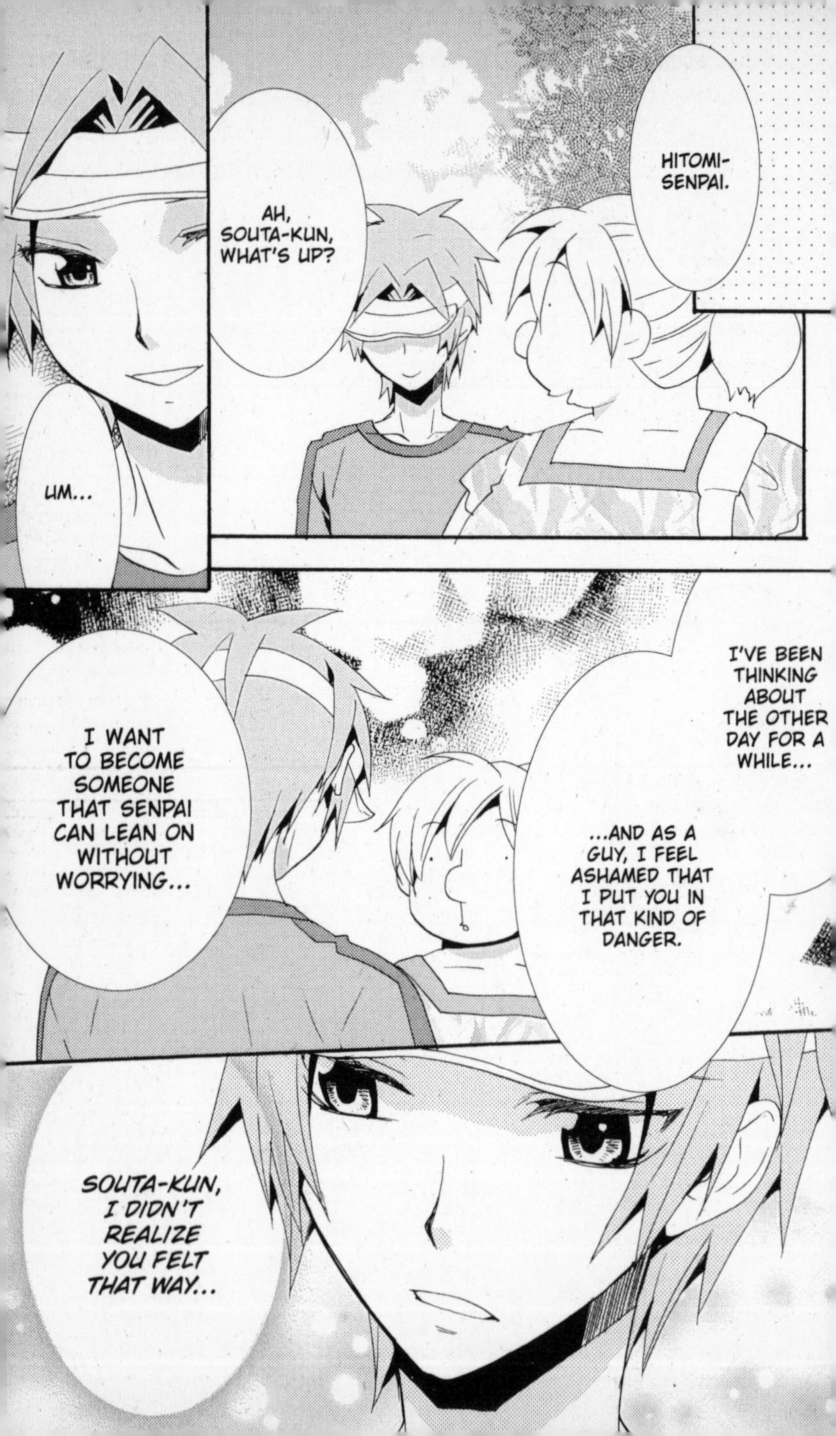
HITOMI-SENPAI.
AH, SOUTA-KUN, WHAT'S UP?
UM...
I'VE BEEN THINKING ABOUT THE OTHER DAY FOR A WHILE...
...AND AS A GUY, I FEEL ASHAMED THAT I PUT YOU IN THAT KIND OF DANGER.
I WANT TO BECOME SOMEONE THAT SENPAI CAN LEAN ON WITHOUT WORRYING...
SOUTA-KUN, I DIDN'T REALIZE YOU FELT THAT WAY...

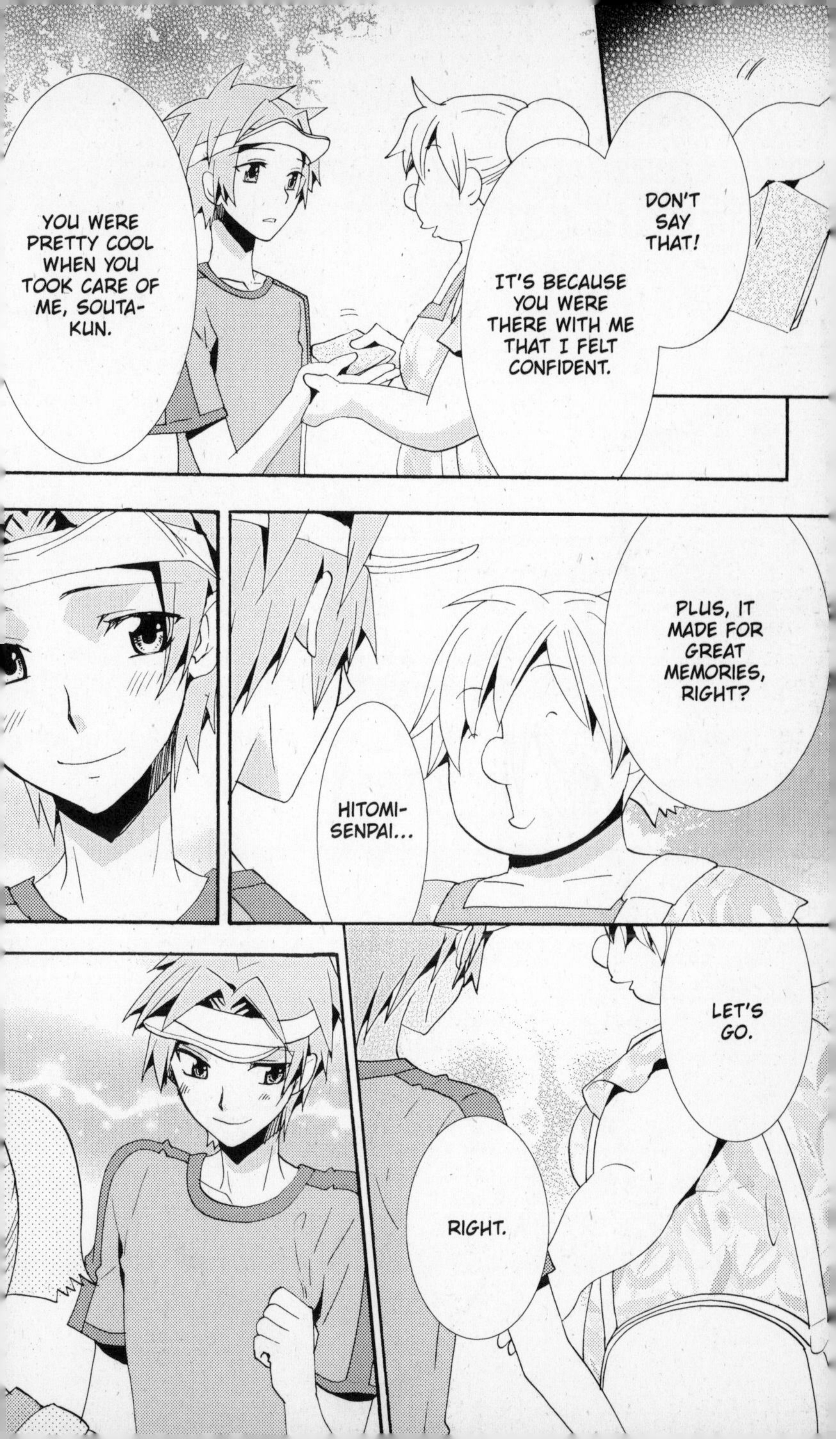
DON'T SAY THAT!
IT'S BECAUSE YOU WERE THERE WITH ME THAT I FELT CONFIDENT.
YOU WERE PRETTY COOL WHEN YOU TOOK CARE OF ME, SOUTA-KUN.
PLUS, IT MADE FOR GREAT MEMORIES, RIGHT?
HITOMI-SENPAI...
LET'S GO.
RIGHT.

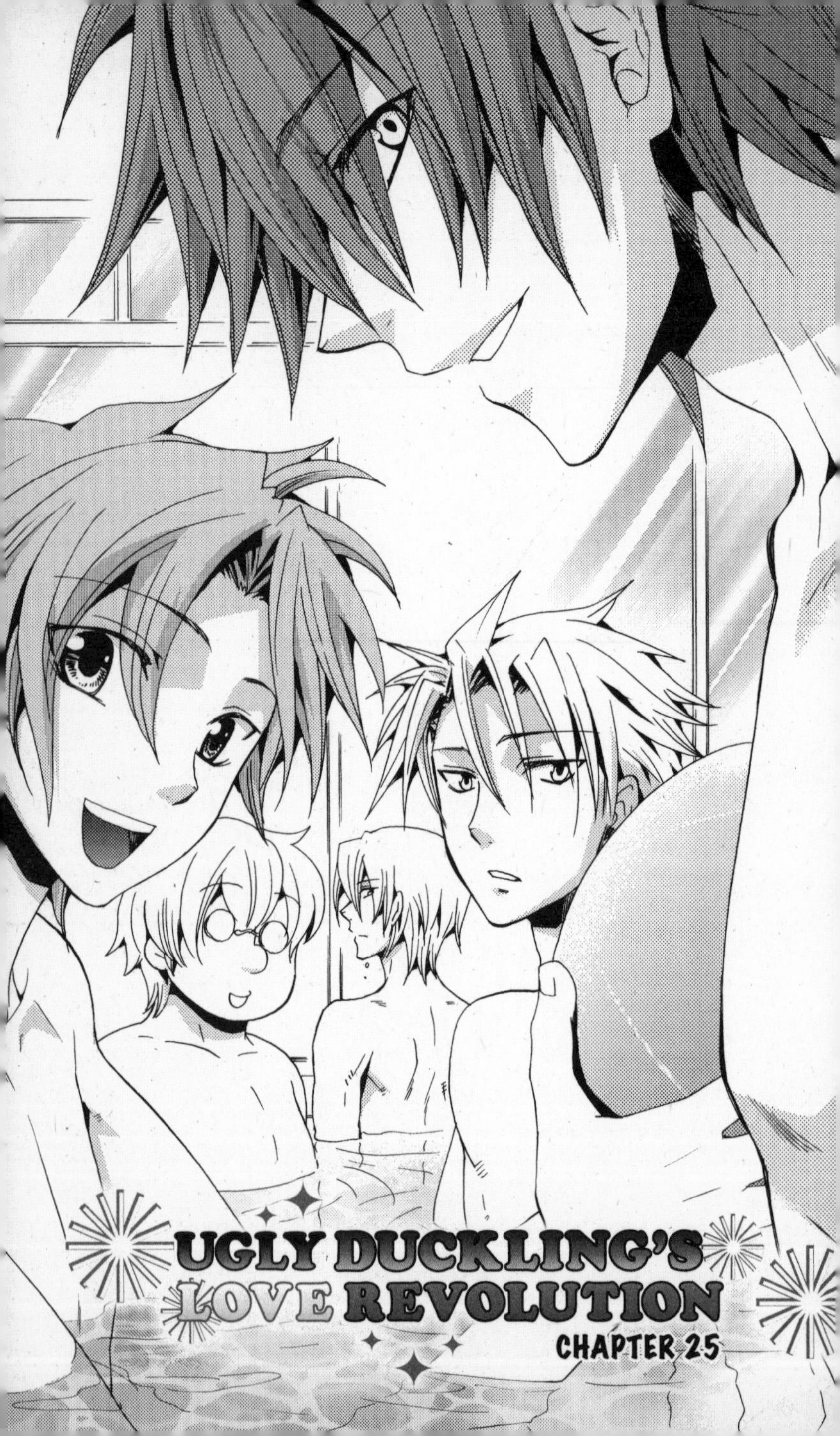
UGLY DUCKLING'S LOVE REVOLUTION
CHAPTER 25

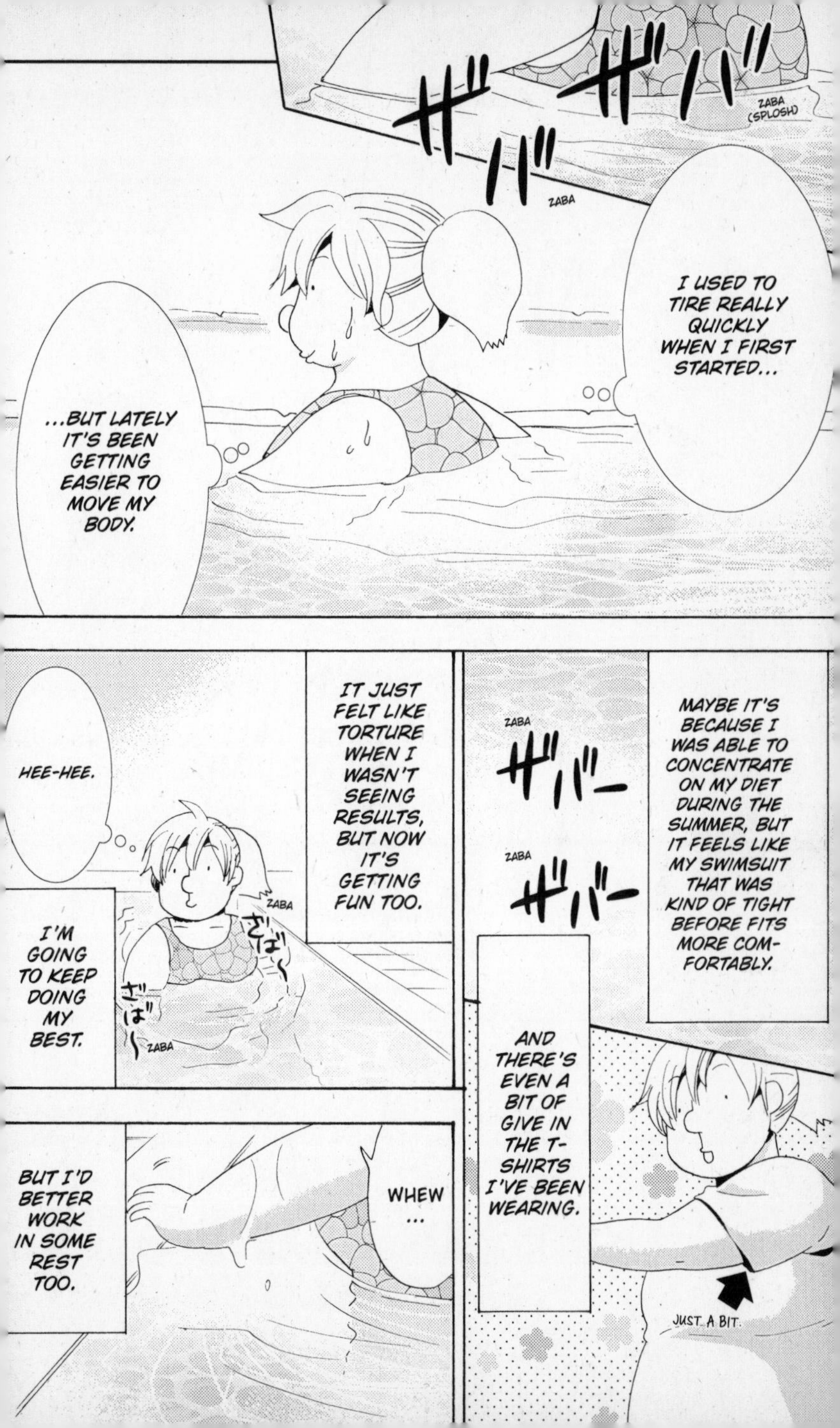

ZABA (SPLOSH)
ZABA
I USED TO TIRE REALLY QUICKLY WHEN I FIRST STARTED...
...BUT LATELY IT'S BEEN GETTING EASIER TO MOVE MY BODY.
ZABA
ZABA
MAYBE IT'S BECAUSE I WAS ABLE TO CONCENTRATE ON MY DIET DURING THE SUMMER, BUT IT FEELS LIKE MY SWIMSUIT THAT WAS KIND OF TIGHT BEFORE FITS MORE COM-FORTABLY.
AND THERE'S EVEN A BIT OF GIVE IN THE T-SHIRTS I'VE BEEN WEARING.
JUST A BIT.
IT JUST FELT LIKE TORTURE WHEN I WASN'T SEEING RESULTS, BUT NOW IT'S GETTING FUN TOO.
HEE-HEE.
ZABA
ZABA
I'M GOING TO KEEP DOING MY BEST.
WHEW ...
BUT I'D BETTER WORK IN SOME REST TOO.

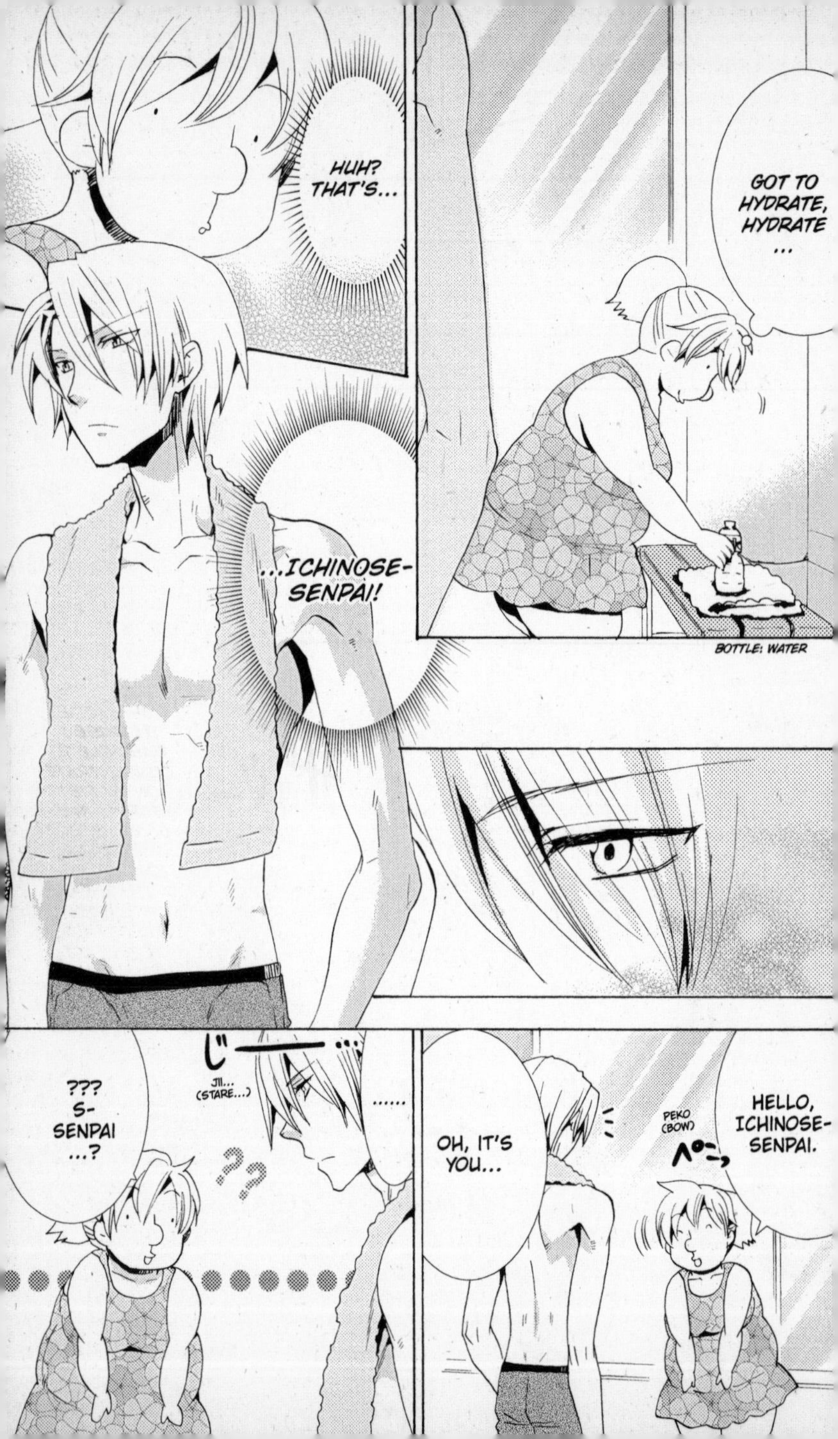
GOT TO HYDRATE, HYDRATE ...
BOTTLE: WATER
HUH? THAT'S...
...ICHINOSE-SENPAI!
HELLO, ICHINOSE-SENPAI.
PEKO (BOW)
OH, IT'S YOU...
......
じ——…
JII... (STARE...)
??? S-SENPAI ...?

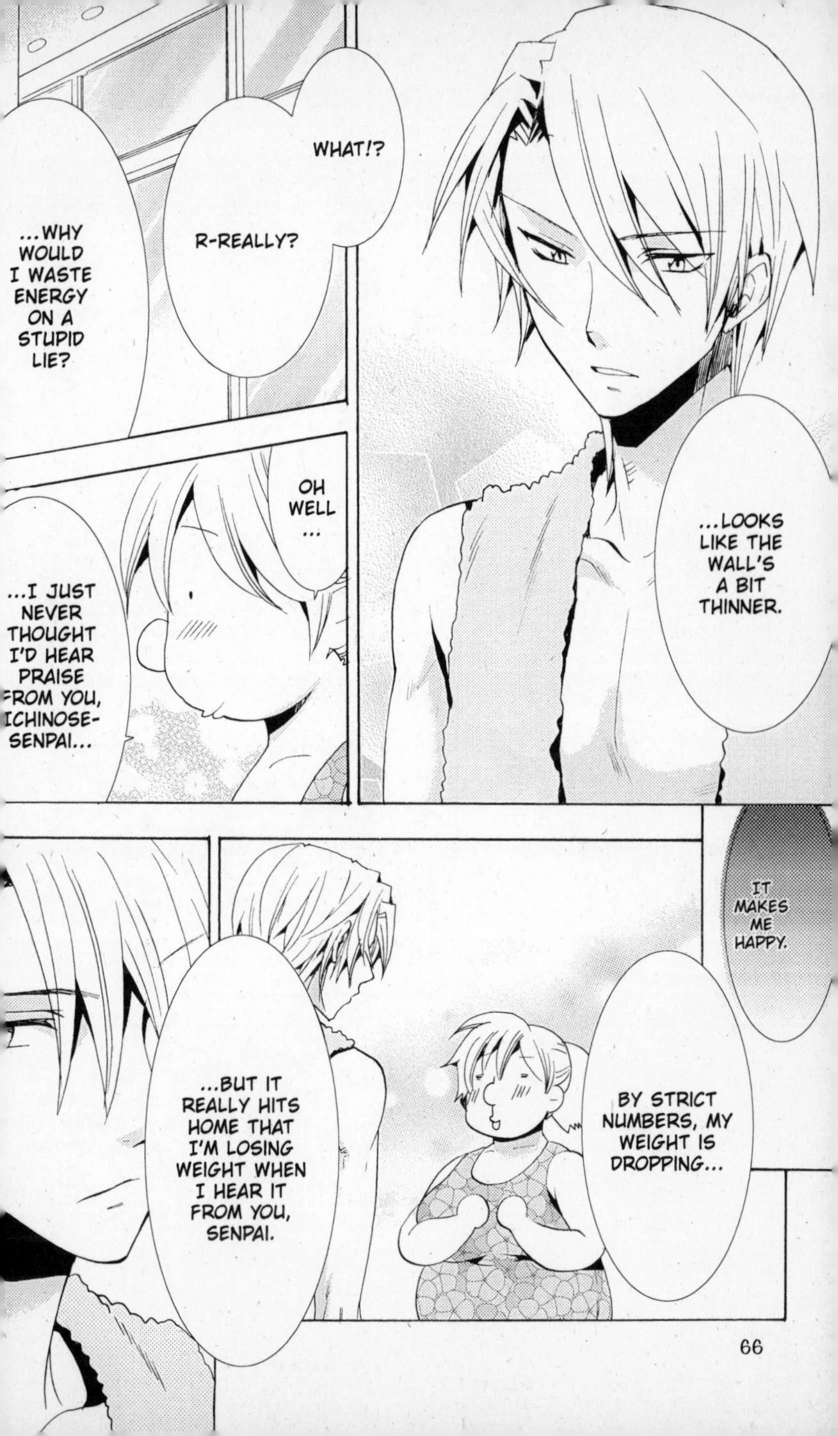
...LOOKS LIKE THE WALL'S A BIT THINNER.
WHAT!?
R-REALLY?
...WHY WOULD I WASTE ENERGY ON A STUPID LIE?
OH WELL...
...I JUST NEVER THOUGHT I'D HEAR PRAISE FROM YOU, ICHINOSE-SENPAI...
IT MAKES ME HAPPY.
BY STRICT NUMBERS, MY WEIGHT IS DROPPING...
...BUT IT REALLY HITS HOME THAT I'M LOSING WEIGHT WHEN I HEAR IT FROM YOU, SENPAI.

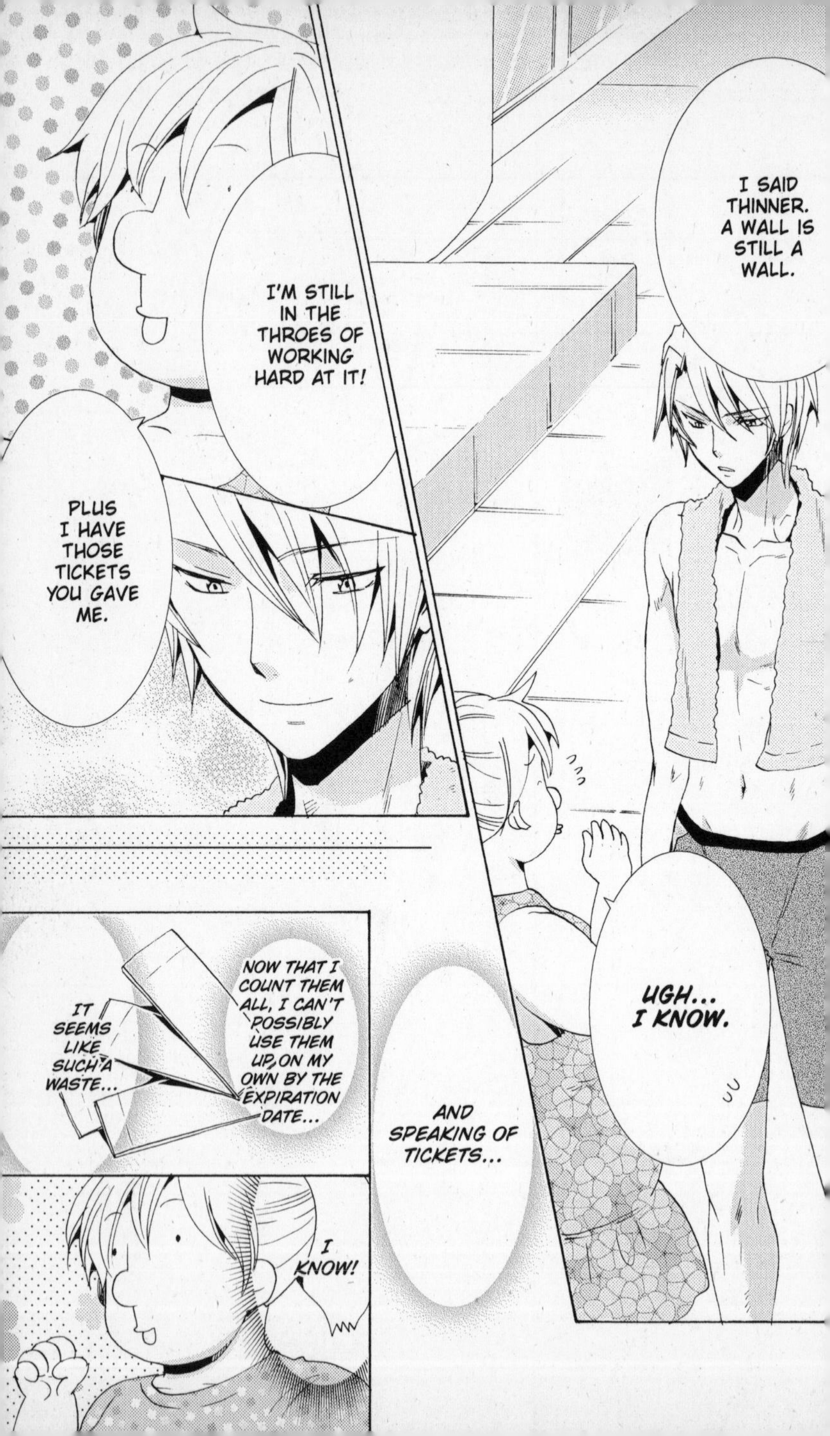
I SAID THINNER. A WALL IS STILL A WALL.
UGH... I KNOW.
I'M STILL IN THE THROES OF WORKING HARD AT IT!
PLUS I HAVE THOSE TICKETS YOU GAVE ME.
NOW THAT I COUNT THEM ALL, I CAN'T POSSIBLY USE THEM UP ON MY OWN BY THE EXPIRATION DATE...
IT SEEMS LIKE SUCH A WASTE...
AND SPEAKING OF TICKETS...
I KNOW!

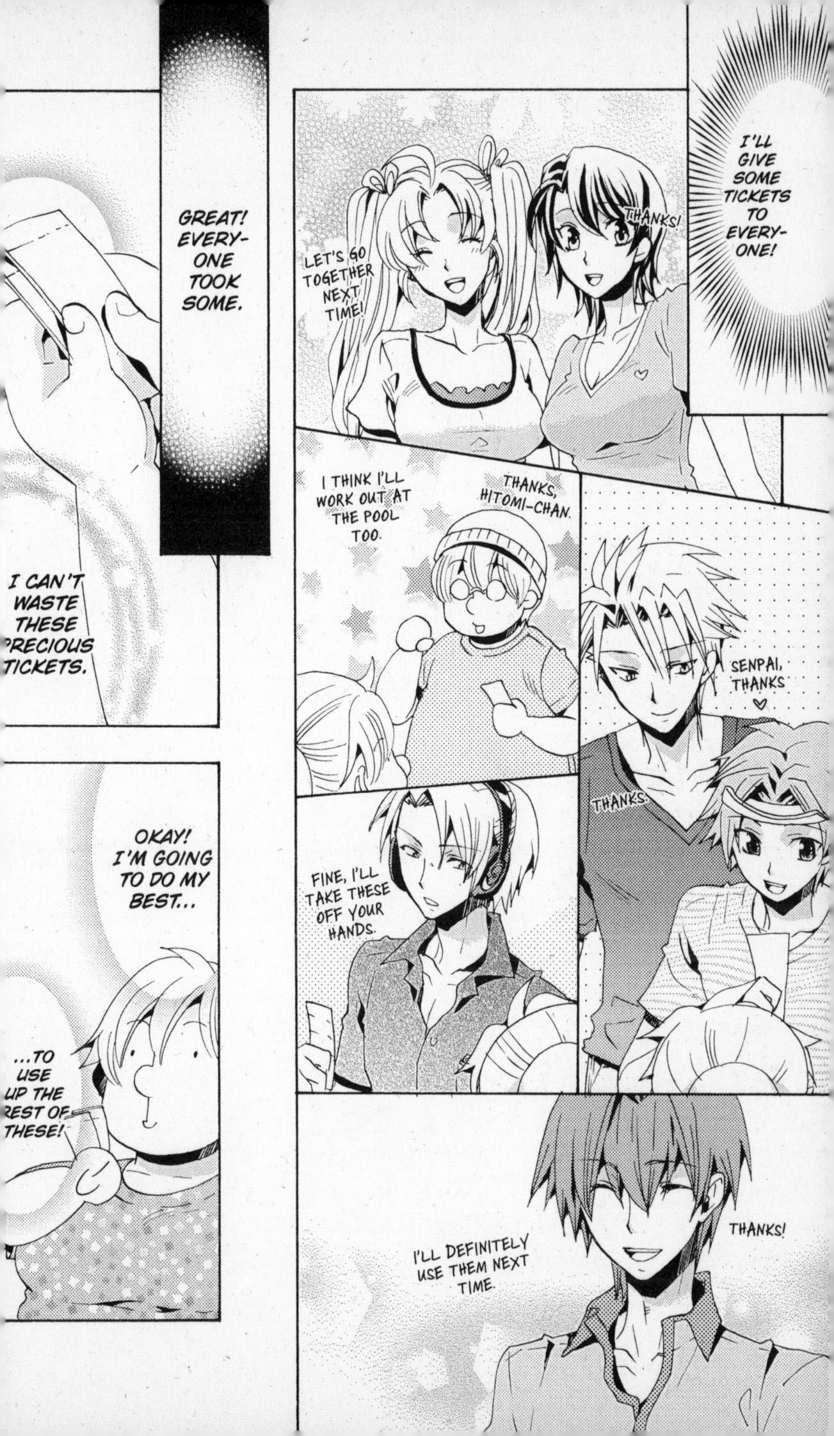
I'LL GIVE SOME TICKETS TO EVERYONE!
THANKS!
LET'S GO TOGETHER NEXT TIME!
SENPAI, THANKS ♡
THANKS.
THANKS, HITOMI-CHAN.
I THINK I'LL WORK OUT AT THE POOL TOO.
FINE, I'LL TAKE THESE OFF YOUR HANDS.
THANKS!
I'LL DEFINITELY USE THEM NEXT TIME.
GREAT! EVERYONE TOOK SOME.
I CAN'T WASTE THESE PRECIOUS TICKETS.
OKAY! I'M GOING TO DO MY BEST...
...TO USE UP THE REST OF THESE!

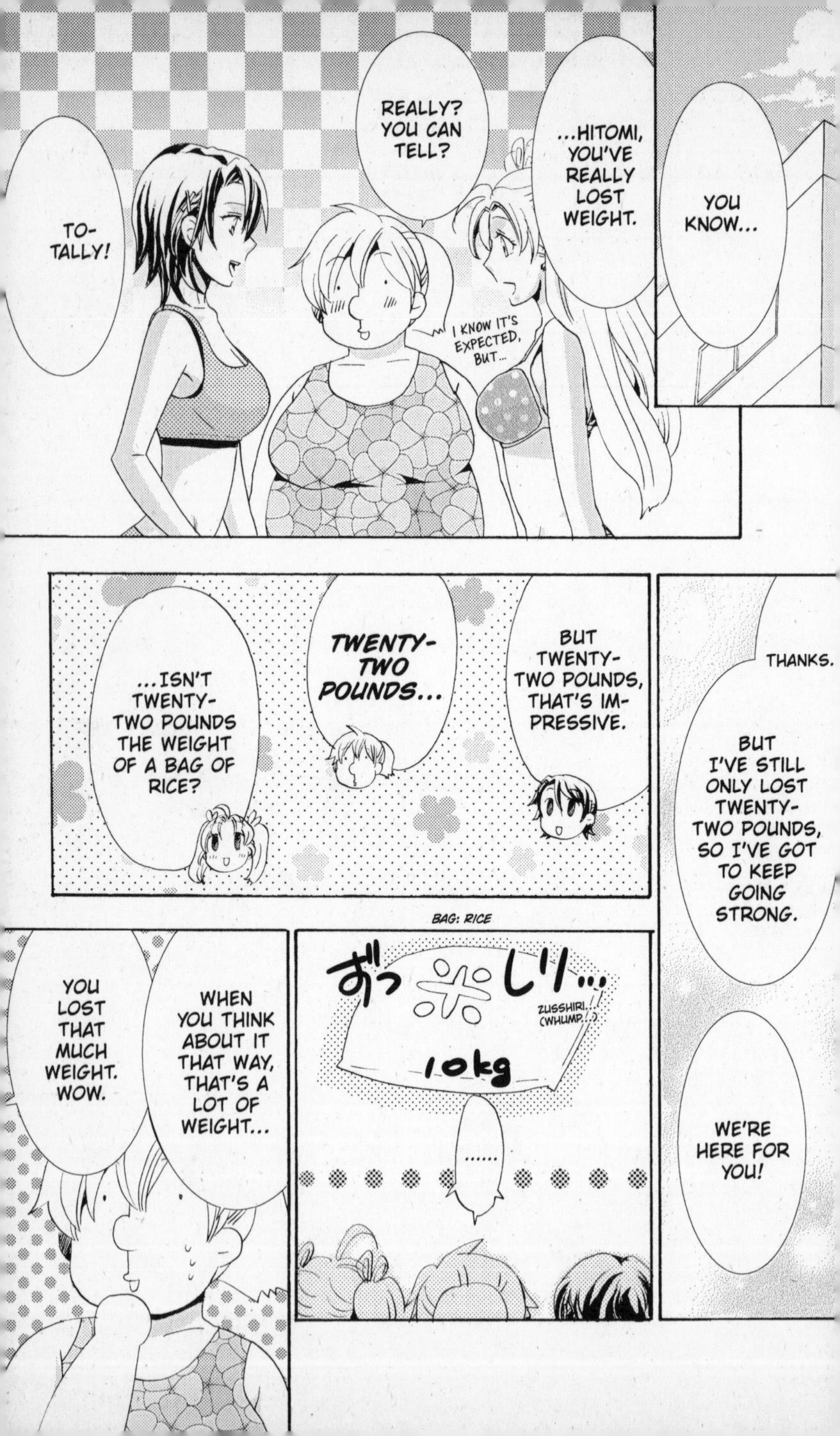
YOU KNOW...
...HITOMI, YOU'VE REALLY LOST WEIGHT.
REALLY? YOU CAN TELL?
I KNOW IT'S EXPECTED, BUT...
TO-TALLY!
THANKS.
BUT I'VE STILL ONLY LOST TWENTY-TWO POUNDS, SO I'VE GOT TO KEEP GOING STRONG.
WE'RE HERE FOR YOU!
BUT TWENTY-TWO POUNDS, THAT'S IM-PRESSIVE.
TWENTY-TWO POUNDS...
...ISN'T TWENTY-TWO POUNDS THE WEIGHT OF A BAG OF RICE?
BAG: RICE
ずっしり...
ZUSSHIRI... (WHUMP...)
10kg
......
WHEN YOU THINK ABOUT IT THAT WAY, THAT'S A LOT OF WEIGHT...
YOU LOST THAT MUCH WEIGHT. WOW.

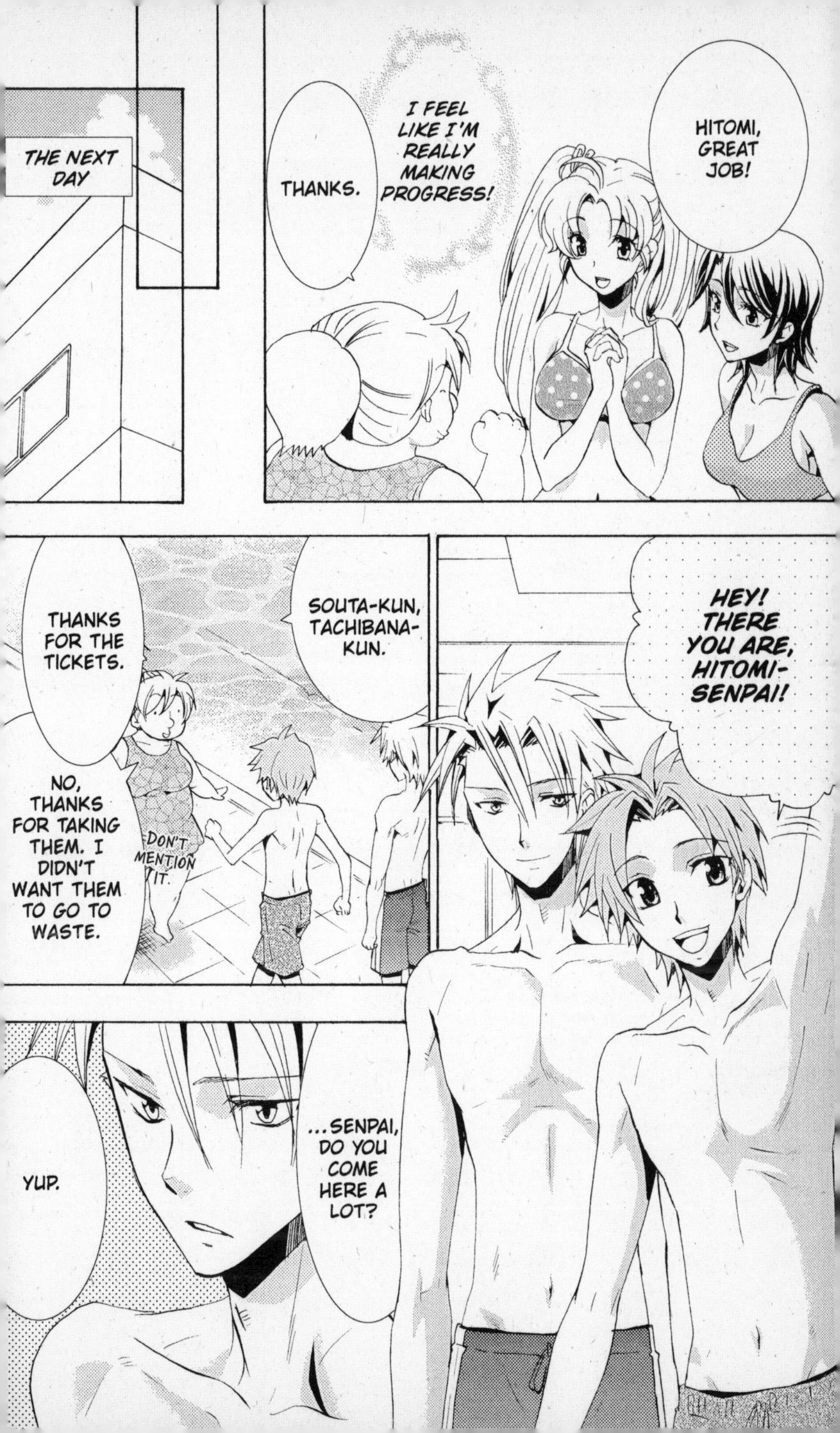
HITOMI, GREAT JOB!
I FEEL LIKE I'M REALLY MAKING PROGRESS!
THANKS.
THE NEXT DAY
HEY! THERE YOU ARE, HITOMI-SENPAI!
SOUTA-KUN, TACHIBANA-KUN.
THANKS FOR THE TICKETS.
DON'T MENTION IT.
NO, THANKS FOR TAKING THEM. I DIDN'T WANT THEM TO GO TO WASTE.
...SENPAI, DO YOU COME HERE A LOT?
YUP.

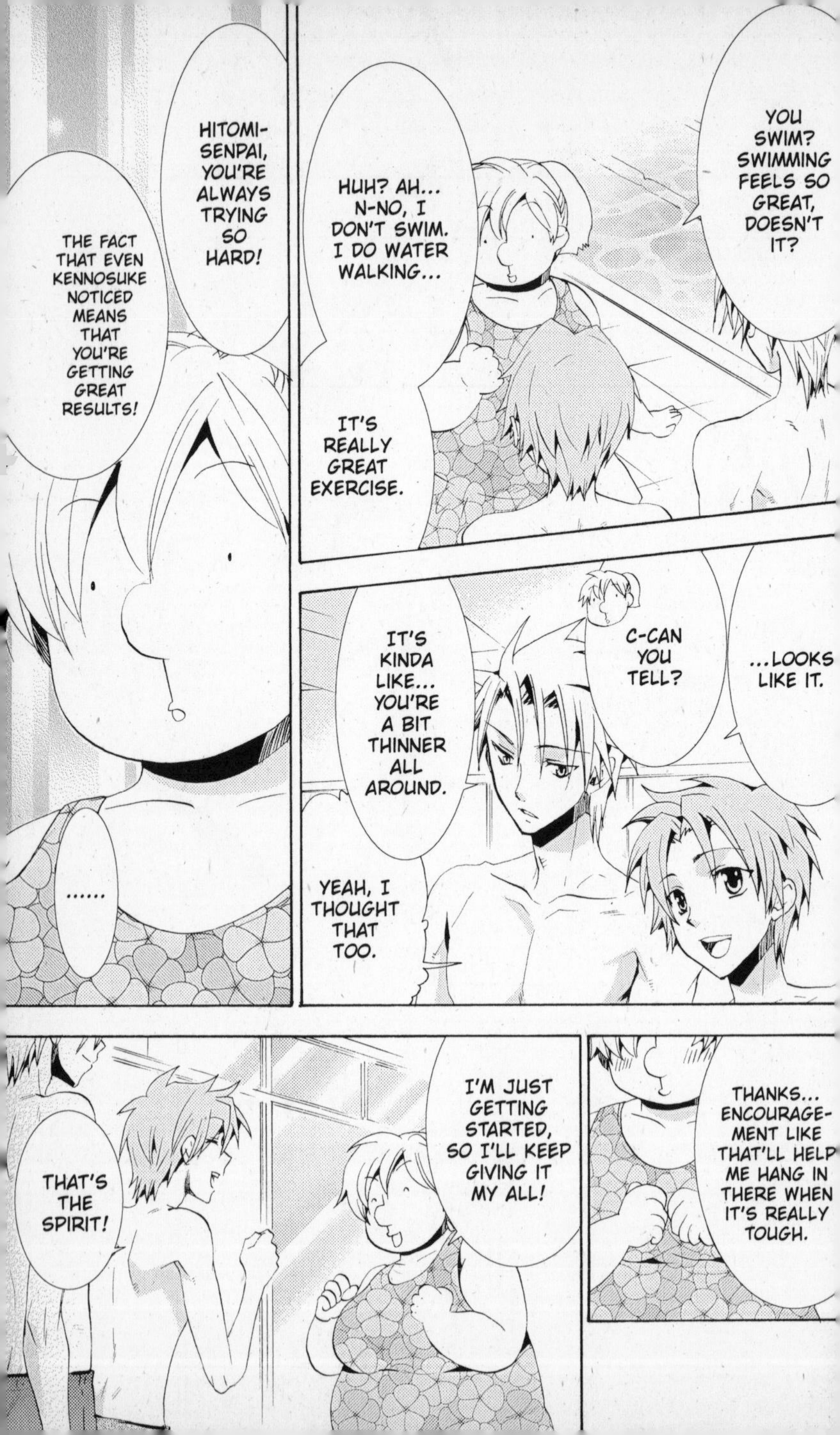
YOU SWIM? SWIMMING FEELS SO GREAT, DOESN'T IT?
HUH? AH... N-NO, I DON'T SWIM. I DO WATER WALKING...
IT'S REALLY GREAT EXERCISE.
...LOOKS LIKE IT.
C-CAN YOU TELL?
IT'S KINDA LIKE... YOU'RE A BIT THINNER ALL AROUND.
YEAH, I THOUGHT THAT TOO.
HITOMI-SENPAI, YOU'RE ALWAYS TRYING SO HARD!
THE FACT THAT EVEN KENNOSUKE NOTICED MEANS THAT YOU'RE GETTING GREAT RESULTS!
......
THANKS... ENCOURAGEMENT LIKE THAT'LL HELP ME HANG IN THERE WHEN IT'S REALLY TOUGH.
I'M JUST GETTING STARTED, SO I'LL KEEP GIVING IT MY ALL!
THAT'S THE SPIRIT!

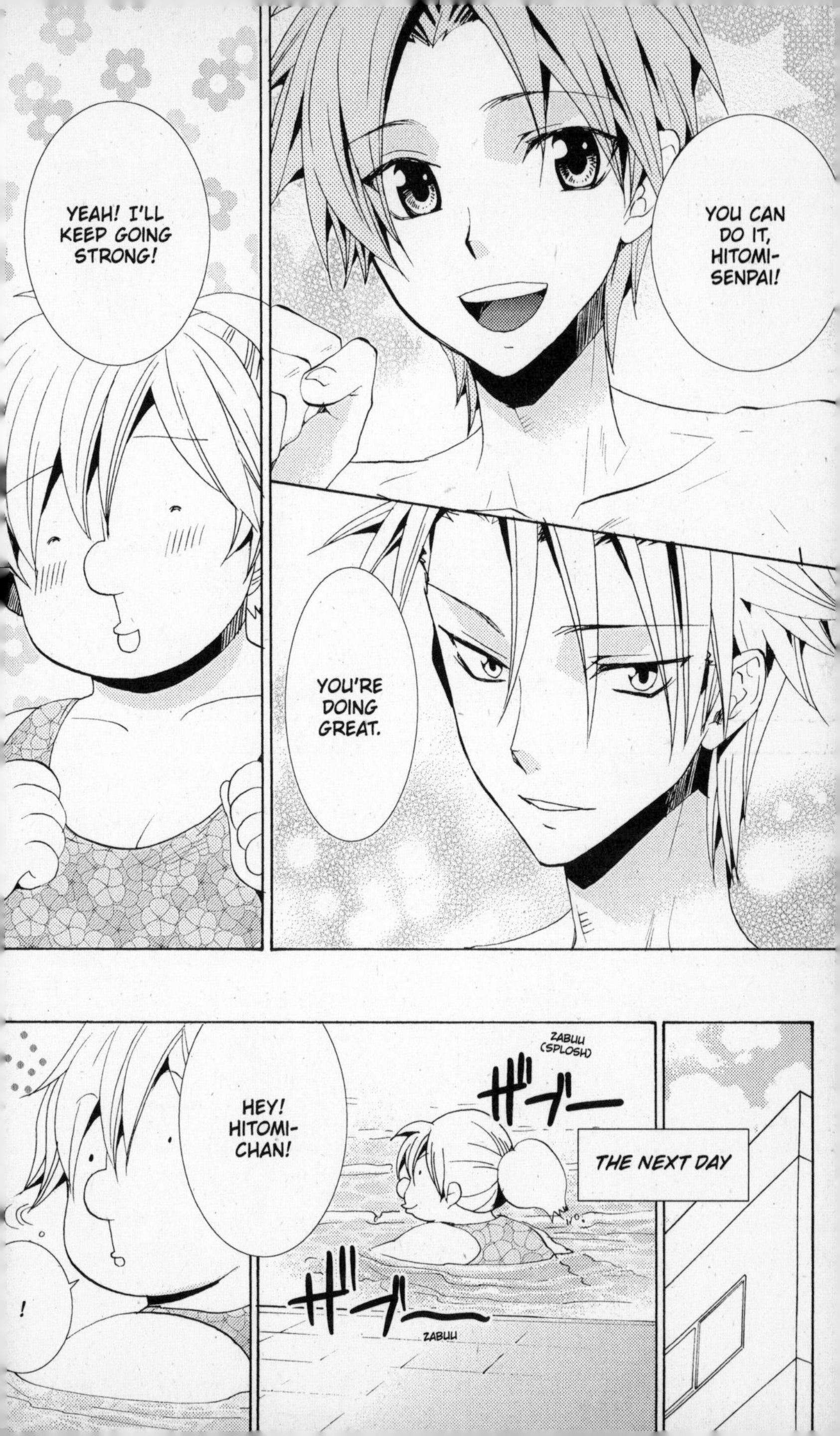
YOU CAN DO IT, HITOMI-SENPAI!
YOU'RE DOING GREAT.
YEAH! I'LL KEEP GOING STRONG!
THE NEXT DAY
ザブー
ZABUU (SPLOSH)
ザブー
ZABUU
HEY! HITOMI-CHAN!
!

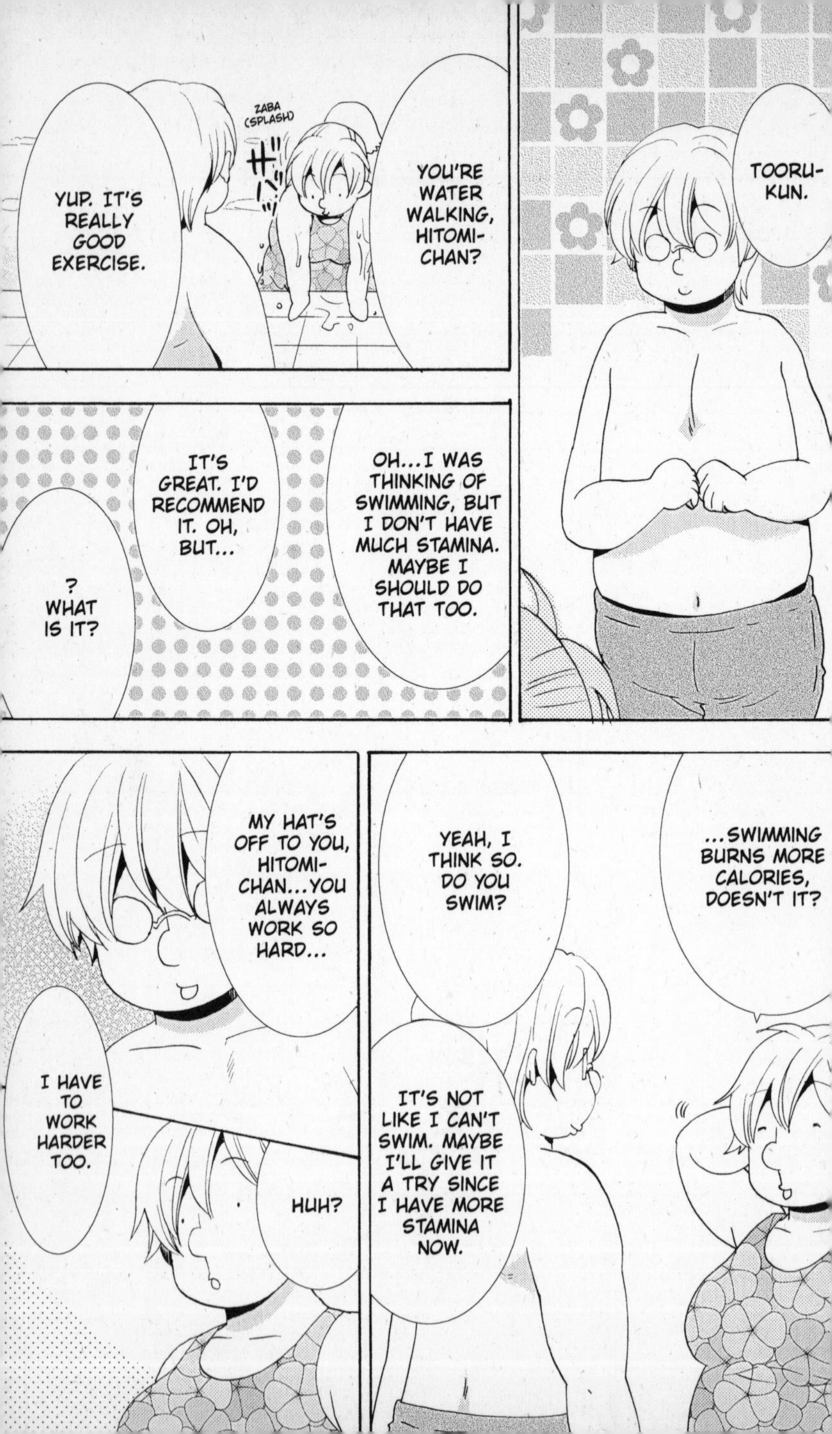
TOORU-KUN.
ZABA (SPLASH)
YOU'RE WATER WALKING, HITOMI-CHAN?
YUP. IT'S REALLY GOOD EXERCISE.
OH...I WAS THINKING OF SWIMMING, BUT I DON'T HAVE MUCH STAMINA. MAYBE I SHOULD DO THAT TOO.
IT'S GREAT. I'D RECOMMEND IT. OH, BUT...
? WHAT IS IT?
...SWIMMING BURNS MORE CALORIES, DOESN'T IT?
YEAH, I THINK SO. DO YOU SWIM?
IT'S NOT LIKE I CAN'T SWIM. MAYBE I'LL GIVE IT A TRY SINCE I HAVE MORE STAMINA NOW.
MY HAT'S OFF TO YOU, HITOMI-CHAN...YOU ALWAYS WORK SO HARD...
I HAVE TO WORK HARDER TOO.
HUH?

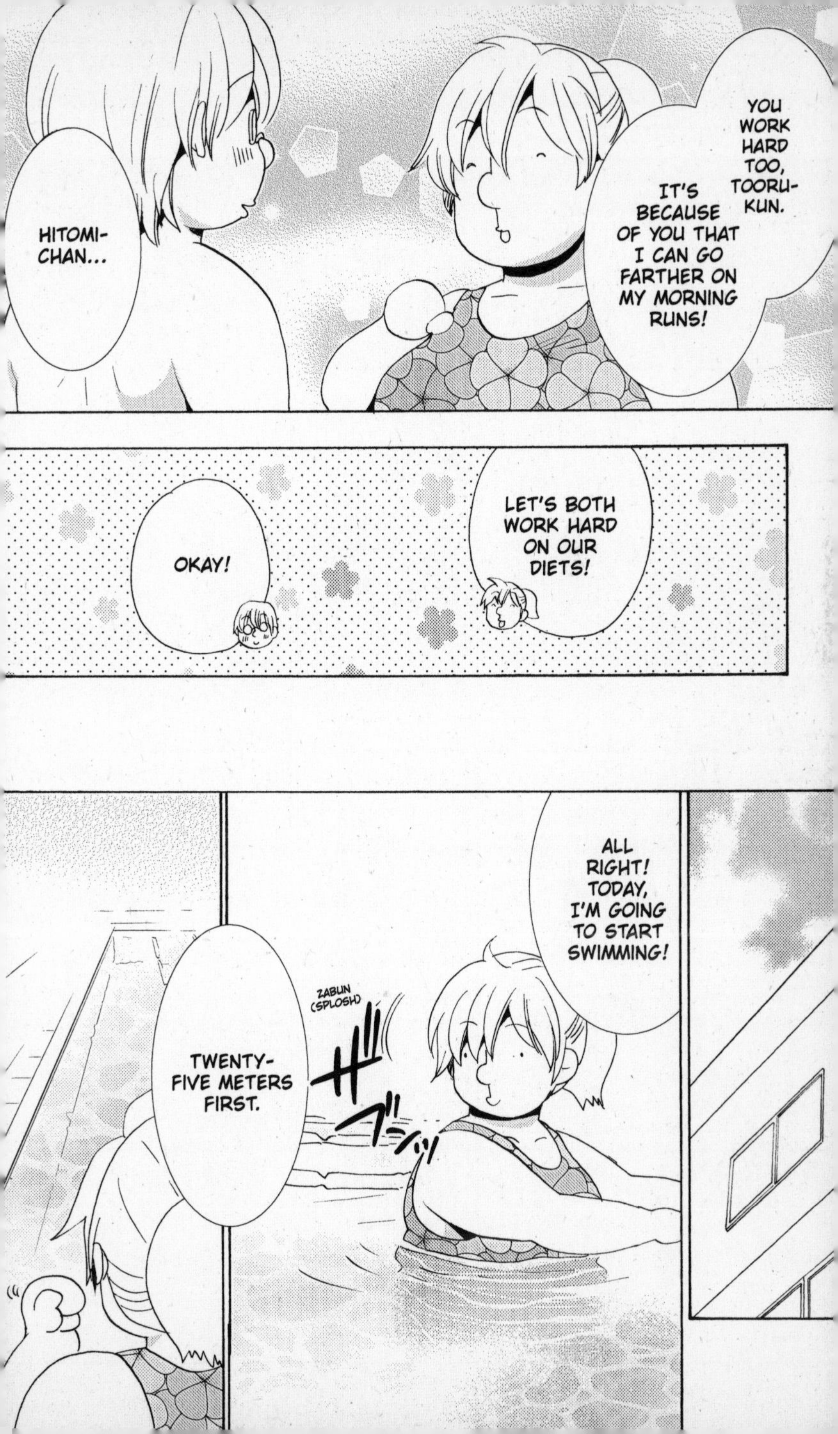
YOU WORK HARD TOO, TOORU-KUN.
IT'S BECAUSE OF YOU THAT I CAN GO FARTHER ON MY MORNING RUNS!
HITOMI-CHAN...
LET'S BOTH WORK HARD ON OUR DIETS!
OKAY!
ALL RIGHT! TODAY, I'M GOING TO START SWIMMING!
ZABUN (SPLOSH)
TWENTY-FIVE METERS FIRST.

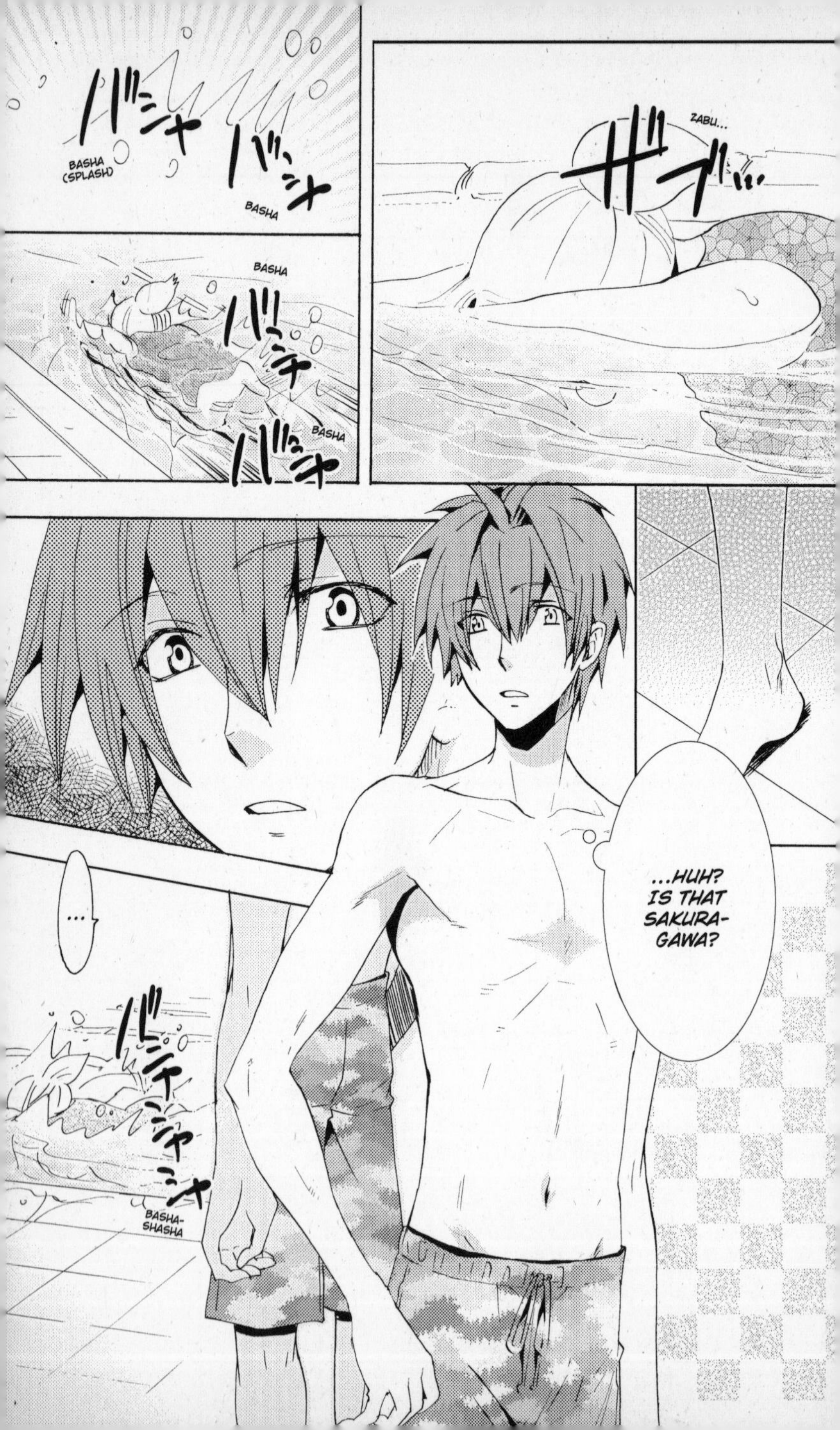
ザブ…
ZABU...
バシャ
BASHA (SPLASH)
バシャ
BASHA
バシャ
BASHA
バシャ
BASHA
...HUH? IS THAT SAKURA-GAWA?
...
バシャシャシャ
BASHA-SHASHA

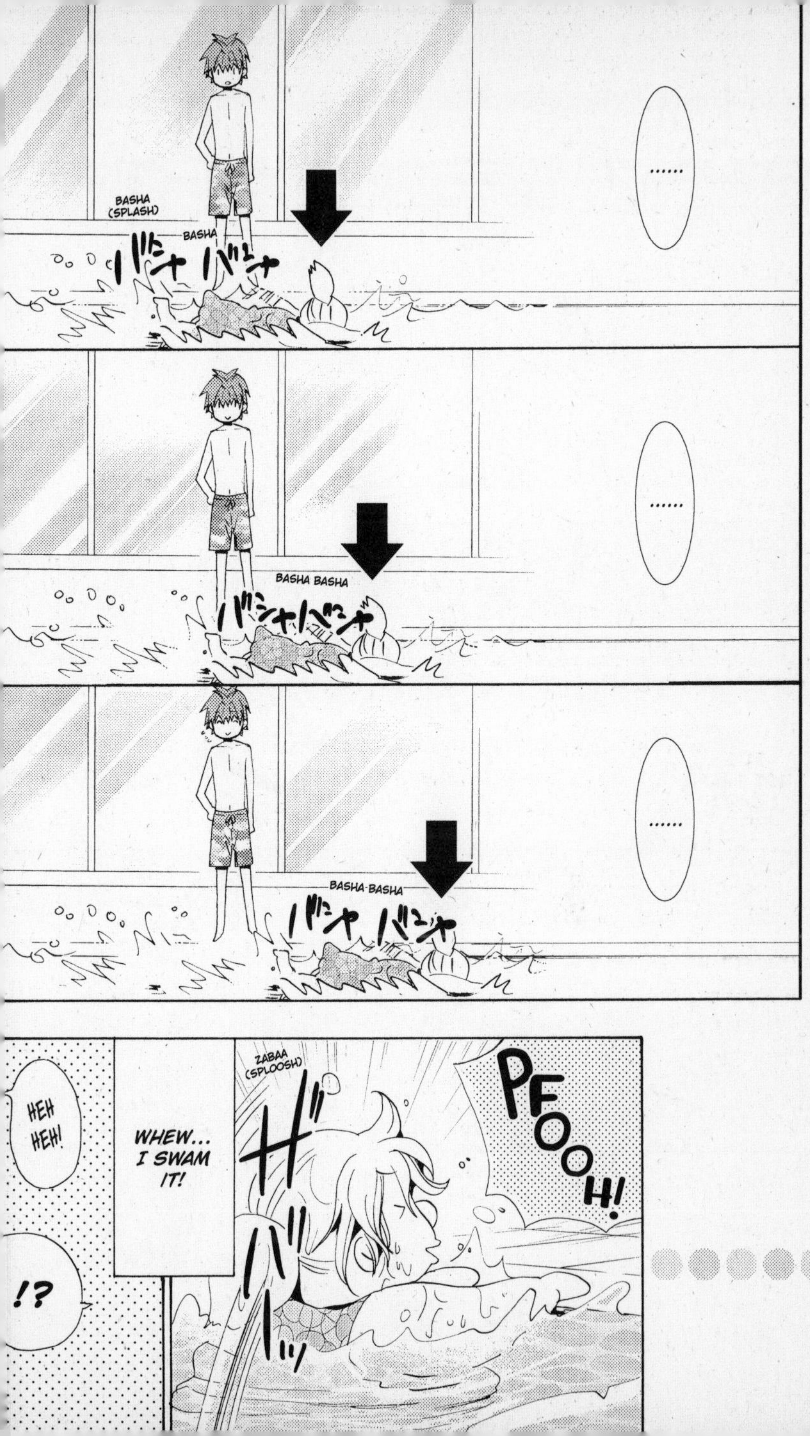

……
BASHA (SPLASH)
BASHA
……
BASHA BASHA
……
BASHA-BASHA
PFOOH!
ZABAA (SPLOOSH)
WHEW… I SWAM IT!
HEH HEH!
!?

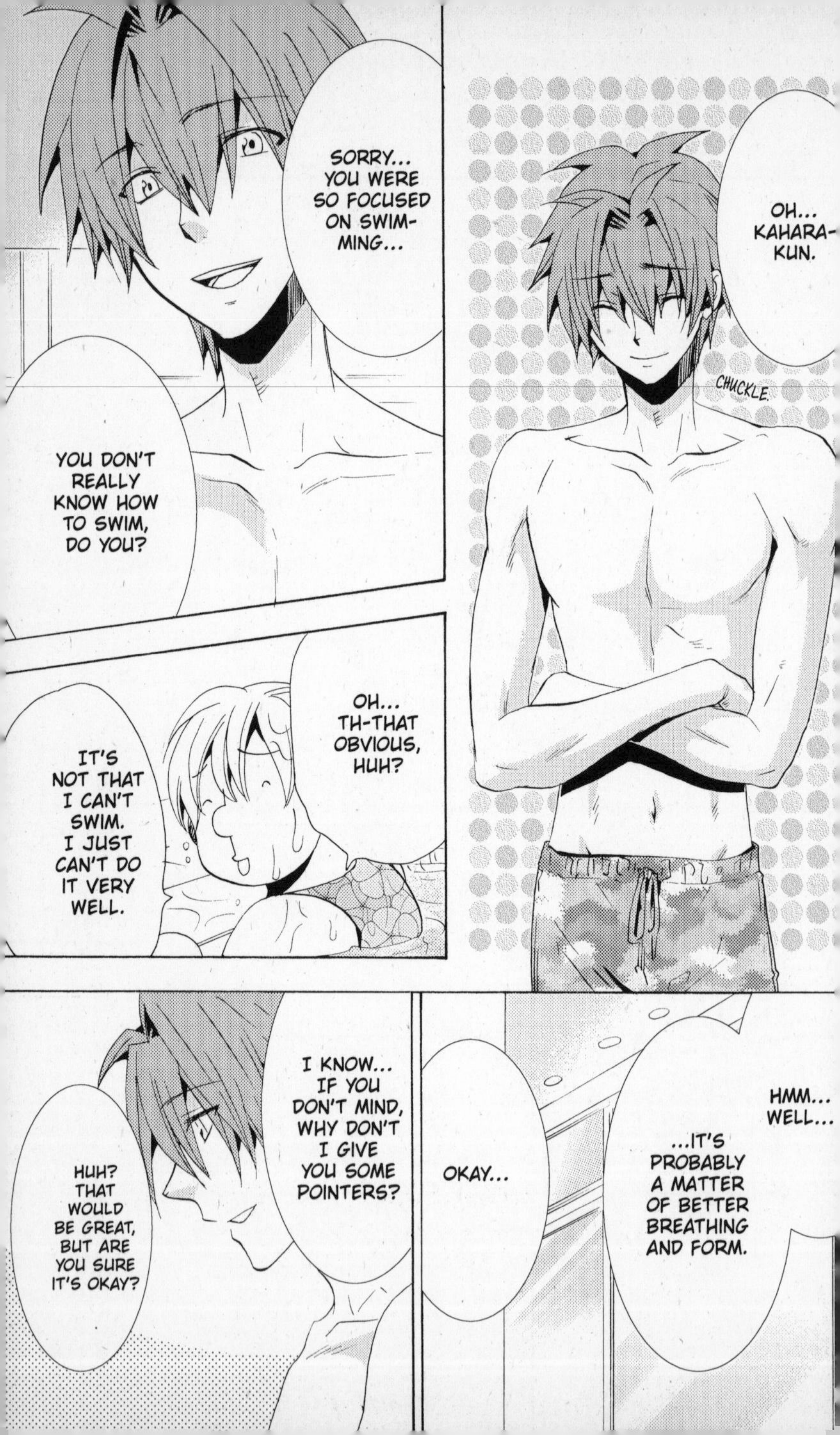
OH... KAHARA-KUN.
CHUCKLE.
SORRY... YOU WERE SO FOCUSED ON SWIMMING...
YOU DON'T REALLY KNOW HOW TO SWIM, DO YOU?
OH... TH-THAT OBVIOUS, HUH?
IT'S NOT THAT I CAN'T SWIM. I JUST CAN'T DO IT VERY WELL.
HMM... WELL...
...IT'S PROBABLY A MATTER OF BETTER BREATHING AND FORM.
OKAY...
I KNOW... IF YOU DON'T MIND, WHY DON'T I GIVE YOU SOME POINTERS?
HUH? THAT WOULD BE GREAT, BUT ARE YOU SURE IT'S OKAY?

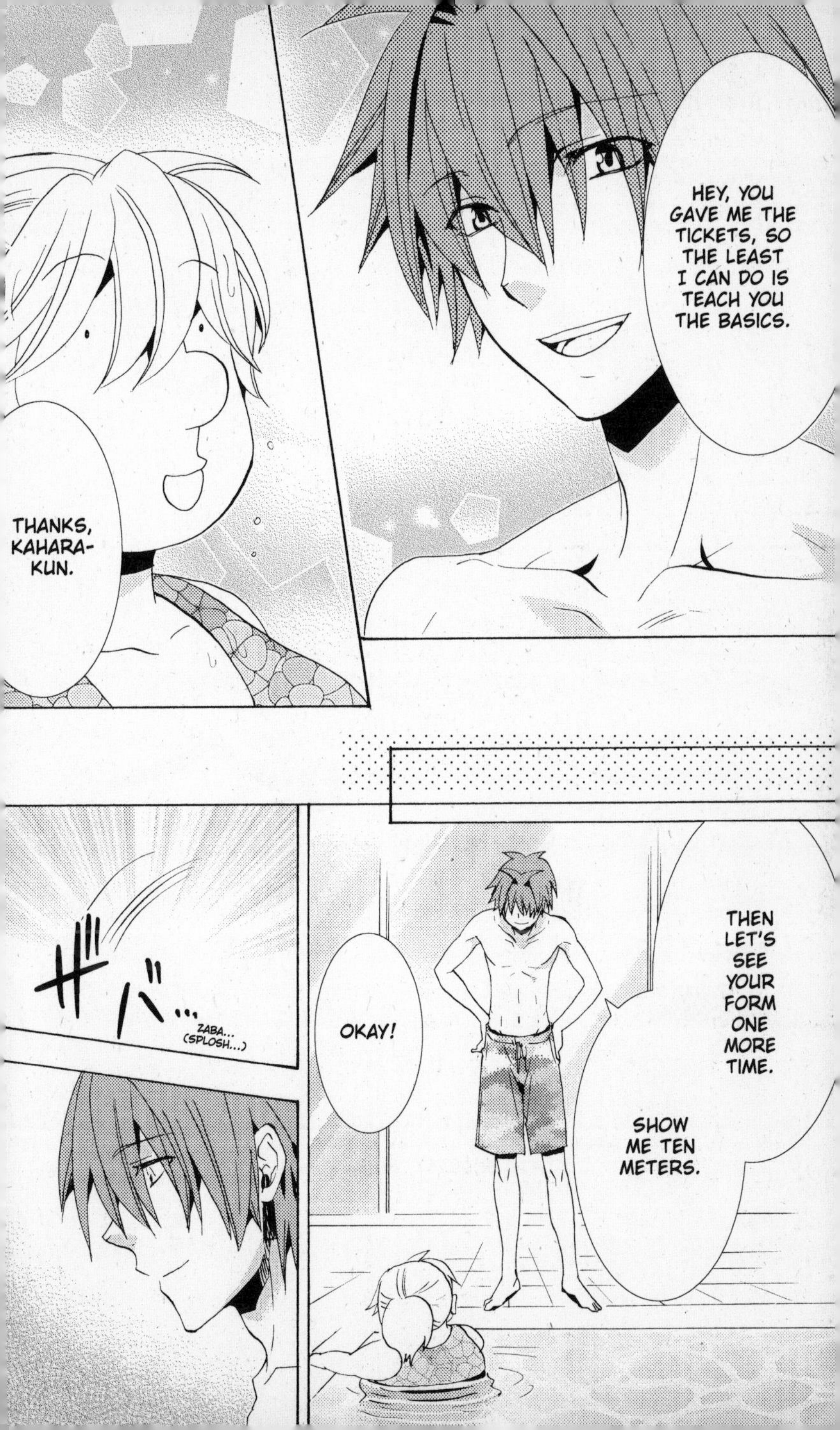
HEY, YOU GAVE ME THE TICKETS, SO THE LEAST I CAN DO IS TEACH YOU THE BASICS.
THANKS, KAHARA-KUN.
THEN LET'S SEE YOUR FORM ONE MORE TIME.
SHOW ME TEN METERS.
OKAY!
ザバ…
ZABA... (SPLOSH...)

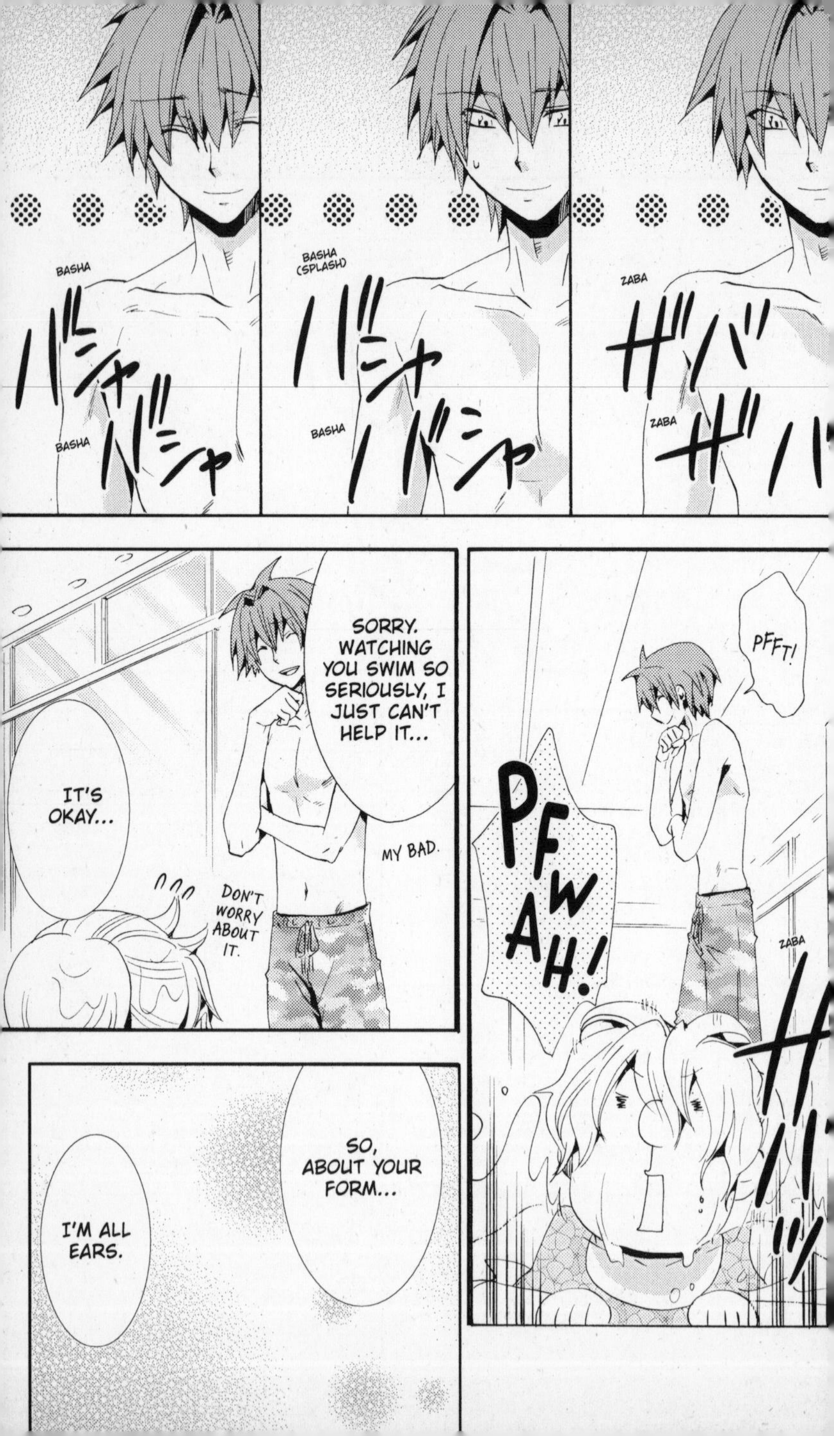
ZABA
ザバ
ZABA
ザバ
BASHA (SPLASH)
バシャ
BASHA
バシャ
BASHA
バシャ
BASHA
バシャ
PFFT!
PFWAH!
ZABA
ザバッ
SORRY. WATCHING YOU SWIM SO SERIOUSLY, I JUST CAN'T HELP IT...
MY BAD.
DON'T WORRY ABOUT IT.
IT'S OKAY...
SO, ABOUT YOUR FORM...
I'M ALL EARS.

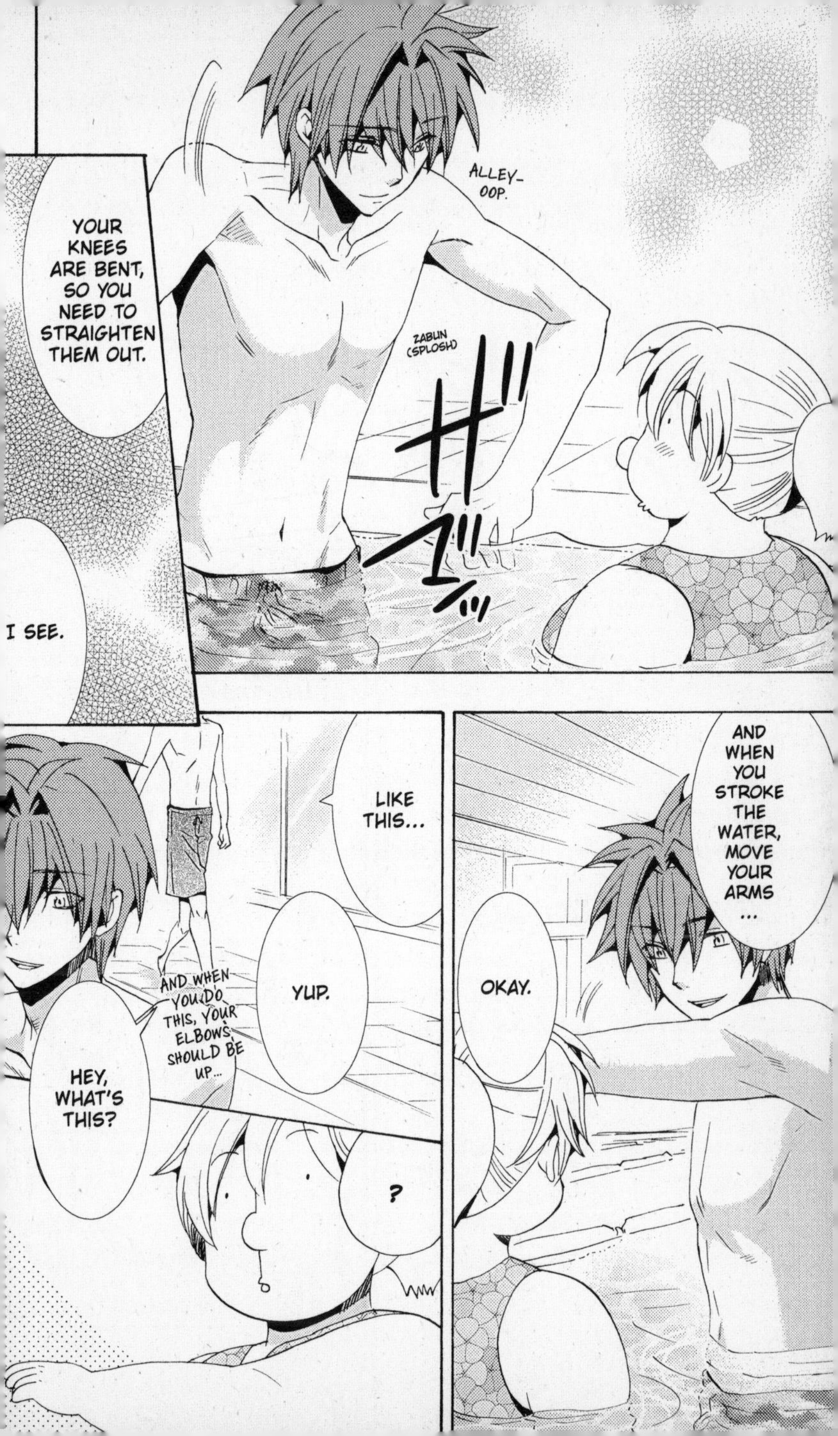
ALLEY-OOP.
YOUR KNEES ARE BENT, SO YOU NEED TO STRAIGHTEN THEM OUT.
ZABUN (SPLOSH)
ザブッ
I SEE.
AND WHEN YOU STROKE THE WATER, MOVE YOUR ARMS ...
OKAY.
LIKE THIS...
YUP.
AND WHEN YOU DO THIS, YOUR ELBOWS SHOULD BE UP...
HEY, WHAT'S THIS?
?

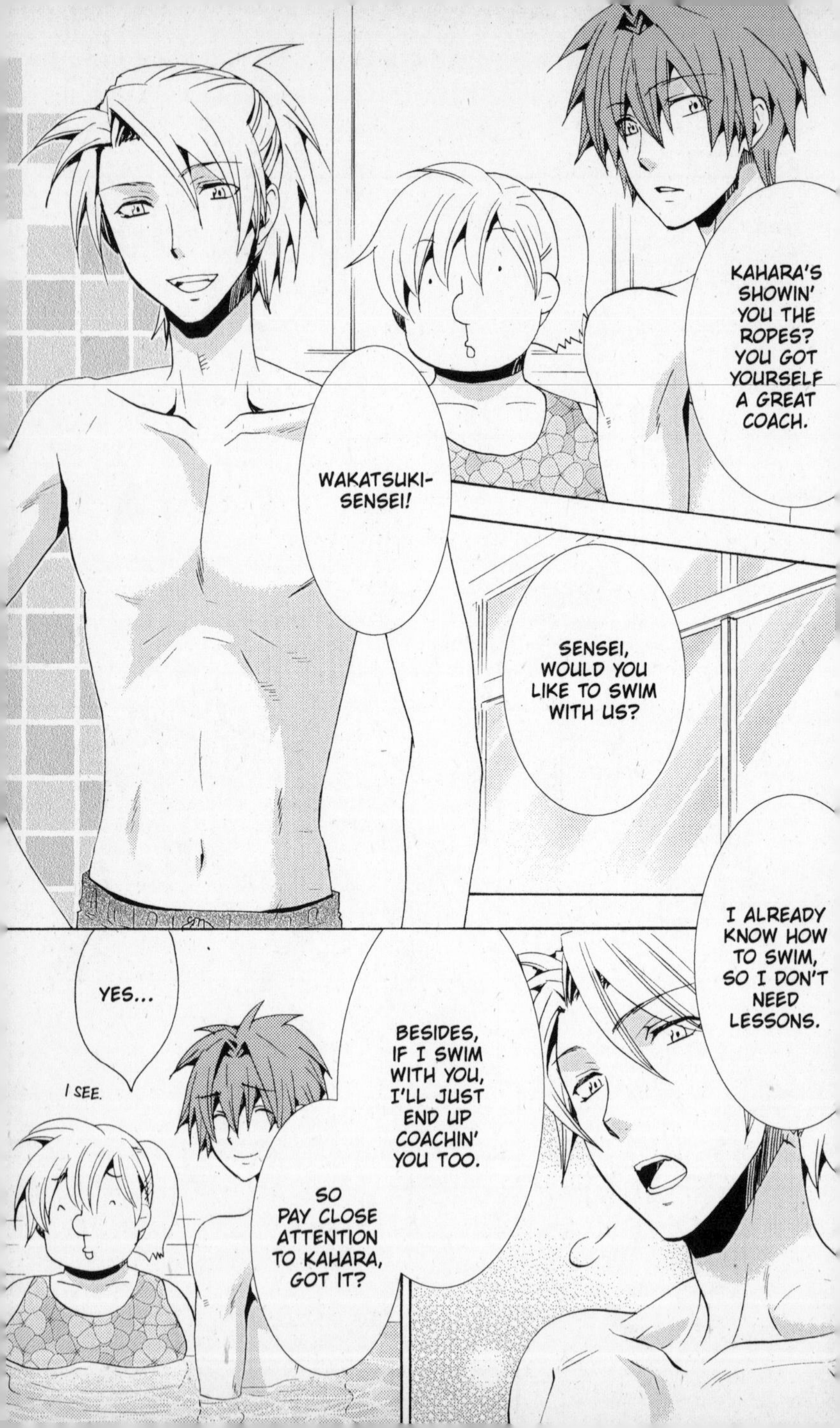
KAHARA'S SHOWIN' YOU THE ROPES? YOU GOT YOURSELF A GREAT COACH.
WAKATSUKI-SENSEI!
SENSEI, WOULD YOU LIKE TO SWIM WITH US?
I ALREADY KNOW HOW TO SWIM, SO I DON'T NEED LESSONS.
BESIDES, IF I SWIM WITH YOU, I'LL JUST END UP COACHIN' YOU TOO.
SO PAY CLOSE ATTENTION TO KAHARA, GOT IT?
YES...
I SEE.

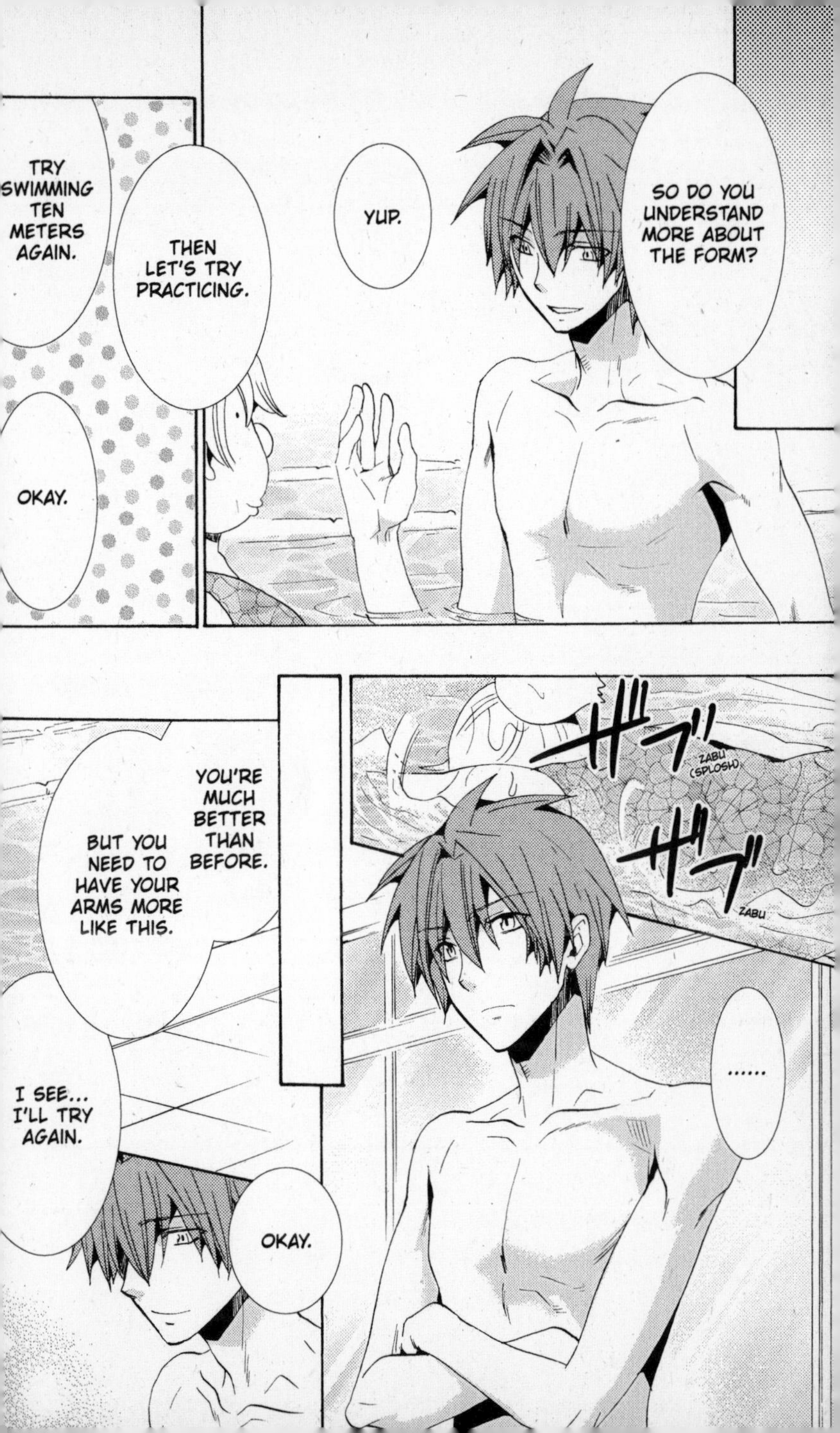
SO DO YOU UNDERSTAND MORE ABOUT THE FORM?
YUP.
THEN LET'S TRY PRACTICING.
TRY SWIMMING TEN METERS AGAIN.
OKAY.
ザブ!
ZABU (SPLOSH)
ザブ
ZABU
......
YOU'RE MUCH BETTER THAN BEFORE.
BUT YOU NEED TO HAVE YOUR ARMS MORE LIKE THIS.
I SEE... I'LL TRY AGAIN.
OKAY.

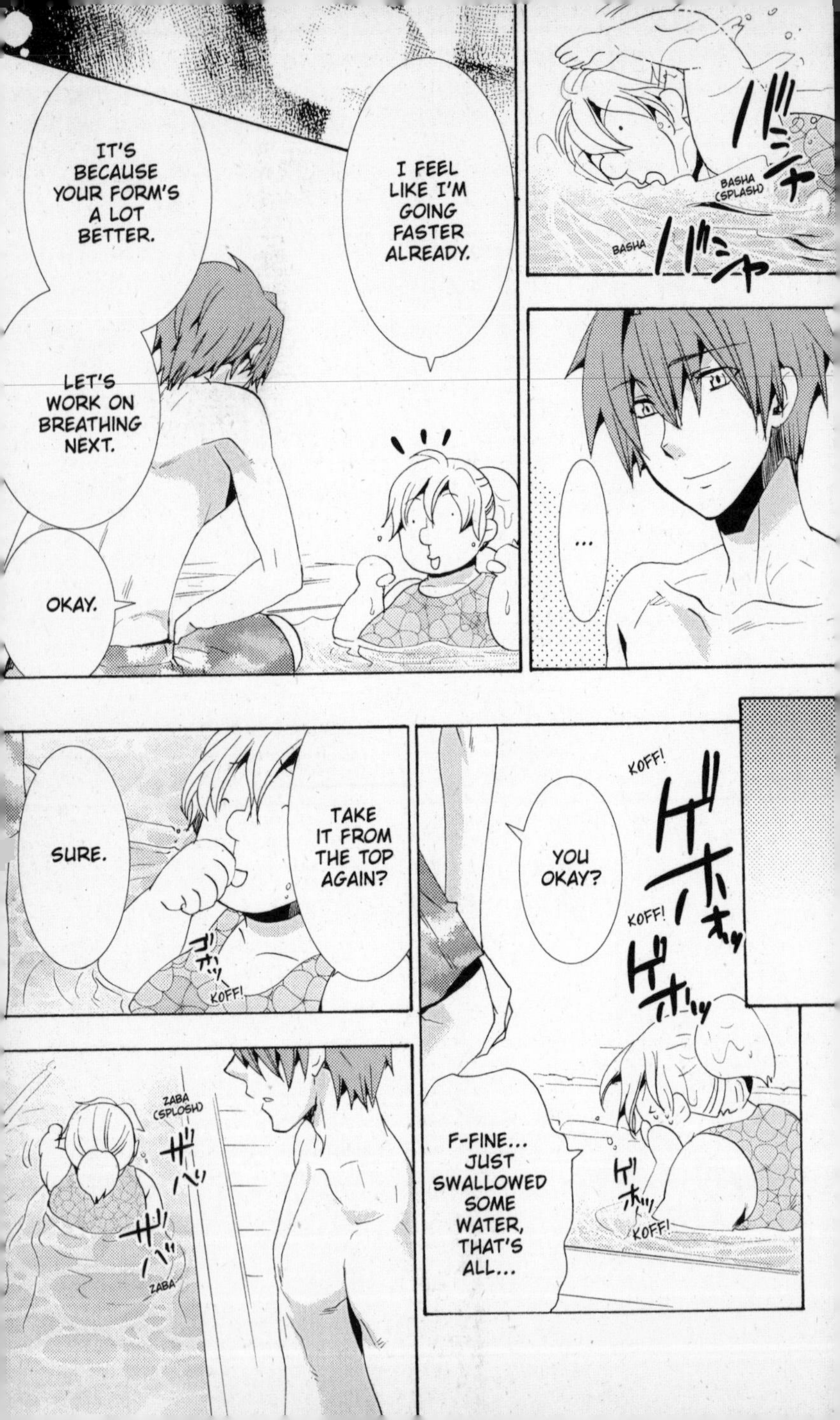

BASHA (SPLASH)
BASHA
...
I FEEL LIKE I'M GOING FASTER ALREADY.
IT'S BECAUSE YOUR FORM'S A LOT BETTER.
LET'S WORK ON BREATHING NEXT.
OKAY.
KOFF!
YOU OKAY?
KOFF!
F-FINE... JUST SWALLOWED SOME WATER, THAT'S ALL...
KOFF!
TAKE IT FROM THE TOP AGAIN?
SURE.
KOFF!
ZABA (SPLOSH)
ZABA

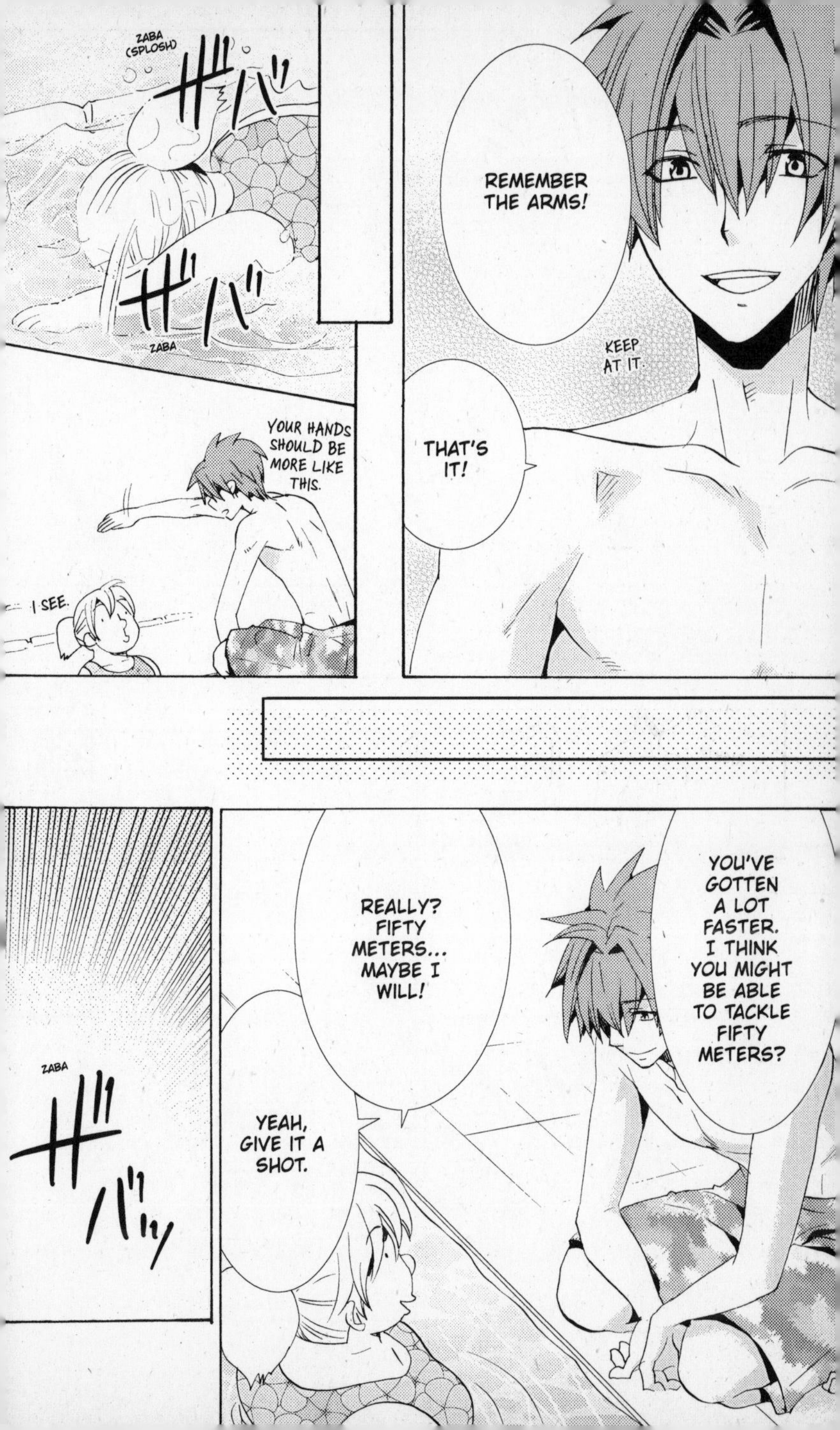
REMEMBER THE ARMS!
KEEP AT IT.
THAT'S IT!
ZABA (SPLOSH)
ZABA
YOUR HANDS SHOULD BE MORE LIKE THIS.
I SEE.
YOU'VE GOTTEN A LOT FASTER. I THINK YOU MIGHT BE ABLE TO TACKLE FIFTY METERS?
REALLY? FIFTY METERS... MAYBE I WILL!
YEAH, GIVE IT A SHOT.
ZABA

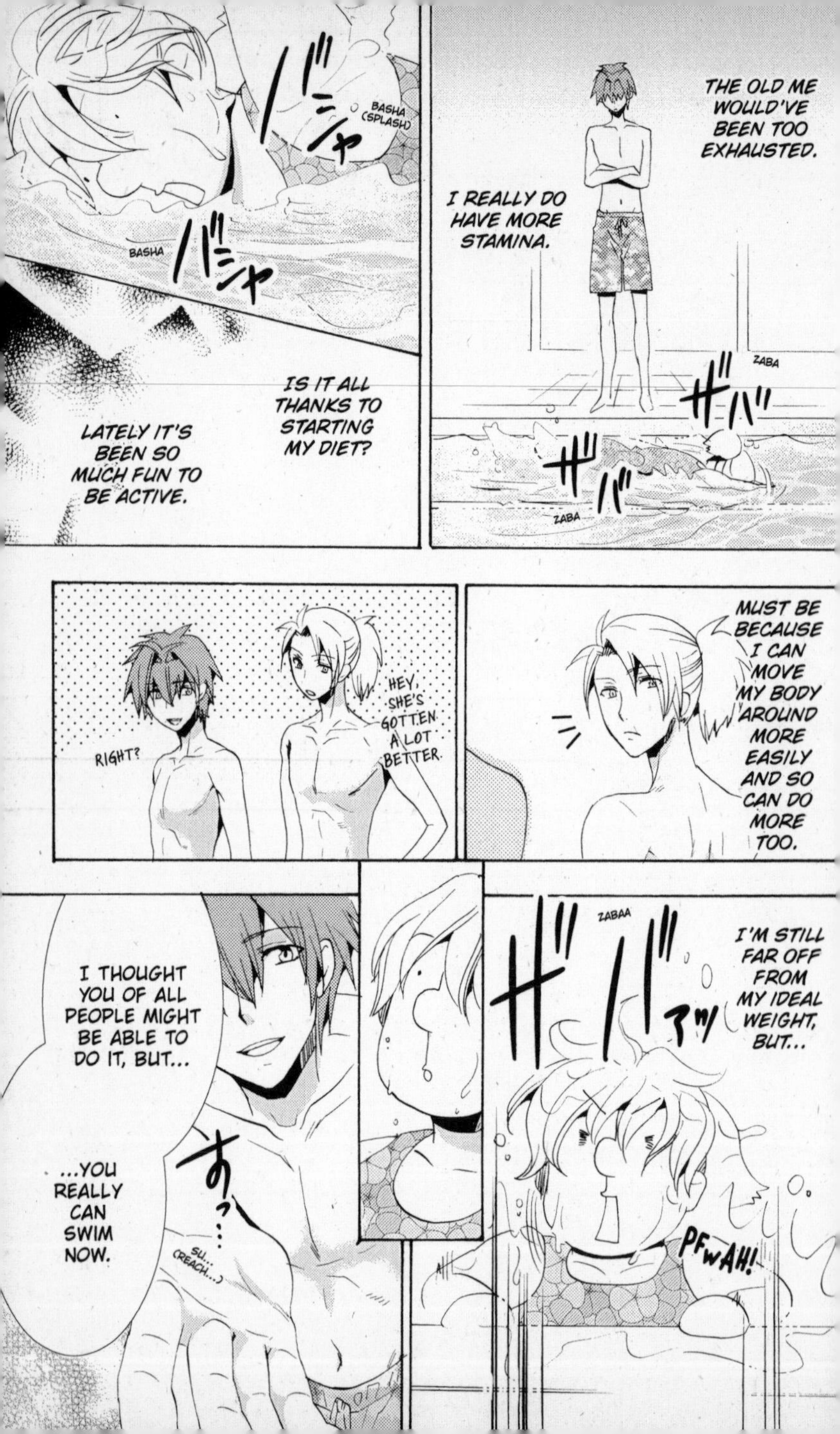
THE OLD ME WOULD'VE BEEN TOO EXHAUSTED.
I REALLY DO HAVE MORE STAMINA.
ZABA
ZABA
BASHA (SPLASH)
BASHA
IS IT ALL THANKS TO STARTING MY DIET?
LATELY IT'S BEEN SO MUCH FUN TO BE ACTIVE.
MUST BE BECAUSE I CAN MOVE MY BODY AROUND MORE EASILY AND SO CAN DO MORE TOO.
HEY, SHE'S GOTTEN A LOT BETTER.
RIGHT?
ZABAA
I'M STILL FAR OFF FROM MY IDEAL WEIGHT, BUT...
PFWAH!
I THOUGHT YOU OF ALL PEOPLE MIGHT BE ABLE TO DO IT, BUT...
...YOU REALLY CAN SWIM NOW.
SU... (REACH...)

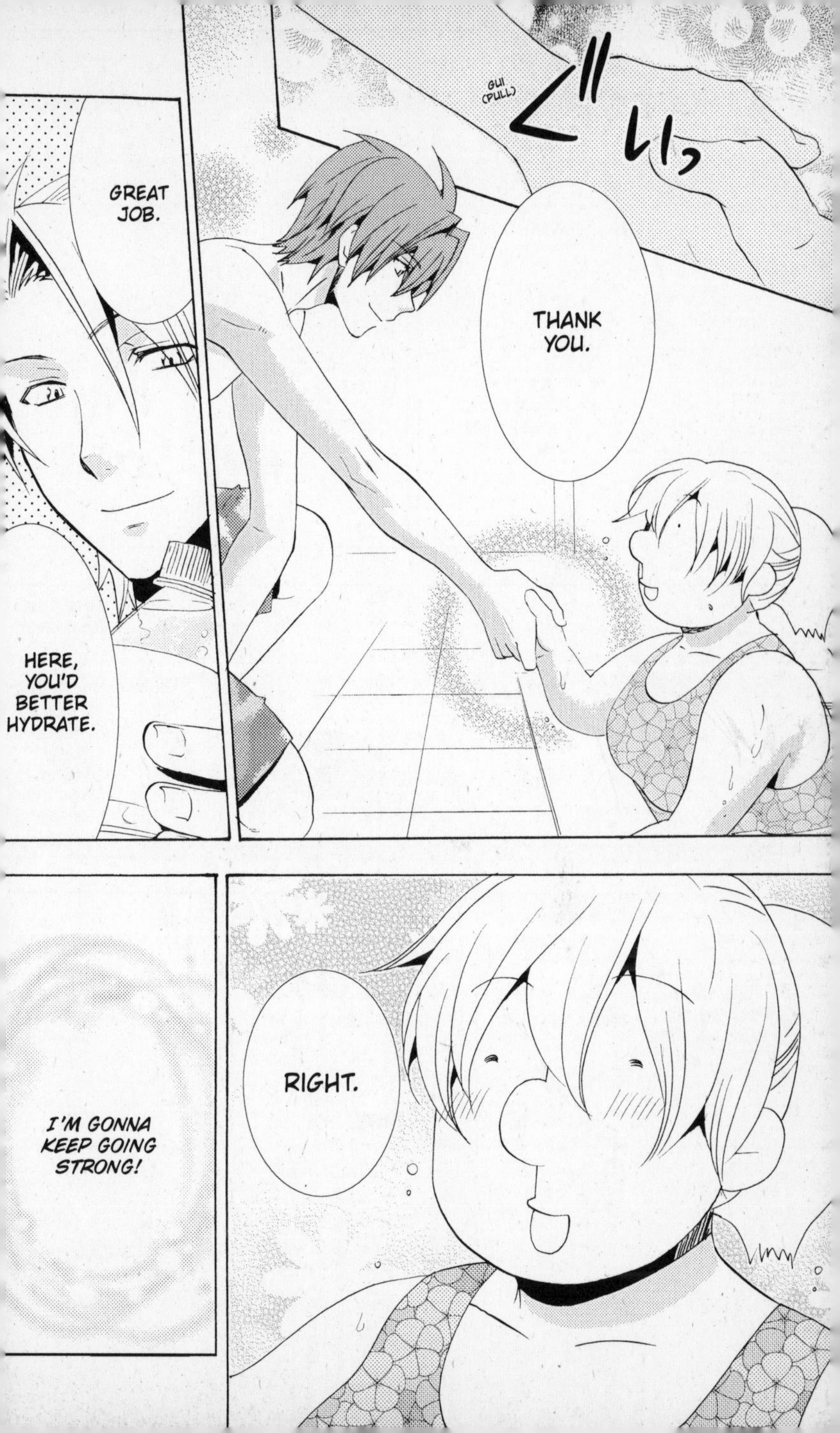
GUI (PULL)
THANK YOU.
GREAT JOB.
HERE, YOU'D BETTER HYDRATE.
RIGHT.
I'M GONNA KEEP GOING STRONG!

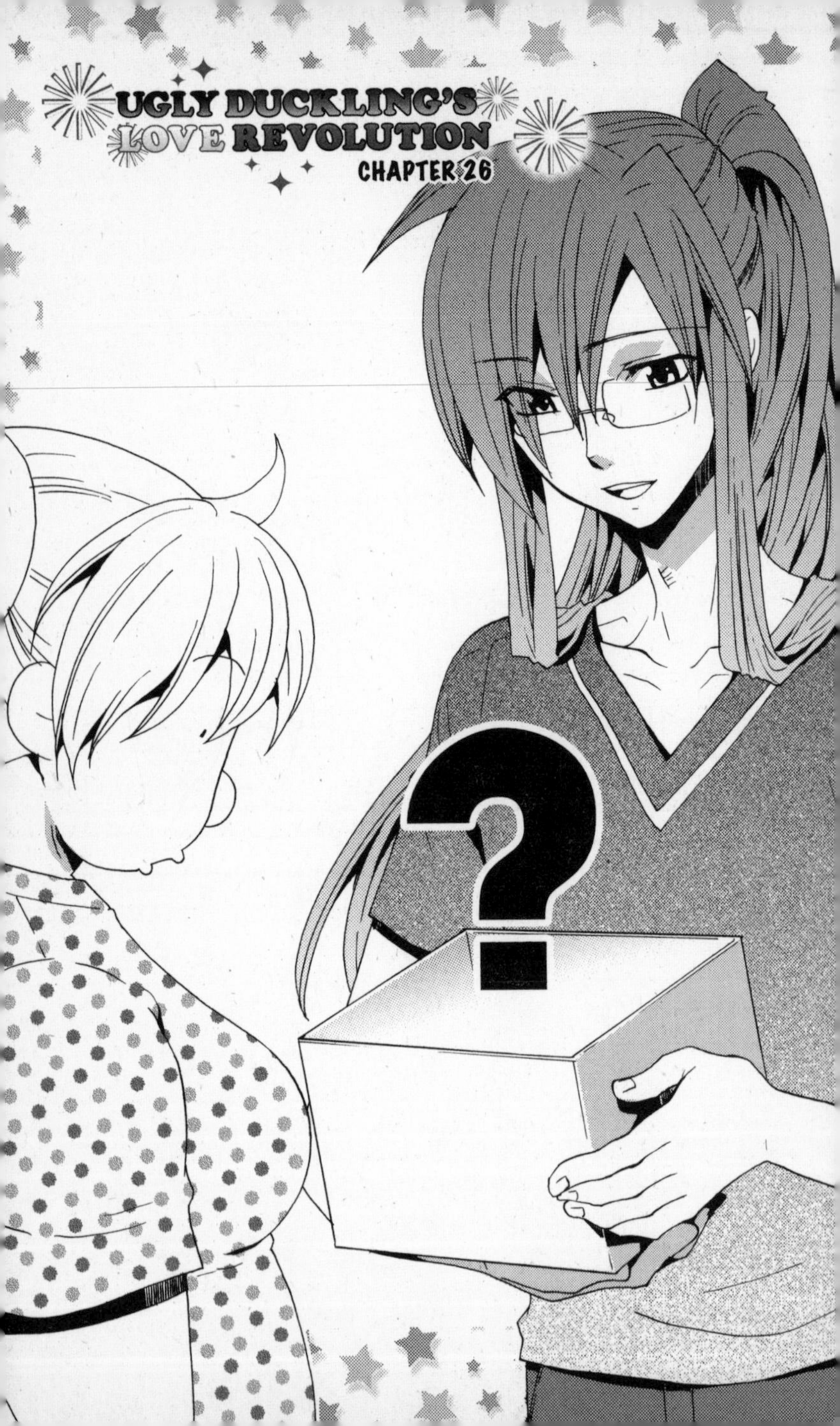
UGLY DUCKLING'S LOVE REVOLUTION
CHAPTER 26
?

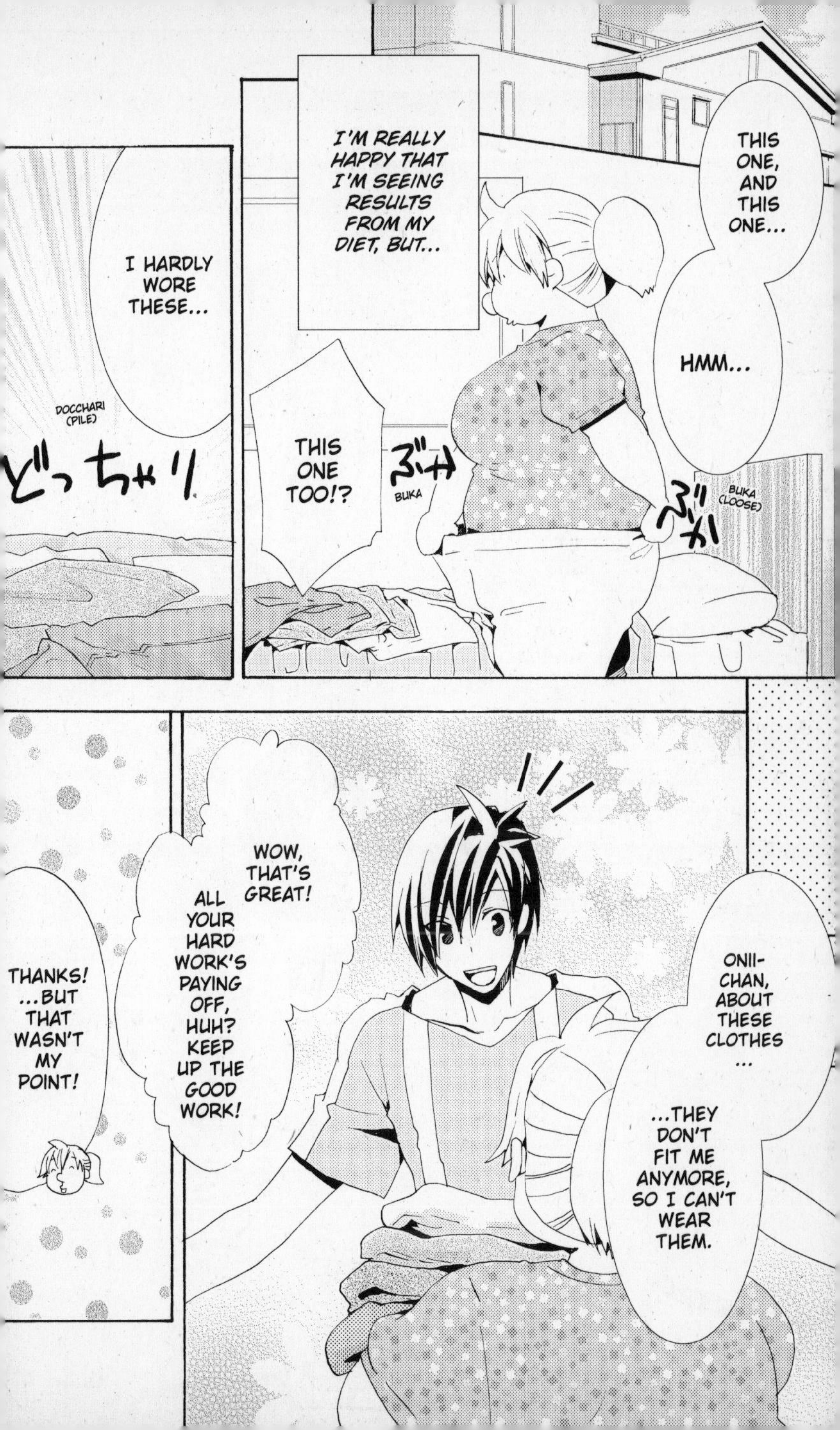
THIS ONE, AND THIS ONE...
I'M REALLY HAPPY THAT I'M SEEING RESULTS FROM MY DIET, BUT...
HMM...
ぶか
BUKA (LOOSE)
ぶか
BUKA
THIS ONE TOO!?
I HARDLY WORE THESE...
どっちゃり
DOCCHARI (PILE)
ONII-CHAN, ABOUT THESE CLOTHES...
...THEY DON'T FIT ME ANYMORE, SO I CAN'T WEAR THEM.
WOW, THAT'S GREAT!
ALL YOUR HARD WORK'S PAYING OFF, HUH? KEEP UP THE GOOD WORK!
THANKS! ...BUT THAT WASN'T MY POINT!

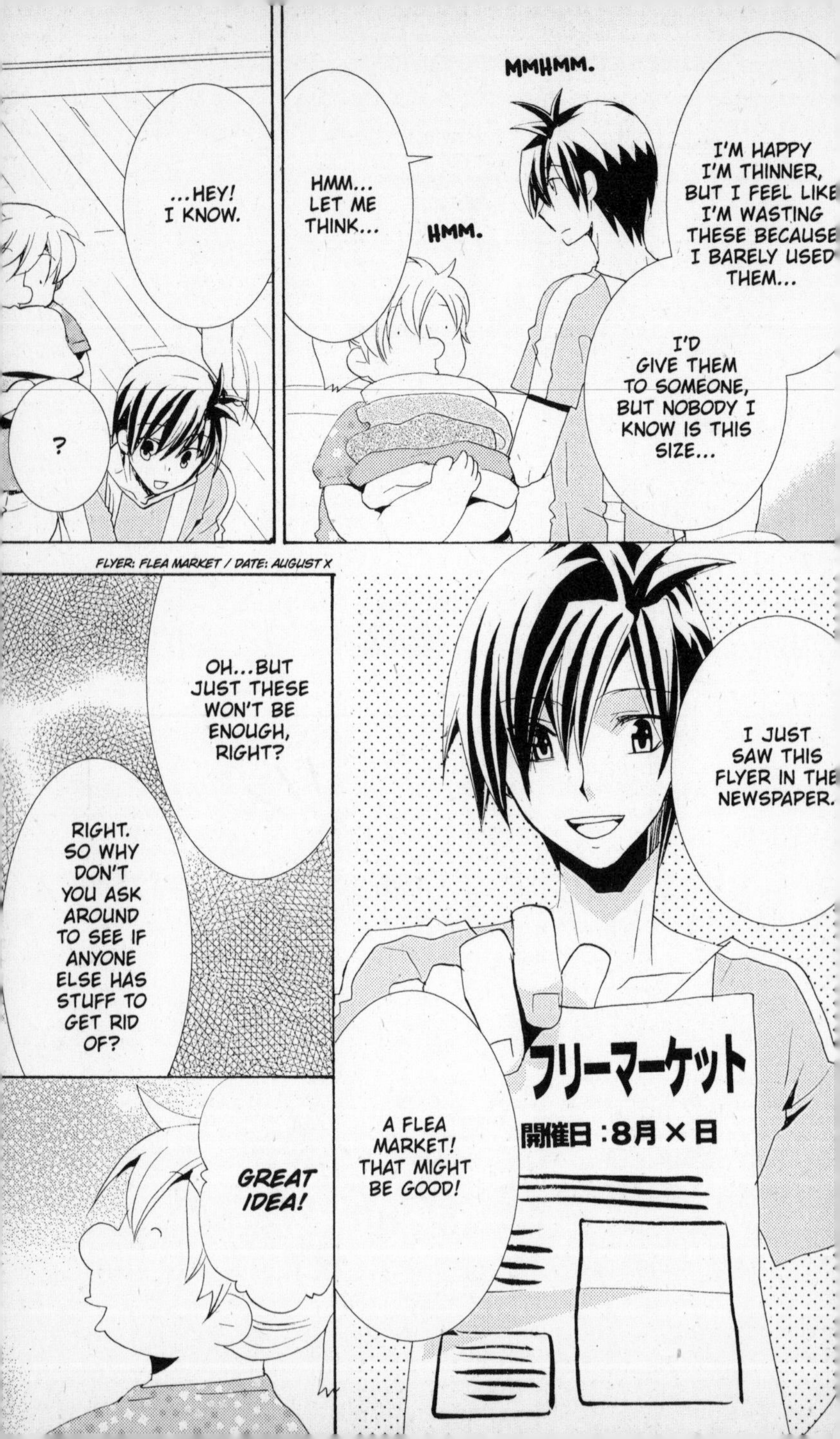
I'M HAPPY I'M THINNER, BUT I FEEL LIKE I'M WASTING THESE BECAUSE I BARELY USED THEM...
MMHMM.
I'D GIVE THEM TO SOMEONE, BUT NOBODY I KNOW IS THIS SIZE...
HMM.
HMM... LET ME THINK...
...HEY! I KNOW.
?
FLYER: FLEA MARKET / DATE: AUGUST X
I JUST SAW THIS FLYER IN THE NEWSPAPER.
フリーマーケット
開催日：8月×日
A FLEA MARKET! THAT MIGHT BE GOOD!
OH...BUT JUST THESE WON'T BE ENOUGH, RIGHT?
RIGHT. SO WHY DON'T YOU ASK AROUND TO SEE IF ANYONE ELSE HAS STUFF TO GET RID OF?
GREAT IDEA!

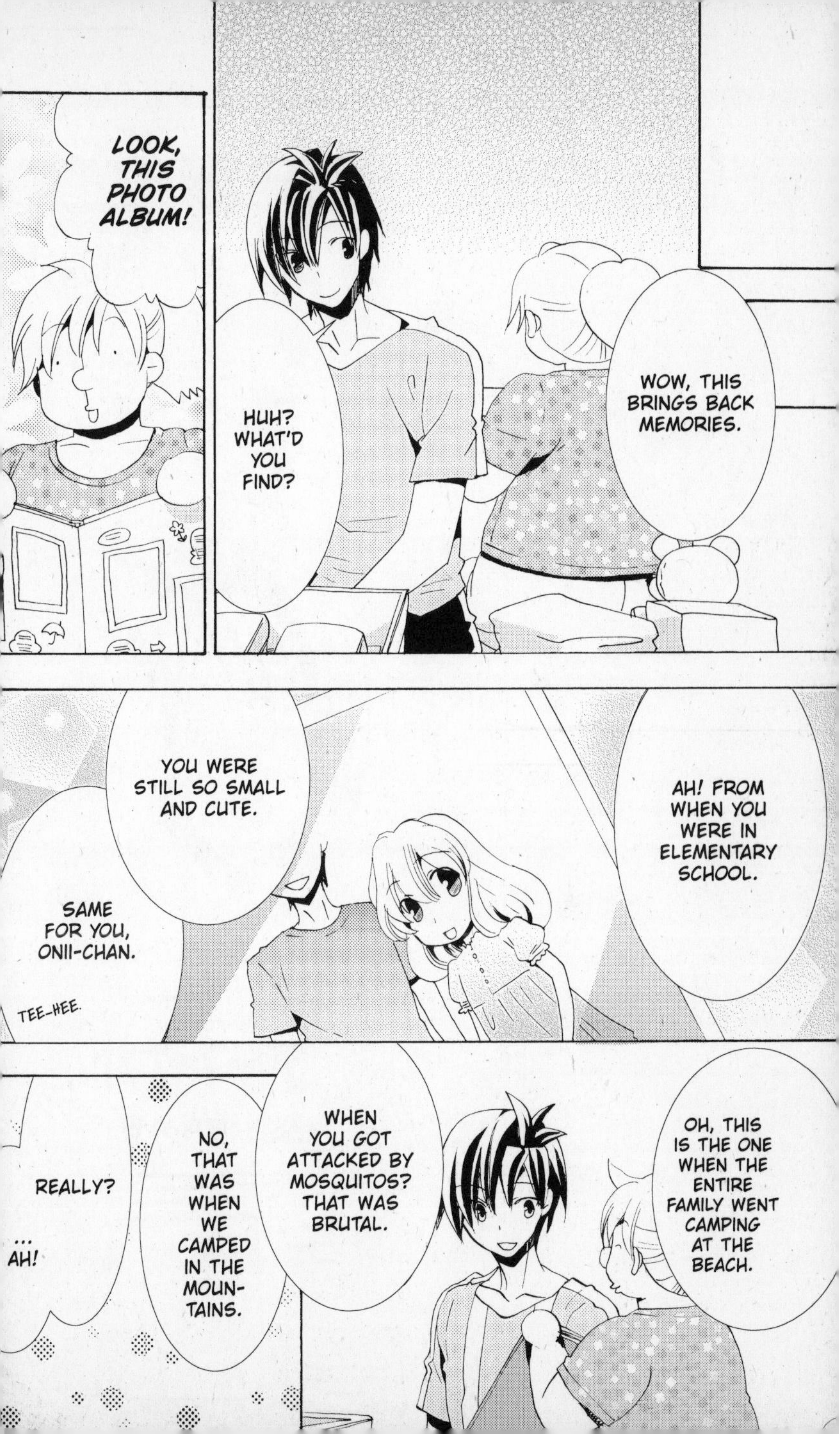
WOW, THIS BRINGS BACK MEMORIES.
HUH? WHAT'D YOU FIND?
LOOK, THIS PHOTO ALBUM!
AH! FROM WHEN YOU WERE IN ELEMENTARY SCHOOL.
YOU WERE STILL SO SMALL AND CUTE.
SAME FOR YOU, ONII-CHAN.
TEE-HEE.
OH, THIS IS THE ONE WHEN THE ENTIRE FAMILY WENT CAMPING AT THE BEACH.
WHEN YOU GOT ATTACKED BY MOSQUITOS? THAT WAS BRUTAL.
NO, THAT WAS WHEN WE CAMPED IN THE MOUN-TAINS.
REALLY?
...AH!

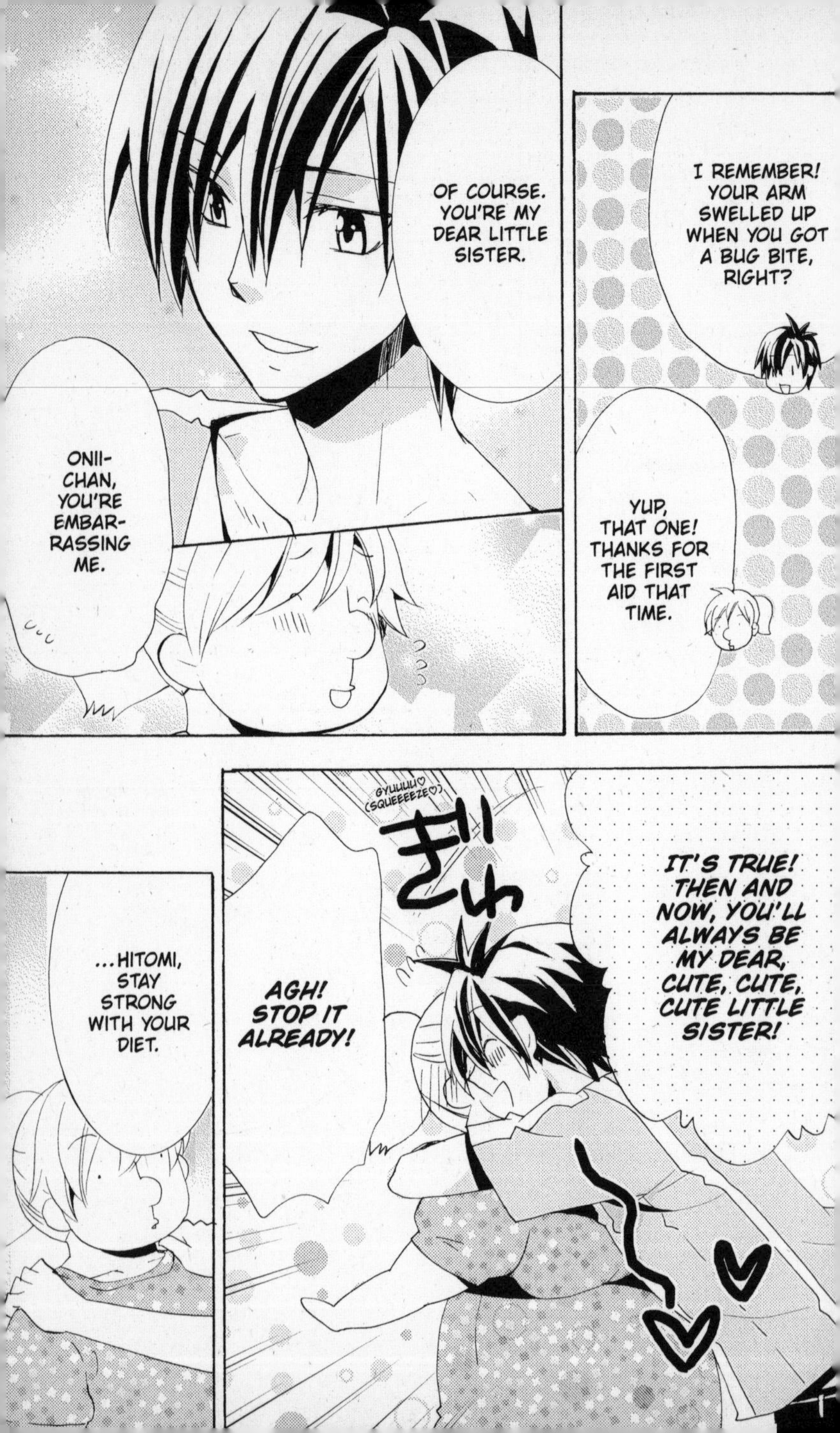
I REMEMBER! YOUR ARM SWELLED UP WHEN YOU GOT A BUG BITE, RIGHT?
YUP, THAT ONE! THANKS FOR THE FIRST AID THAT TIME.
OF COURSE. YOU'RE MY DEAR LITTLE SISTER.
ONII-CHAN, YOU'RE EMBARRASSING ME.
IT'S TRUE! THEN AND NOW, YOU'LL ALWAYS BE MY DEAR, CUTE, CUTE, CUTE LITTLE SISTER!
ぎゅ
GYUUUU♡ (SQUEEEEZE♡)
AGH! STOP IT ALREADY!
...HITOMI, STAY STRONG WITH YOUR DIET.

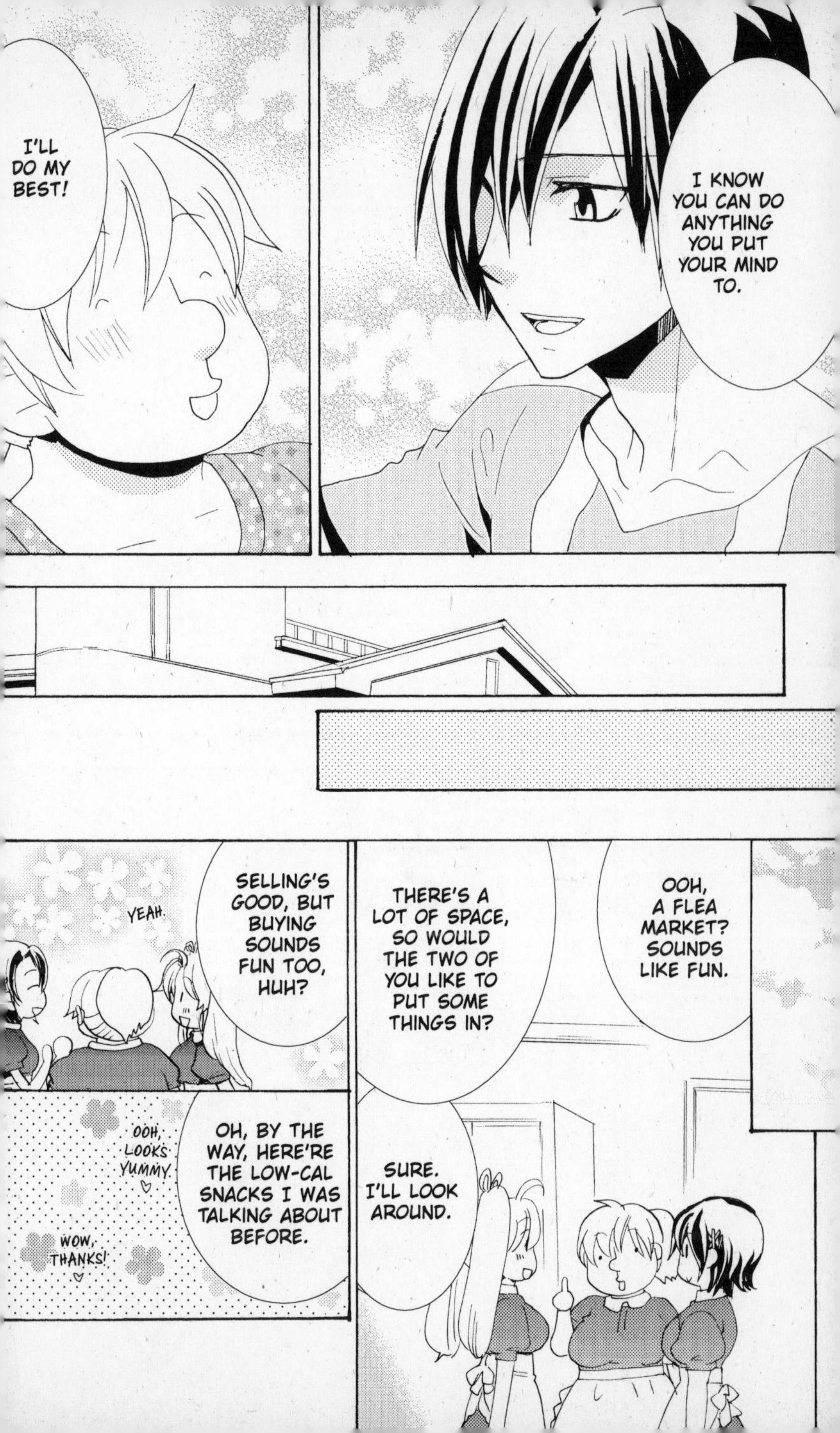
I KNOW YOU CAN DO ANYTHING YOU PUT YOUR MIND TO.
I'LL DO MY BEST!
OOH, A FLEA MARKET? SOUNDS LIKE FUN.
THERE'S A LOT OF SPACE, SO WOULD THE TWO OF YOU LIKE TO PUT SOME THINGS IN?
SURE. I'LL LOOK AROUND.
SELLING'S GOOD, BUT BUYING SOUNDS FUN TOO, HUH?
YEAH.
OH, BY THE WAY, HERE'RE THE LOW-CAL SNACKS I WAS TALKING ABOUT BEFORE.
OOH, LOOKS YUMMY ♡
WOW, THANKS! ♡

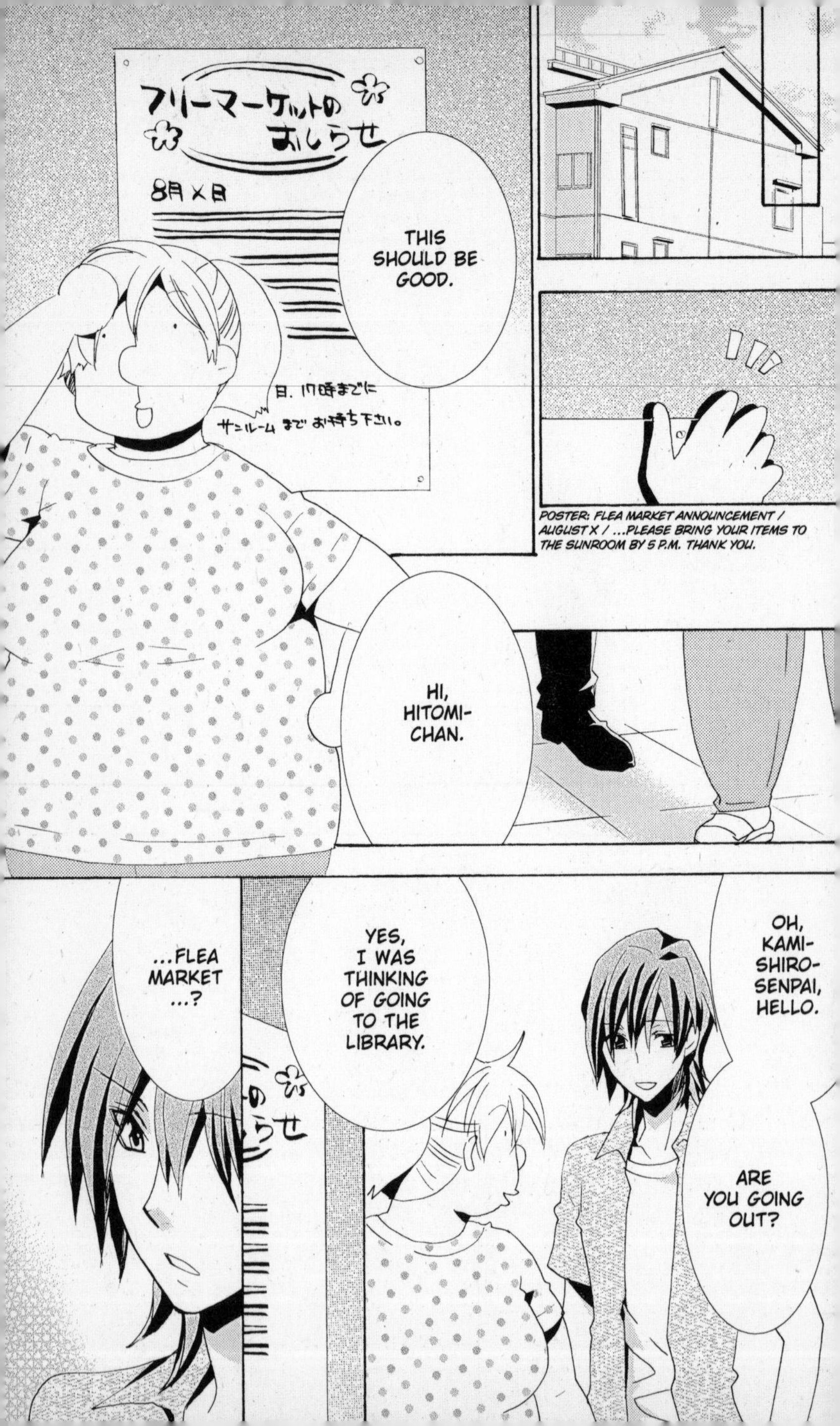

POSTER: FLEA MARKET ANNOUNCEMENT / AUGUST X / ...PLEASE BRING YOUR ITEMS TO THE SUNROOM BY 5 P.M. THANK YOU.
フリーマーケットの おしらせ
8月×日
日. 17時までに サンルーム まで お持ち下さい。
THIS SHOULD BE GOOD.
HI, HITOMI-CHAN.
OH, KAMI-SHIRO-SENPAI, HELLO.
ARE YOU GOING OUT?
YES, I WAS THINKING OF GOING TO THE LIBRARY.
...FLEA MARKET ...?

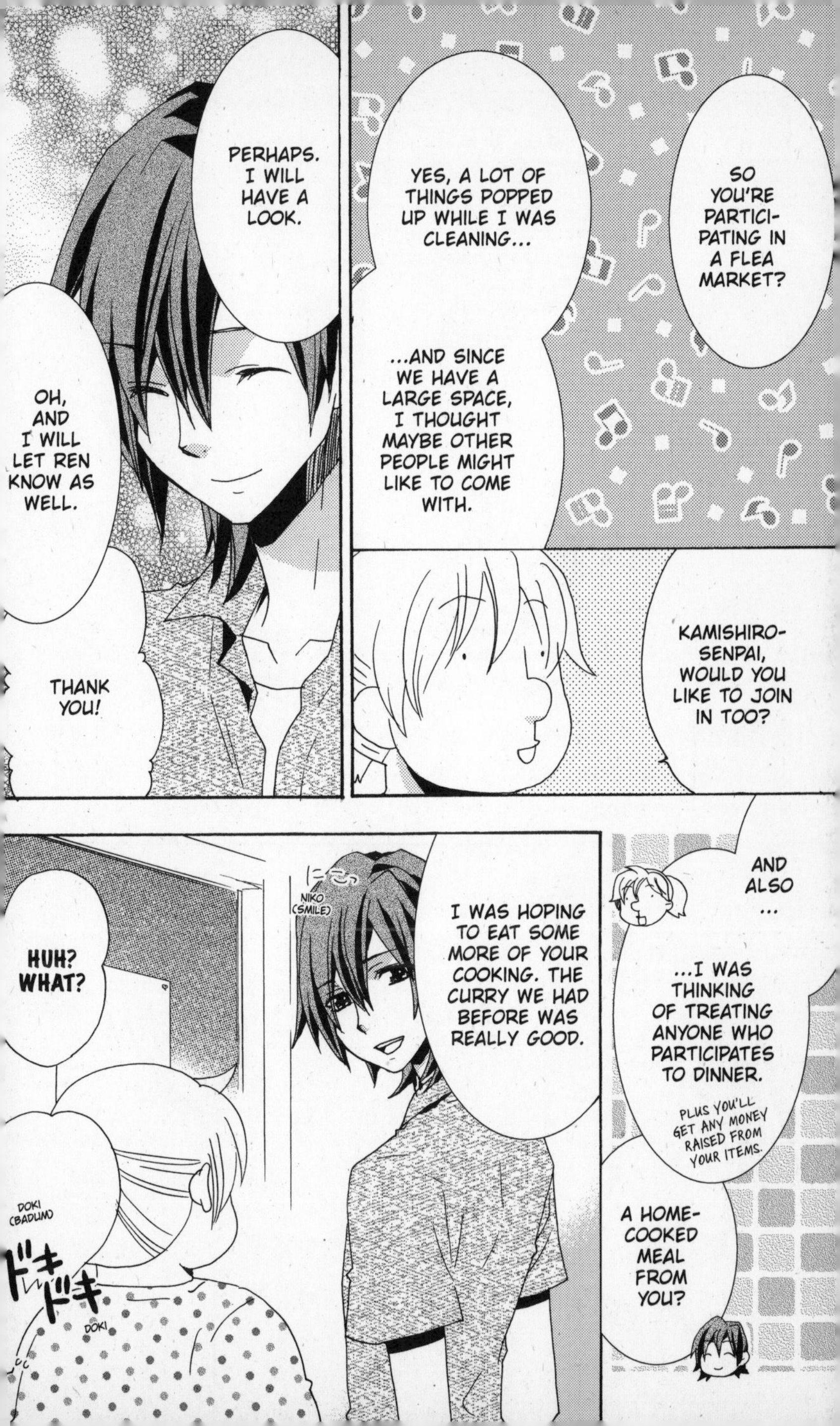
SO YOU'RE PARTICI-PATING IN A FLEA MARKET?
YES, A LOT OF THINGS POPPED UP WHILE I WAS CLEANING...
...AND SINCE WE HAVE A LARGE SPACE, I THOUGHT MAYBE OTHER PEOPLE MIGHT LIKE TO COME WITH.
KAMISHIRO-SENPAI, WOULD YOU LIKE TO JOIN IN TOO?
PERHAPS. I WILL HAVE A LOOK.
OH, AND I WILL LET REN KNOW AS WELL.
THANK YOU!
AND ALSO ...
...I WAS THINKING OF TREATING ANYONE WHO PARTICIPATES TO DINNER.
PLUS YOU'LL GET ANY MONEY RAISED FROM YOUR ITEMS.
A HOME-COOKED MEAL FROM YOU?
NIKO (SMILE)
I WAS HOPING TO EAT SOME MORE OF YOUR COOKING. THE CURRY WE HAD BEFORE WAS REALLY GOOD.
HUH? WHAT?
DOKI (BADUM)
DOKI

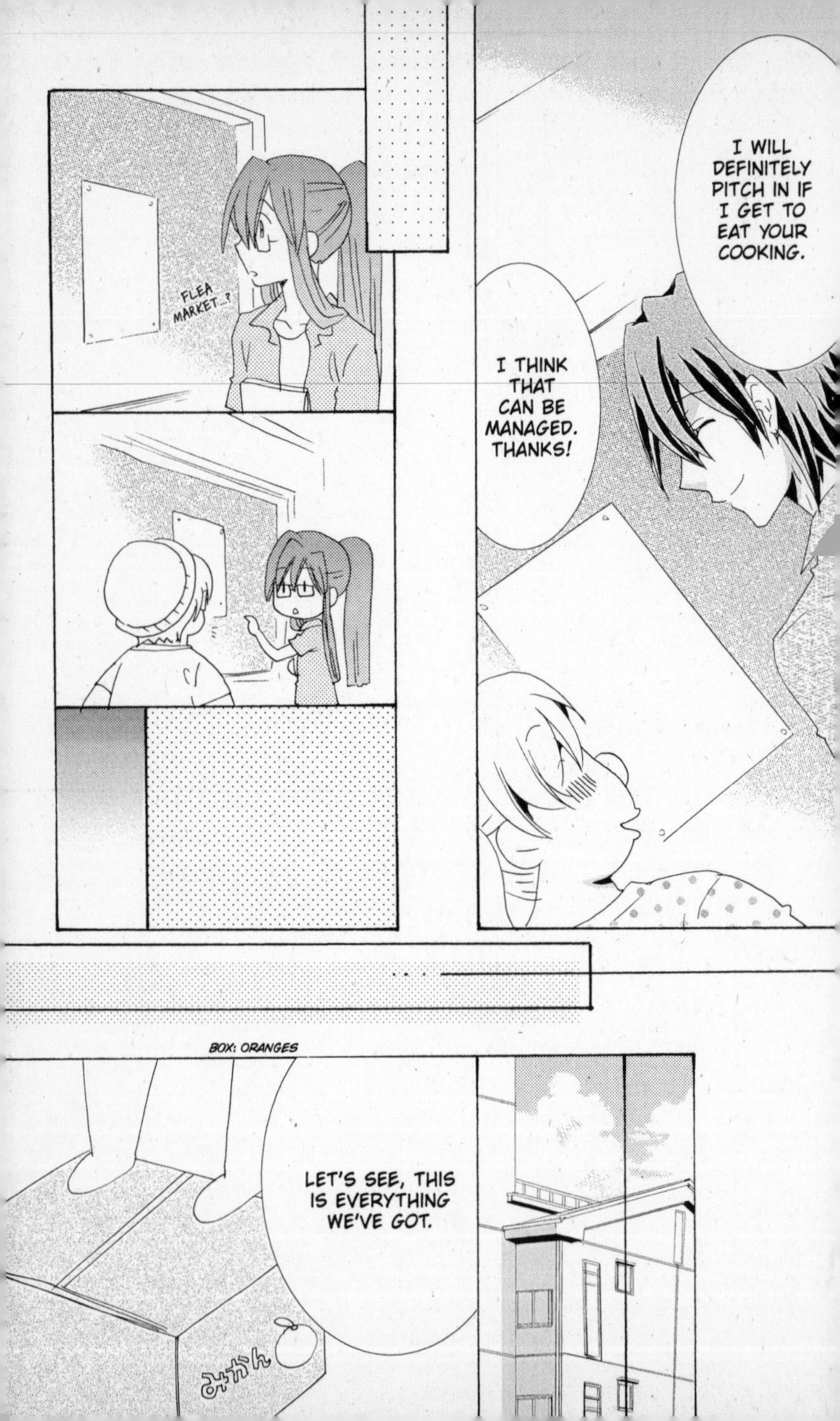
I WILL DEFINITELY PITCH IN IF I GET TO EAT YOUR COOKING.
I THINK THAT CAN BE MANAGED. THANKS!
FLEA MARKET...?
. . .
BOX: ORANGES
LET'S SEE, THIS IS EVERYTHING WE'VE GOT.
みかん

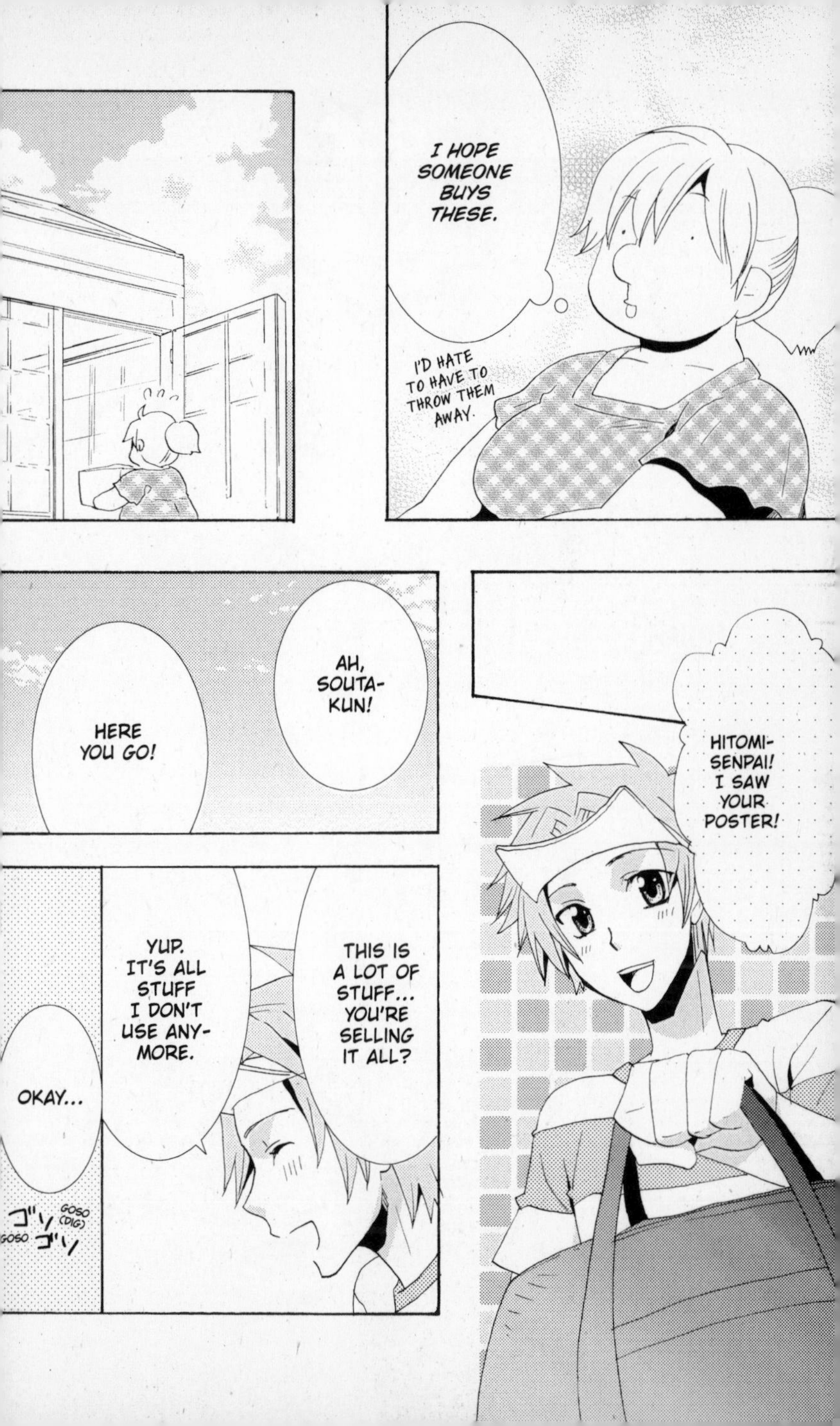
I HOPE SOMEONE BUYS THESE.
I'D HATE TO HAVE TO THROW THEM AWAY.
HITOMI-SENPAI! I SAW YOUR POSTER!
AH, SOUTA-KUN!
HERE YOU GO!
THIS IS A LOT OF STUFF... YOU'RE SELLING IT ALL?
YUP. IT'S ALL STUFF I DON'T USE ANY-MORE.
OKAY...
ゴソ GOSO (DIG)
GOSO ゴソ

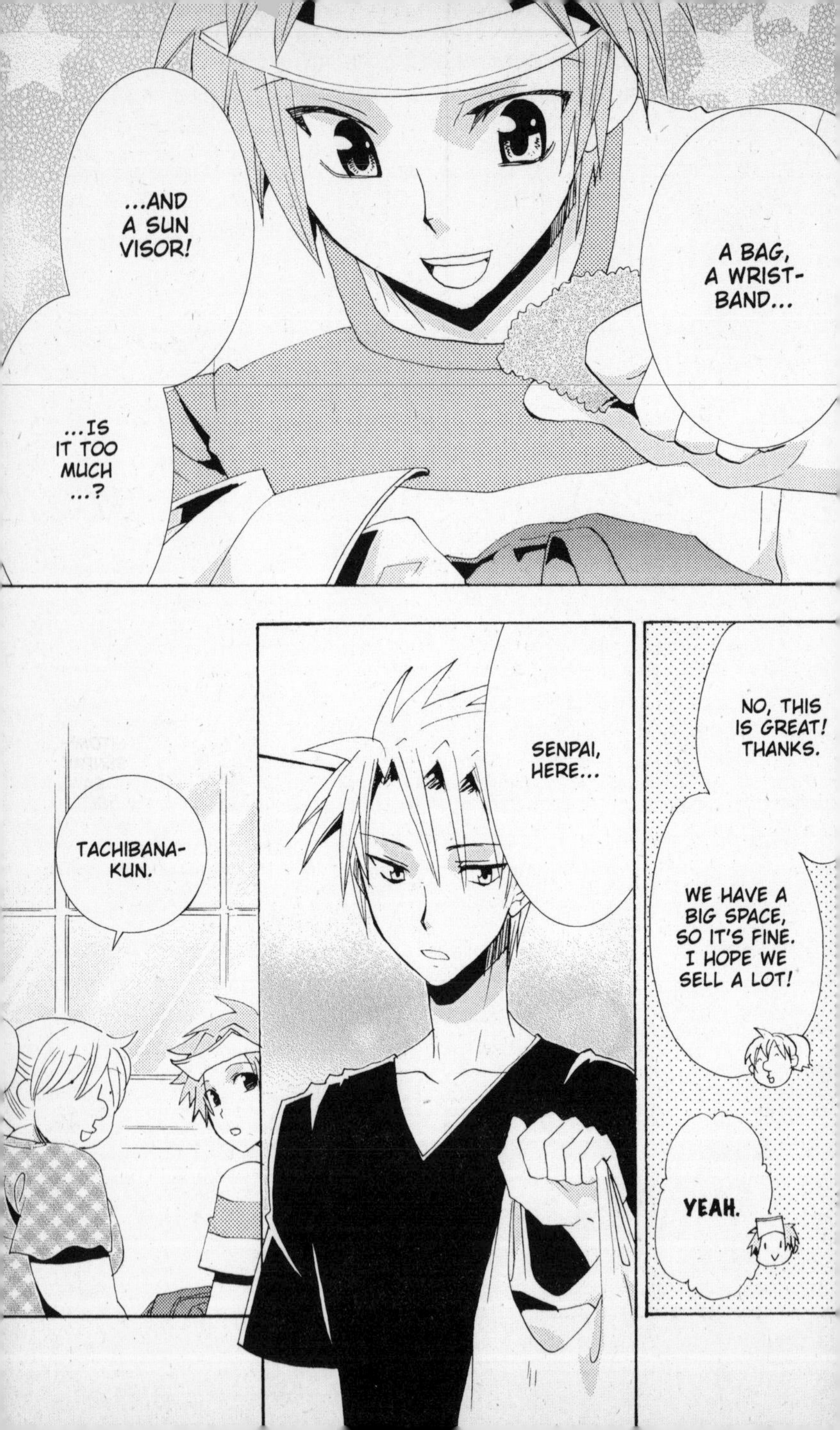
A BAG, A WRIST-BAND...
...AND A SUN VISOR!
...IS IT TOO MUCH ...?
NO, THIS IS GREAT! THANKS.
WE HAVE A BIG SPACE, SO IT'S FINE. I HOPE WE SELL A LOT!
YEAH.
SENPAI, HERE...
TACHIBANA-KUN.

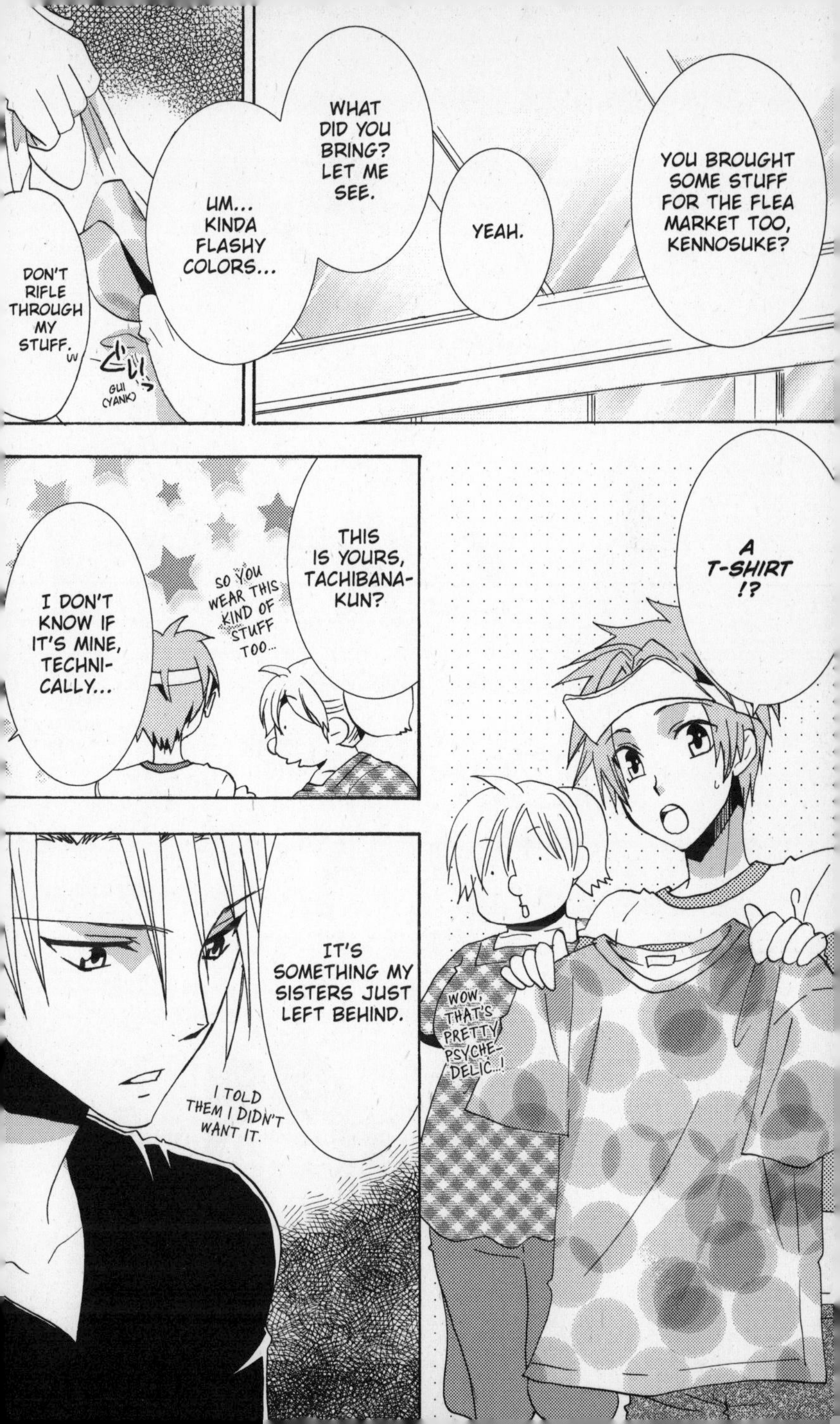
YOU BROUGHT SOME STUFF FOR THE FLEA MARKET TOO, KENNOSUKE?
YEAH.
WHAT DID YOU BRING? LET ME SEE.
UM... KINDA FLASHY COLORS...
DON'T RIFLE THROUGH MY STUFF.
ぐい
GUI (YANK)
A T-SHIRT!?
WOW, THAT'S PRETTY PSYCHE-DELIC...!
THIS IS YOURS, TACHIBANA-KUN?
SO YOU WEAR THIS KIND OF STUFF TOO...
I DON'T KNOW IF IT'S MINE, TECHNI-CALLY...
IT'S SOMETHING MY SISTERS JUST LEFT BEHIND.
I TOLD THEM I DIDN'T WANT IT.

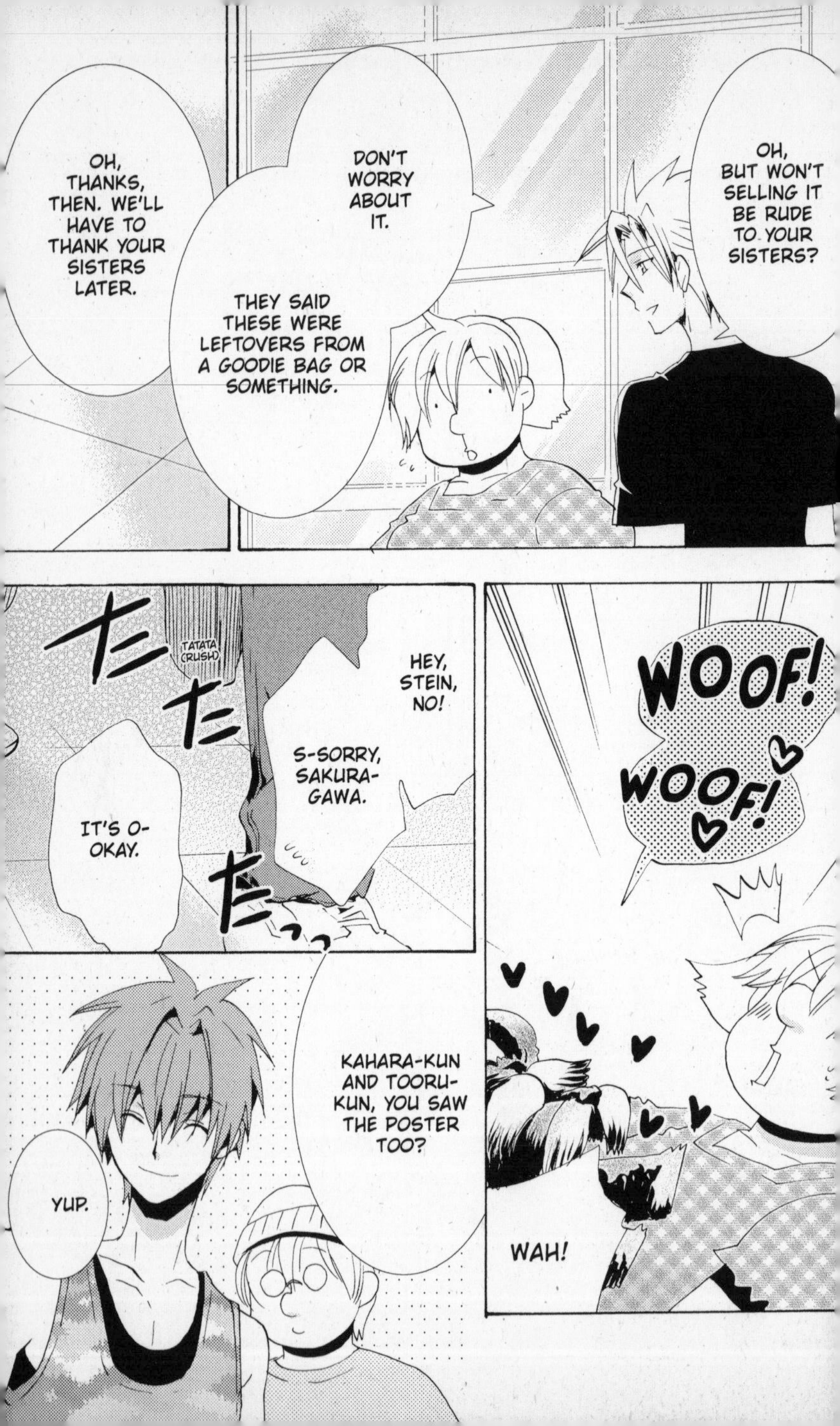
OH, BUT WON'T SELLING IT BE RUDE TO YOUR SISTERS?
DON'T WORRY ABOUT IT.
THEY SAID THESE WERE LEFTOVERS FROM A GOODIE BAG OR SOMETHING.
OH, THANKS, THEN. WE'LL HAVE TO THANK YOUR SISTERS LATER.
WOOF! WOOF!
WAH!
HEY, STEIN, NO!
S-SORRY, SAKURA-GAWA.
TATATA (CRUSH)
IT'S O-OKAY.
KAHARA-KUN AND TOORU-KUN, YOU SAW THE POSTER TOO?
YUP.

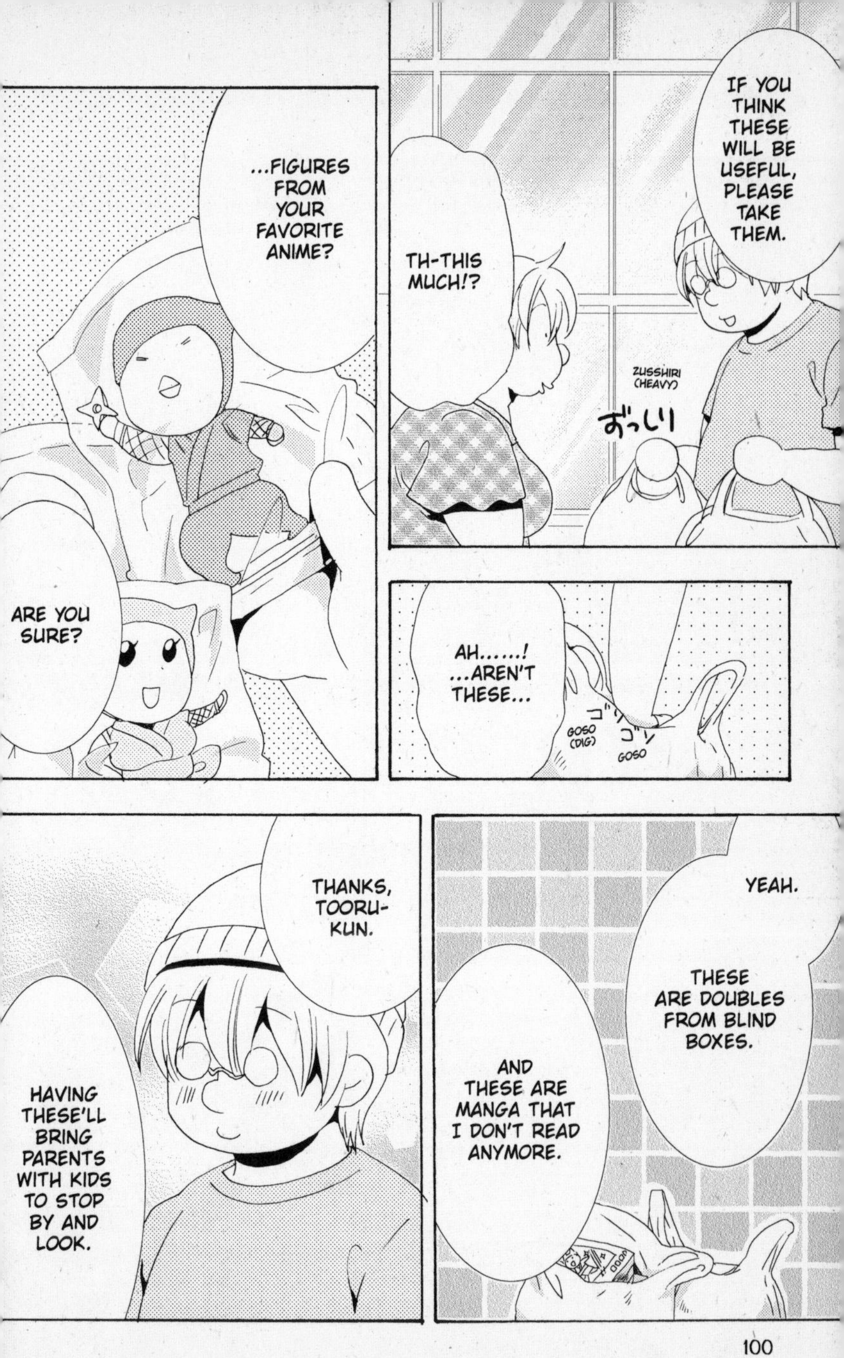
IF YOU THINK THESE WILL BE USEFUL, PLEASE TAKE THEM.
TH-THIS MUCH!?
ZUSSHIRI (HEAVY)
ずっしり
AH......! ...AREN'T THESE...
ゴソ
GOSO (DIG)
ゴソ
GOSO
...FIGURES FROM YOUR FAVORITE ANIME?
ARE YOU SURE?
YEAH.
THESE ARE DOUBLES FROM BLIND BOXES.
AND THESE ARE MANGA THAT I DON'T READ ANYMORE.
THANKS, TOORU-KUN.
HAVING THESE'LL BRING PARENTS WITH KIDS TO STOP BY AND LOOK.

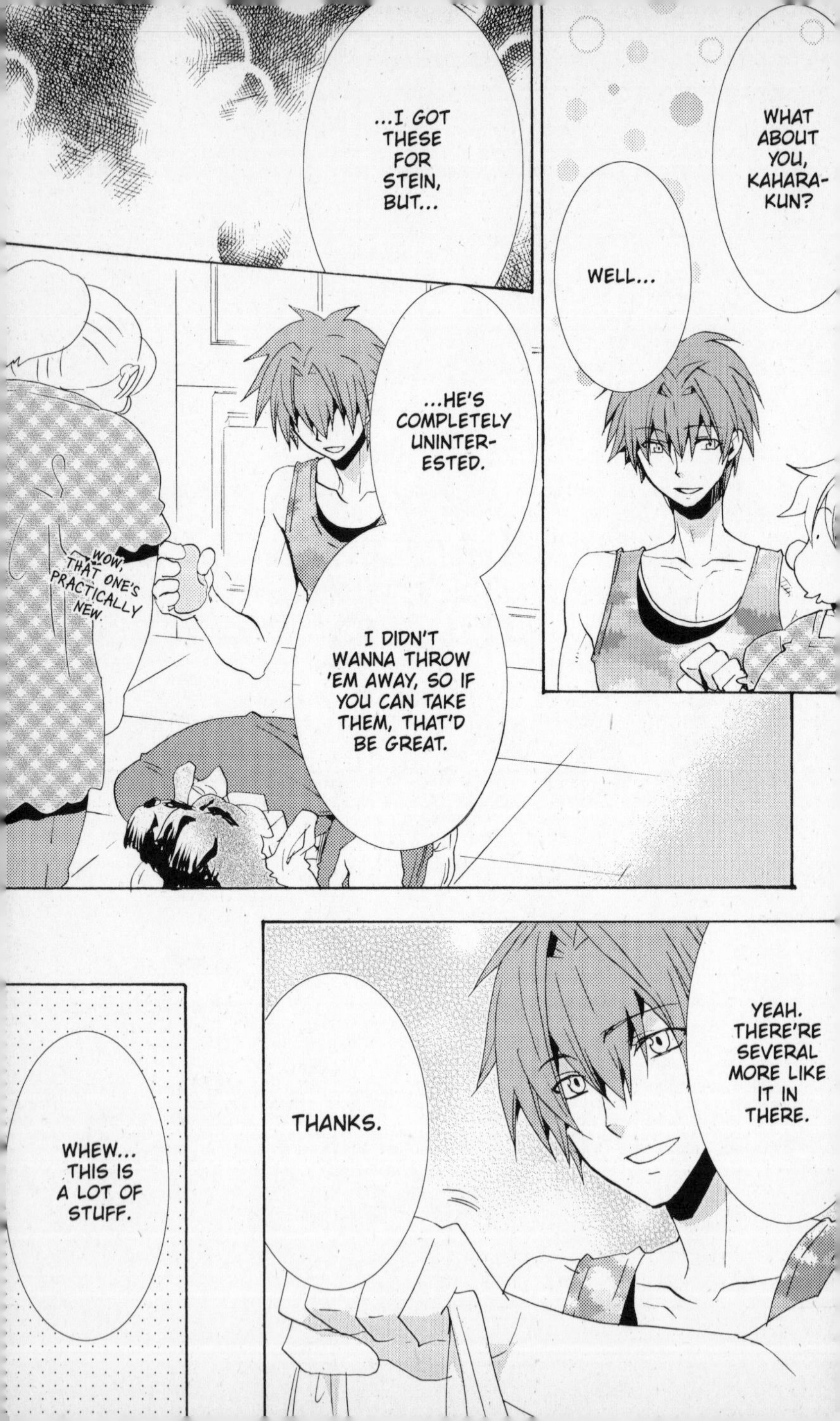
WHAT ABOUT YOU, KAHARA-KUN?
WELL...
...I GOT THESE FOR STEIN, BUT...
...HE'S COMPLETELY UNINTER-ESTED.
I DIDN'T WANNA THROW 'EM AWAY, SO IF YOU CAN TAKE THEM, THAT'D BE GREAT.
WOW, THAT ONE'S PRACTICALLY NEW.
YEAH. THERE'RE SEVERAL MORE LIKE IT IN THERE.
THANKS.
WHEW... THIS IS A LOT OF STUFF.

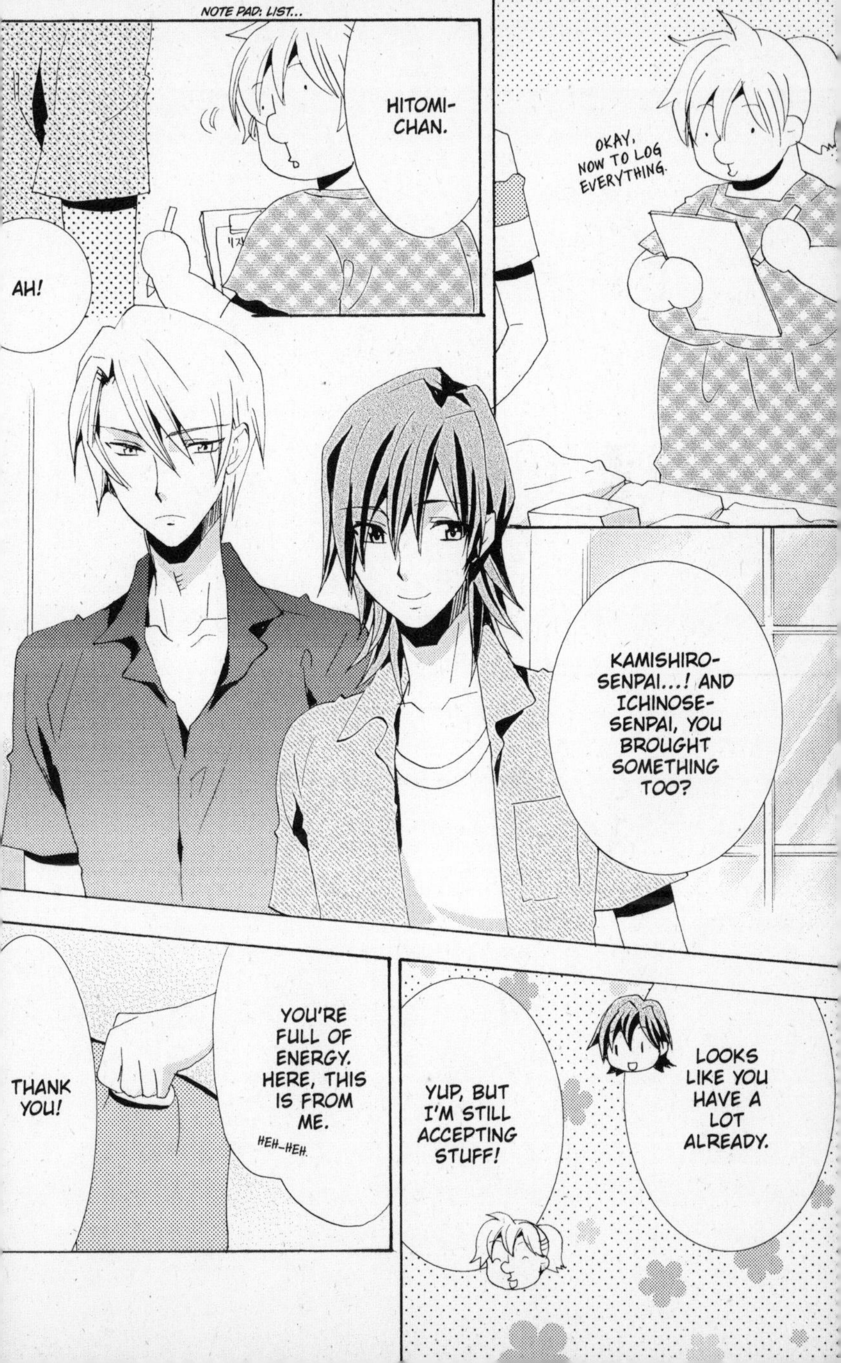
OKAY, NOW TO LOG EVERYTHING.
NOTE PAD: LIST...
HITOMI-CHAN.
AH!
KAMISHIRO-SENPAI...! AND ICHINOSE-SENPAI, YOU BROUGHT SOMETHING TOO?
LOOKS LIKE YOU HAVE A LOT ALREADY.
YUP, BUT I'M STILL ACCEPTING STUFF!
YOU'RE FULL OF ENERGY. HERE, THIS IS FROM ME.
HEH-HEH.
THANK YOU!

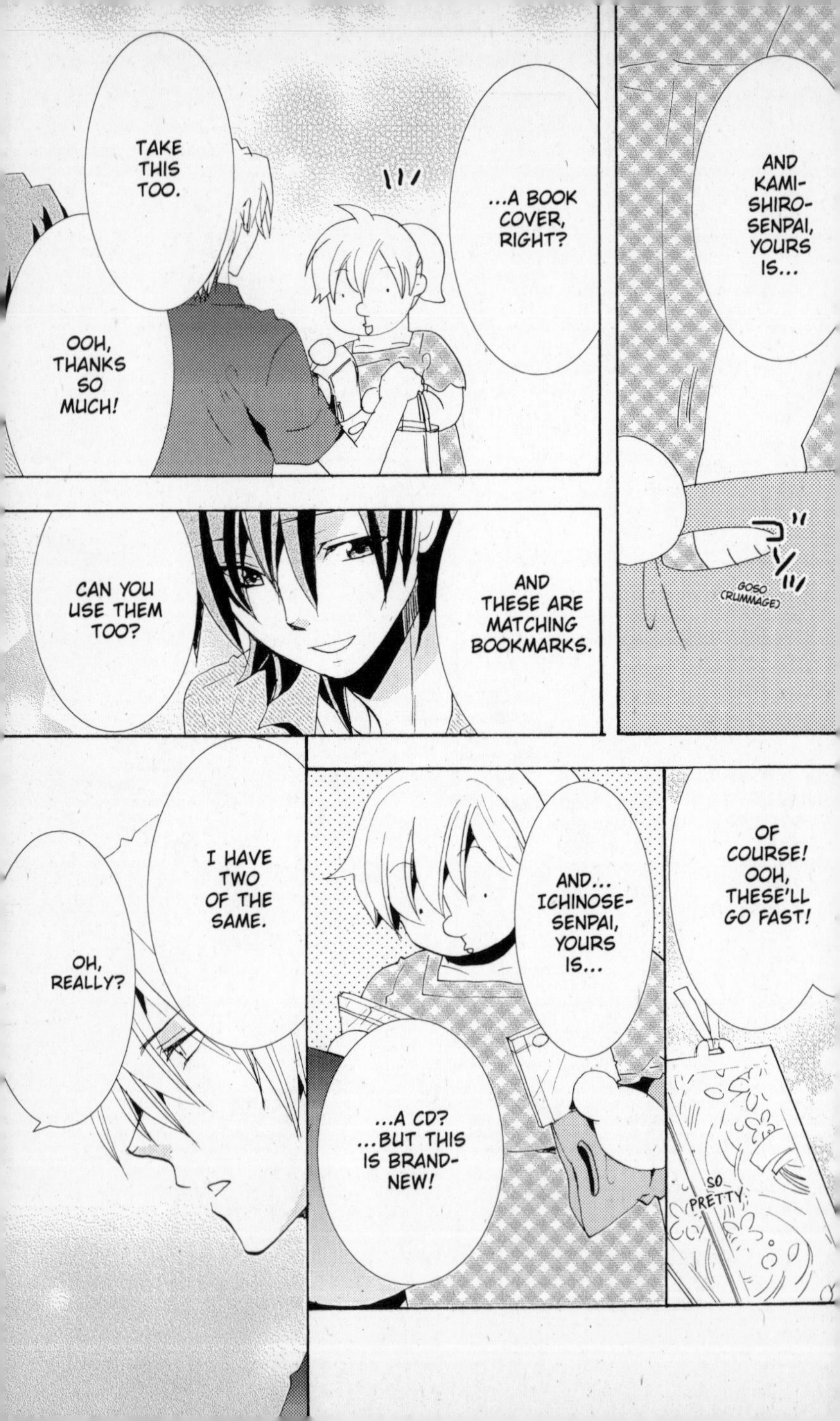
AND KAMI-SHIRO-SENPAI, YOURS IS...
...A BOOK COVER, RIGHT?
TAKE THIS TOO.
OOH, THANKS SO MUCH!
GOSO (RUMMAGE)
AND THESE ARE MATCHING BOOKMARKS.
CAN YOU USE THEM TOO?
OF COURSE! OOH, THESE'LL GO FAST!
SO PRETTY
AND... ICHINOSE-SENPAI, YOURS IS...
...A CD? ...BUT THIS IS BRAND-NEW!
I HAVE TWO OF THE SAME.
OH, REALLY?

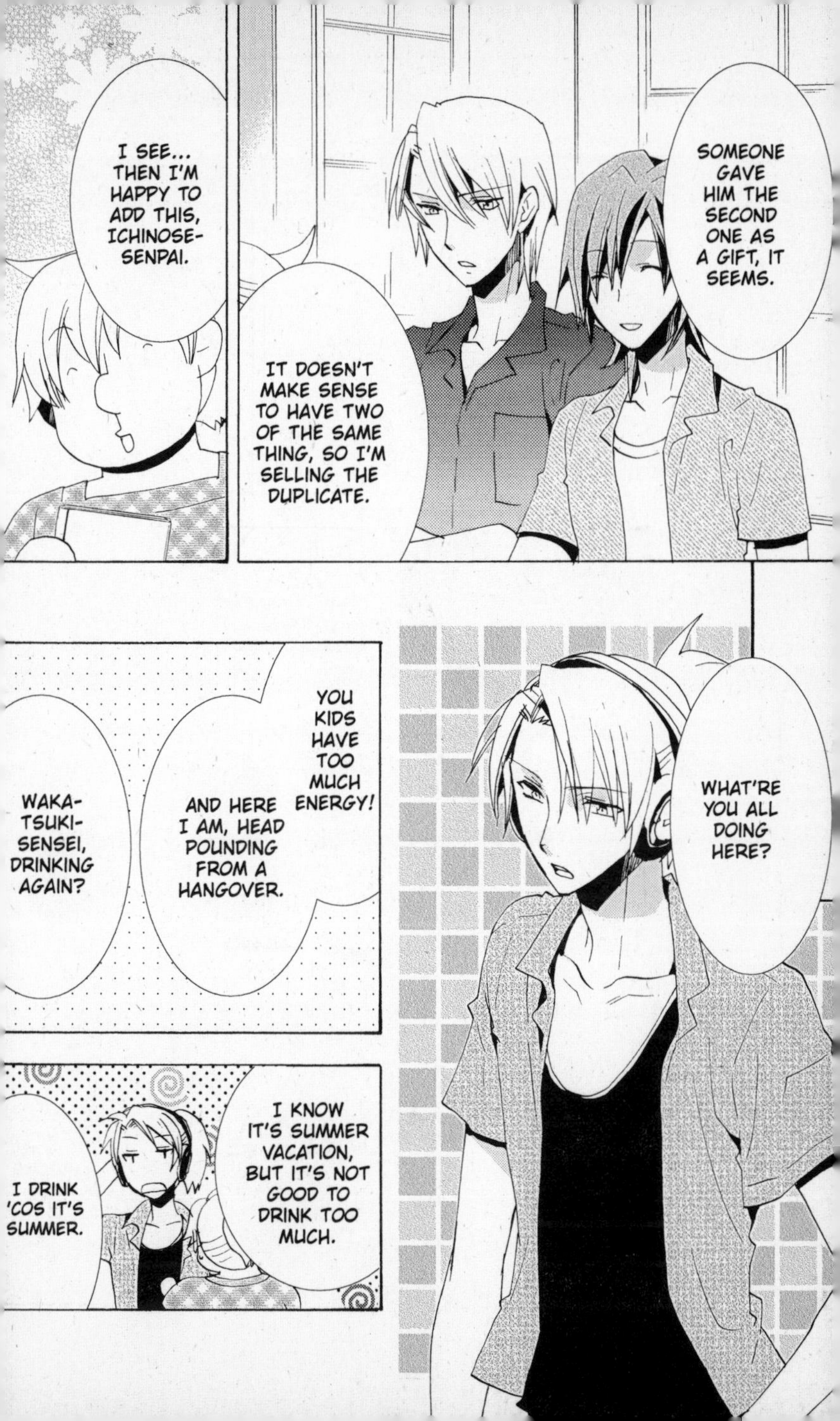
SOMEONE GAVE HIM THE SECOND ONE AS A GIFT, IT SEEMS.
IT DOESN'T MAKE SENSE TO HAVE TWO OF THE SAME THING, SO I'M SELLING THE DUPLICATE.
I SEE... THEN I'M HAPPY TO ADD THIS, ICHINOSE-SENPAI.
WHAT'RE YOU ALL DOING HERE?
YOU KIDS HAVE TOO MUCH ENERGY!
AND HERE I AM, HEAD POUNDING FROM A HANGOVER.
WAKATSUKI-SENSEI, DRINKING AGAIN?
I KNOW IT'S SUMMER VACATION, BUT IT'S NOT GOOD TO DRINK TOO MUCH.
I DRINK 'COS IT'S SUMMER.

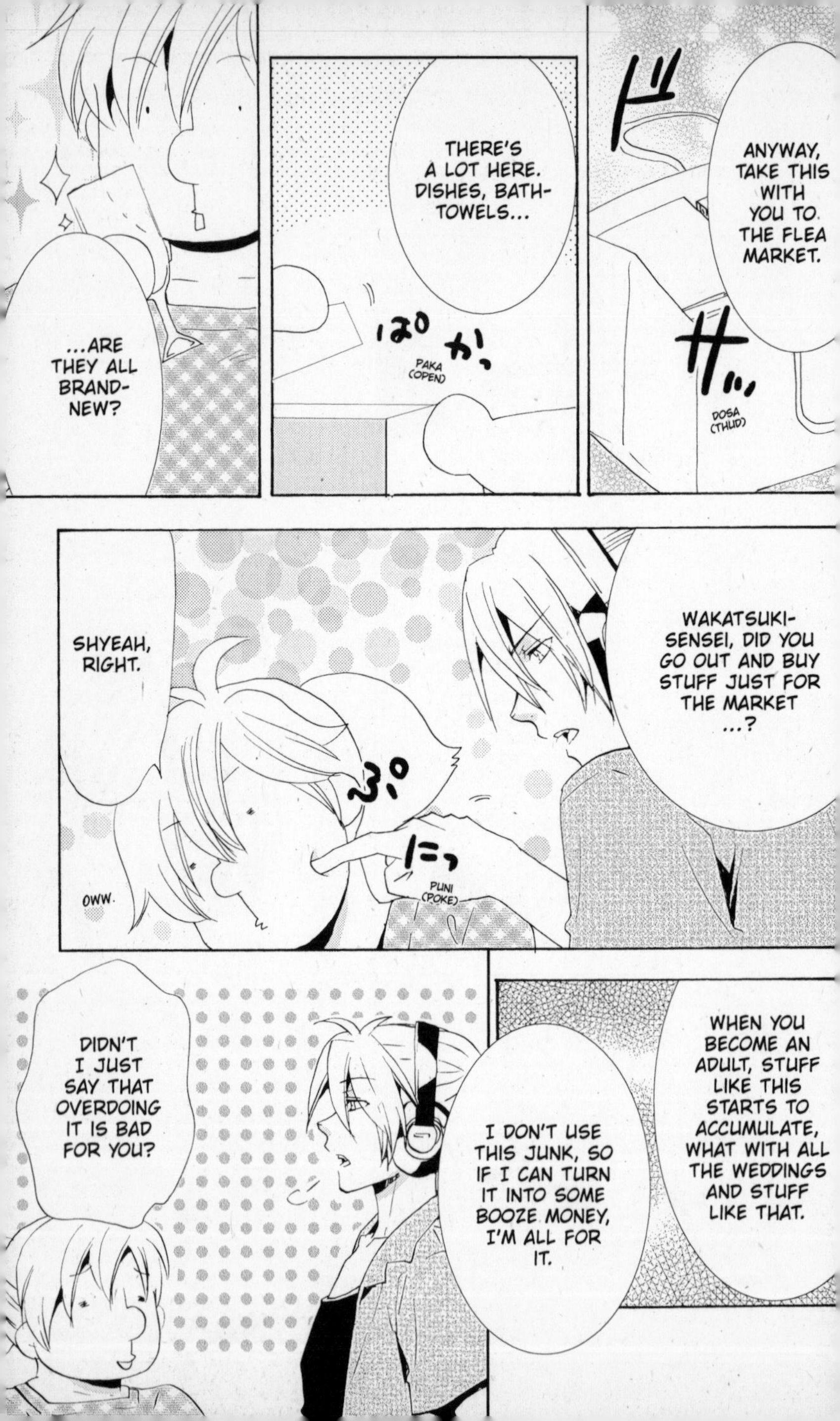
ド
ANYWAY, TAKE THIS WITH YOU TO THE FLEA MARKET.
ザッ
DOSA (THUD)
THERE'S A LOT HERE. DISHES, BATH-TOWELS...
ぱかっ
PAKA (OPEN)
...ARE THEY ALL BRAND-NEW?
WAKATSUKI-SENSEI, DID YOU GO OUT AND BUY STUFF JUST FOR THE MARKET ...?
SHYEAH, RIGHT.
ぷ
にっ
PUNI (POKE)
OWW.
WHEN YOU BECOME AN ADULT, STUFF LIKE THIS STARTS TO ACCUMULATE, WHAT WITH ALL THE WEDDINGS AND STUFF LIKE THAT.
I DON'T USE THIS JUNK, SO IF I CAN TURN IT INTO SOME BOOZE MONEY, I'M ALL FOR IT.
DIDN'T I JUST SAY THAT OVERDOING IT IS BAD FOR YOU?

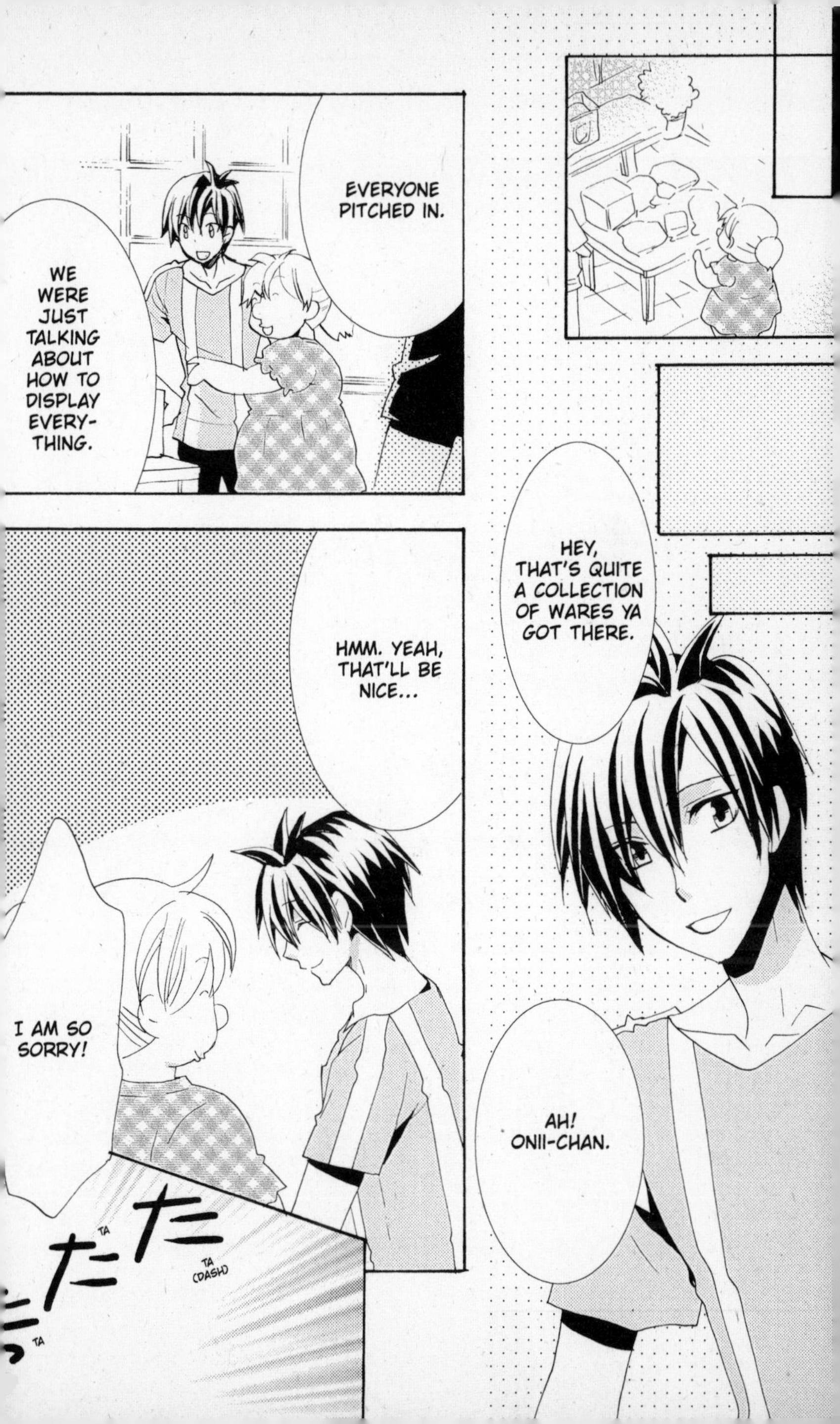
HEY, THAT'S QUITE A COLLECTION OF WARES YA GOT THERE.
AH! ONII-CHAN.
EVERYONE PITCHED IN.
WE WERE JUST TALKING ABOUT HOW TO DISPLAY EVERY-THING.
HMM. YEAH, THAT'LL BE NICE...
I AM SO SORRY!
TA
TA (DASH)
TA

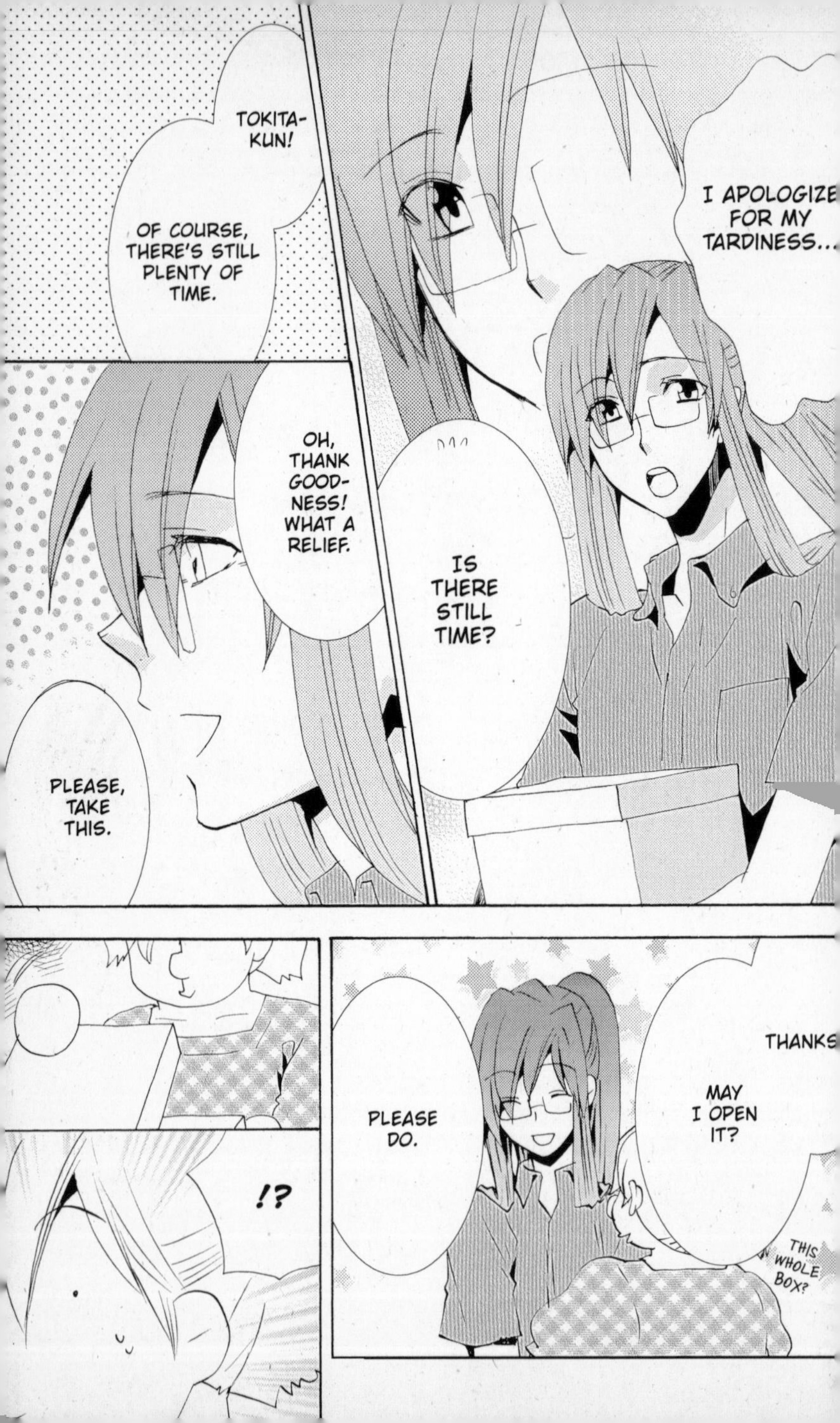
I APOLOGIZE FOR MY TARDINESS...
IS THERE STILL TIME?
TOKITA-KUN!
OF COURSE, THERE'S STILL PLENTY OF TIME.
OH, THANK GOODNESS! WHAT A RELIEF.
PLEASE, TAKE THIS.
THANKS
MAY I OPEN IT?
THIS WHOLE BOX?
PLEASE DO.
!?

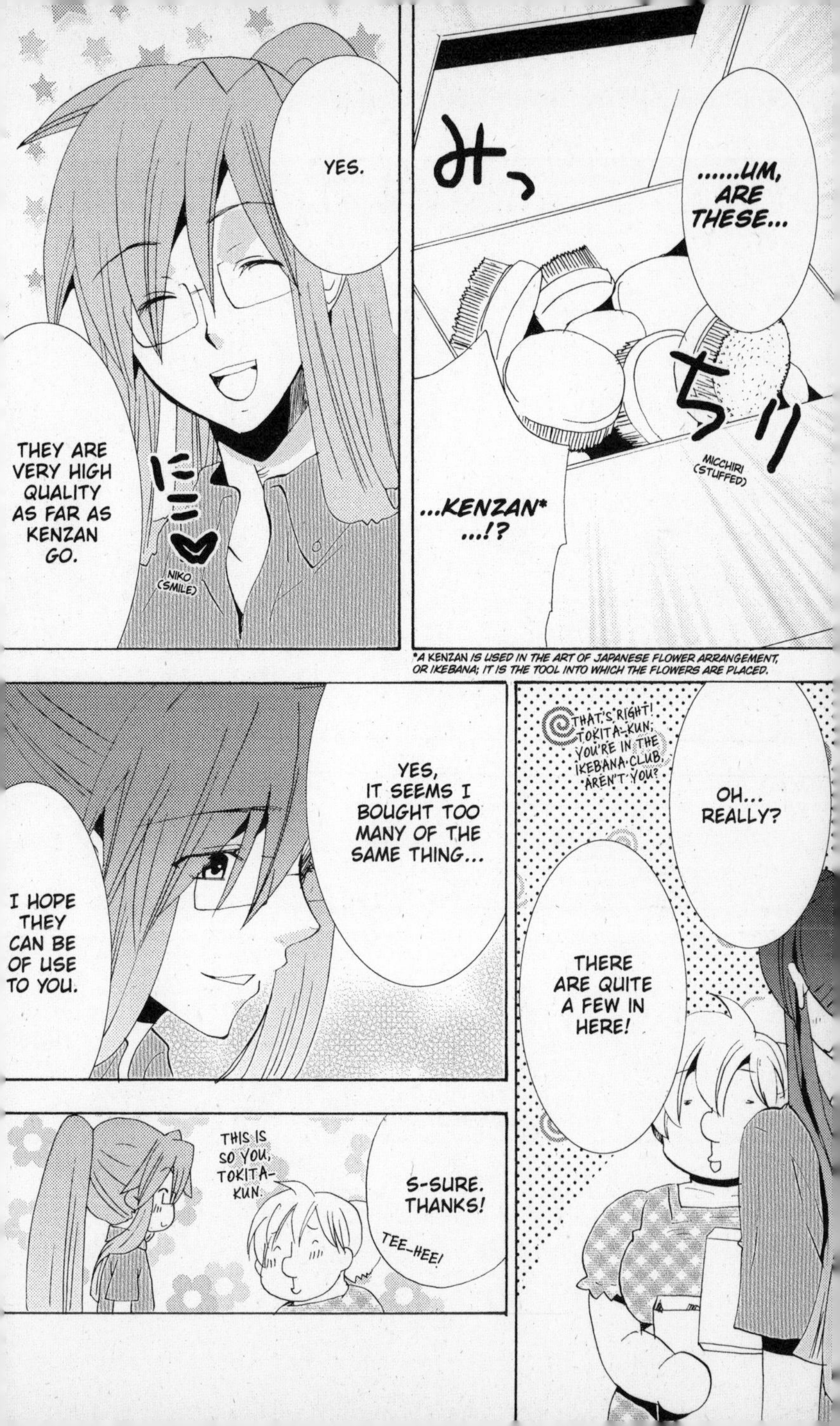
みっ
......UM, ARE THESE...
ちり
MICCHIRI (STUFFED)
...KENZAN* ...!?
YES.
THEY ARE VERY HIGH QUALITY AS FAR AS KENZAN GO.
にこ
NIKO (SMILE)
OH... REALLY?
THAT'S RIGHT! TOKITA-KUN, YOU'RE IN THE IKEBANA CLUB, AREN'T YOU?
THERE ARE QUITE A FEW IN HERE!
YES, IT SEEMS I BOUGHT TOO MANY OF THE SAME THING...
I HOPE THEY CAN BE OF USE TO YOU.
S-SURE. THANKS!
TEE-HEE!
THIS IS SO YOU, TOKITA-KUN.

*A KENZAN IS USED IN THE ART OF JAPANESE FLOWER ARRANGEMENT, OR IKEBANA; IT IS THE TOOL INTO WHICH THE FLOWERS ARE PLACED.

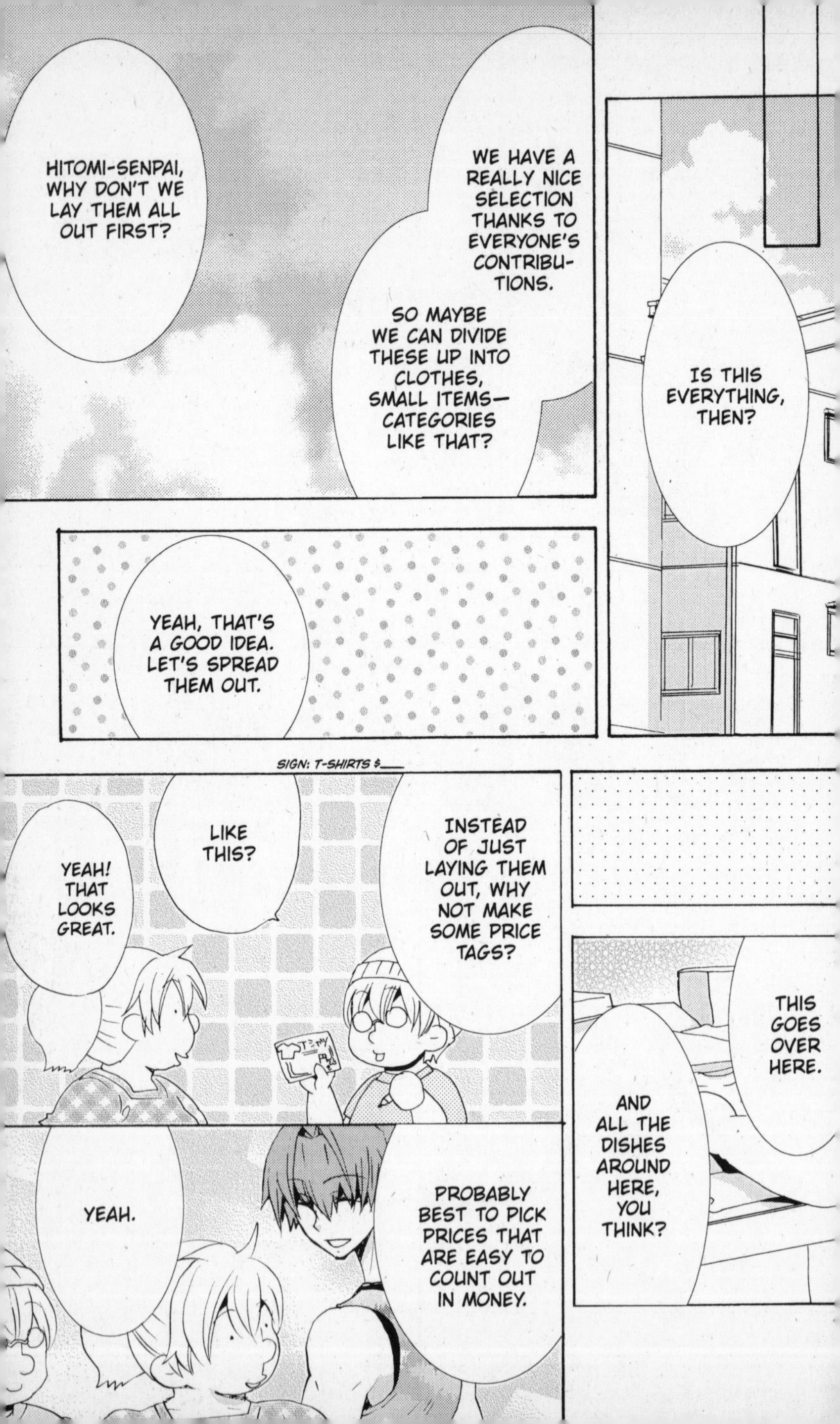
IS THIS EVERYTHING, THEN?
WE HAVE A REALLY NICE SELECTION THANKS TO EVERYONE'S CONTRIBU- TIONS.
SO MAYBE WE CAN DIVIDE THESE UP INTO CLOTHES, SMALL ITEMS— CATEGORIES LIKE THAT?
HITOMI-SENPAI, WHY DON'T WE LAY THEM ALL OUT FIRST?
YEAH, THAT'S A GOOD IDEA. LET'S SPREAD THEM OUT.
SIGN: T-SHIRTS $___
INSTEAD OF JUST LAYING THEM OUT, WHY NOT MAKE SOME PRICE TAGS?
LIKE THIS?
YEAH! THAT LOOKS GREAT.
THIS GOES OVER HERE.
AND ALL THE DISHES AROUND HERE, YOU THINK?
PROBABLY BEST TO PICK PRICES THAT ARE EASY TO COUNT OUT IN MONEY.
YEAH.

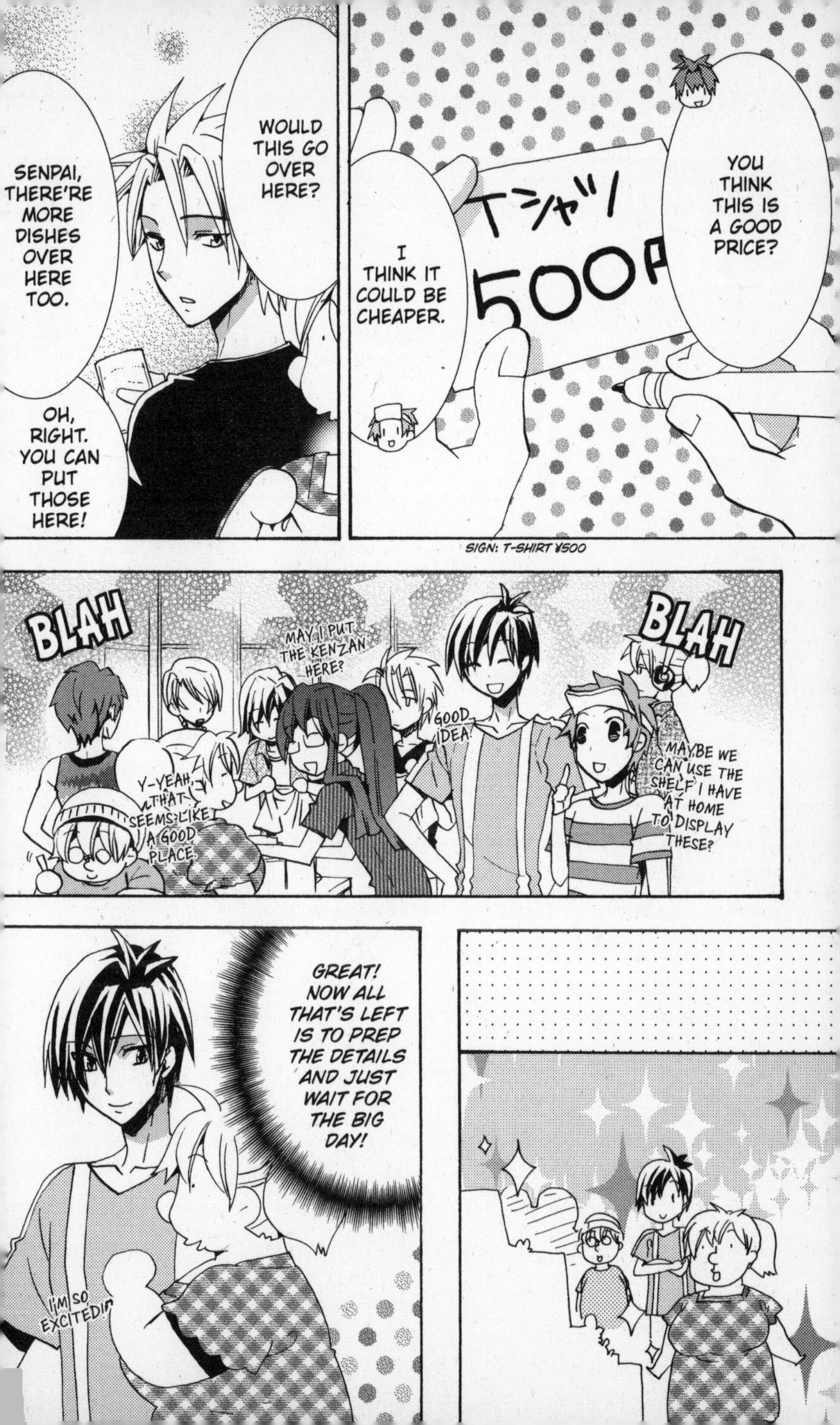
YOU THINK THIS IS A GOOD PRICE?
I THINK IT COULD BE CHEAPER.
Tシャツ
500
SIGN: T-SHIRT ¥500
WOULD THIS GO OVER HERE?
SENPAI, THERE'RE MORE DISHES OVER HERE TOO.
OH, RIGHT. YOU CAN PUT THOSE HERE!
BLAH
MAYBE WE CAN USE THE SHELF I HAVE AT HOME TO DISPLAY THESE?
GOOD IDEA.
MAY I PUT THE KENZAN HERE?
Y-YEAH, THAT SEEMS LIKE A GOOD PLACE.
BLAH
GREAT! NOW ALL THAT'S LEFT IS TO PREP THE DETAILS AND JUST WAIT FOR THE BIG DAY!
I'M SO EXCITED!

LOVEREVO!!

LOVEREVO!!

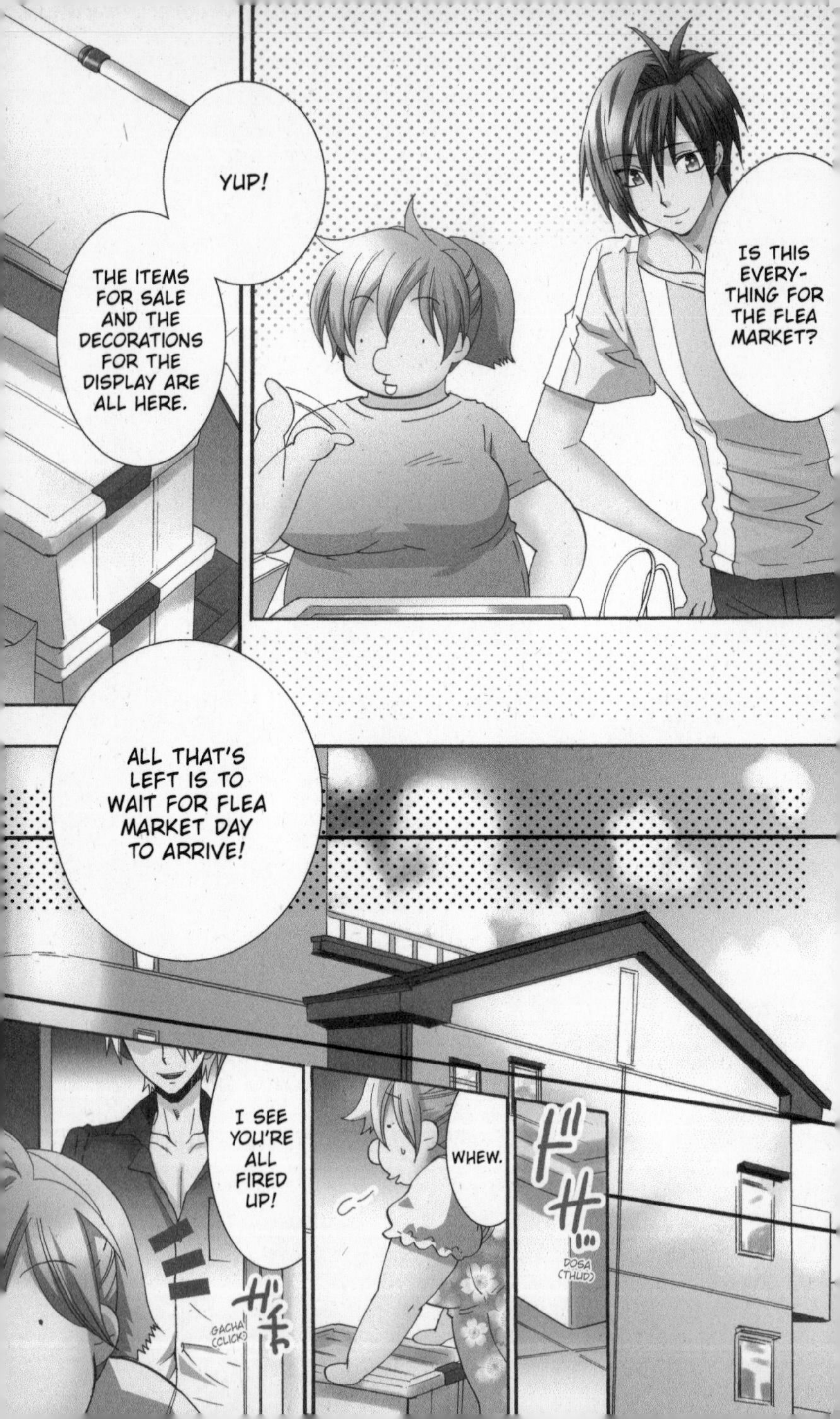

IS THIS EVERY-THING FOR THE FLEA MARKET?
YUP!
THE ITEMS FOR SALE AND THE DECORATIONS FOR THE DISPLAY ARE ALL HERE.
ALL THAT'S LEFT IS TO WAIT FOR FLEA MARKET DAY TO ARRIVE!
DOSA (THUD)
WHEW.
I SEE YOU'RE ALL FIRED UP!
GACHA (CLICK)

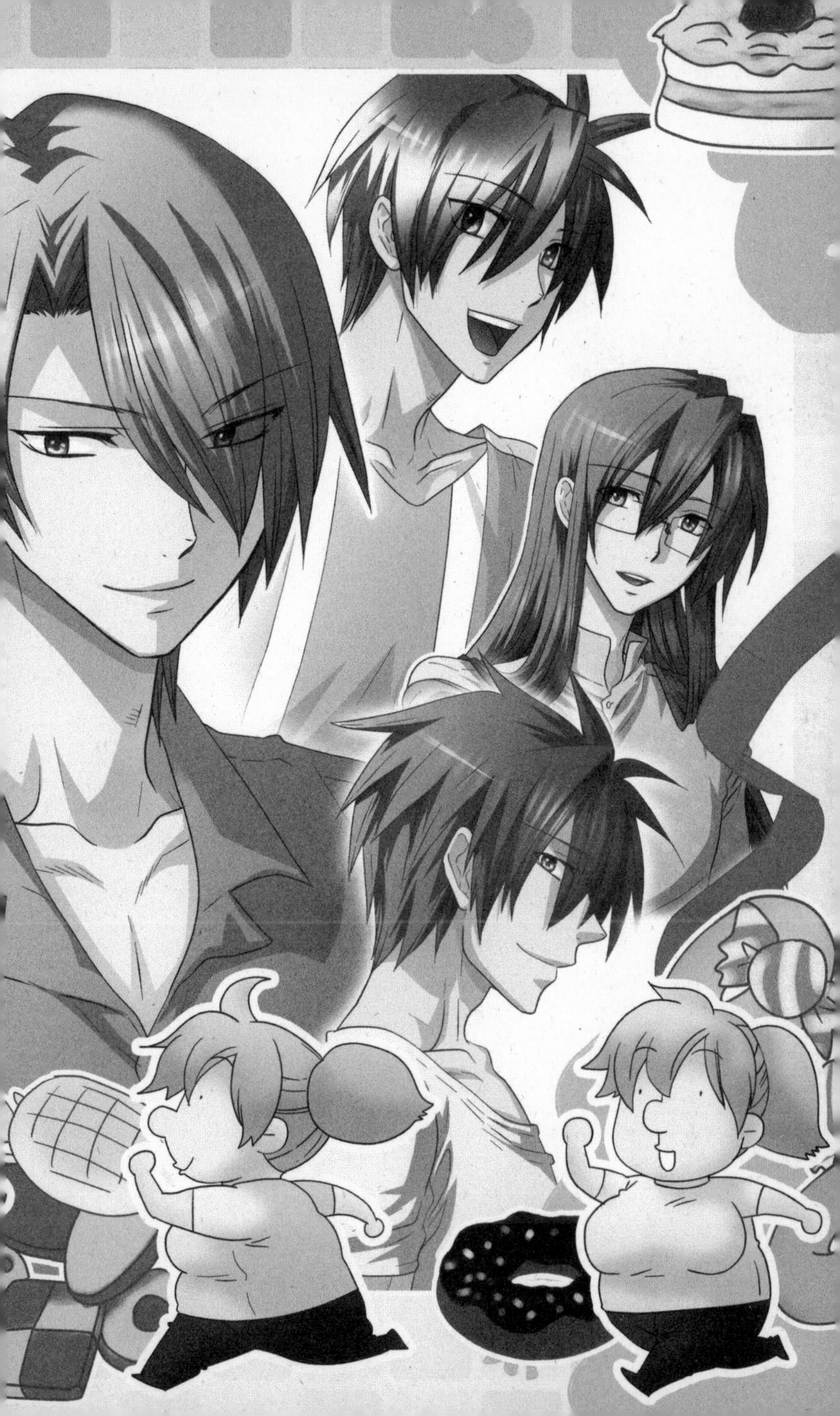

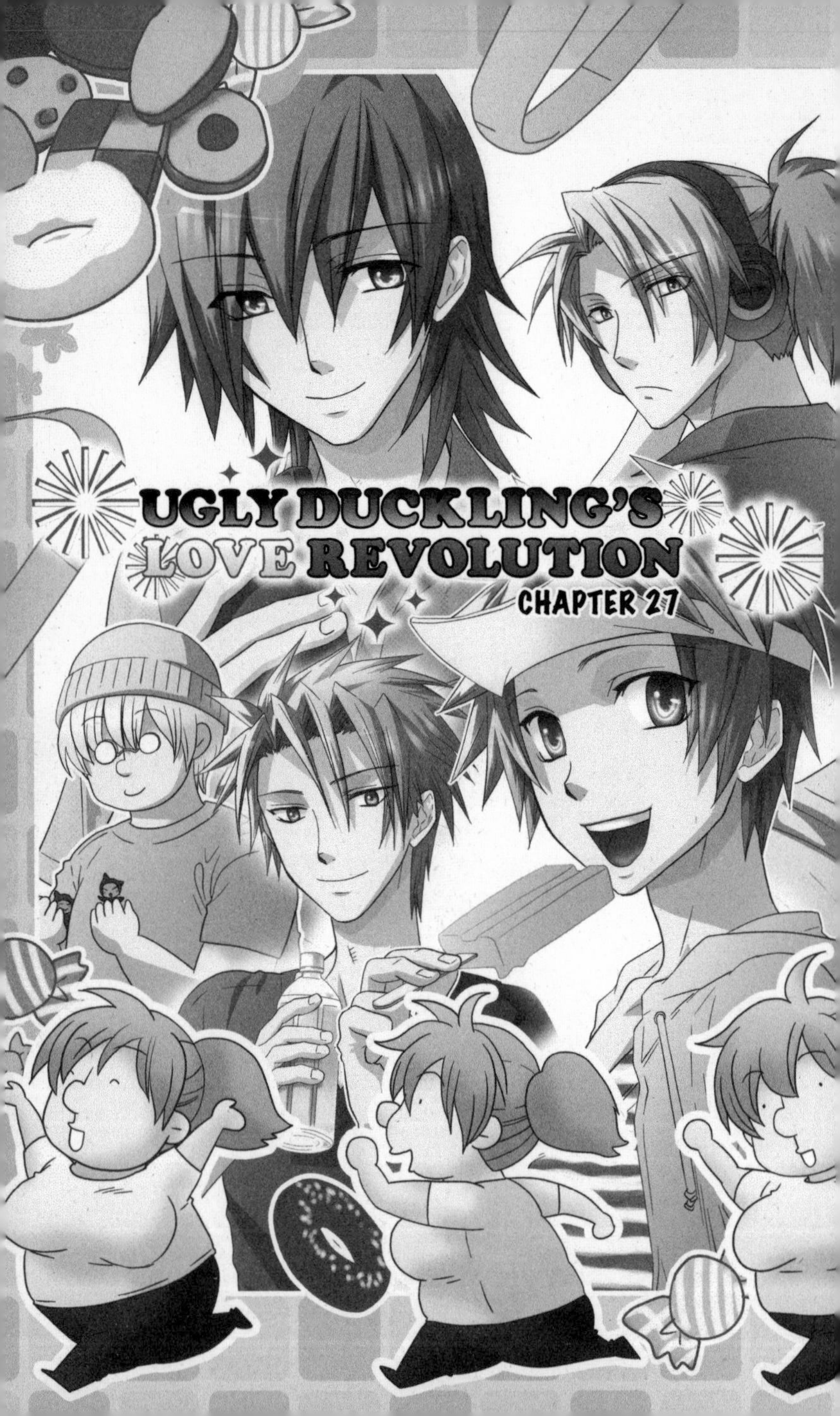
UGLY DUCKLING'S LOVE REVOLUTION
CHAPTER 27

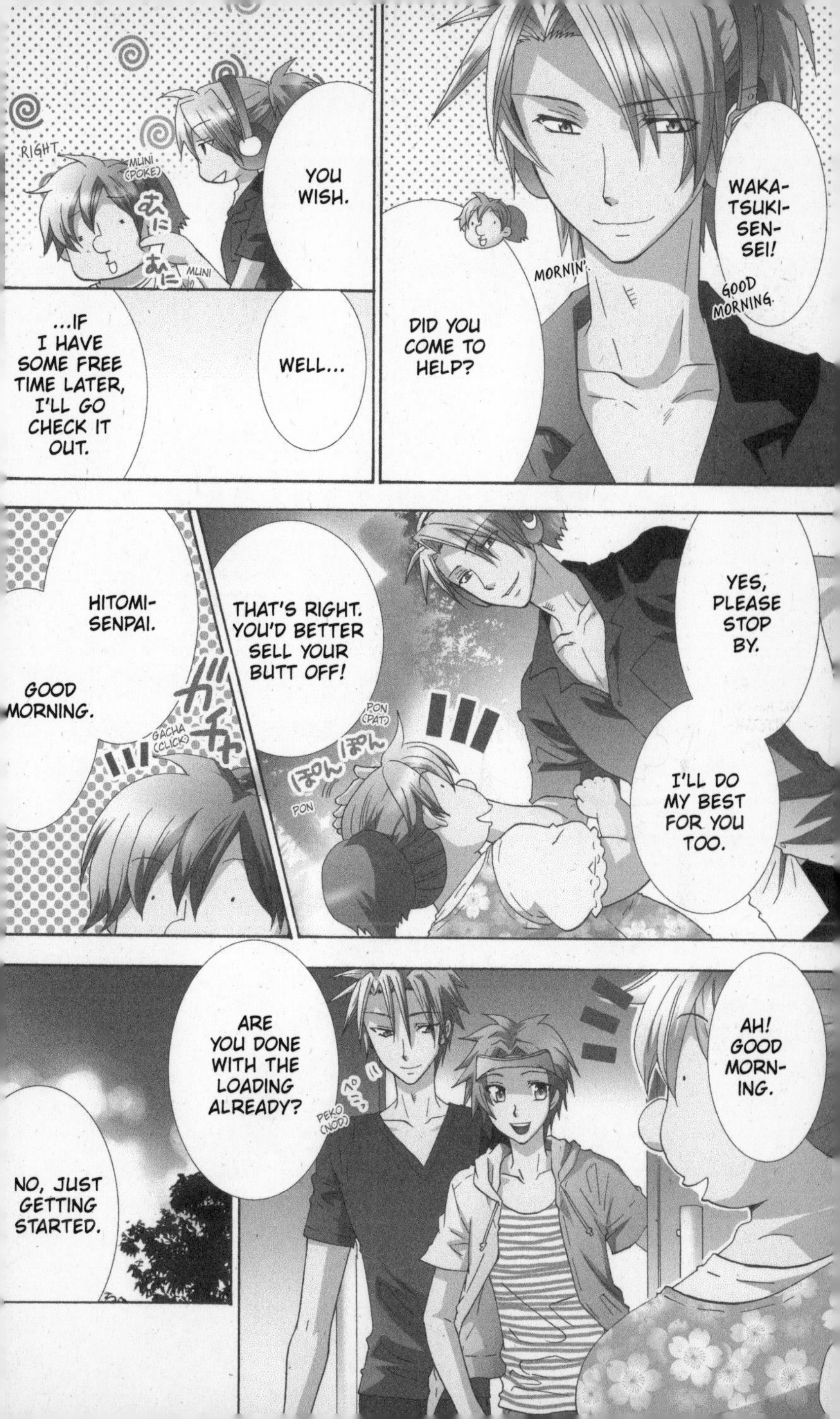
WAKA-TSUKI-SEN-SEI!
GOOD MORNING.
MORNIN'.
DID YOU COME TO HELP?
YOU WISH.
RIGHT
むに MUNI (POKE)
むに MUNI
WELL...
...IF I HAVE SOME FREE TIME LATER, I'LL GO CHECK IT OUT.
YES, PLEASE STOP BY.
I'LL DO MY BEST FOR YOU TOO.
THAT'S RIGHT. YOU'D BETTER SELL YOUR BUTT OFF!
ぽん PON (PAT)
ぽん PON
HITOMI-SENPAI.
ガチャ GACHA (CLICK)
GOOD MORNING.
AH! GOOD MORN-ING.
ARE YOU DONE WITH THE LOADING ALREADY?
PEKO (NOD)
NO, JUST GETTING STARTED.

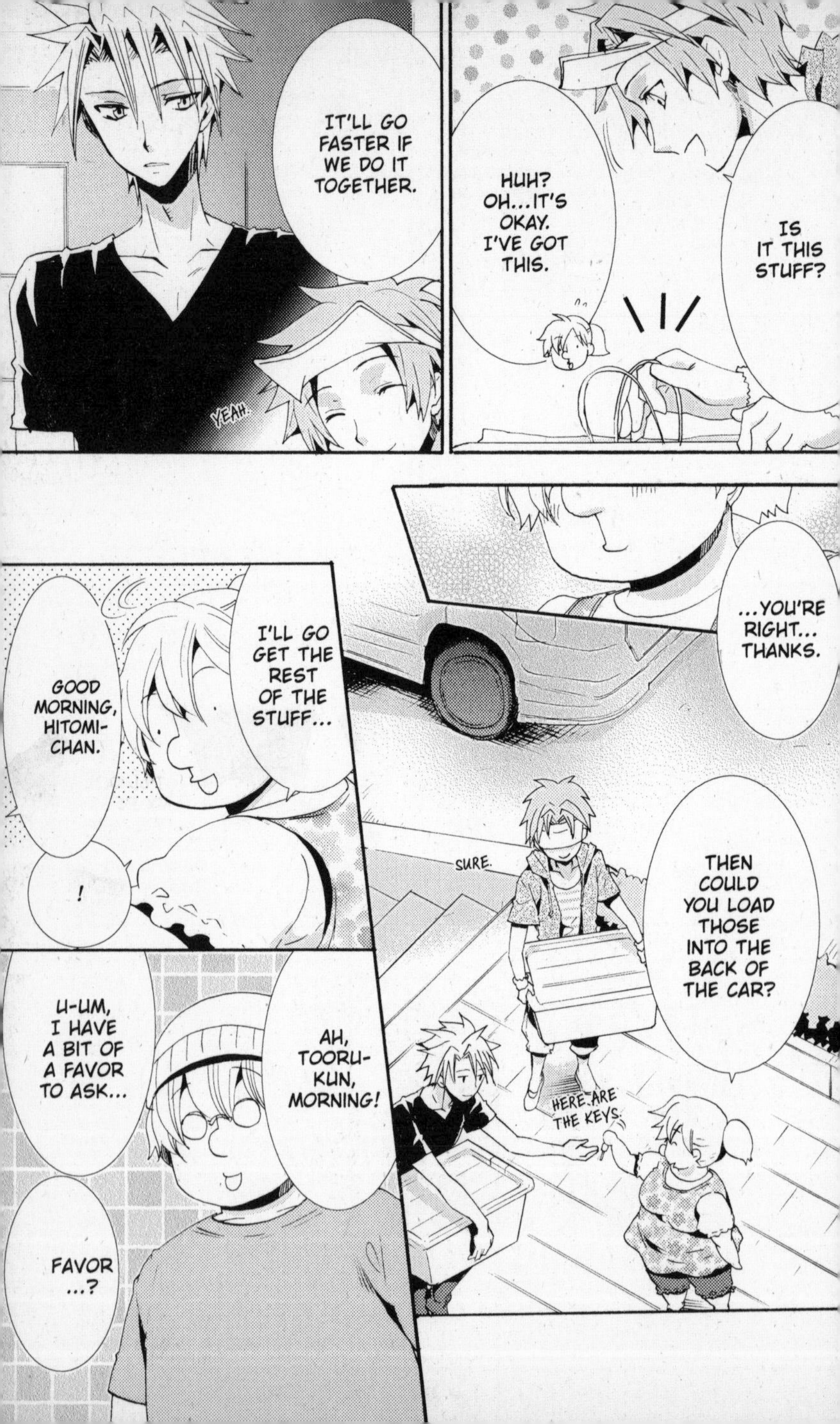
IS IT THIS STUFF?
HUH? OH...IT'S OKAY. I'VE GOT THIS.
IT'LL GO FASTER IF WE DO IT TOGETHER.
YEAH.
...YOU'RE RIGHT... THANKS.
THEN COULD YOU LOAD THOSE INTO THE BACK OF THE CAR?
SURE.
HERE ARE THE KEYS.
I'LL GO GET THE REST OF THE STUFF...
GOOD MORNING, HITOMI-CHAN.
!
AH, TOORU-KUN, MORNING!
U-UM, I HAVE A BIT OF A FAVOR TO ASK...
FAVOR ...?

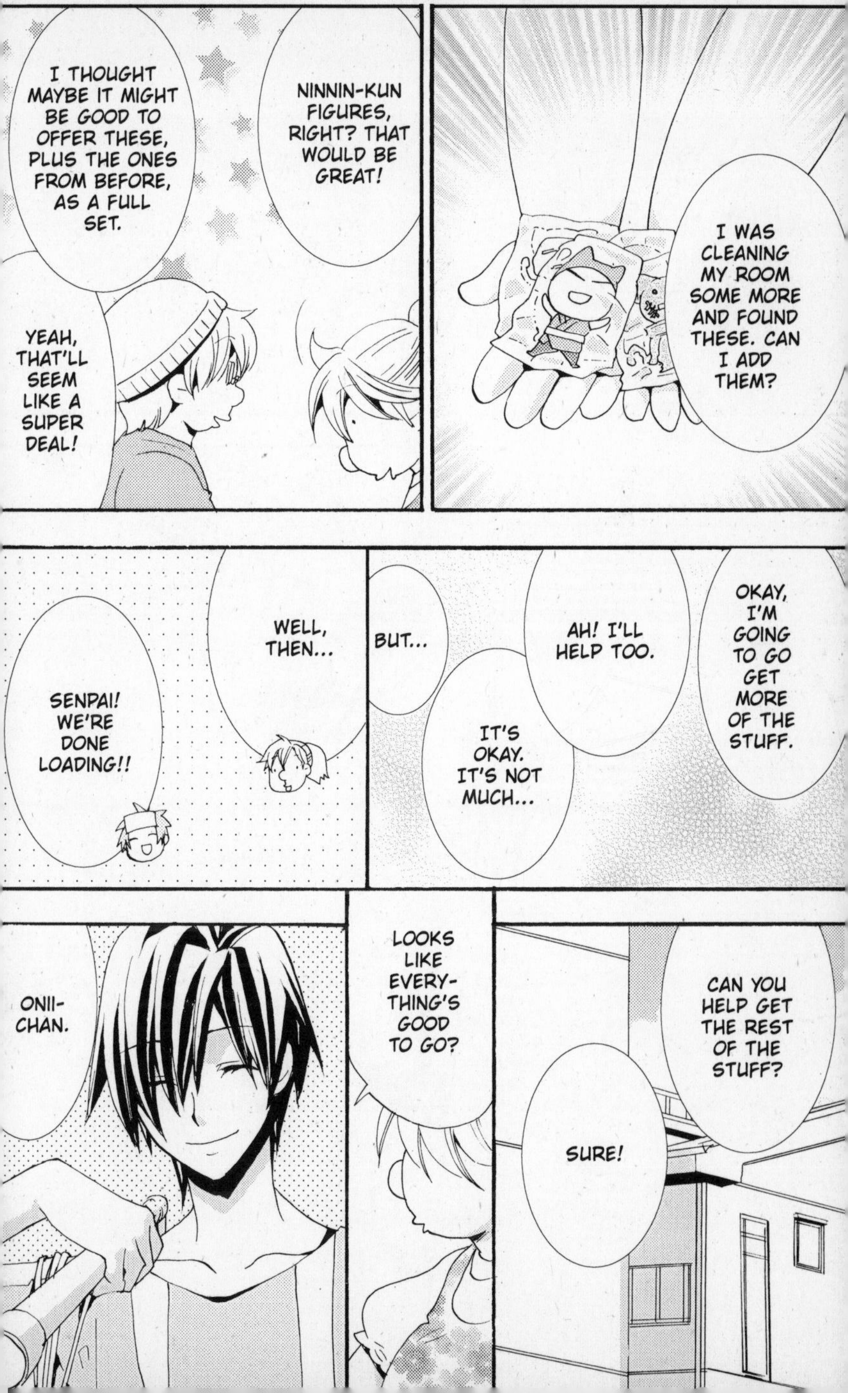
I WAS CLEANING MY ROOM SOME MORE AND FOUND THESE. CAN I ADD THEM?
NINNIN-KUN FIGURES, RIGHT? THAT WOULD BE GREAT!
I THOUGHT MAYBE IT MIGHT BE GOOD TO OFFER THESE, PLUS THE ONES FROM BEFORE, AS A FULL SET.
YEAH, THAT'LL SEEM LIKE A SUPER DEAL!
OKAY, I'M GOING TO GO GET MORE OF THE STUFF.
AH! I'LL HELP TOO.
BUT...
IT'S OKAY. IT'S NOT MUCH...
WELL, THEN...
SENPAI! WE'RE DONE LOADING!!
CAN YOU HELP GET THE REST OF THE STUFF?
SURE!
LOOKS LIKE EVERY-THING'S GOOD TO GO?
ONII-CHAN.

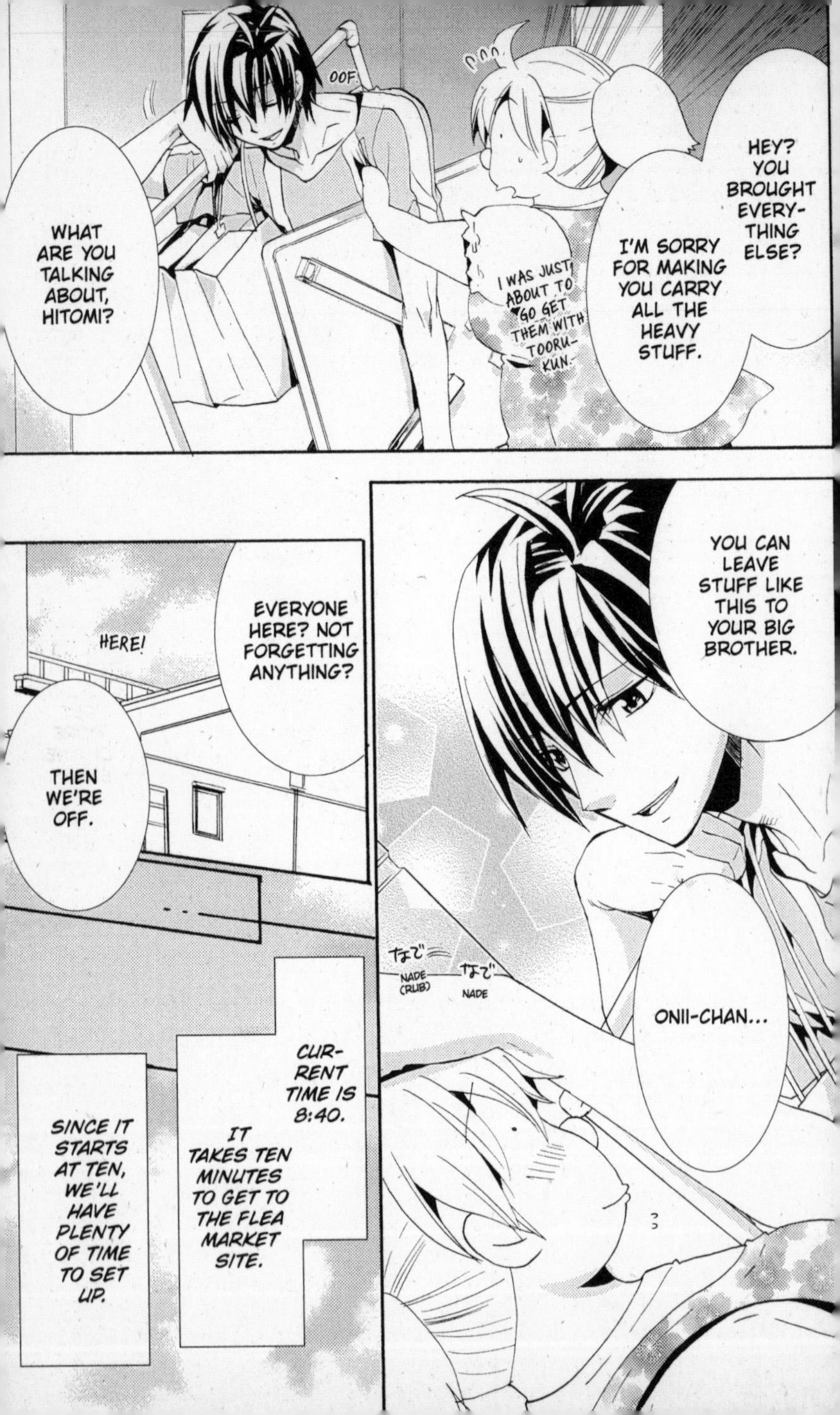
HEY? YOU BROUGHT EVERY-THING ELSE?
I'M SORRY FOR MAKING YOU CARRY ALL THE HEAVY STUFF.
I WAS JUST ABOUT TO GO GET THEM WITH TOORU-KUN.
OOF
WHAT ARE YOU TALKING ABOUT, HITOMI?
YOU CAN LEAVE STUFF LIKE THIS TO YOUR BIG BROTHER.
なで NADE (RUB)
なで NADE
ONII-CHAN...
EVERYONE HERE? NOT FORGETTING ANYTHING?
HERE!
THEN WE'RE OFF.
CUR-RENT TIME IS 8:40.
IT TAKES TEN MINUTES TO GET TO THE FLEA MARKET SITE.
SINCE IT STARTS AT TEN, WE'LL HAVE PLENTY OF TIME TO SET UP.

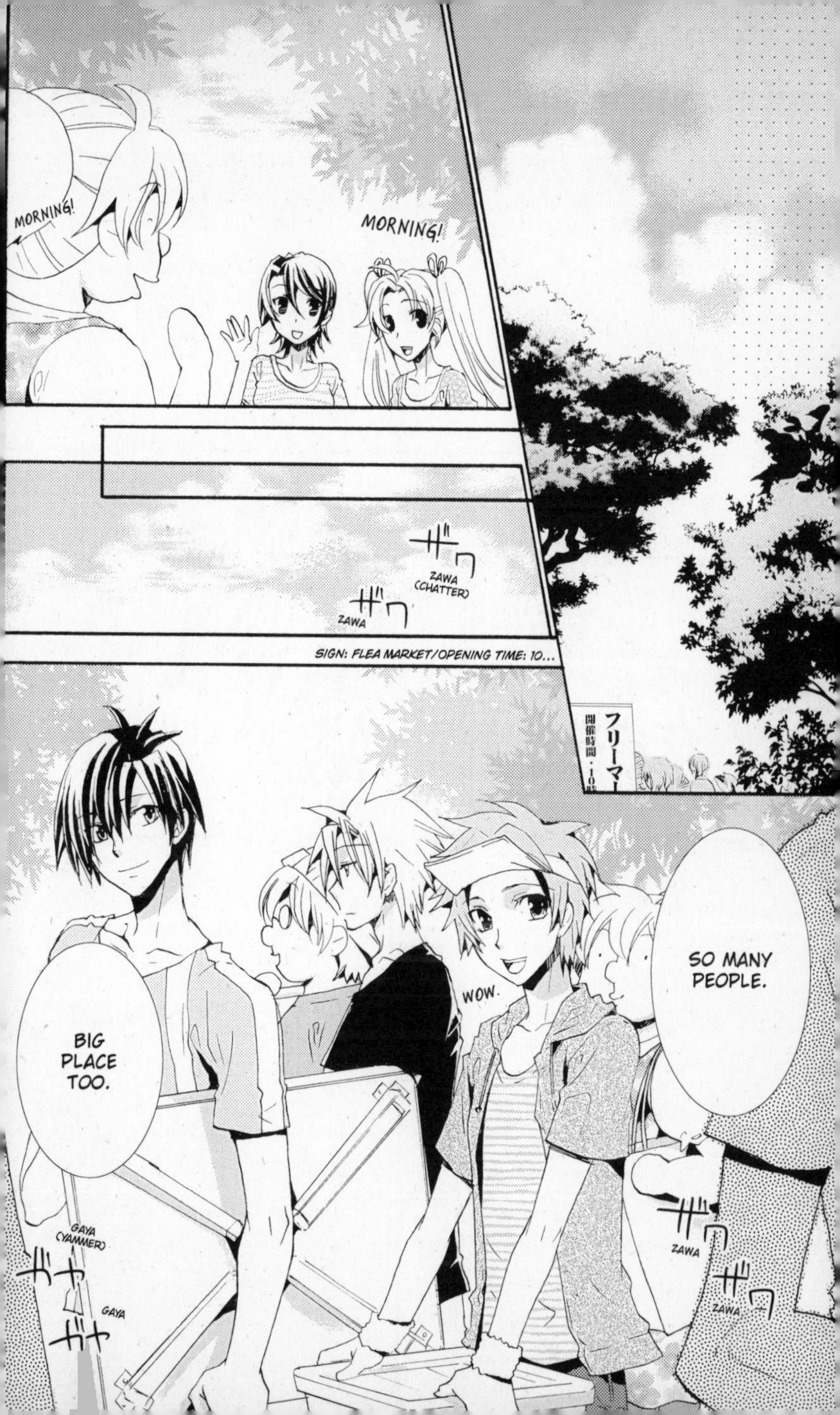
MORNING!
MORNING!
ザワ
ZAWA (CHATTER)
ザワ
ZAWA
SIGN: FLEA MARKET/OPENING TIME: 10...
フリーマ
SO MANY PEOPLE.
ザワ
ZAWA
ザワ
ZAWA
WOW.
BIG PLACE TOO.
ガヤ
GAYA (YAMMER)
ガヤ
GAYA

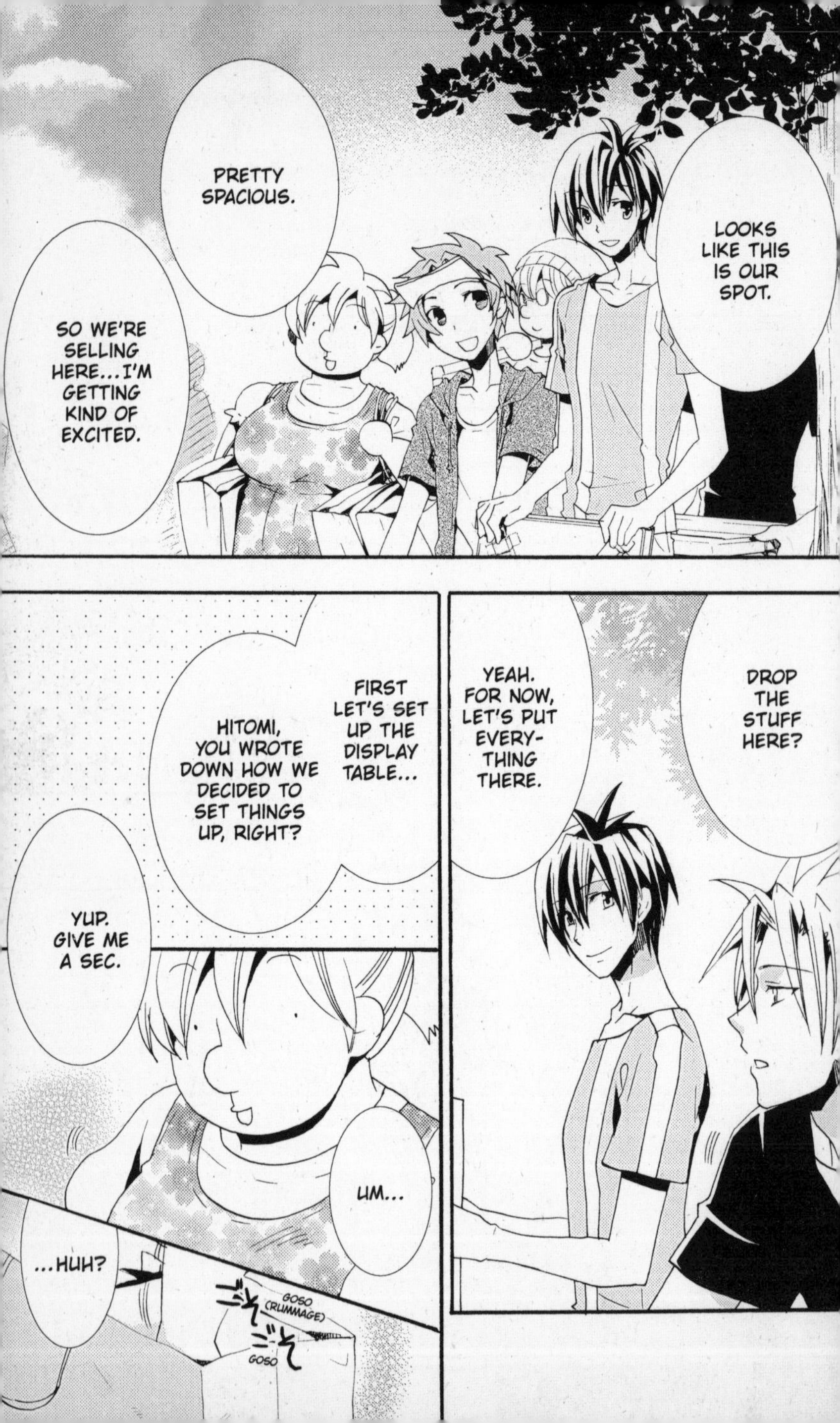
LOOKS LIKE THIS IS OUR SPOT.
PRETTY SPACIOUS.
SO WE'RE SELLING HERE...I'M GETTING KIND OF EXCITED.
DROP THE STUFF HERE?
YEAH. FOR NOW, LET'S PUT EVERY-THING THERE.
FIRST LET'S SET UP THE DISPLAY TABLE...
HITOMI, YOU WROTE DOWN HOW WE DECIDED TO SET THINGS UP, RIGHT?
YUP. GIVE ME A SEC.
UM...
GOSO (RUMMAGE)
GOSO
...HUH?

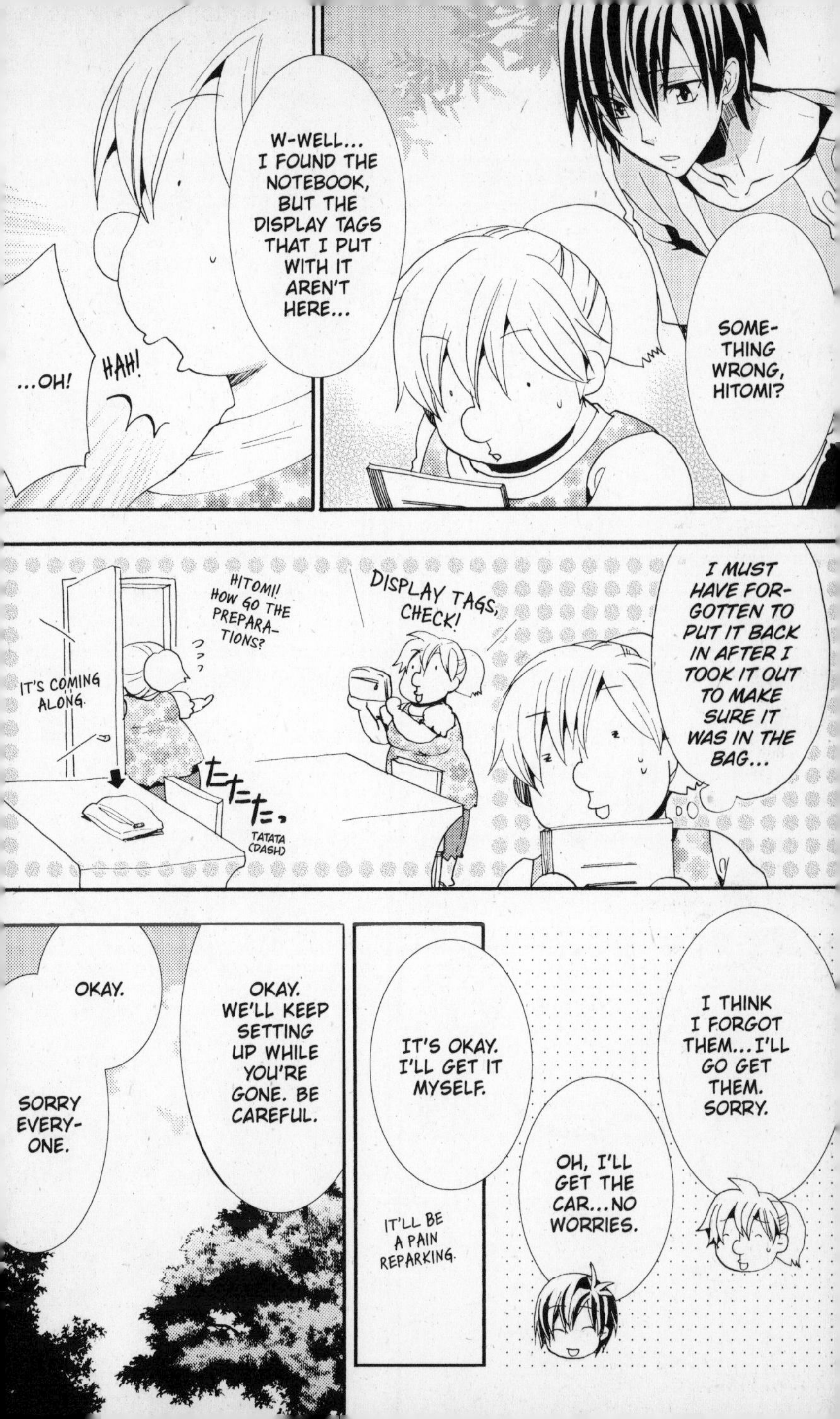
SOME-THING WRONG, HITOMI?
W-WELL... I FOUND THE NOTEBOOK, BUT THE DISPLAY TAGS THAT I PUT WITH IT AREN'T HERE...
HAH!
...OH!
I MUST HAVE FOR-GOTTEN TO PUT IT BACK IN AFTER I TOOK IT OUT TO MAKE SURE IT WAS IN THE BAG...
DISPLAY TAGS, CHECK!
HITOMI! HOW GO THE PREPARA-TIONS?
IT'S COMING ALONG.
TATATA (DASH)
I THINK I FORGOT THEM...I'LL GO GET THEM. SORRY.
IT'S OKAY. I'LL GET IT MYSELF.
OH, I'LL GET THE CAR...NO WORRIES.
IT'LL BE A PAIN REPARKING.
OKAY. WE'LL KEEP SETTING UP WHILE YOU'RE GONE. BE CAREFUL.
OKAY.
SORRY EVERY-ONE.

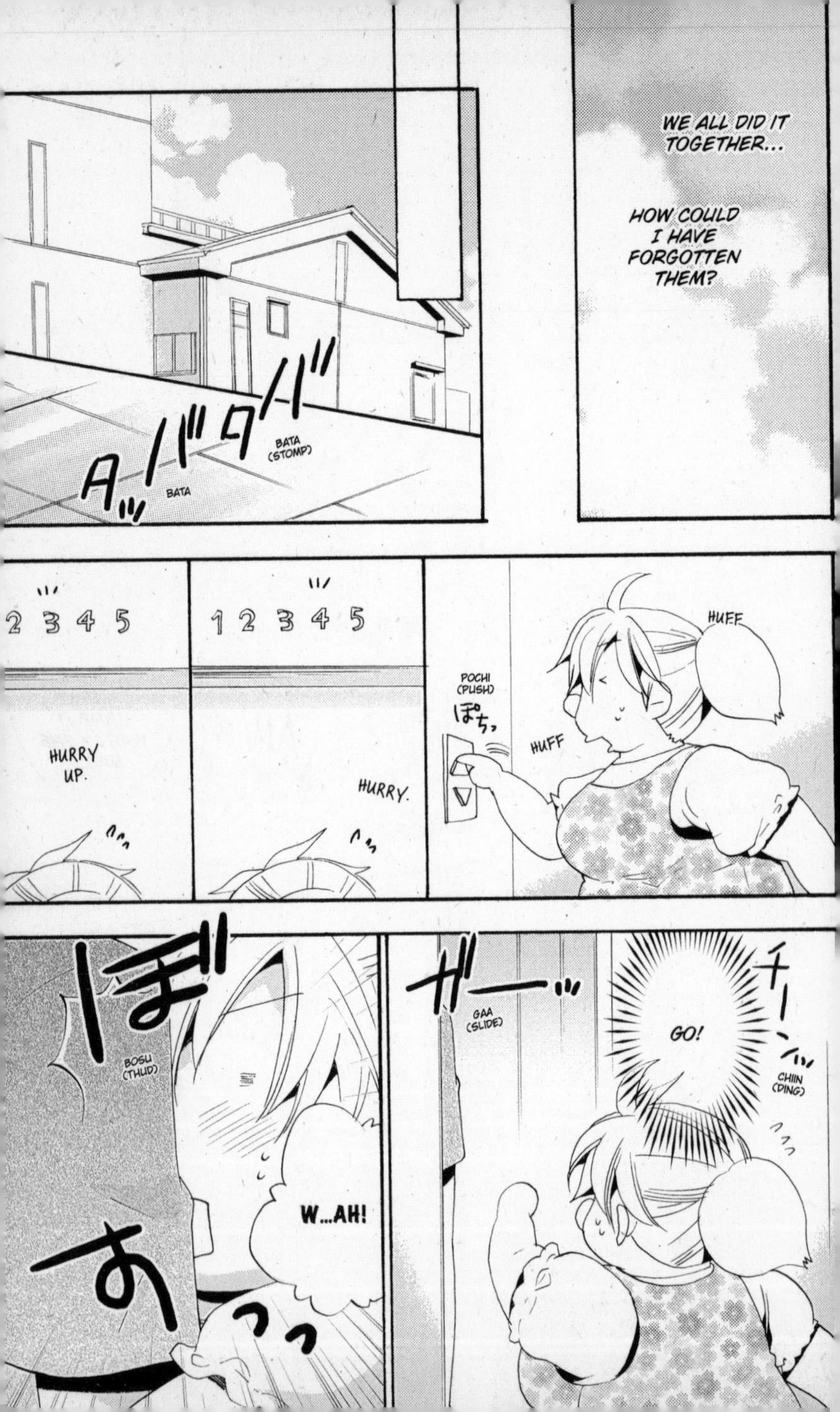
WE ALL DID IT TOGETHER...
HOW COULD I HAVE FORGOTTEN THEM?
BATA (STOMP)
BATA
HUFF
POCHI (PUSH)
HUFF
1 2 3 4 5
HURRY.
2 3 4 5
HURRY UP.
CHIIN (DING)
GO!
GAA (SLIDE)
BOSU (THUD)
W...AH!

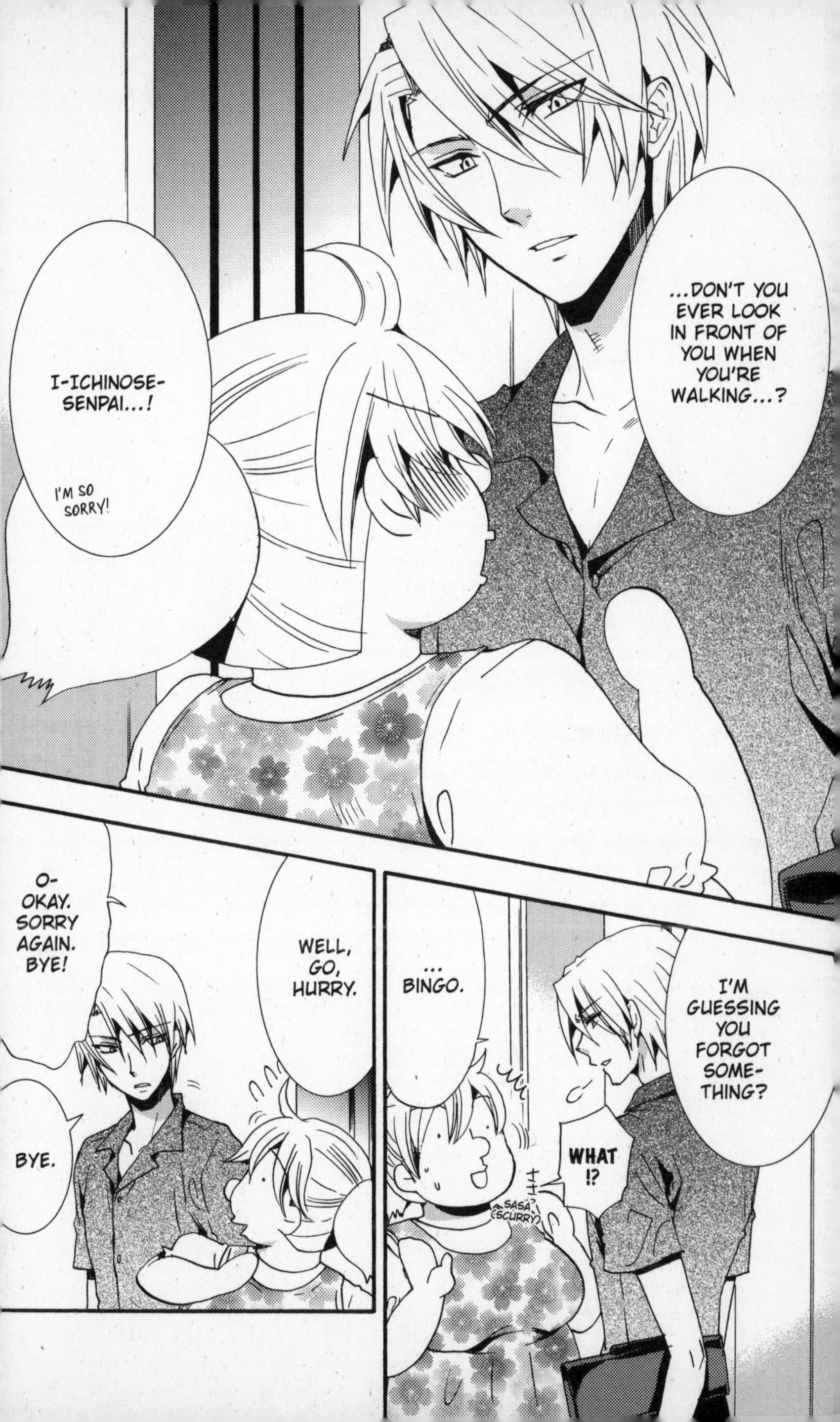
...DON'T YOU EVER LOOK IN FRONT OF YOU WHEN YOU'RE WALKING...?
I-ICHINOSE-SENPAI...!
I'M SO SORRY!
I'M GUESSING YOU FORGOT SOME-THING?
WHAT!?
SASA (SCURRY)
...BINGO.
WELL, GO, HURRY.
O-OKAY. SORRY AGAIN. BYE!
BYE.

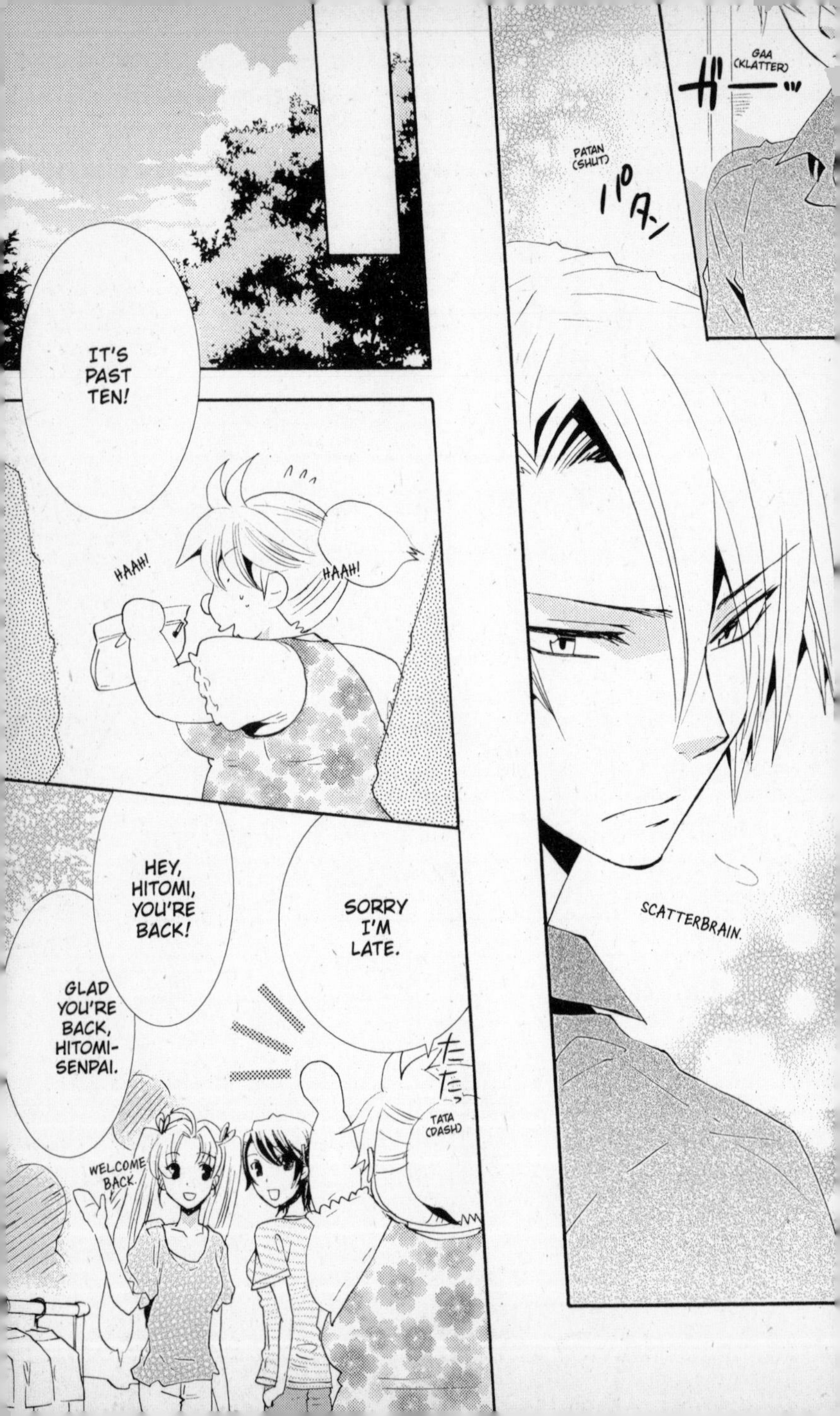

ガーッ
GAA (KLATTER)
パタン
PATAN (SHUT)
SCATTERBRAIN.
IT'S PAST TEN!
HAAH!
HAAH!
SORRY I'M LATE.
たたっ
TATA (DASH)
HEY, HITOMI, YOU'RE BACK!
GLAD YOU'RE BACK, HITOMI-SENPAI.
WELCOME BACK.

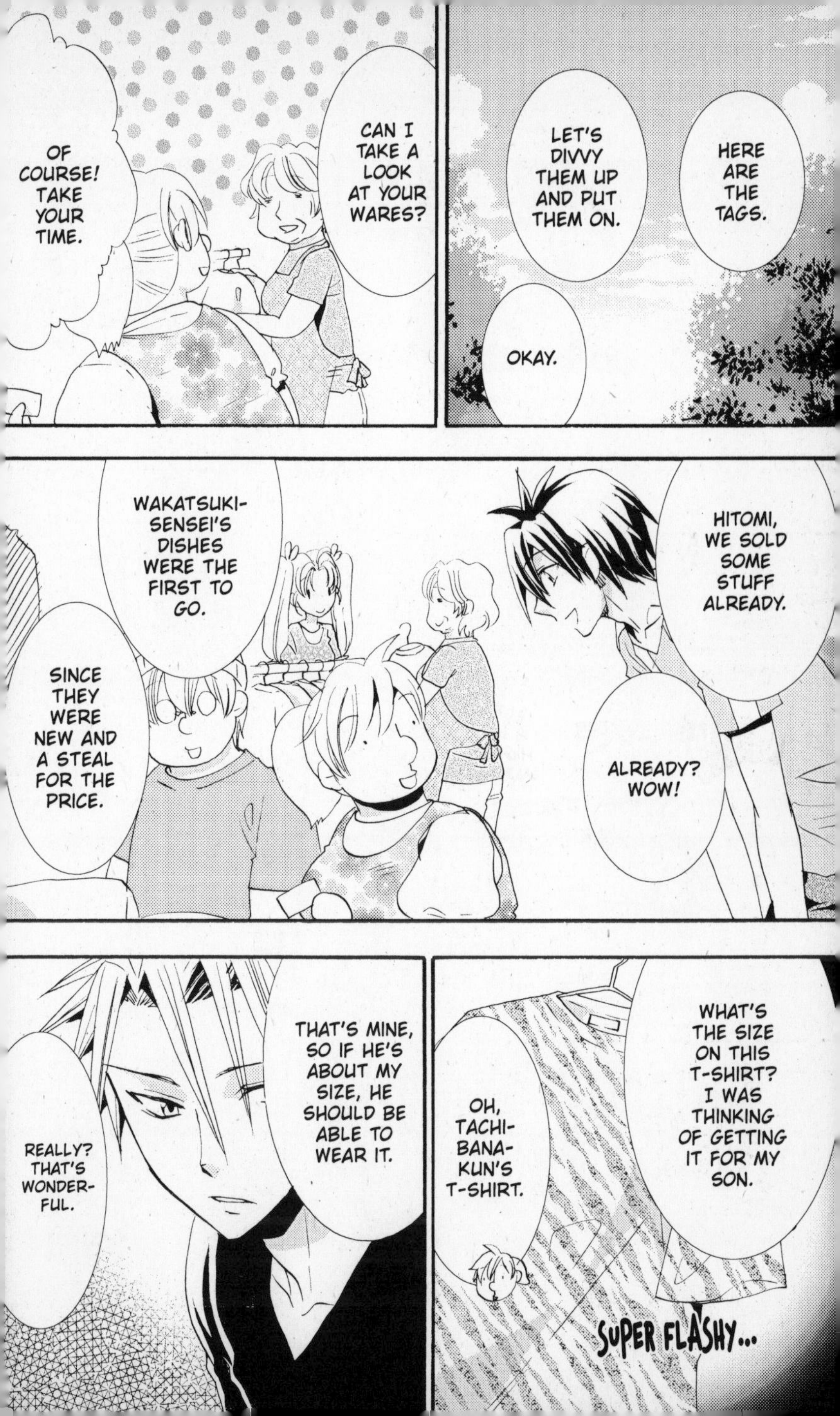
HERE ARE THE TAGS.
LET'S DIVVY THEM UP AND PUT THEM ON.
OKAY.
CAN I TAKE A LOOK AT YOUR WARES?
OF COURSE! TAKE YOUR TIME.
HITOMI, WE SOLD SOME STUFF ALREADY.
ALREADY? WOW!
WAKATSUKI-SENSEI'S DISHES WERE THE FIRST TO GO.
SINCE THEY WERE NEW AND A STEAL FOR THE PRICE.
WHAT'S THE SIZE ON THIS T-SHIRT? I WAS THINKING OF GETTING IT FOR MY SON.
OH, TACHIBANA-KUN'S T-SHIRT.
SUPER FLASHY...
THAT'S MINE, SO IF HE'S ABOUT MY SIZE, HE SHOULD BE ABLE TO WEAR IT.
REALLY? THAT'S WONDERFUL.

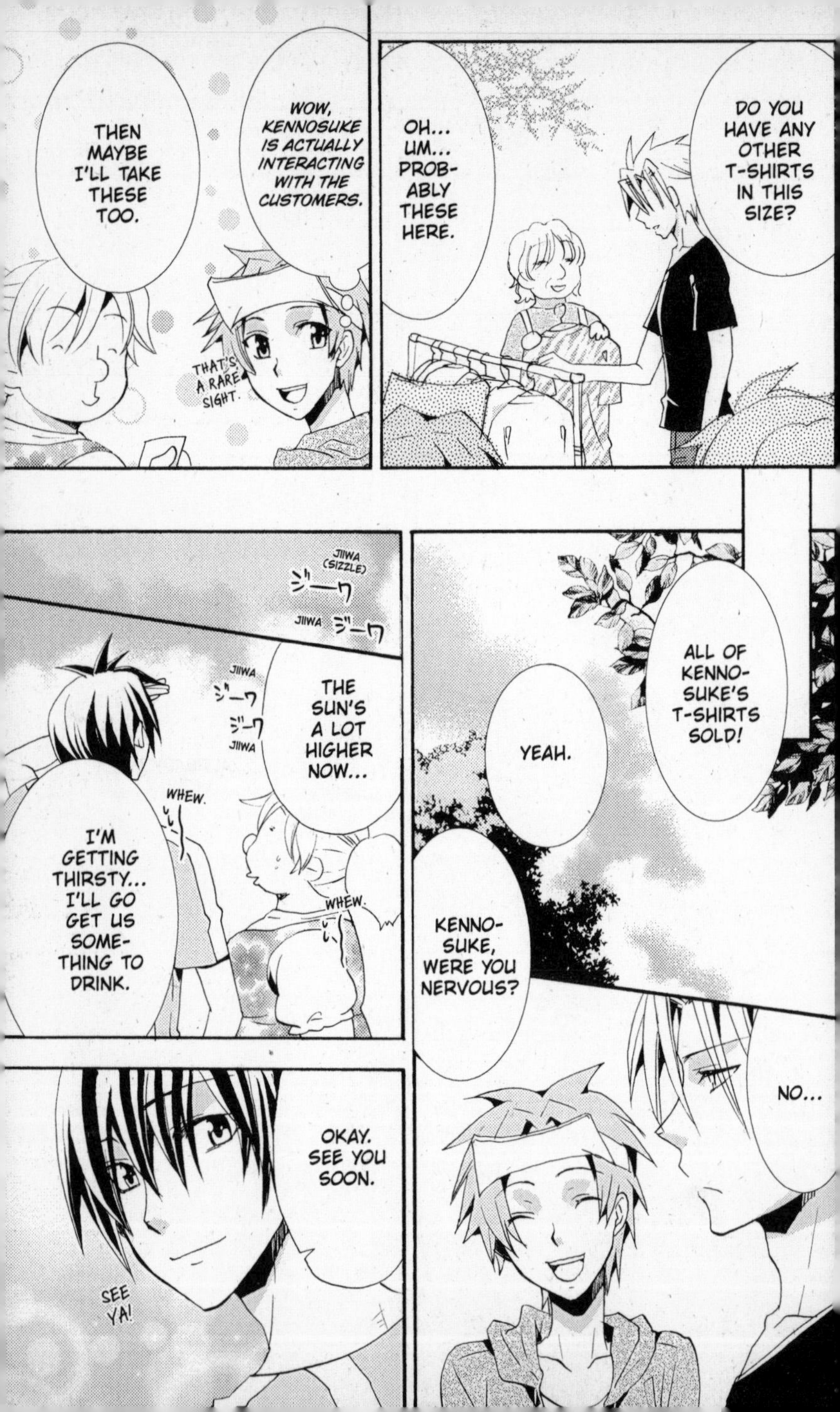
DO YOU HAVE ANY OTHER T-SHIRTS IN THIS SIZE?
OH... UM... PROBABLY THESE HERE.
WOW, KENNOSUKE IS ACTUALLY INTERACTING WITH THE CUSTOMERS.
THAT'S A RARE SIGHT.
THEN MAYBE I'LL TAKE THESE TOO.
ALL OF KENNOSUKE'S T-SHIRTS SOLD!
YEAH.
KENNOSUKE, WERE YOU NERVOUS?
NO...
JIIWA (SIZZLE)
ジーワ
JIIWA ジーワ
JIIWA
ジーワ
ジーワ
JIIWA
THE SUN'S A LOT HIGHER NOW...
WHEW.
WHEW.
I'M GETTING THIRSTY... I'LL GO GET US SOMETHING TO DRINK.
OKAY. SEE YOU SOON.
SEE YA!

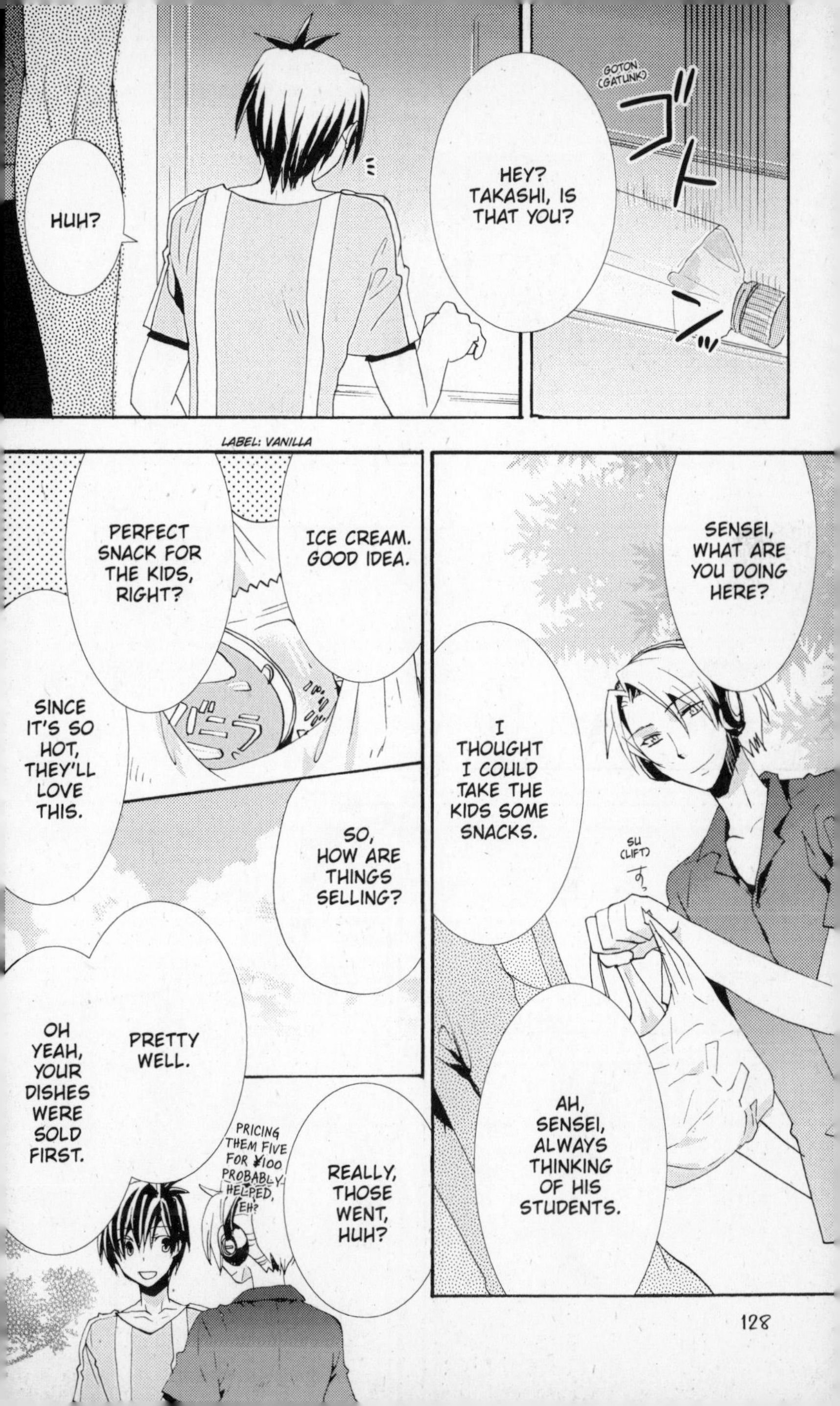
GOTON (GATUNK)
HEY? TAKASHI, IS THAT YOU?
HUH?
SENSEI, WHAT ARE YOU DOING HERE?
I THOUGHT I COULD TAKE THE KIDS SOME SNACKS.
SU (LIFT)
AH, SENSEI, ALWAYS THINKING OF HIS STUDENTS.
LABEL: VANILLA
ICE CREAM. GOOD IDEA.
PERFECT SNACK FOR THE KIDS, RIGHT?
SINCE IT'S SO HOT, THEY'LL LOVE THIS.
SO, HOW ARE THINGS SELLING?
PRETTY WELL.
OH YEAH, YOUR DISHES WERE SOLD FIRST.
REALLY, THOSE WENT, HUH?
PRICING THEM FIVE FOR ¥100 PROBABLY HELPED, EH?

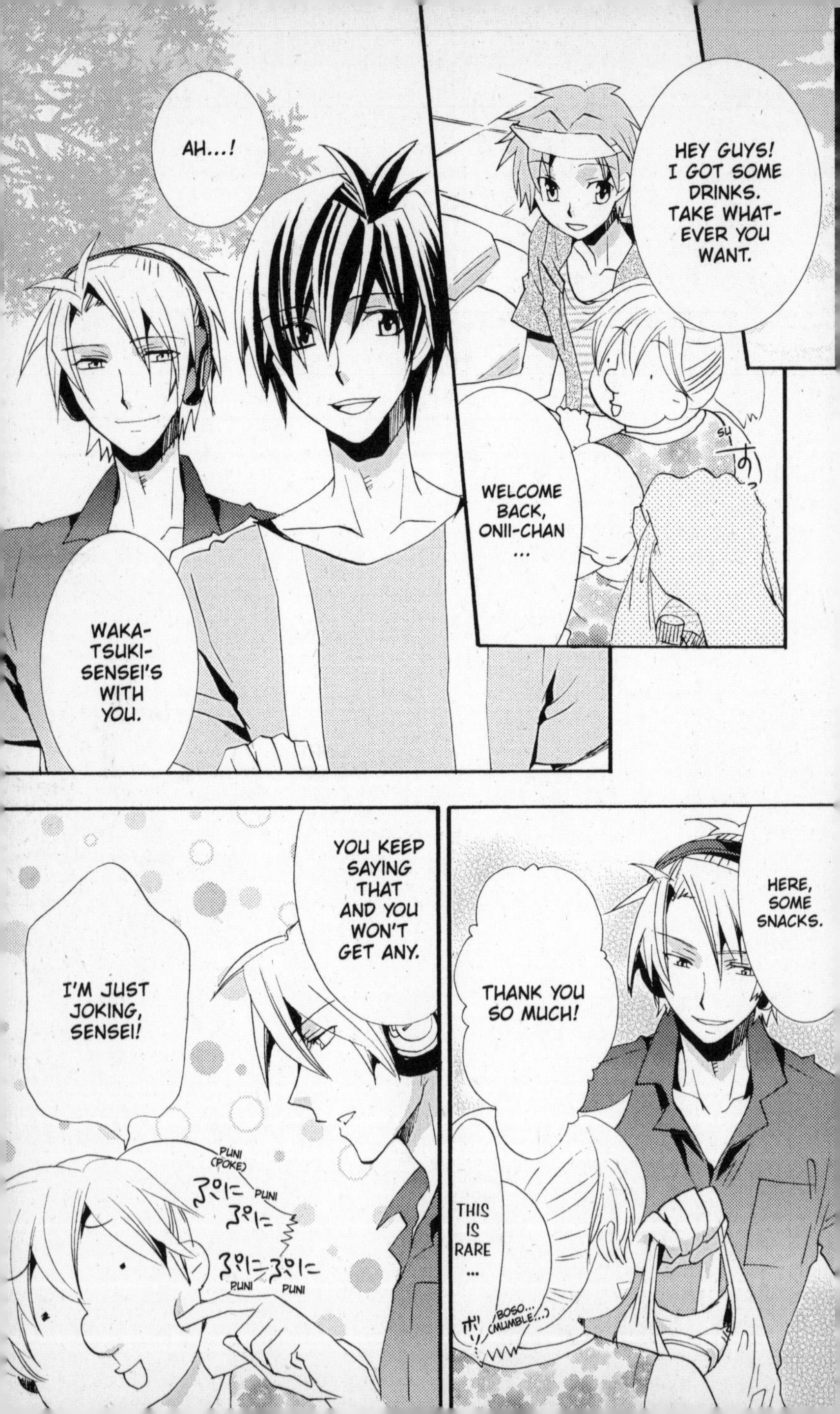

HEY GUYS! I GOT SOME DRINKS. TAKE WHATEVER YOU WANT.
SU
WELCOME BACK, ONII-CHAN ...
AH...!
WAKA-TSUKI-SENSEI'S WITH YOU.
HERE, SOME SNACKS.
THANK YOU SO MUCH!
THIS IS RARE ...
BOSO... (MUMBLE...)
YOU KEEP SAYING THAT AND YOU WON'T GET ANY.
I'M JUST JOKING, SENSEI!
PUNI (POKE)
PUNI
PUNI
PUNI

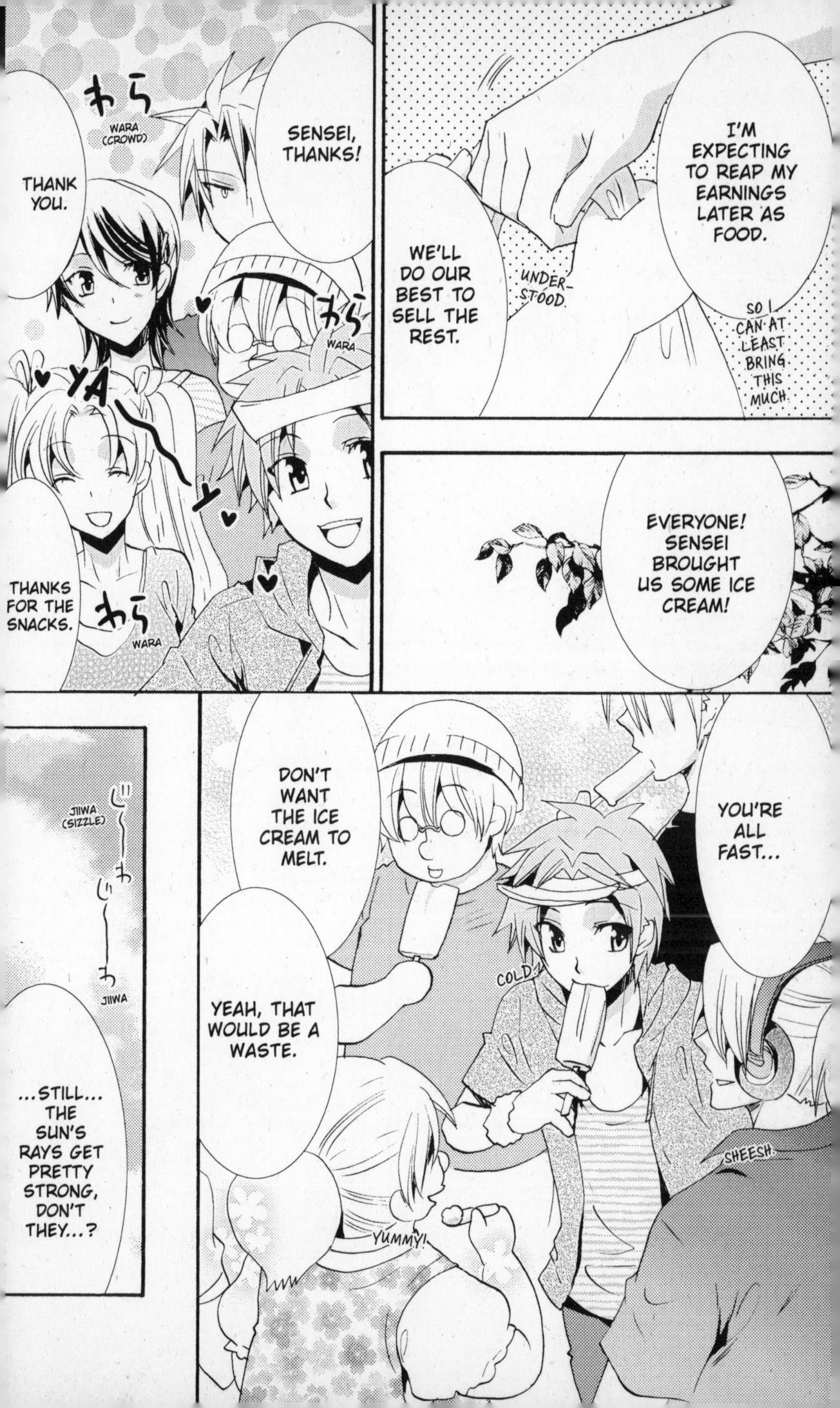
I'M EXPECTING TO REAP MY EARNINGS LATER AS FOOD.
SO I CAN AT LEAST BRING THIS MUCH.
UNDER-STOOD.
WE'LL DO OUR BEST TO SELL THE REST.
EVERYONE! SENSEI BROUGHT US SOME ICE CREAM!
SENSEI, THANKS!
わら
WARA (CROWD)
THANK YOU.
わら
WARA
YA~
THANKS FOR THE SNACKS.
わら
WARA
YOU'RE ALL FAST...
DON'T WANT THE ICE CREAM TO MELT.
COLD
YEAH, THAT WOULD BE A WASTE.
SHEESH.
YUMMY!
じ〜わ
JIIWA (SIZZLE)
じ〜わ
JIIWA
...STILL... THE SUN'S RAYS GET PRETTY STRONG, DON'T THEY...?

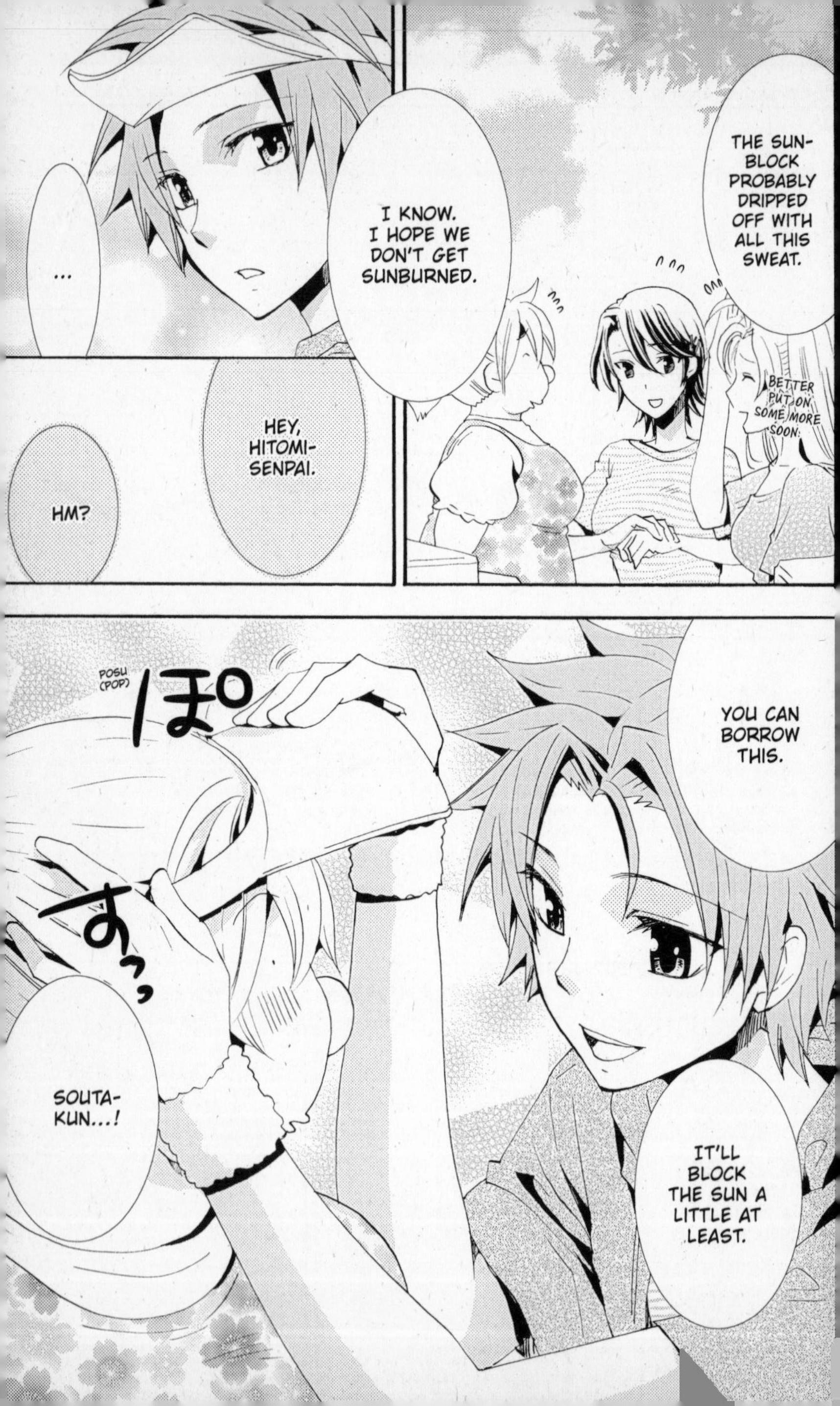
THE SUN-BLOCK PROBABLY DRIPPED OFF WITH ALL THIS SWEAT.
BETTER PUT ON SOME MORE SOON.
I KNOW. I HOPE WE DON'T GET SUNBURNED.
...
HEY, HITOMI-SENPAI.
HM?
YOU CAN BORROW THIS.
POSU (POP)
ぽ
IT'LL BLOCK THE SUN A LITTLE AT LEAST.
すっ
SOUTA-KUN...!

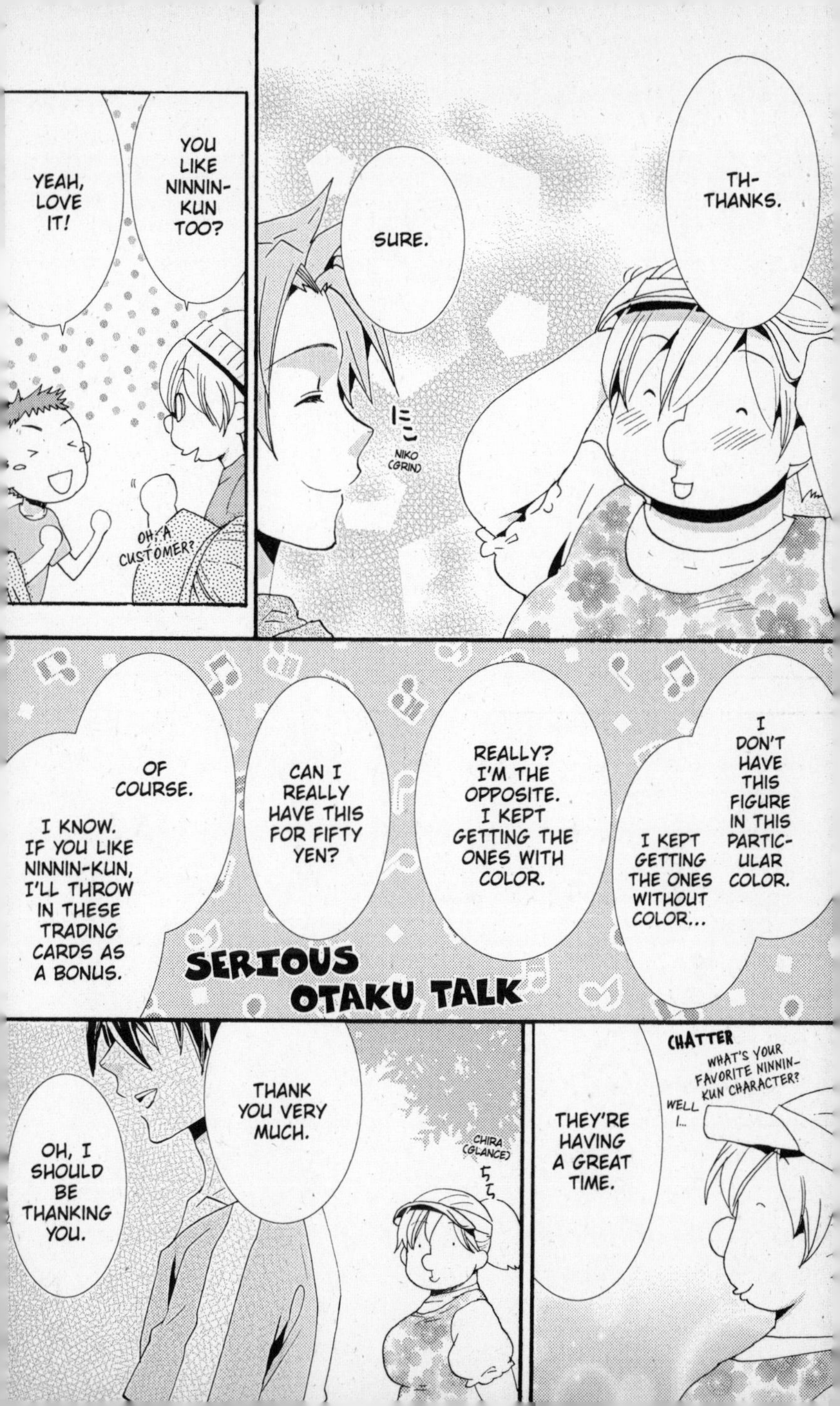
TH-THANKS.
SURE.
NIKO (GRIN)
YOU LIKE NINNIN-KUN TOO?
YEAH, LOVE IT!
OH, A CUSTOMER?
I DON'T HAVE THIS FIGURE IN THIS PARTICULAR COLOR.
I KEPT GETTING THE ONES WITHOUT COLOR...
REALLY? I'M THE OPPOSITE. I KEPT GETTING THE ONES WITH COLOR.
CAN I REALLY HAVE THIS FOR FIFTY YEN?
OF COURSE.
I KNOW. IF YOU LIKE NINNIN-KUN, I'LL THROW IN THESE TRADING CARDS AS A BONUS.
SERIOUS OTAKU TALK
CHATTER
WHAT'S YOUR FAVORITE NINNIN-KUN CHARACTER?
WELL I...
THEY'RE HAVING A GREAT TIME.
THANK YOU VERY MUCH.
CHIRA (GLANCE)
OH, I SHOULD BE THANKING YOU.

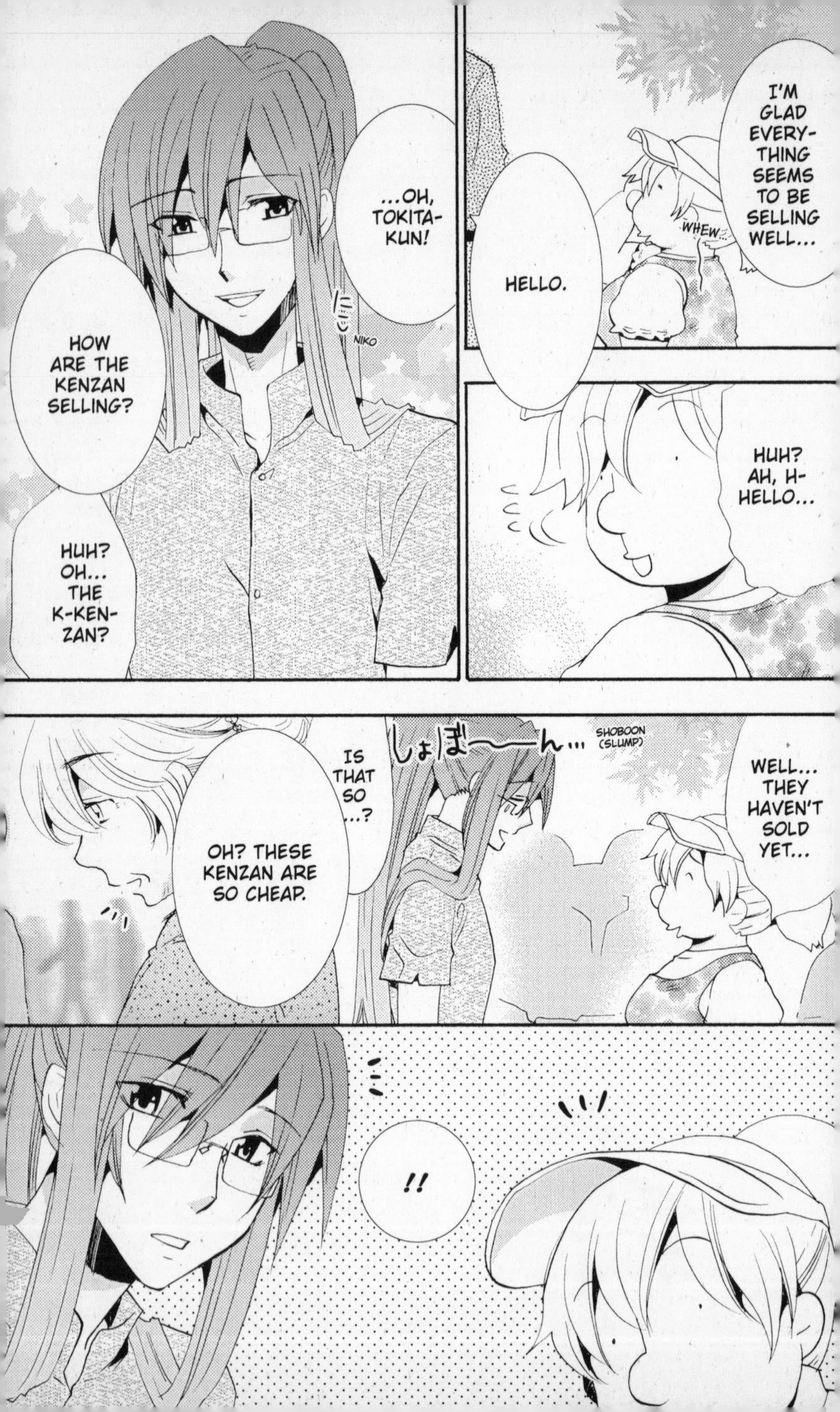
I'M GLAD EVERY-THING SEEMS TO BE SELLING WELL...
WHEW
HELLO.
...OH, TOKITA-KUN!
NIKO
HOW ARE THE KENZAN SELLING?
HUH? AH, H-HELLO...
HUH? OH... THE K-KEN-ZAN?
WELL... THEY HAVEN'T SOLD YET...
しょぼーーん...
SHOBOON (SLUMP)
IS THAT SO ...?
OH? THESE KENZAN ARE SO CHEAP.
!!

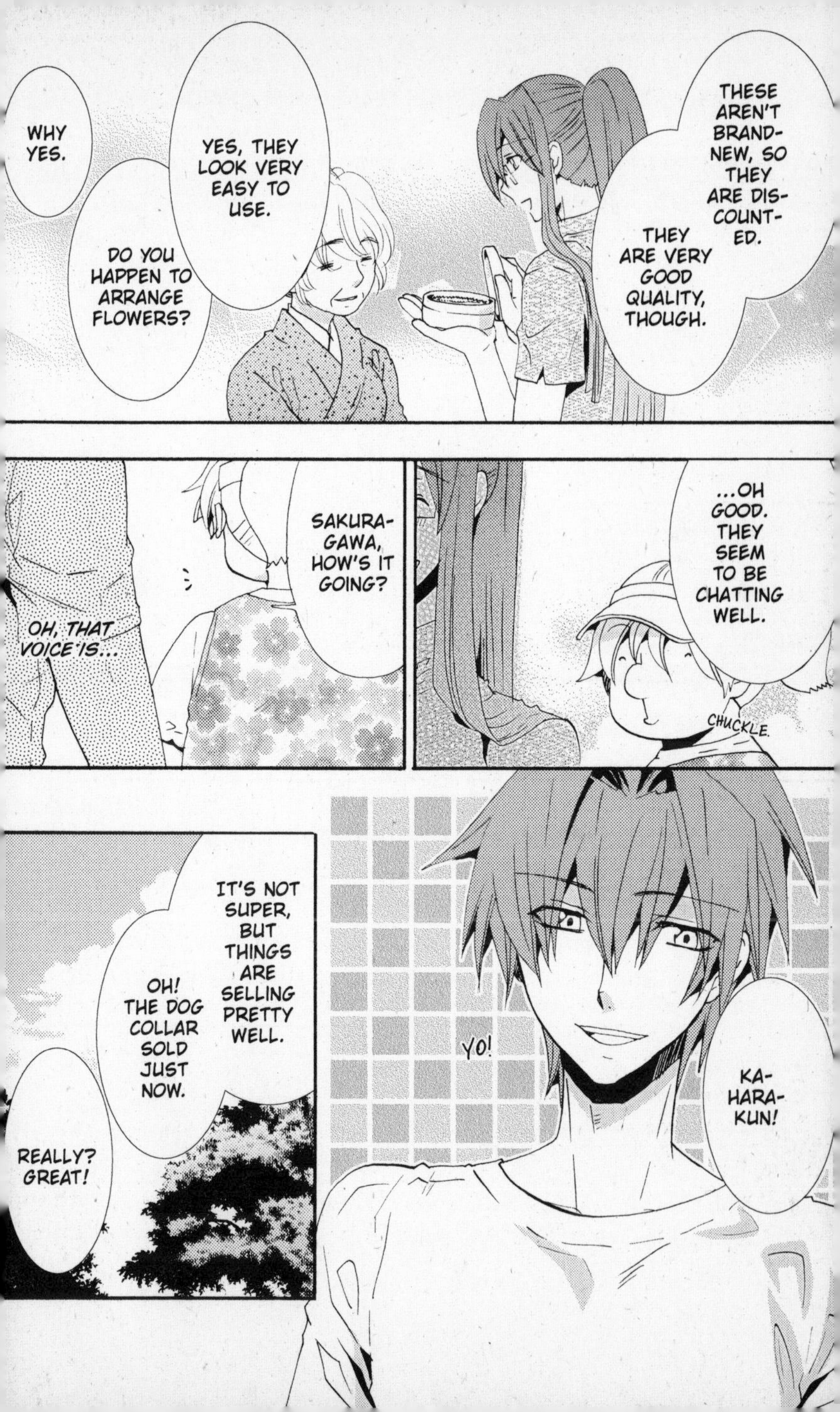
THESE AREN'T BRAND-NEW, SO THEY ARE DISCOUNTED.
THEY ARE VERY GOOD QUALITY, THOUGH.
YES, THEY LOOK VERY EASY TO USE.
DO YOU HAPPEN TO ARRANGE FLOWERS?
WHY YES.
...OH GOOD. THEY SEEM TO BE CHATTING WELL.
CHUCKLE.
SAKURAGAWA, HOW'S IT GOING?
OH, THAT VOICE IS...
KA-HARA-KUN!
YO!
IT'S NOT SUPER, BUT THINGS ARE SELLING PRETTY WELL.
OH! THE DOG COLLAR SOLD JUST NOW.
REALLY? GREAT!

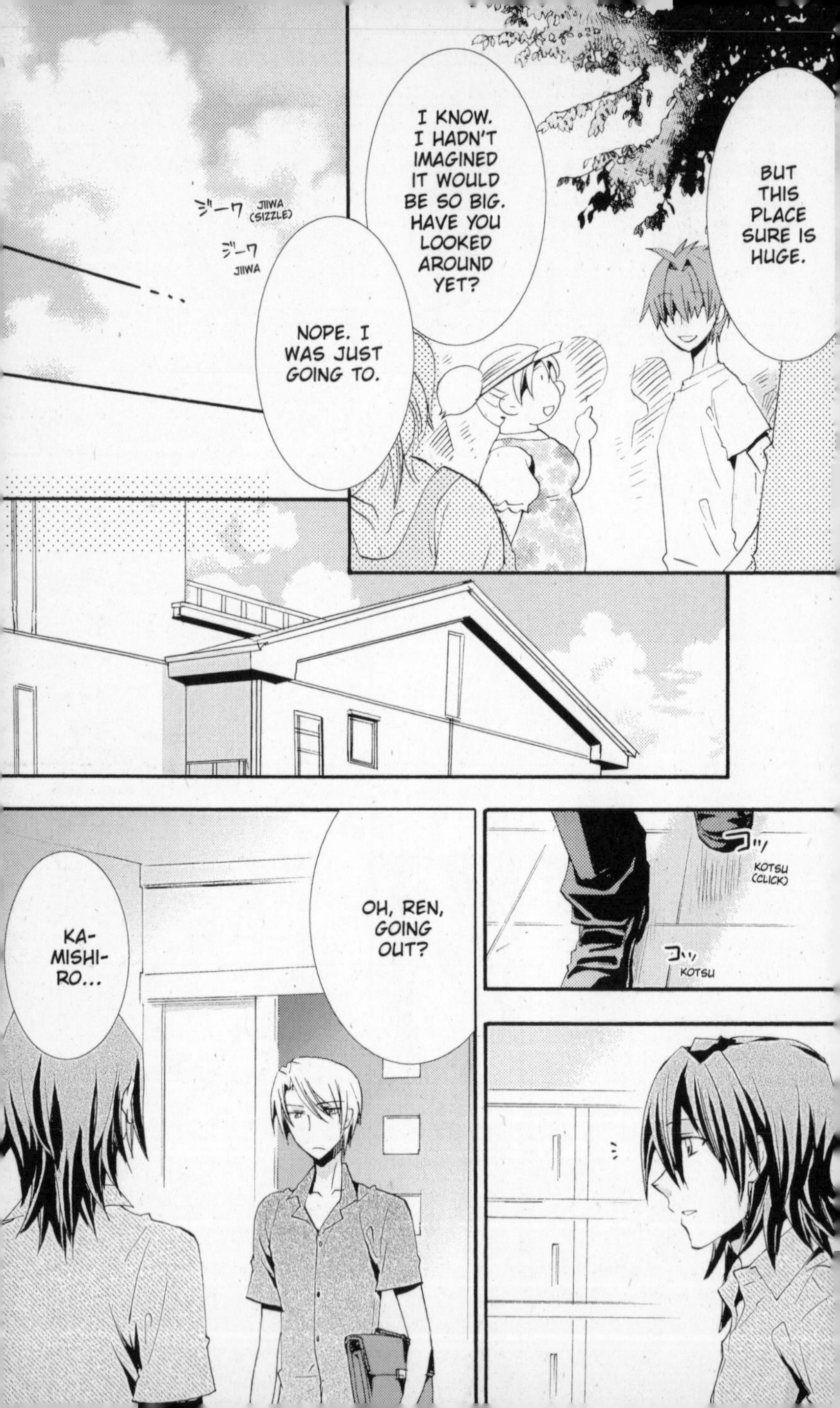

BUT THIS PLACE SURE IS HUGE.
I KNOW. I HADN'T IMAGINED IT WOULD BE SO BIG. HAVE YOU LOOKED AROUND YET?
NOPE. I WAS JUST GOING TO.
ジーワ JIIWA (SIZZLE)
ジーワ JIIWA
コッ KOTSU (CLICK)
コッ KOTSU
OH, REN, GOING OUT?
KA-MISHI-RO...

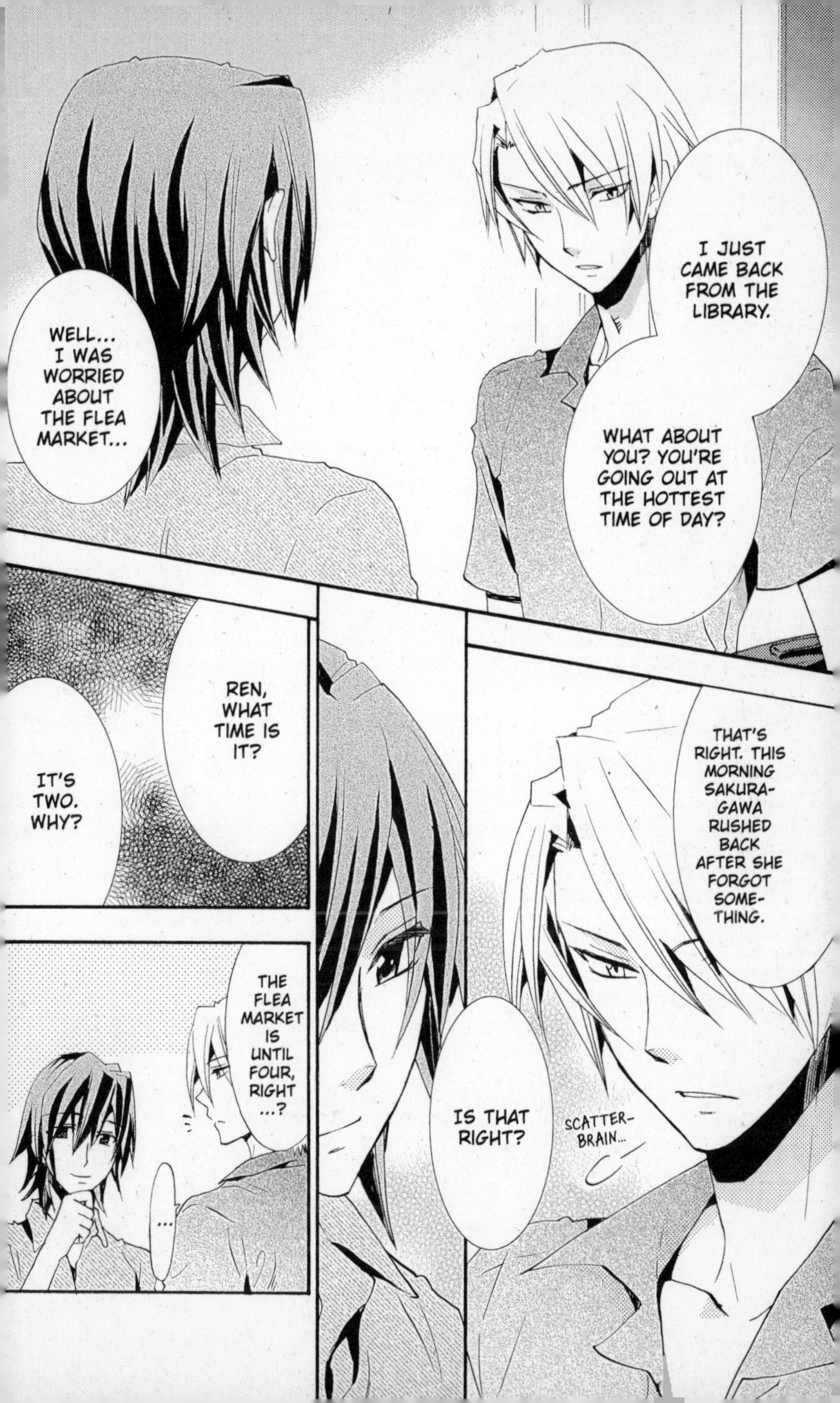
I JUST CAME BACK FROM THE LIBRARY.
WHAT ABOUT YOU? YOU'RE GOING OUT AT THE HOTTEST TIME OF DAY?
WELL... I WAS WORRIED ABOUT THE FLEA MARKET...
THAT'S RIGHT. THIS MORNING SAKURA-GAWA RUSHED BACK AFTER SHE FORGOT SOME-THING.
SCATTER-BRAIN...
IS THAT RIGHT?
REN, WHAT TIME IS IT?
IT'S TWO. WHY?
THE FLEA MARKET IS UNTIL FOUR, RIGHT...?
...

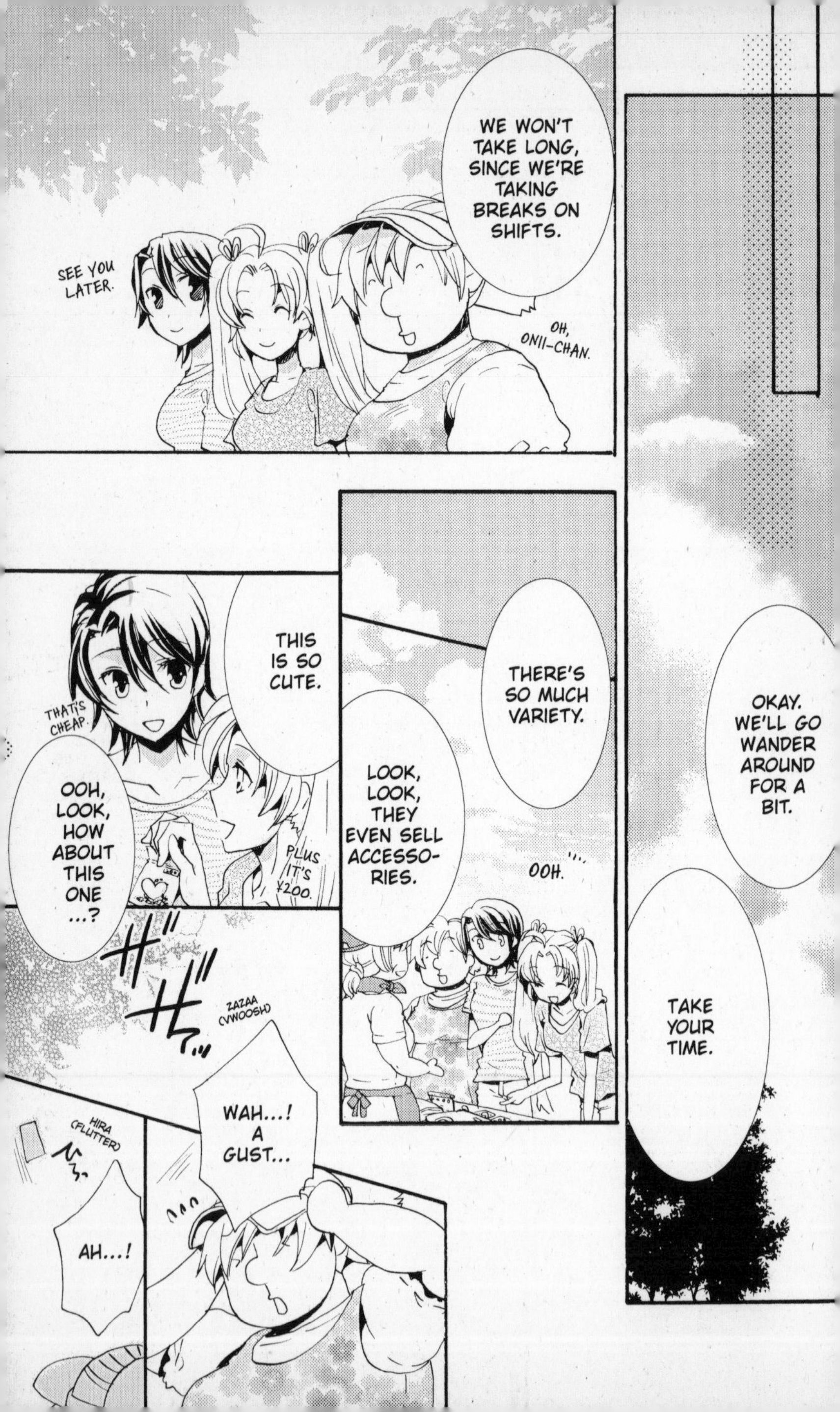
OH, ONII-CHAN.
WE WON'T TAKE LONG, SINCE WE'RE TAKING BREAKS ON SHIFTS.
SEE YOU LATER.
OKAY. WE'LL GO WANDER AROUND FOR A BIT.
TAKE YOUR TIME.
THERE'S SO MUCH VARIETY.
OOH.
LOOK, LOOK, THEY EVEN SELL ACCESSO-RIES.
THIS IS SO CUTE.
PLUS IT'S ¥200.
THAT'S CHEAP.
OOH, LOOK, HOW ABOUT THIS ONE ...?
ZAZAA (VWOOSH)
WAH...! A GUST...
HIRA (FLUTTER)
AH...!

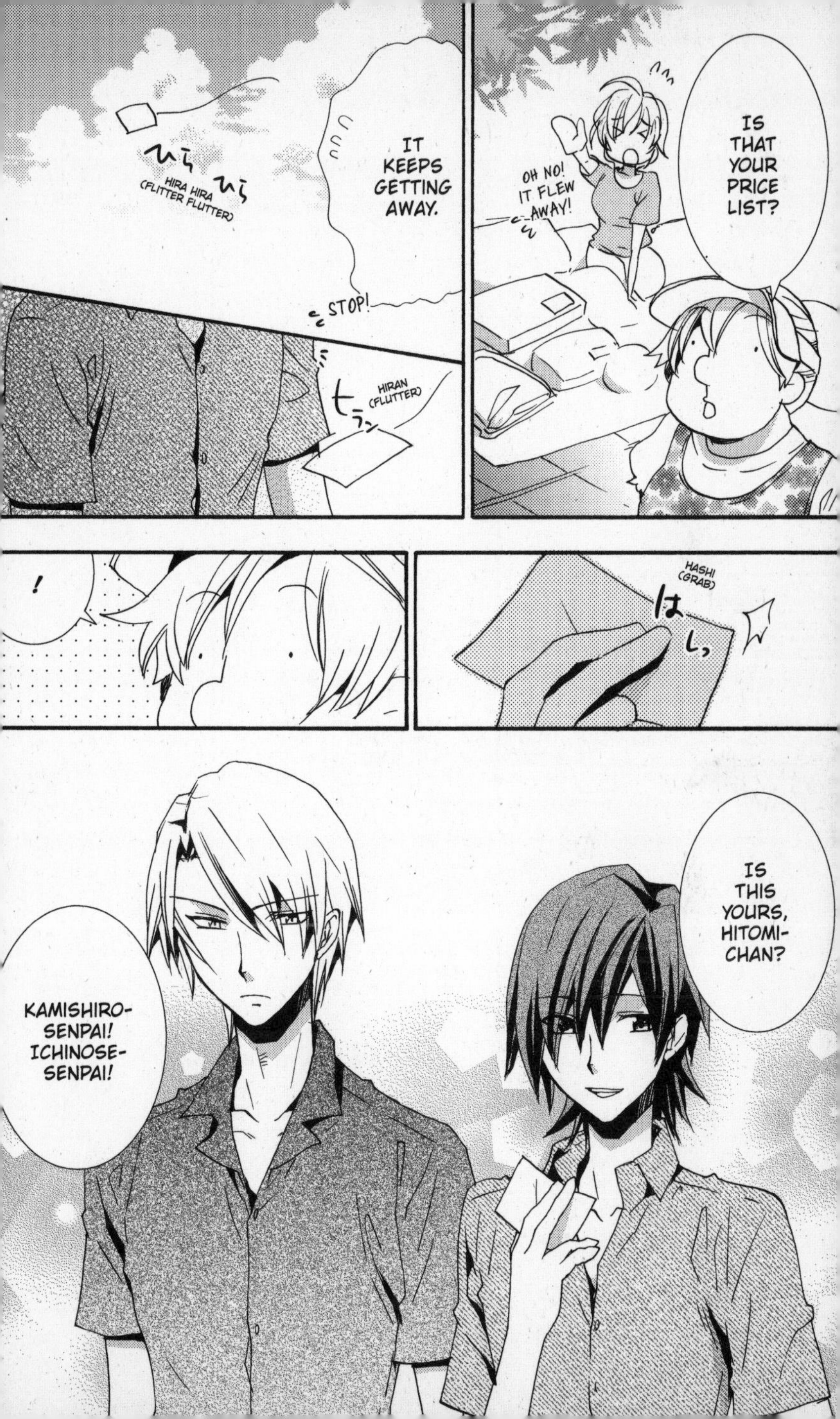
IS THAT YOUR PRICE LIST?
OH NO! IT FLEW AWAY!
HIRA HIRA (FLITTER FLUTTER)
IT KEEPS GETTING AWAY.
STOP!
HIRAN (FLUTTER)
HASHI (GRAB)
!
IS THIS YOURS, HITOMI-CHAN?
KAMISHIRO-SENPAI! ICHINOSE-SENPAI!

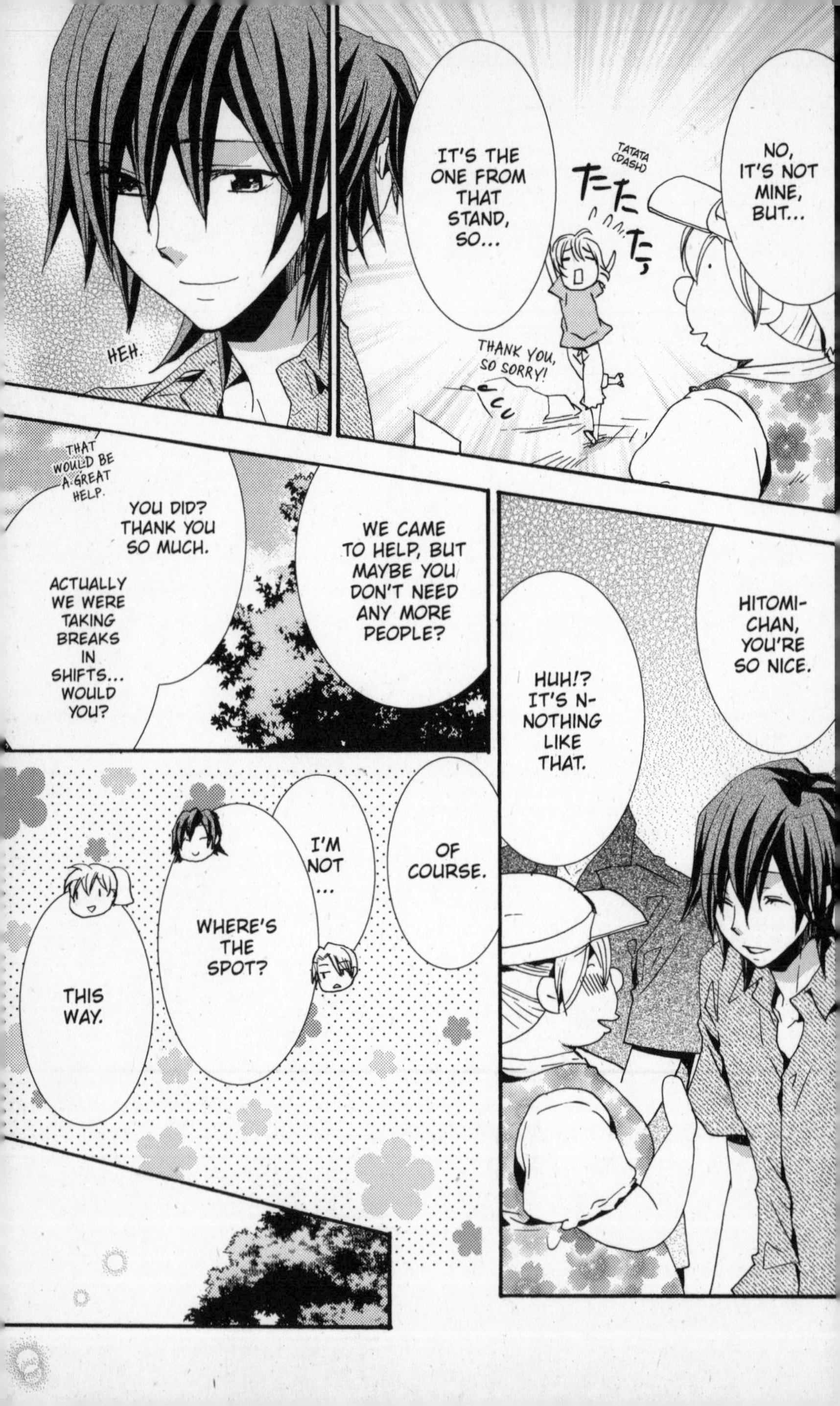
NO, IT'S NOT MINE, BUT...
TATATA (DASH)
たたた
IT'S THE ONE FROM THAT STAND, SO...
THANK YOU, SO SORRY!
HEH.
HITOMI-CHAN, YOU'RE SO NICE.
HUH!? IT'S N-NOTHING LIKE THAT.
WE CAME TO HELP, BUT MAYBE YOU DON'T NEED ANY MORE PEOPLE?
YOU DID? THANK YOU SO MUCH.
ACTUALLY WE WERE TAKING BREAKS IN SHIFTS... WOULD YOU?
THAT WOULD BE A GREAT HELP.
OF COURSE.
I'M NOT...
WHERE'S THE SPOT?
THIS WAY.

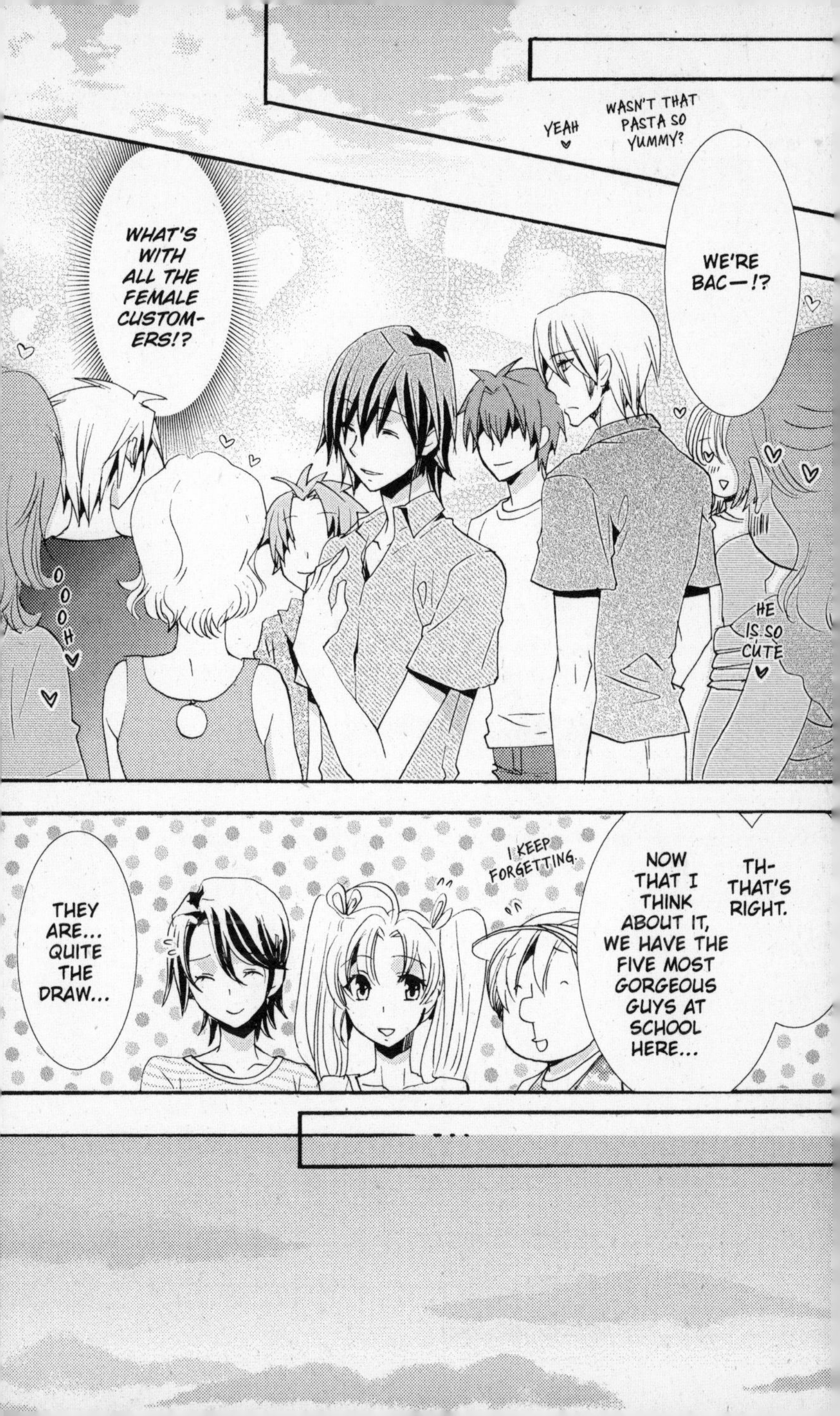
WASN'T THAT PASTA SO YUMMY?
YEAH ♥
WE'RE BAC—!?
HE IS SO CUTE ♥
WHAT'S WITH ALL THE FEMALE CUSTOMERS!?
OOOOH ♥
TH- THAT'S RIGHT.
NOW THAT I THINK ABOUT IT, WE HAVE THE FIVE MOST GORGEOUS GUYS AT SCHOOL HERE...
I KEEP FORGETTING.
THEY ARE... QUITE THE DRAW...

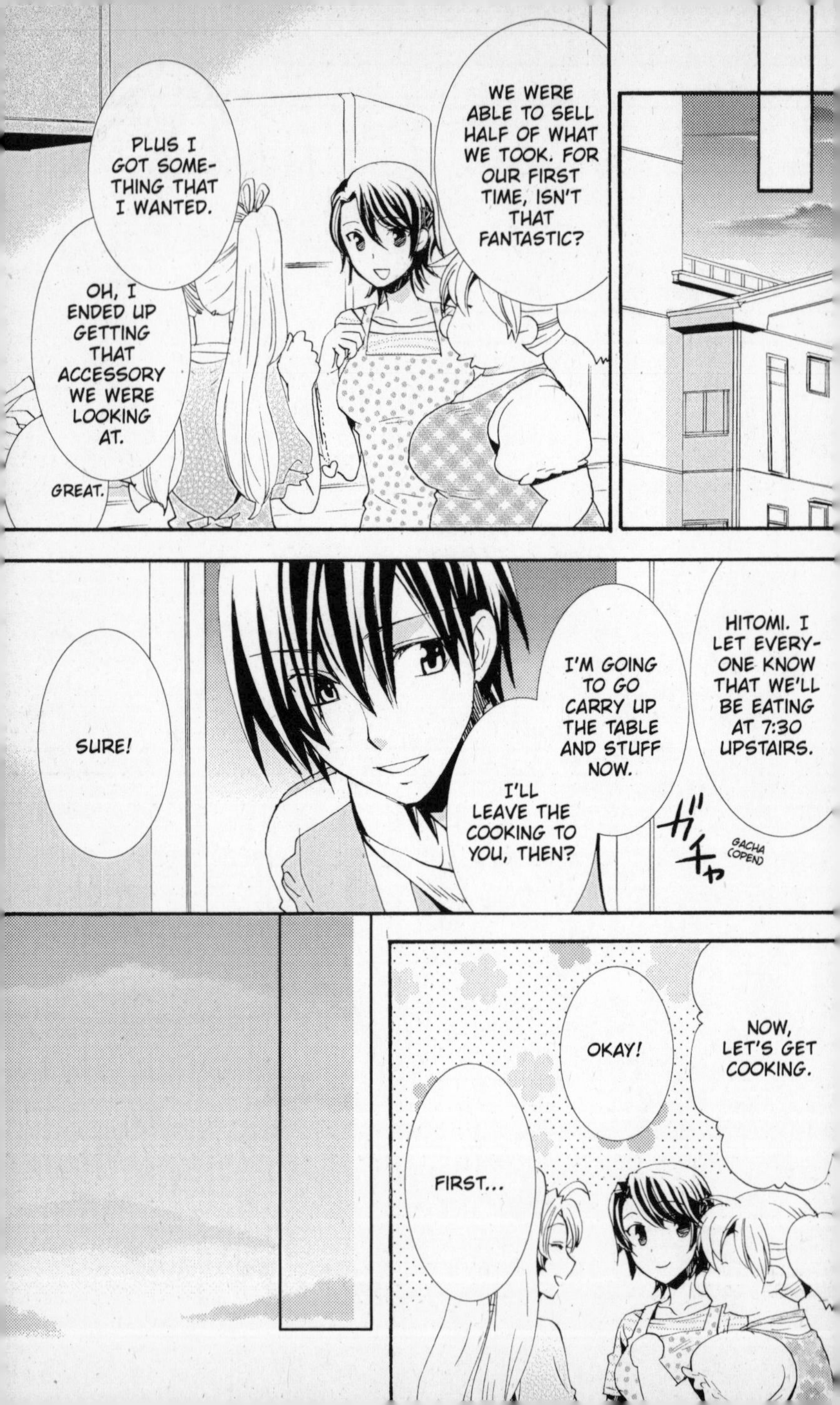
WE WERE ABLE TO SELL HALF OF WHAT WE TOOK. FOR OUR FIRST TIME, ISN'T THAT FANTASTIC?
PLUS I GOT SOME-THING THAT I WANTED.
OH, I ENDED UP GETTING THAT ACCESSORY WE WERE LOOKING AT.
GREAT.
HITOMI. I LET EVERY-ONE KNOW THAT WE'LL BE EATING AT 7:30 UPSTAIRS.
ガチャ
GACHA (OPEN)
I'M GOING TO GO CARRY UP THE TABLE AND STUFF NOW.
I'LL LEAVE THE COOKING TO YOU, THEN?
SURE!
NOW, LET'S GET COOKING.
OKAY!
FIRST...

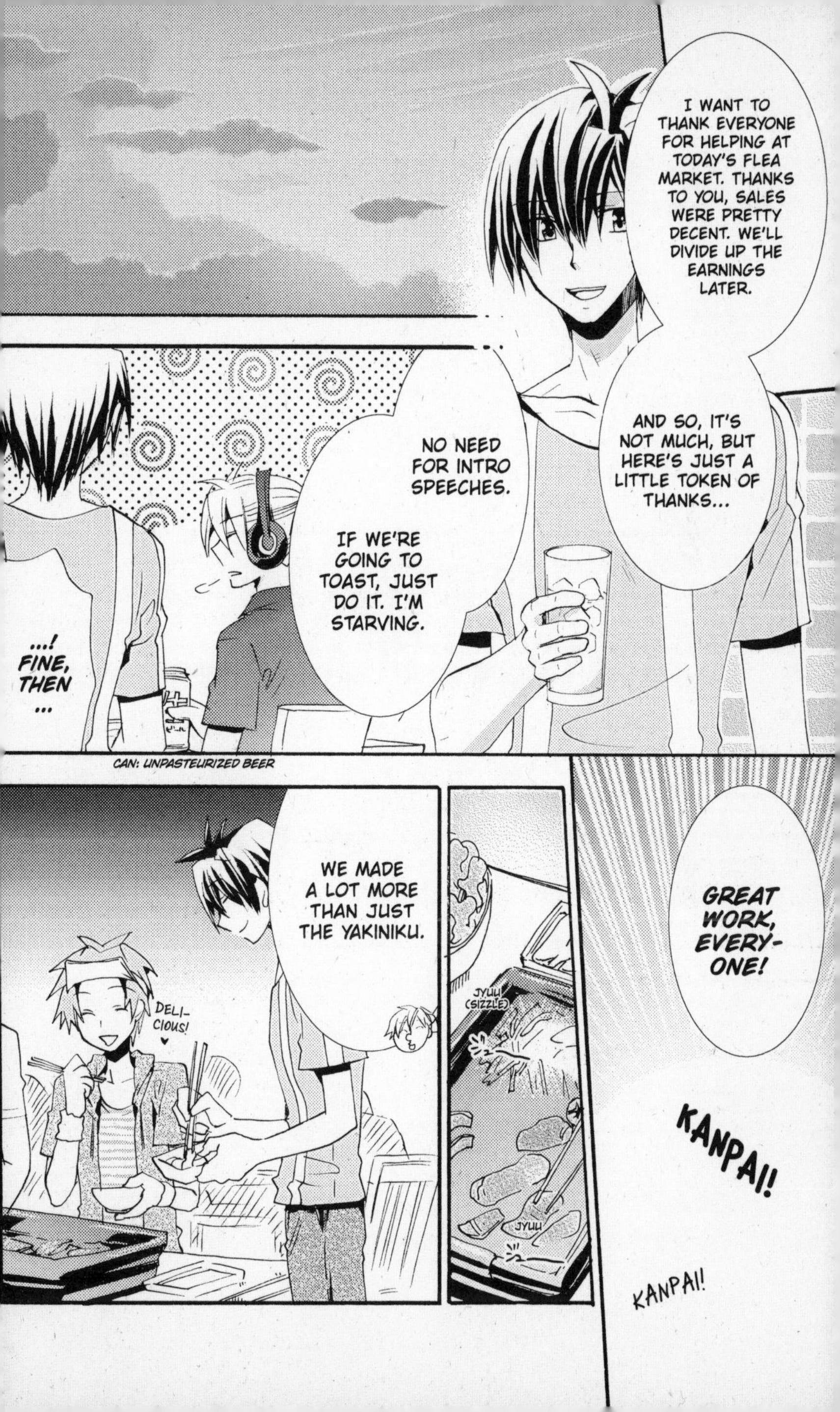
I WANT TO THANK EVERYONE FOR HELPING AT TODAY'S FLEA MARKET. THANKS TO YOU, SALES WERE PRETTY DECENT. WE'LL DIVIDE UP THE EARNINGS LATER.
AND SO, IT'S NOT MUCH, BUT HERE'S JUST A LITTLE TOKEN OF THANKS...
NO NEED FOR INTRO SPEECHES.
IF WE'RE GOING TO TOAST, JUST DO IT. I'M STARVING.
...! FINE, THEN ...
CAN: UNPASTEURIZED BEER
GREAT WORK, EVERY-ONE!
KANPAI!
KANPAI!
JYUU (SIZZLE)
JYUU
WE MADE A LOT MORE THAN JUST THE YAKINIKU.
DELI-CIOUS! ♥

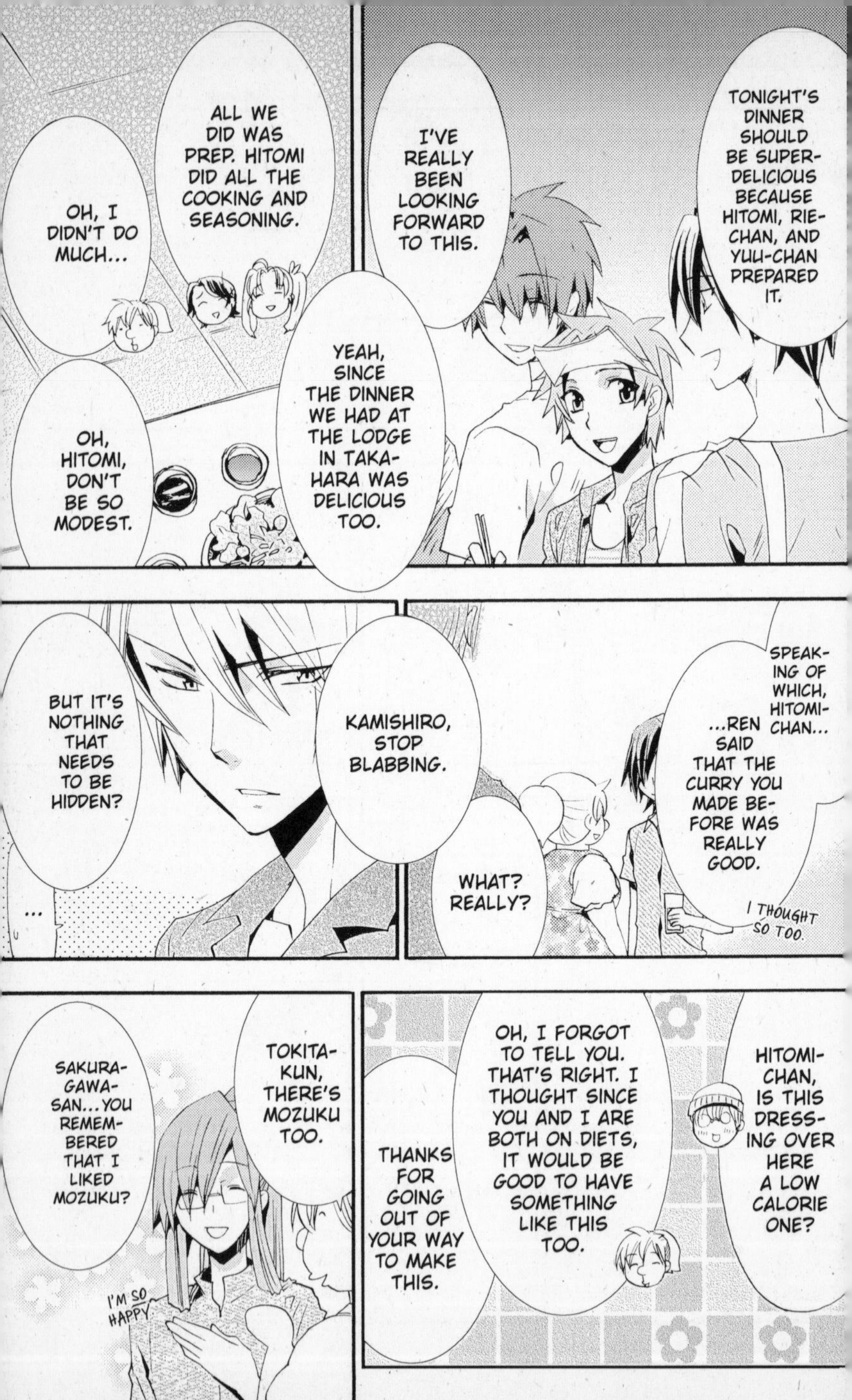
TONIGHT'S DINNER SHOULD BE SUPER-DELICIOUS BECAUSE HITOMI, RIE-CHAN, AND YUU-CHAN PREPARED IT.
I'VE REALLY BEEN LOOKING FORWARD TO THIS.
YEAH, SINCE THE DINNER WE HAD AT THE LODGE IN TAKA-HARA WAS DELICIOUS TOO.
ALL WE DID WAS PREP. HITOMI DID ALL THE COOKING AND SEASONING.
OH, I DIDN'T DO MUCH...
OH, HITOMI, DON'T BE SO MODEST.
SPEAKING OF WHICH, HITOMI-CHAN...
...REN SAID THAT THE CURRY YOU MADE BE-FORE WAS REALLY GOOD.
I THOUGHT SO TOO.
WHAT? REALLY?
KAMISHIRO, STOP BLABBING.
BUT IT'S NOTHING THAT NEEDS TO BE HIDDEN?
...
HITOMI-CHAN, IS THIS DRESS-ING OVER HERE A LOW CALORIE ONE?
OH, I FORGOT TO TELL YOU. THAT'S RIGHT. I THOUGHT SINCE YOU AND I ARE BOTH ON DIETS, IT WOULD BE GOOD TO HAVE SOMETHING LIKE THIS TOO.
THANKS FOR GOING OUT OF YOUR WAY TO MAKE THIS.
TOKITA-KUN, THERE'S MOZUKU TOO.
SAKURA-GAWA-SAN...YOU REMEM-BERED THAT I LIKED MOZUKU?
I'M SO HAPPY

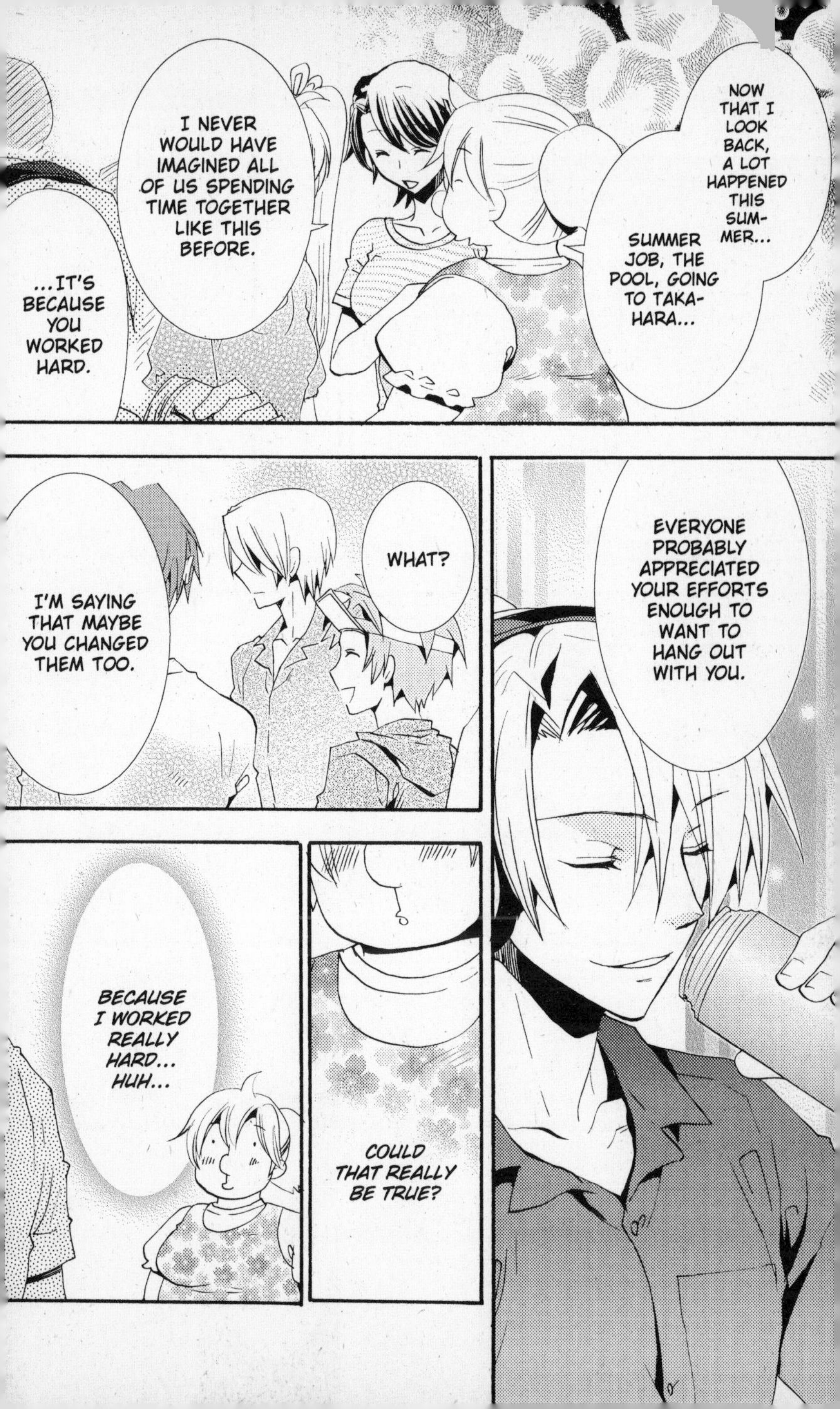
NOW THAT I LOOK BACK, A LOT HAPPENED THIS SUM-MER...
SUMMER JOB, THE POOL, GOING TO TAKA-HARA...
I NEVER WOULD HAVE IMAGINED ALL OF US SPENDING TIME TOGETHER LIKE THIS BEFORE.
...IT'S BECAUSE YOU WORKED HARD.
EVERYONE PROBABLY APPRECIATED YOUR EFFORTS ENOUGH TO WANT TO HANG OUT WITH YOU.
WHAT?
I'M SAYING THAT MAYBE YOU CHANGED THEM TOO.
COULD THAT REALLY BE TRUE?
BECAUSE I WORKED REALLY HARD... HUH...

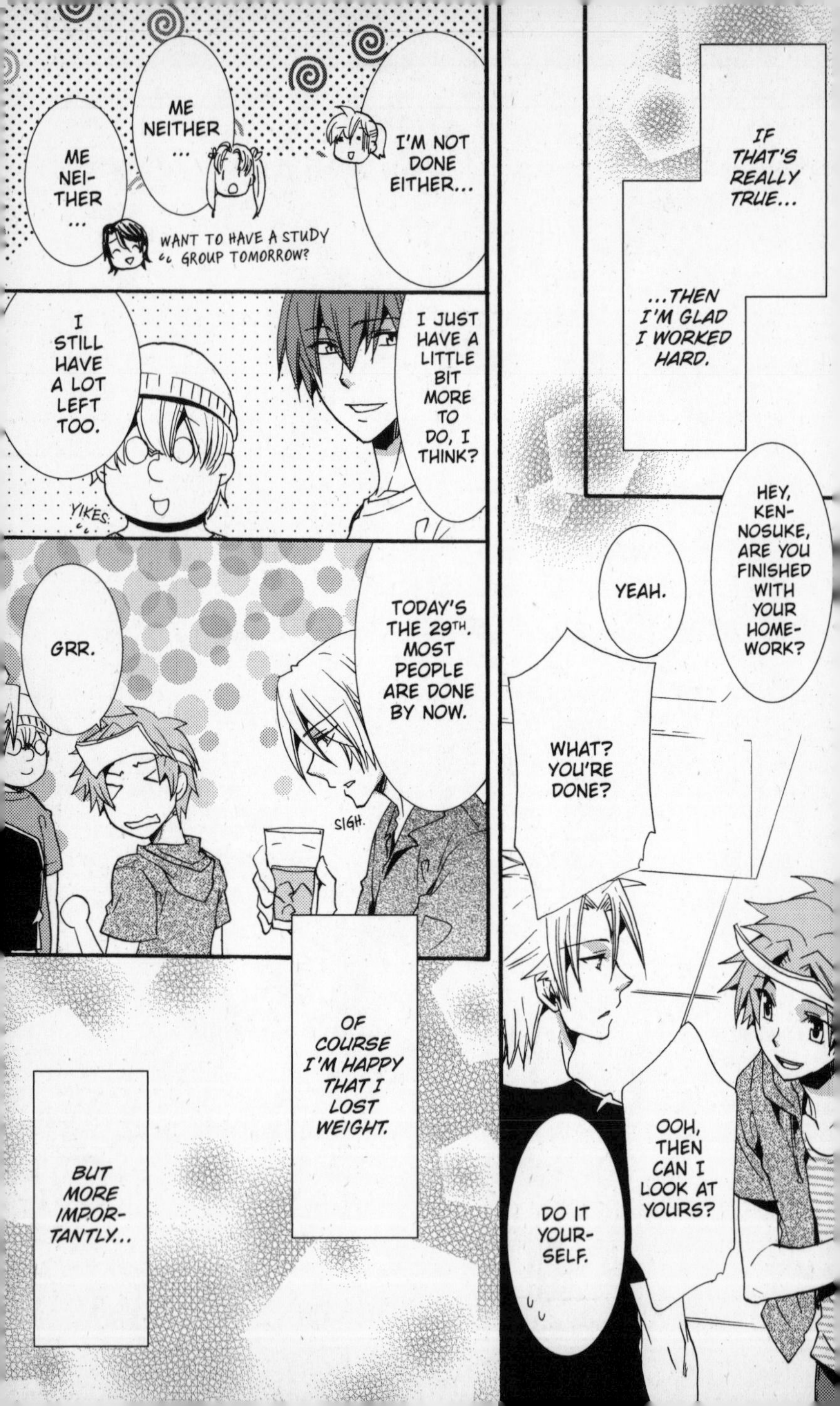
IF THAT'S REALLY TRUE...
...THEN I'M GLAD I WORKED HARD.
HEY, KENNOSUKE, ARE YOU FINISHED WITH YOUR HOMEWORK?
YEAH.
WHAT? YOU'RE DONE?
OOH, THEN CAN I LOOK AT YOURS?
DO IT YOURSELF.
I'M NOT DONE EITHER...
ME NEITHER...
ME NEITHER...
WANT TO HAVE A STUDY GROUP TOMORROW?
I JUST HAVE A LITTLE BIT MORE TO DO, I THINK?
I STILL HAVE A LOT LEFT TOO.
YIKES.
TODAY'S THE 29TH. MOST PEOPLE ARE DONE BY NOW.
SIGH.
GRR.
OF COURSE I'M HAPPY THAT I LOST WEIGHT.
BUT MORE IMPORTANTLY...

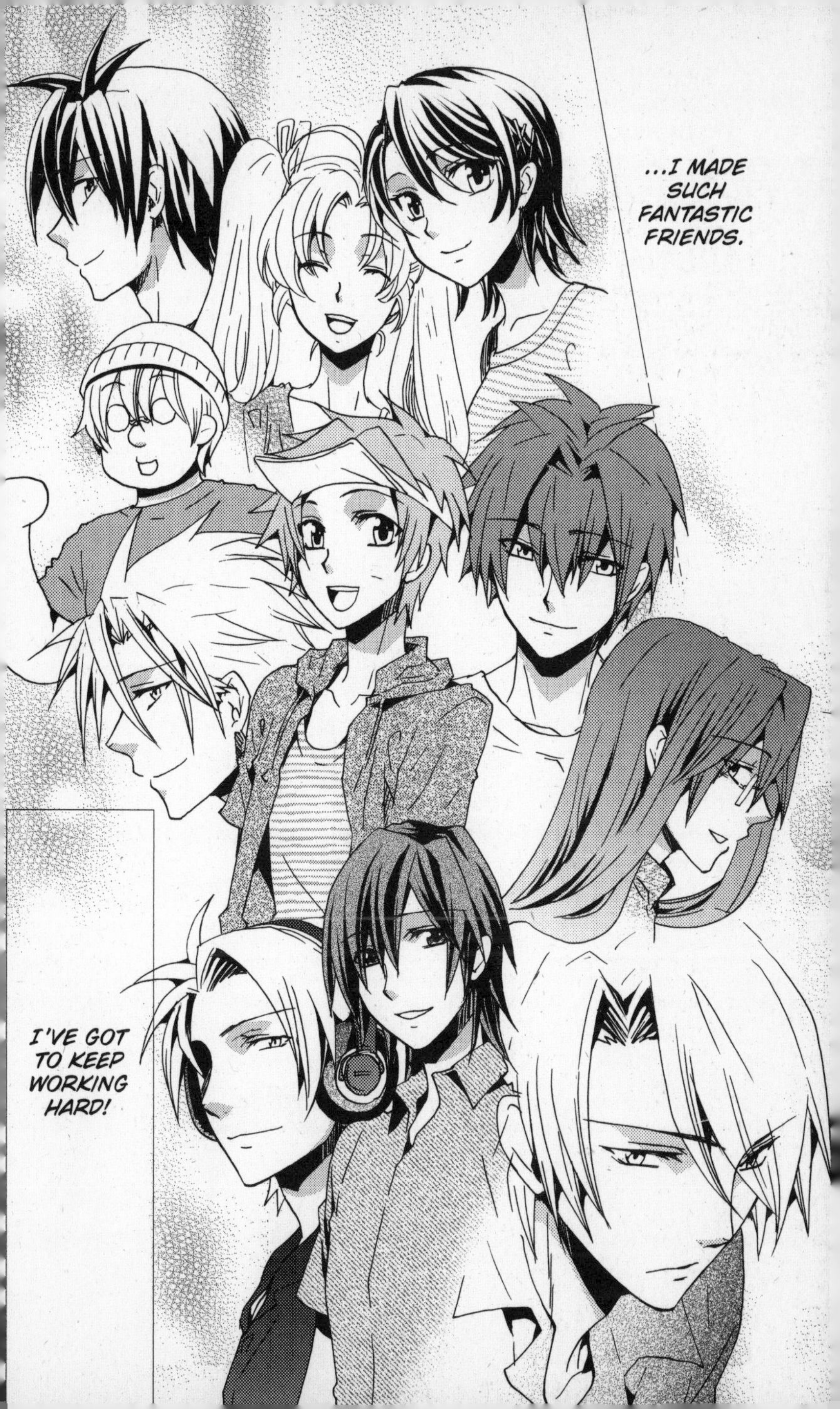
...I MADE SUCH FANTASTIC FRIENDS.
I'VE GOT TO KEEP WORKING HARD!

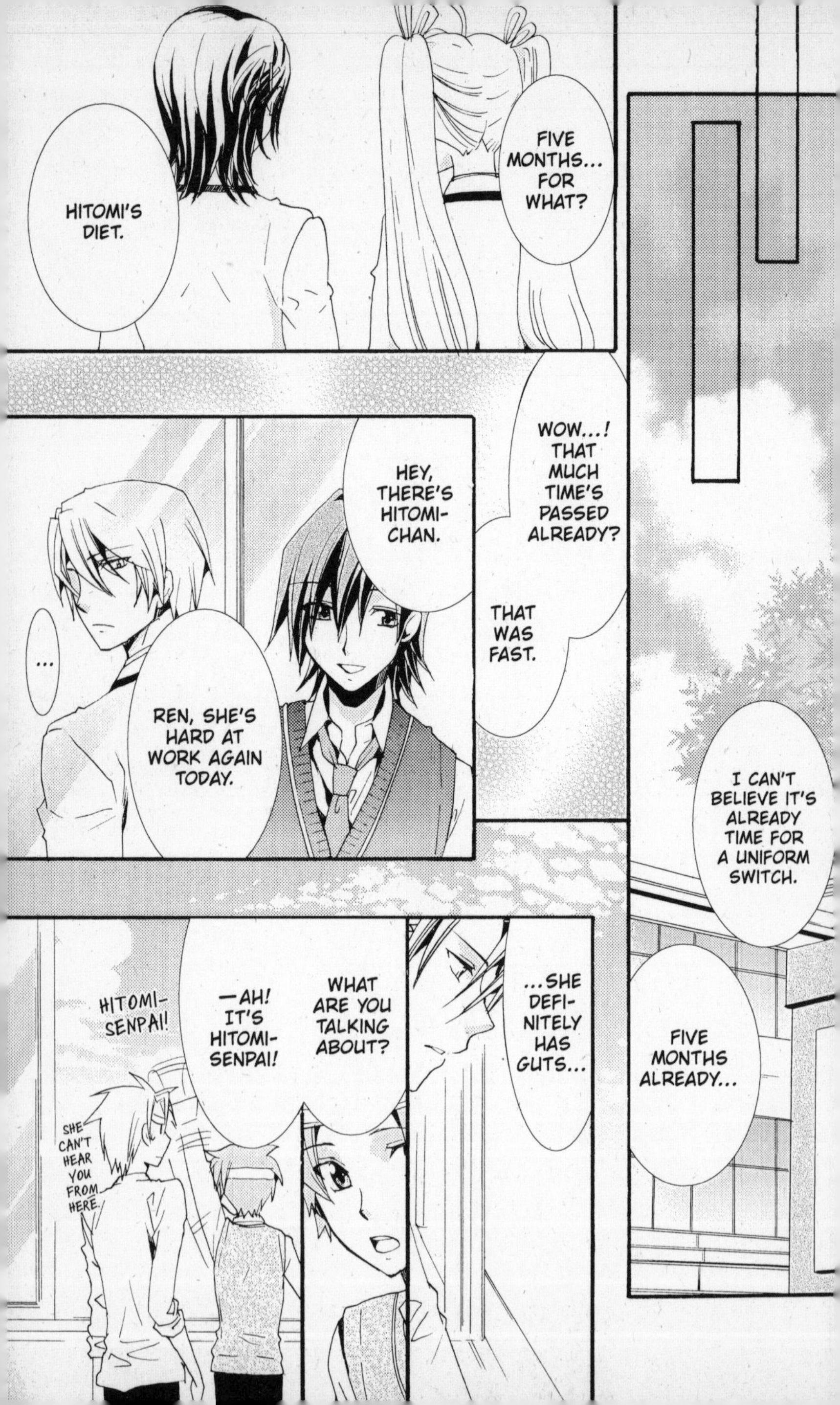
I CAN'T BELIEVE IT'S ALREADY TIME FOR A UNIFORM SWITCH.
FIVE MONTHS ALREADY...
FIVE MONTHS... FOR WHAT?
HITOMI'S DIET.
WOW...! THAT MUCH TIME'S PASSED ALREADY?
THAT WAS FAST.
HEY, THERE'S HITOMI-CHAN.
REN, SHE'S HARD AT WORK AGAIN TODAY.
...
...SHE DEFINITELY HAS GUTS...
WHAT ARE YOU TALKING ABOUT?
—AH! IT'S HITOMI-SENPAI!
HITOMI-SENPAI!
SHE CAN'T HEAR YOU FROM HERE.

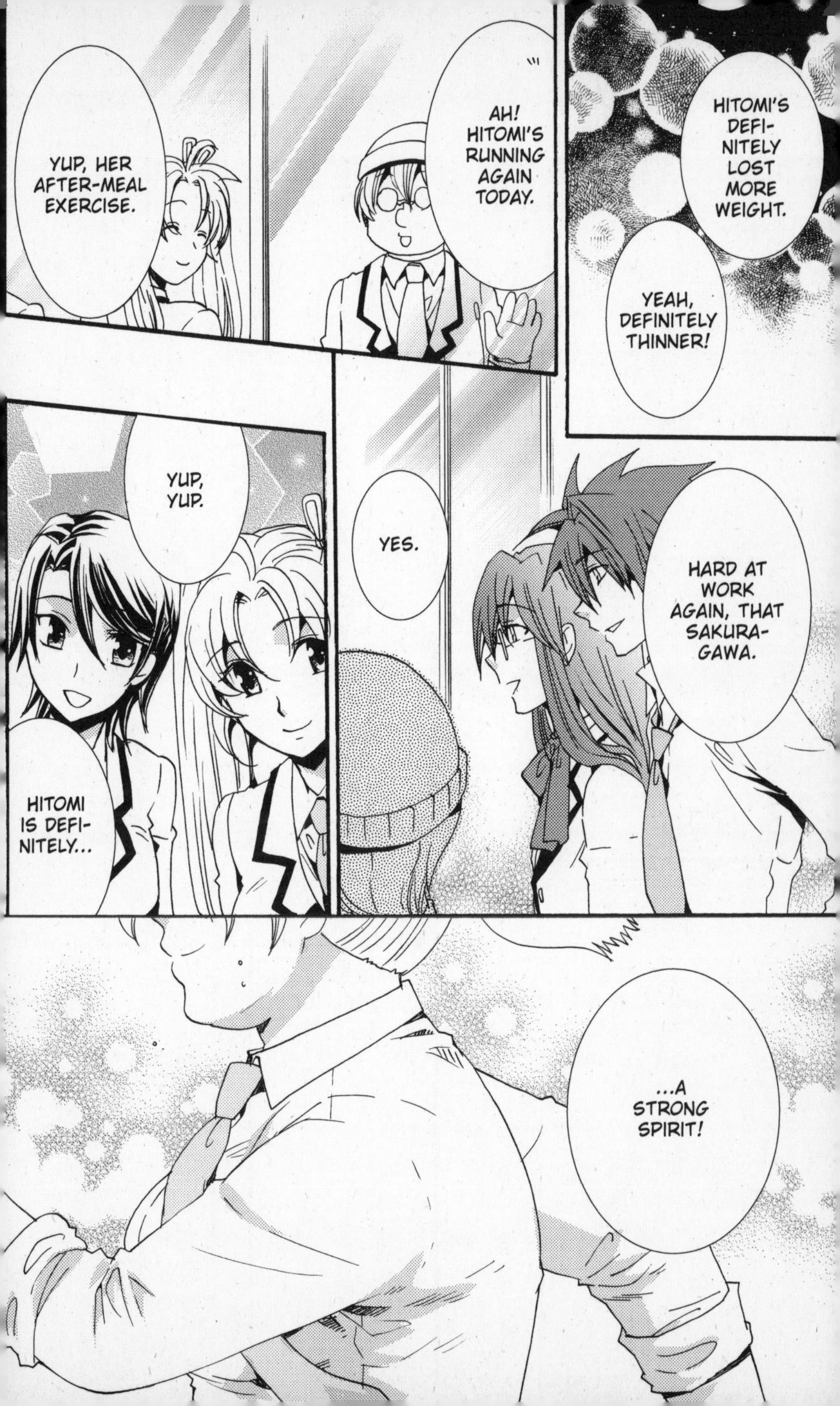

HITOMI'S DEFINITELY LOST MORE WEIGHT.
YEAH, DEFINITELY THINNER!
AH! HITOMI'S RUNNING AGAIN TODAY.
YUP, HER AFTER-MEAL EXERCISE.
HARD AT WORK AGAIN, THAT SAKURAGAWA.
YES.
YUP, YUP.
HITOMI IS DEFINITELY...
...A STRONG SPIRIT!

LOVEREVO!!

LOVEREVO!!

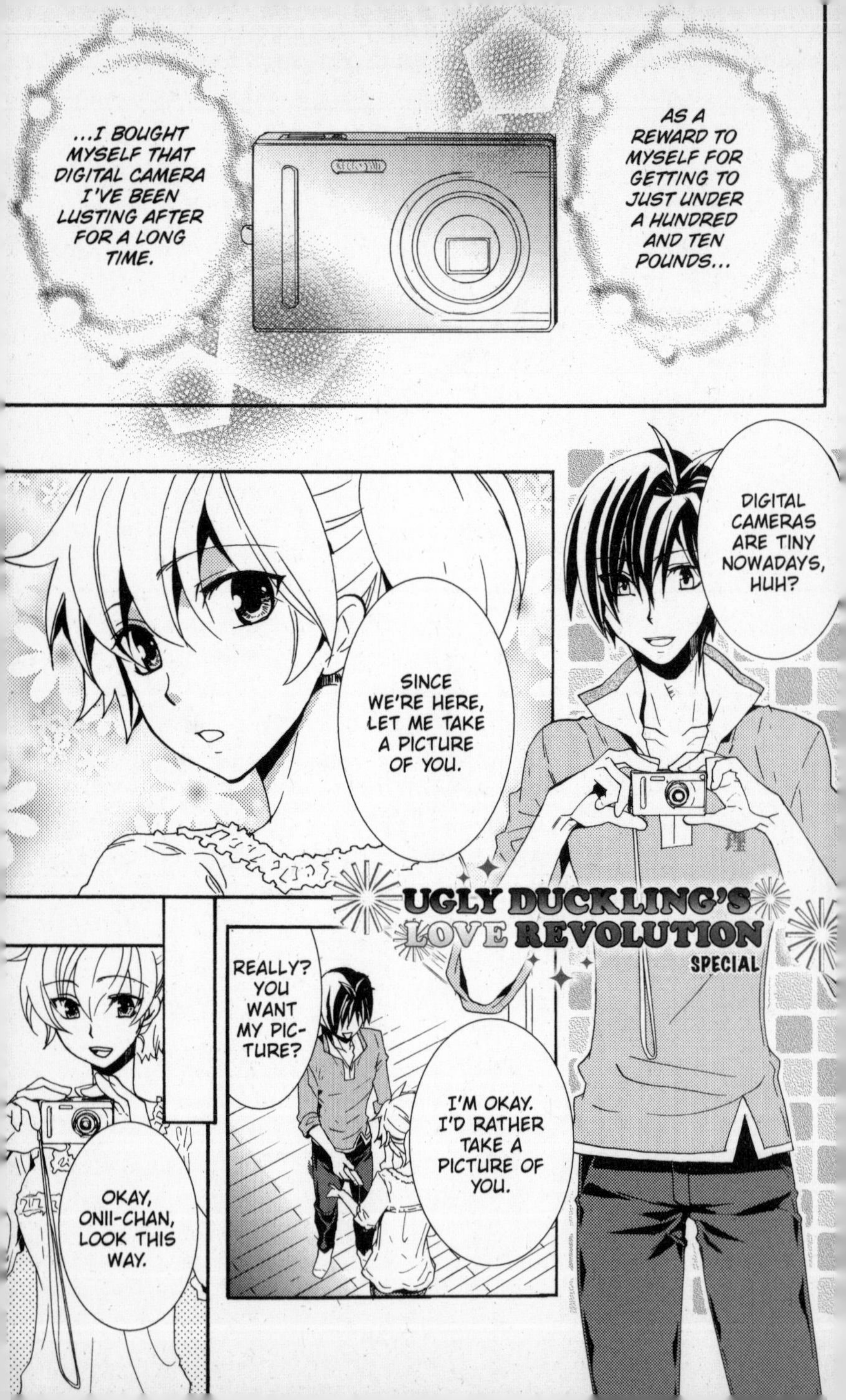
AS A REWARD TO MYSELF FOR GETTING TO JUST UNDER A HUNDRED AND TEN POUNDS...
...I BOUGHT MYSELF THAT DIGITAL CAMERA I'VE BEEN LUSTING AFTER FOR A LONG TIME.
DIGITAL CAMERAS ARE TINY NOWADAYS, HUH?
UGLY DUCKLING'S LOVE REVOLUTION
SPECIAL
SINCE WE'RE HERE, LET ME TAKE A PICTURE OF YOU.
REALLY? YOU WANT MY PIC-TURE?
I'M OKAY. I'D RATHER TAKE A PICTURE OF YOU.
OKAY, ONII-CHAN, LOOK THIS WAY.

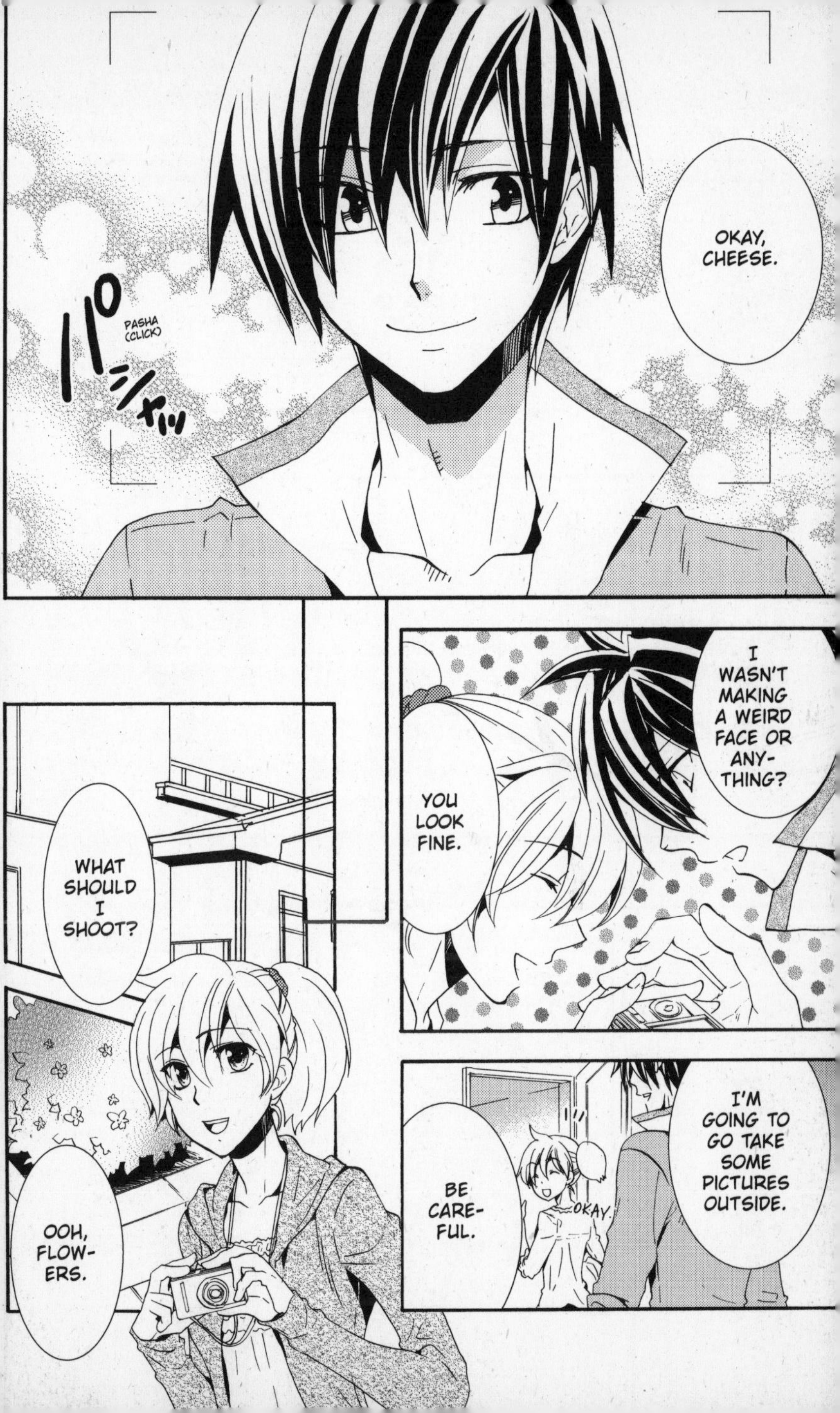
OKAY, CHEESE.
PASHA (CLICK)
I WASN'T MAKING A WEIRD FACE OR ANY-THING?
YOU LOOK FINE.
I'M GOING TO GO TAKE SOME PICTURES OUTSIDE.
OKAY.
BE CARE-FUL.
WHAT SHOULD I SHOOT?
OOH, FLOW-ERS.

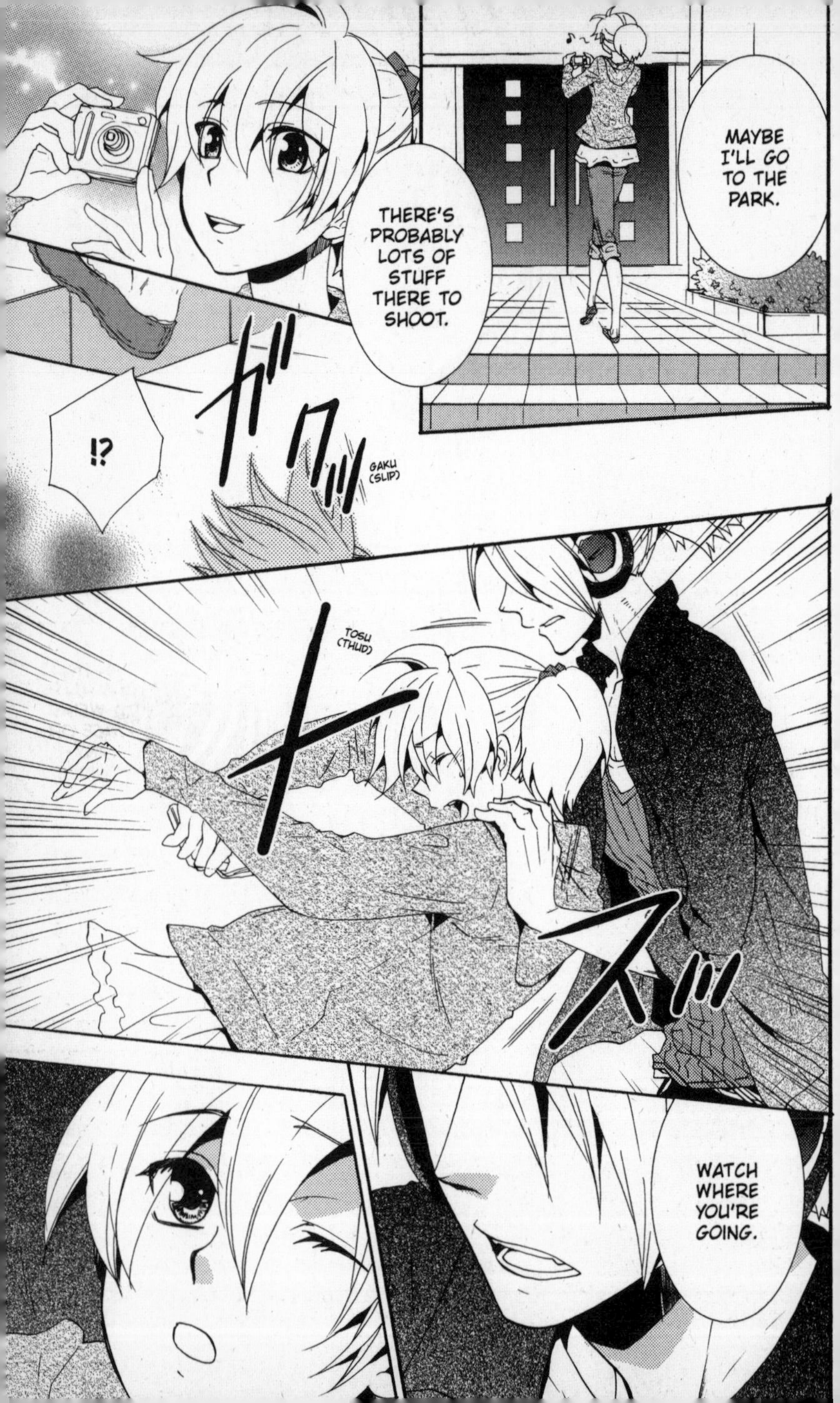
MAYBE I'LL GO TO THE PARK.
THERE'S PROBABLY LOTS OF STUFF THERE TO SHOOT.
GAKU (SLIP)
!?
TOSU (THUD)
WATCH WHERE YOU'RE GOING.

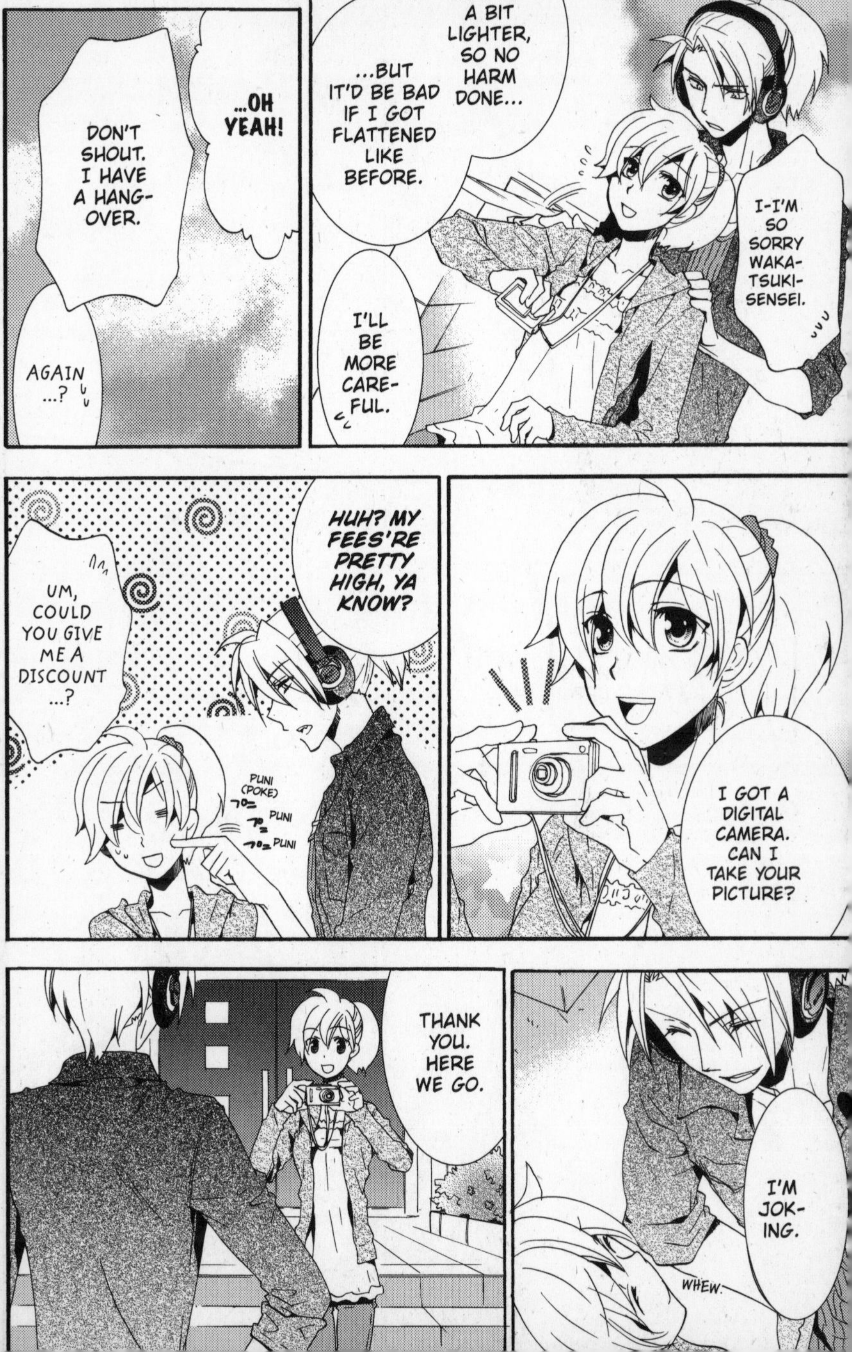
I-I'M SO SORRY WAKATSUKI-SENSEI.
YOU'RE A BIT LIGHTER, SO NO HARM DONE...
...BUT IT'D BE BAD IF I GOT FLATTENED LIKE BEFORE.
I'LL BE MORE CAREFUL.
...OH YEAH!
DON'T SHOUT. I HAVE A HANG-OVER.
AGAIN ...?
I GOT A DIGITAL CAMERA. CAN I TAKE YOUR PICTURE?
HUH? MY FEES'RE PRETTY HIGH, YA KNOW?
UM, COULD YOU GIVE ME A DISCOUNT ...?
PUNI (POKE)
PUNI
PUNI
I'M JOK-ING.
WHEW.
THANK YOU. HERE WE GO.

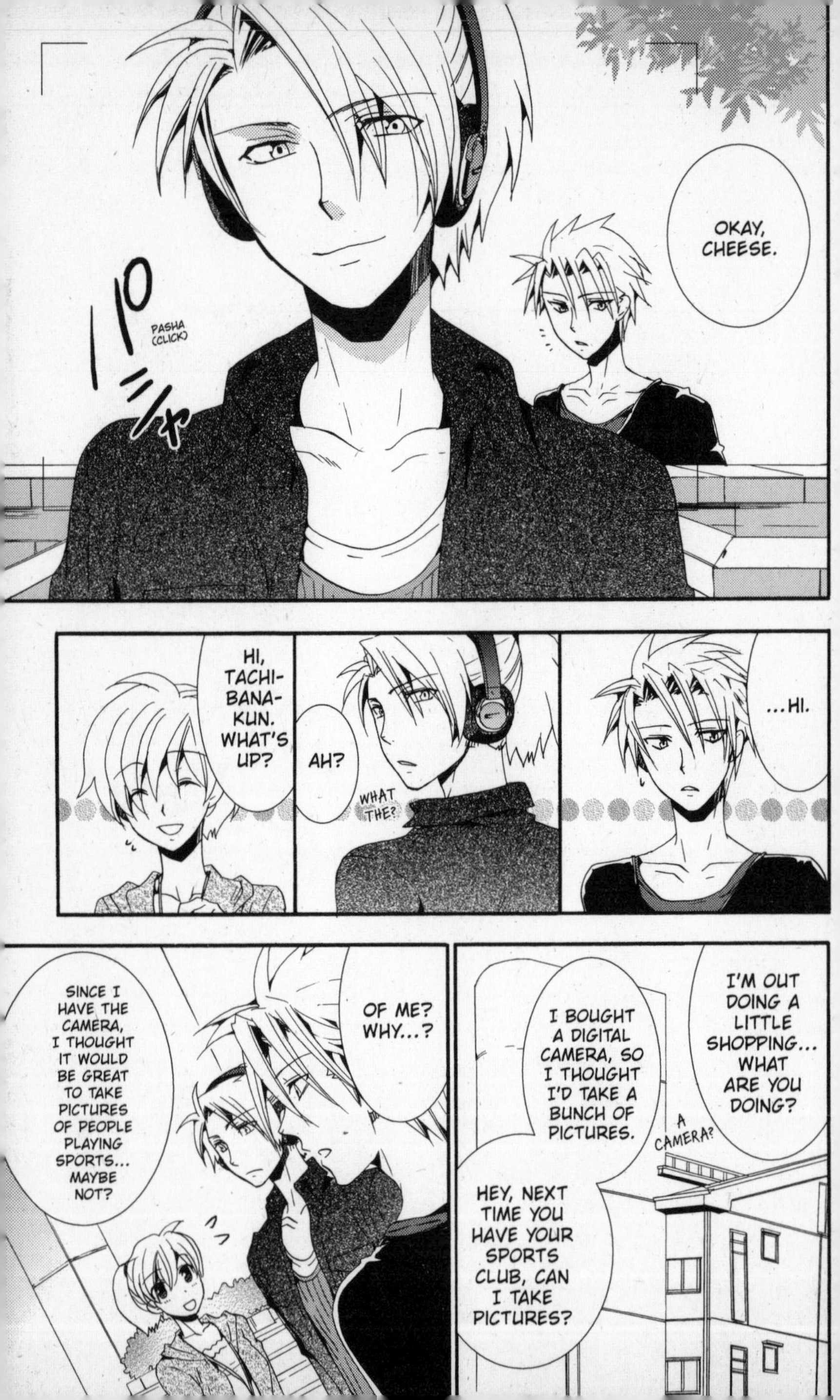
OKAY, CHEESE.
パシャ
PASHA (CLICK)
...HI.
AH?
WHAT THE?
HI, TACHIBANA-KUN. WHAT'S UP?
I'M OUT DOING A LITTLE SHOPPING... WHAT ARE YOU DOING?
A CAMERA?
I BOUGHT A DIGITAL CAMERA, SO I THOUGHT I'D TAKE A BUNCH OF PICTURES.
HEY, NEXT TIME YOU HAVE YOUR SPORTS CLUB, CAN I TAKE PICTURES?
OF ME? WHY...?
SINCE I HAVE THE CAMERA, I THOUGHT IT WOULD BE GREAT TO TAKE PICTURES OF PEOPLE PLAYING SPORTS... MAYBE NOT?

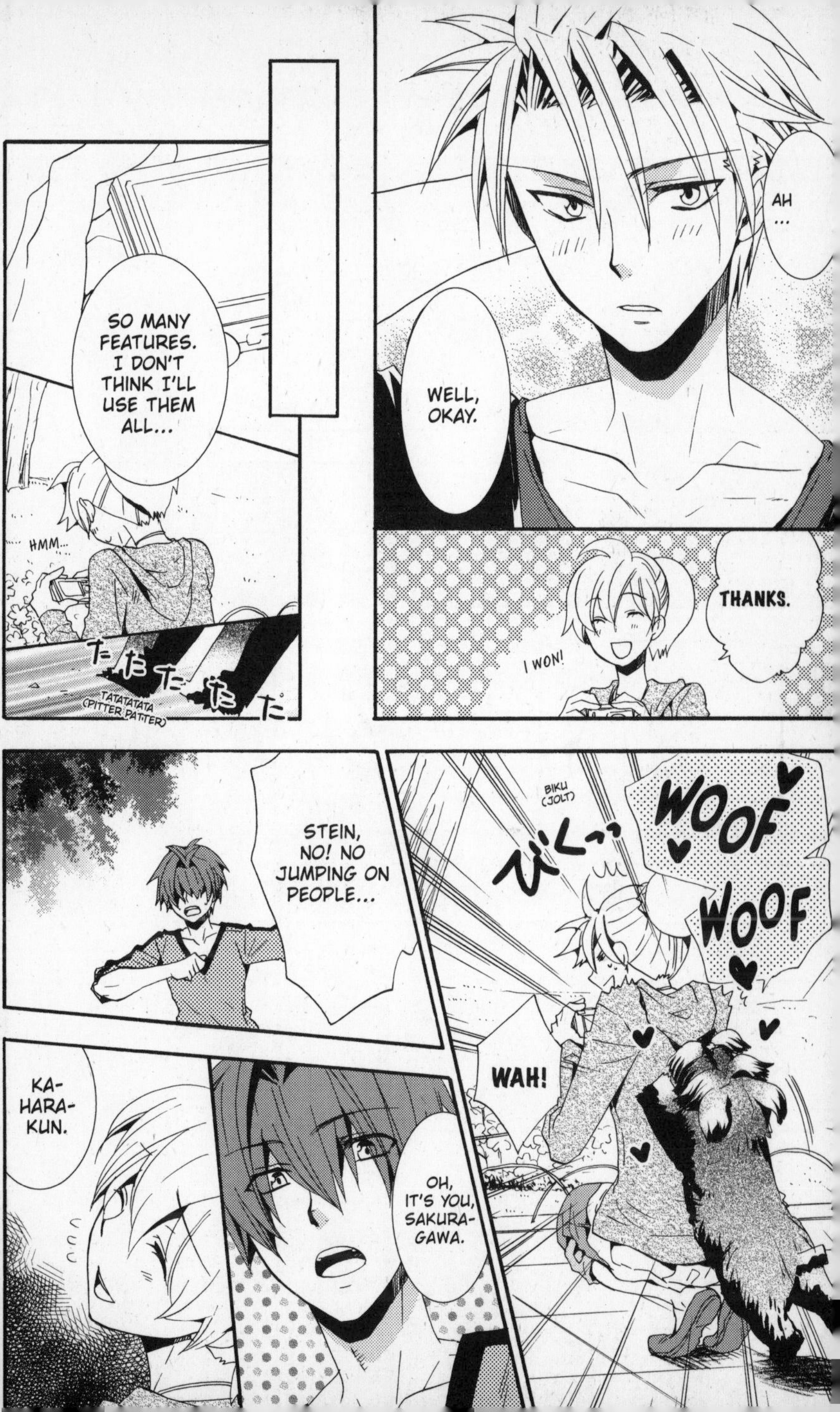
AH ...
WELL, OKAY.
THANKS.
I WON!
SO MANY FEATURES. I DON'T THINK I'LL USE THEM ALL...
...HMM...
たたたたた
TATATATATA (PITTER PATTER)
びくっ
BIKU (JOLT)
WOOF WOOF
WAH!
STEIN, NO! NO JUMPING ON PEOPLE...
KA-HARA-KUN.
OH, IT'S YOU, SAKURA-GAWA.

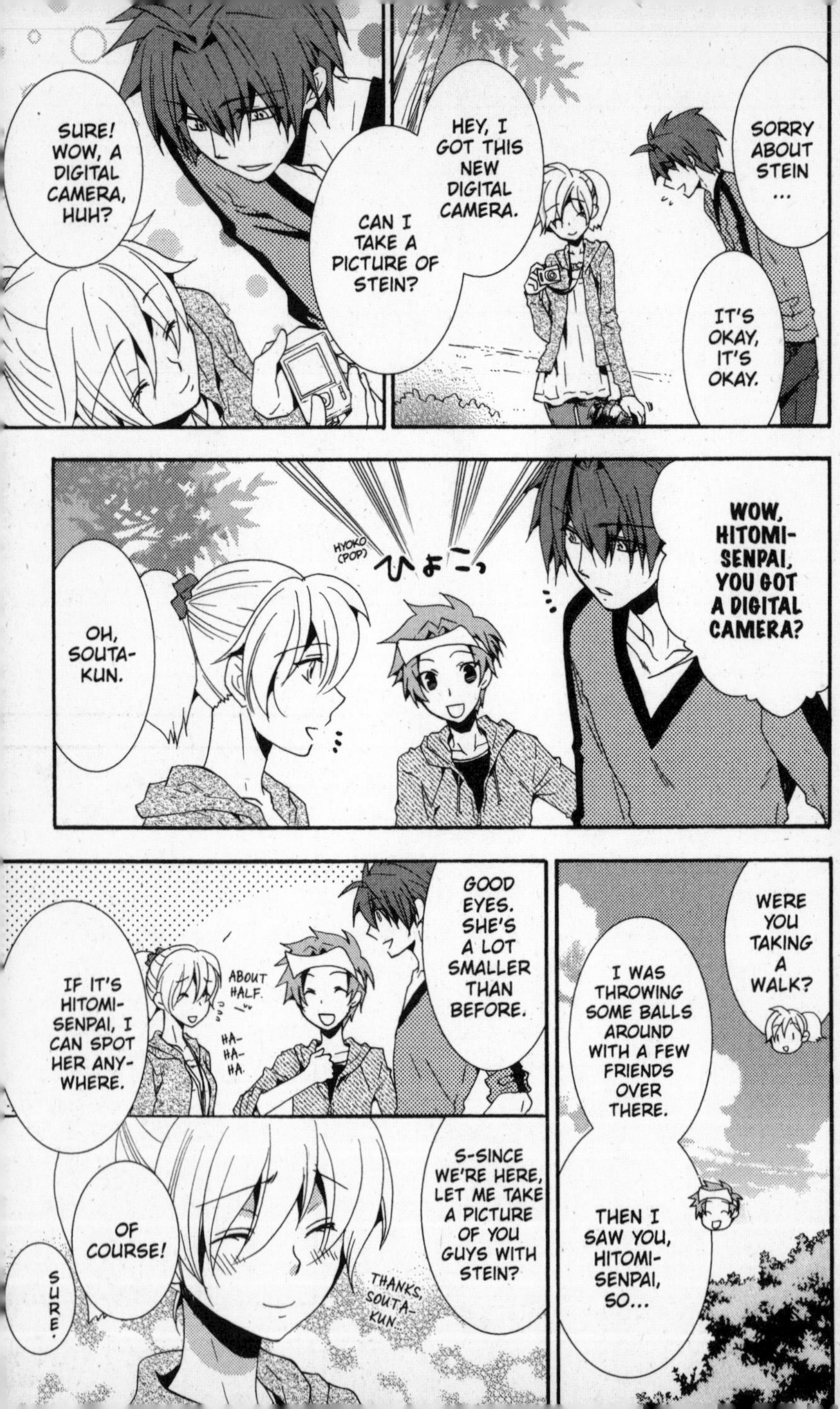
SORRY ABOUT STEIN ...
IT'S OKAY, IT'S OKAY.
HEY, I GOT THIS NEW DIGITAL CAMERA.
CAN I TAKE A PICTURE OF STEIN?
SURE! WOW, A DIGITAL CAMERA, HUH?
WOW, HITOMI-SENPAI, YOU GOT A DIGITAL CAMERA?
HYOKO (POP)
ひょこっ
OH, SOUTA-KUN.
WERE YOU TAKING A WALK?
I WAS THROWING SOME BALLS AROUND WITH A FEW FRIENDS OVER THERE.
THEN I SAW YOU, HITOMI-SENPAI, SO...
GOOD EYES. SHE'S A LOT SMALLER THAN BEFORE.
ABOUT HALF.
HA-HA-HA.
IF IT'S HITOMI-SENPAI, I CAN SPOT HER ANYWHERE.
S-SINCE WE'RE HERE, LET ME TAKE A PICTURE OF YOU GUYS WITH STEIN?
THANKS, SOUTA-KUN.
OF COURSE!
SURE.

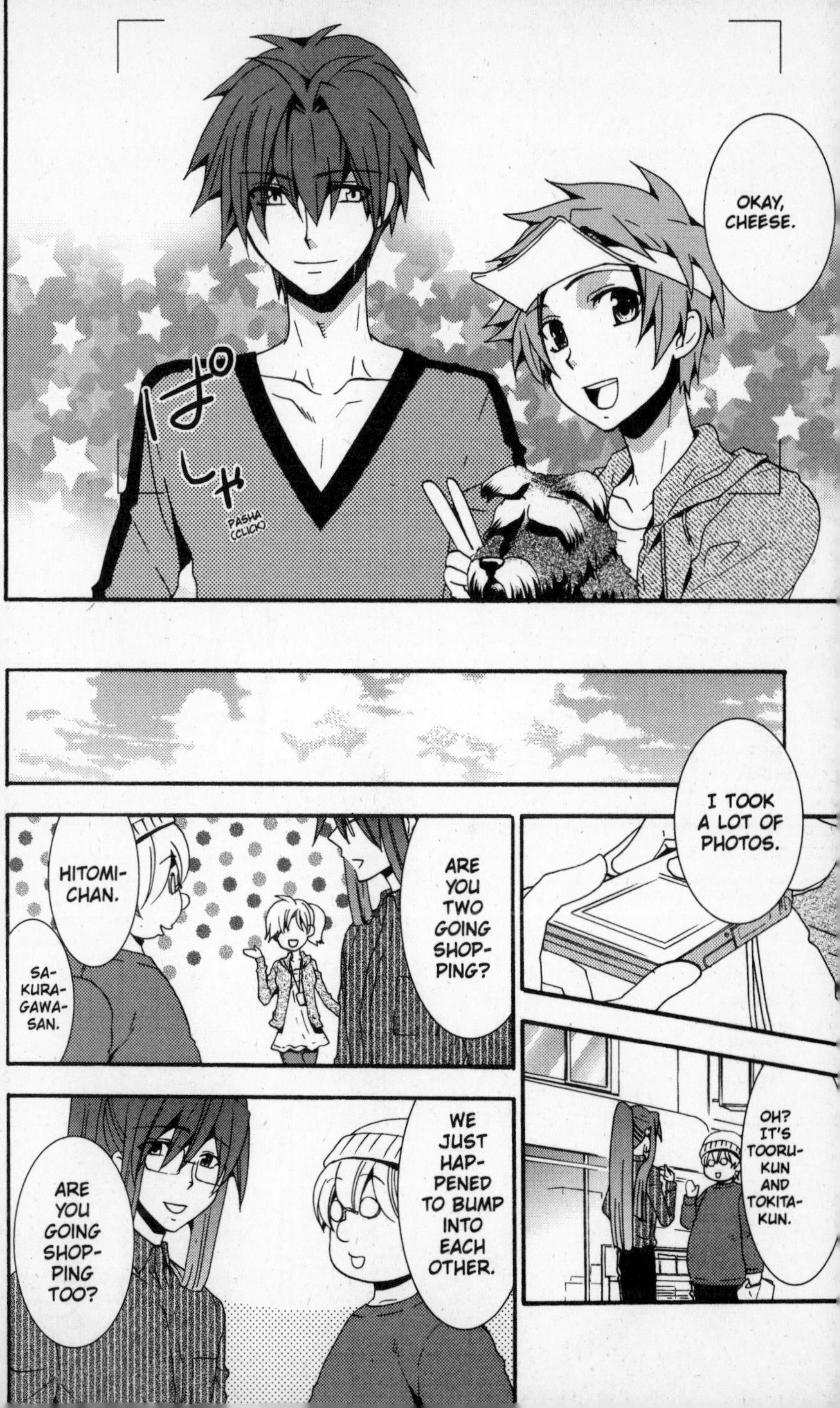

OKAY, CHEESE.
ぱしゃ
PASHA (CLICK)
I TOOK A LOT OF PHOTOS.
ARE YOU TWO GOING SHOP-PING?
HITOMI-CHAN.
SA-KURA-GAWA-SAN.
OH? IT'S TOORU-KUN AND TOKITA-KUN.
WE JUST HAP-PENED TO BUMP INTO EACH OTHER.
ARE YOU GOING SHOP-PING TOO?

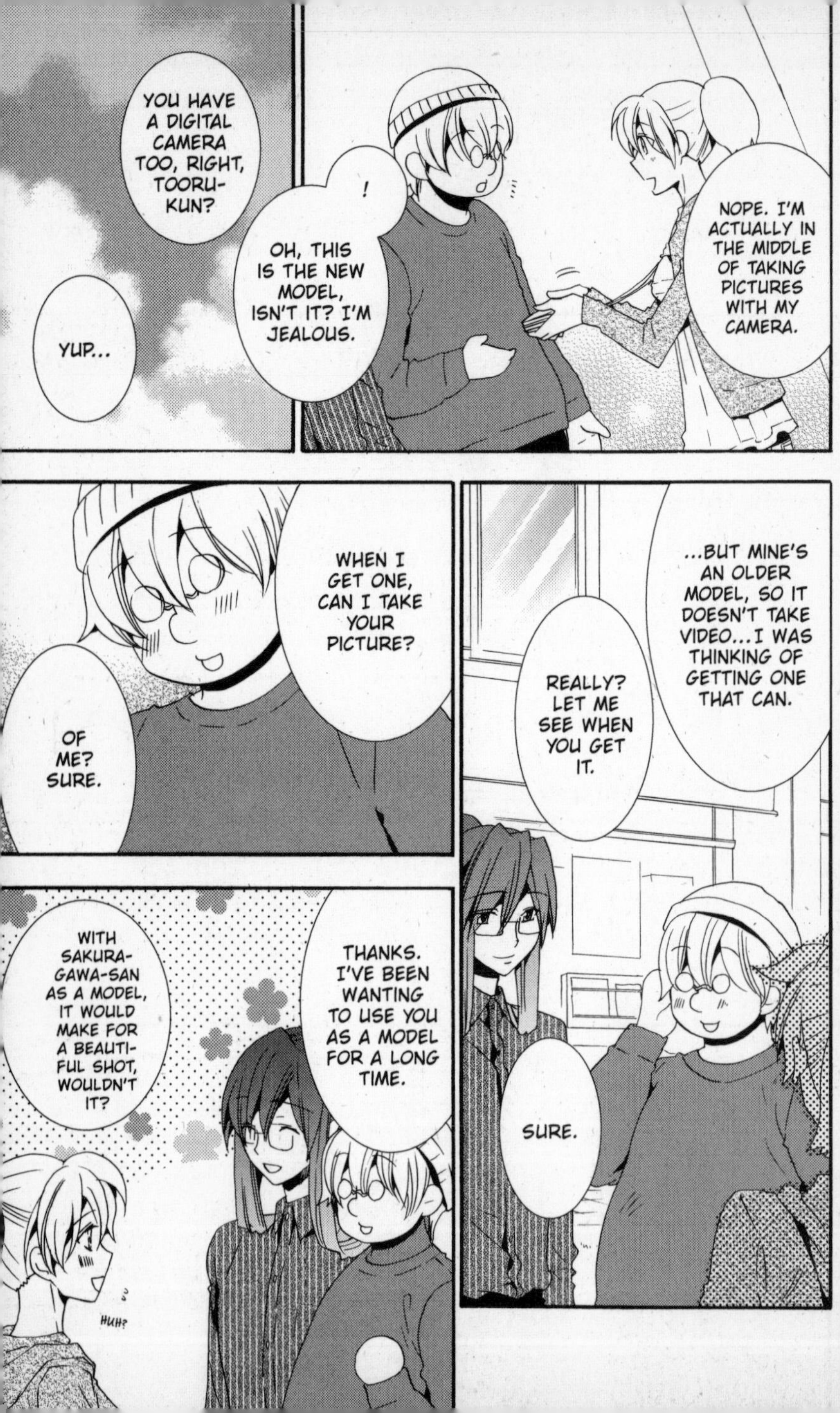
NOPE. I'M ACTUALLY IN THE MIDDLE OF TAKING PICTURES WITH MY CAMERA.
!
OH, THIS IS THE NEW MODEL, ISN'T IT? I'M JEALOUS.
YOU HAVE A DIGITAL CAMERA TOO, RIGHT, TOORU-KUN?
YUP...
...BUT MINE'S AN OLDER MODEL, SO IT DOESN'T TAKE VIDEO...I WAS THINKING OF GETTING ONE THAT CAN.
REALLY? LET ME SEE WHEN YOU GET IT.
SURE.
WHEN I GET ONE, CAN I TAKE YOUR PICTURE?
OF ME? SURE.
THANKS. I'VE BEEN WANTING TO USE YOU AS A MODEL FOR A LONG TIME.
WITH SAKURA-GAWA-SAN AS A MODEL, IT WOULD MAKE FOR A BEAUTI-FUL SHOT, WOULDN'T IT?
HUH?

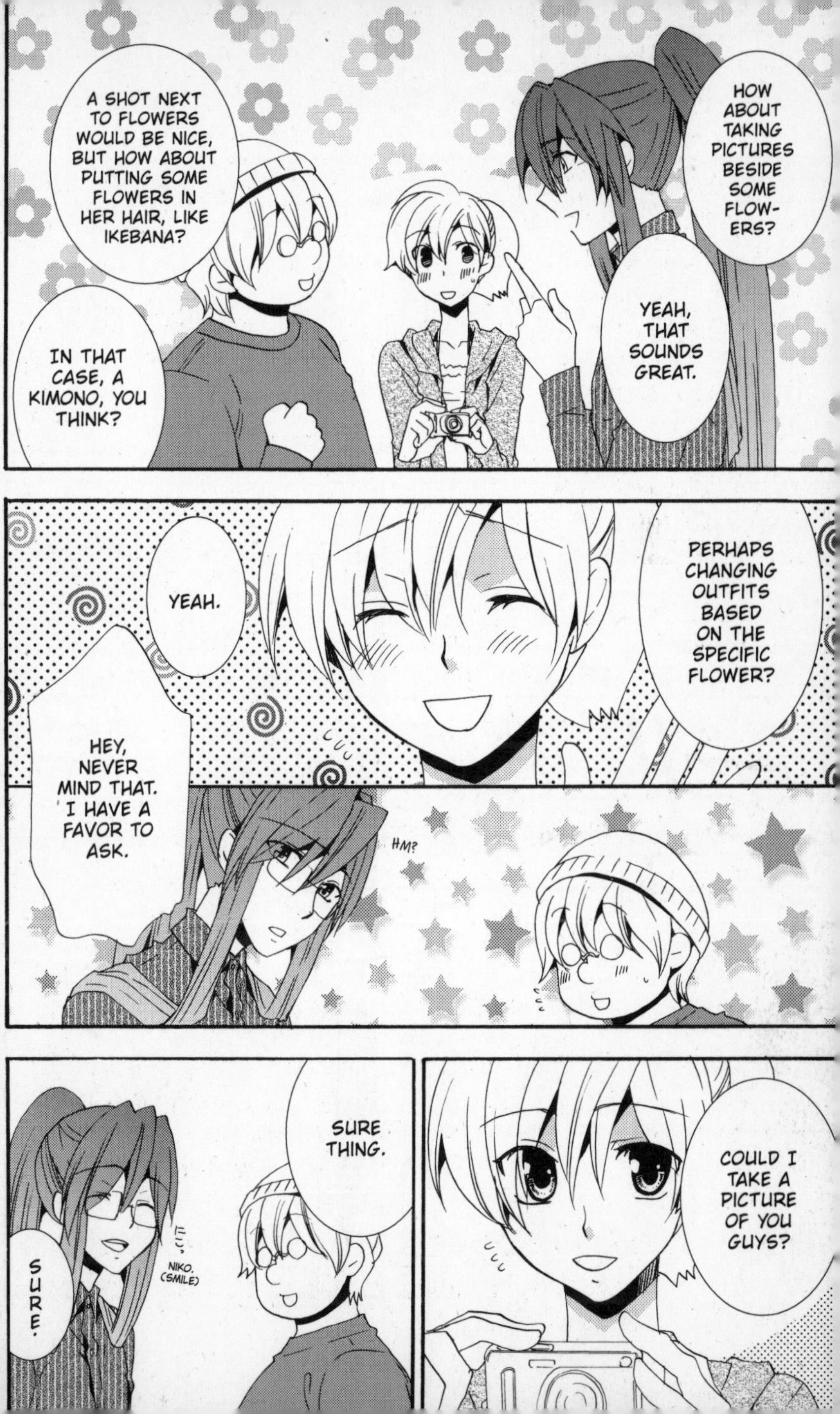
HOW ABOUT TAKING PICTURES BESIDE SOME FLOW-ERS?
YEAH, THAT SOUNDS GREAT.
A SHOT NEXT TO FLOWERS WOULD BE NICE, BUT HOW ABOUT PUTTING SOME FLOWERS IN HER HAIR, LIKE IKEBANA?
IN THAT CASE, A KIMONO, YOU THINK?
PERHAPS CHANGING OUTFITS BASED ON THE SPECIFIC FLOWER?
YEAH.
HEY, NEVER MIND THAT. I HAVE A FAVOR TO ASK.
HM?
COULD I TAKE A PICTURE OF YOU GUYS?
SURE THING.
NIKO. (SMILE)
SURE.

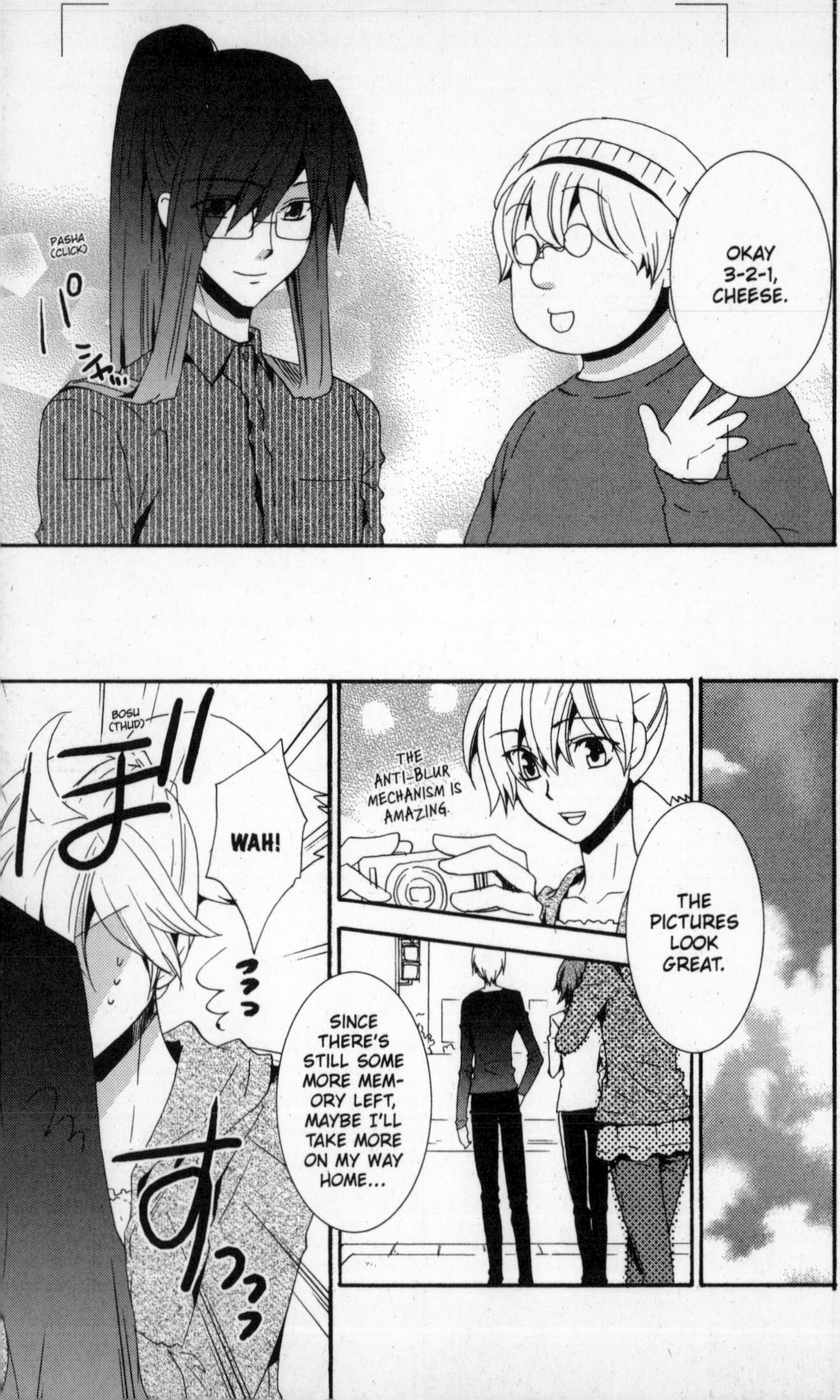
OKAY 3-2-1, CHEESE.
PASHA (CLICK)
THE PICTURES LOOK GREAT.
THE ANTI-BLUR MECHANISM IS AMAZING.
SINCE THERE'S STILL SOME MORE MEMORY LEFT, MAYBE I'LL TAKE MORE ON MY WAY HOME...
BOSU (THUD)
WAH!

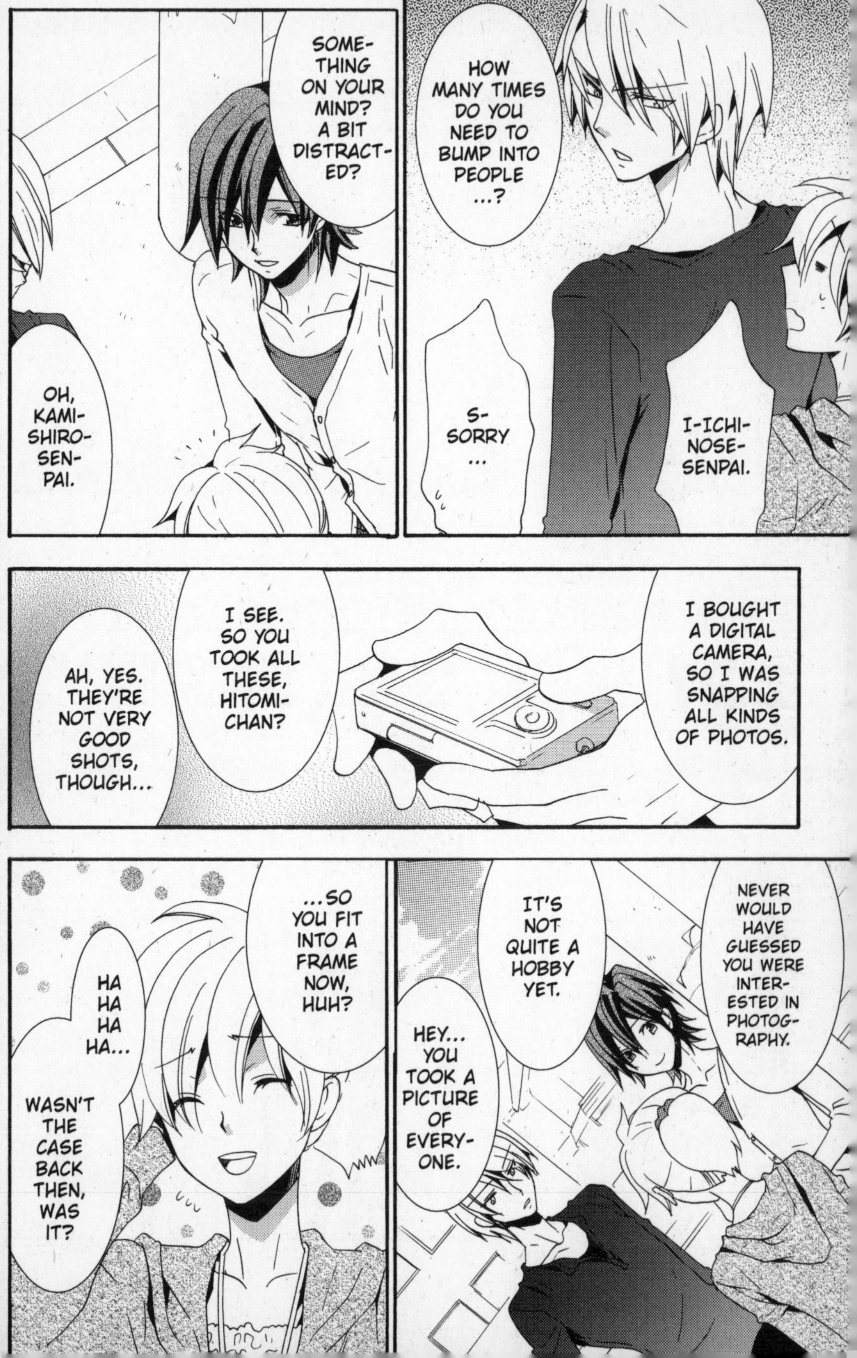
HOW MANY TIMES DO YOU NEED TO BUMP INTO PEOPLE ...?
I-ICHINOSE-SENPAI.
S-SORRY ...
SOMETHING ON YOUR MIND? A BIT DISTRACTED?
OH, KAMISHIRO-SENPAI.
I BOUGHT A DIGITAL CAMERA, SO I WAS SNAPPING ALL KINDS OF PHOTOS.
I SEE. SO YOU TOOK ALL THESE, HITOMI-CHAN?
AH, YES. THEY'RE NOT VERY GOOD SHOTS, THOUGH...
NEVER WOULD HAVE GUESSED YOU WERE INTERESTED IN PHOTOGRAPHY.
IT'S NOT QUITE A HOBBY YET.
HEY... YOU TOOK A PICTURE OF EVERYONE.
...SO YOU FIT INTO A FRAME NOW, HUH?
HA HA HA HA...
WASN'T THE CASE BACK THEN, WAS IT?

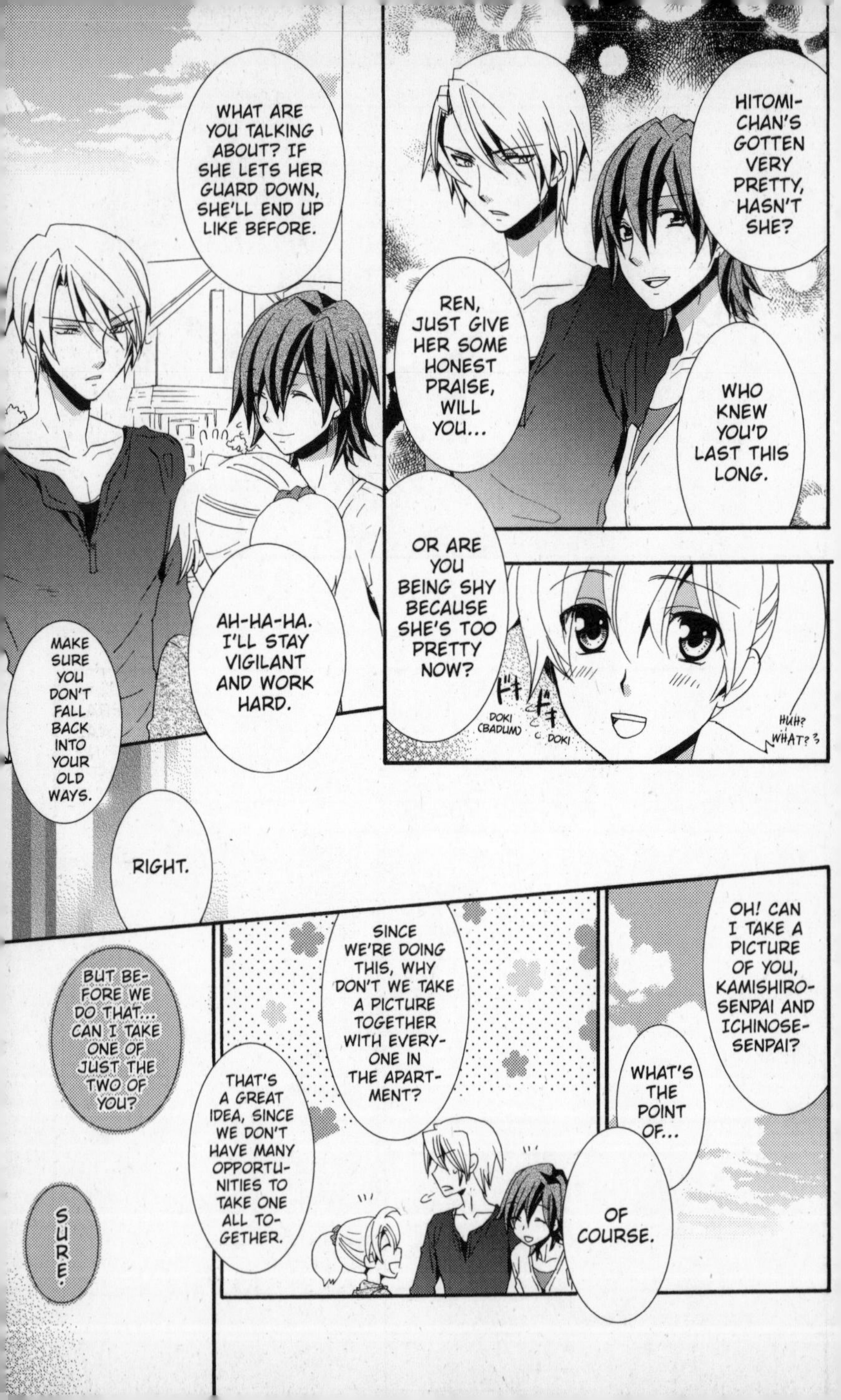
HITOMI-CHAN'S GOTTEN VERY PRETTY, HASN'T SHE?
WHO KNEW YOU'D LAST THIS LONG.
REN, JUST GIVE HER SOME HONEST PRAISE, WILL YOU...
OR ARE YOU BEING SHY BECAUSE SHE'S TOO PRETTY NOW?
ドキ DOKI (BADUM)
ドキ DOKI
HUH? WHAT??
WHAT ARE YOU TALKING ABOUT? IF SHE LETS HER GUARD DOWN, SHE'LL END UP LIKE BEFORE.
AH-HA-HA. I'LL STAY VIGILANT AND WORK HARD.
MAKE SURE YOU DON'T FALL BACK INTO YOUR OLD WAYS.
RIGHT.
OH! CAN I TAKE A PICTURE OF YOU, KAMISHIRO-SENPAI AND ICHINOSE-SENPAI?
WHAT'S THE POINT OF...
OF COURSE.
SINCE WE'RE DOING THIS, WHY DON'T WE TAKE A PICTURE TOGETHER WITH EVERYONE IN THE APARTMENT?
THAT'S A GREAT IDEA, SINCE WE DON'T HAVE MANY OPPORTUNITIES TO TAKE ONE ALL TOGETHER.
BUT BEFORE WE DO THAT... CAN I TAKE ONE OF JUST THE TWO OF YOU?
SURE.

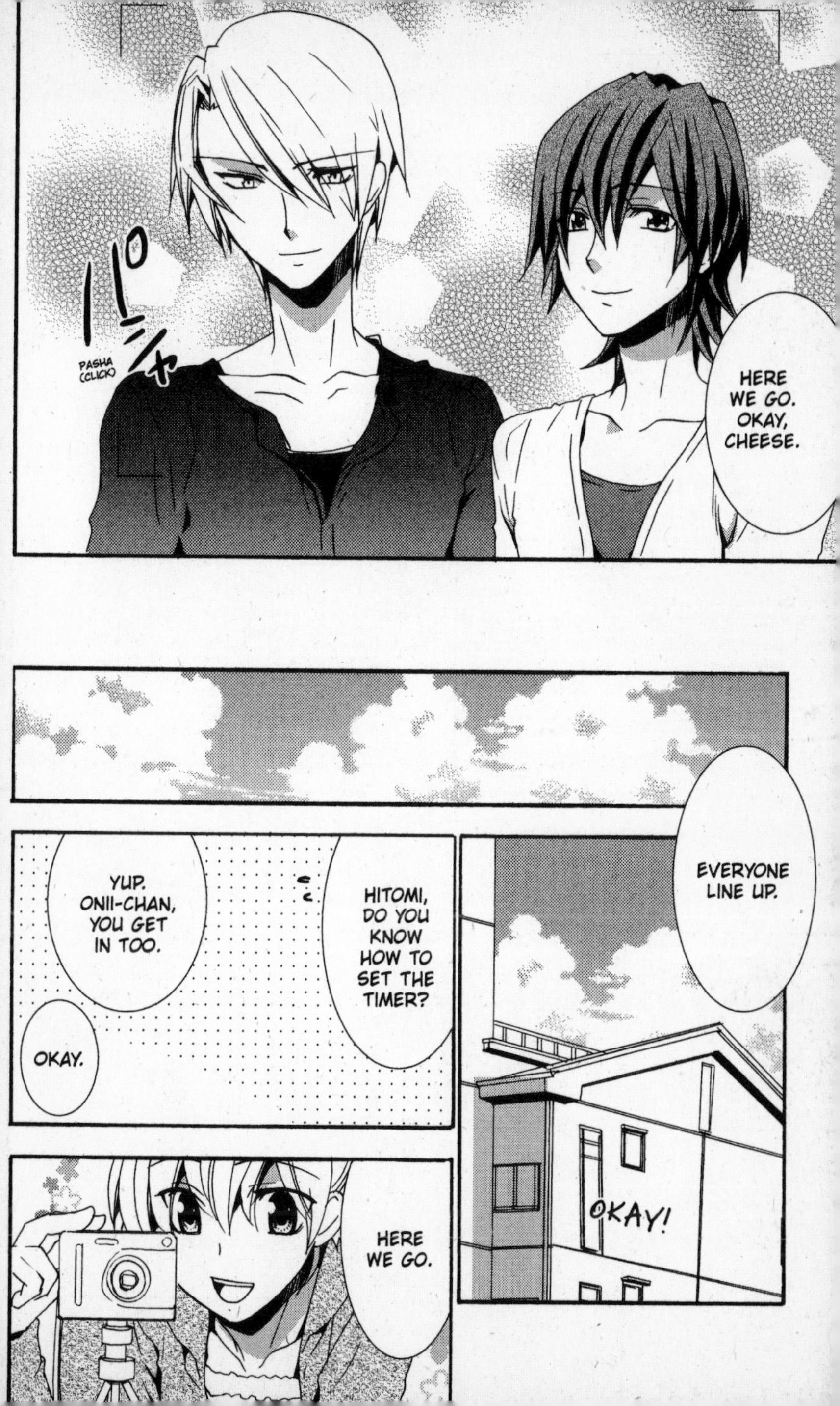
HERE WE GO. OKAY, CHEESE.
パシャ
PASHA (CLICK)
EVERYONE LINE UP.
OKAY!
HITOMI, DO YOU KNOW HOW TO SET THE TIMER?
YUP. ONII-CHAN, YOU GET IN TOO.
OKAY.
HERE WE GO.

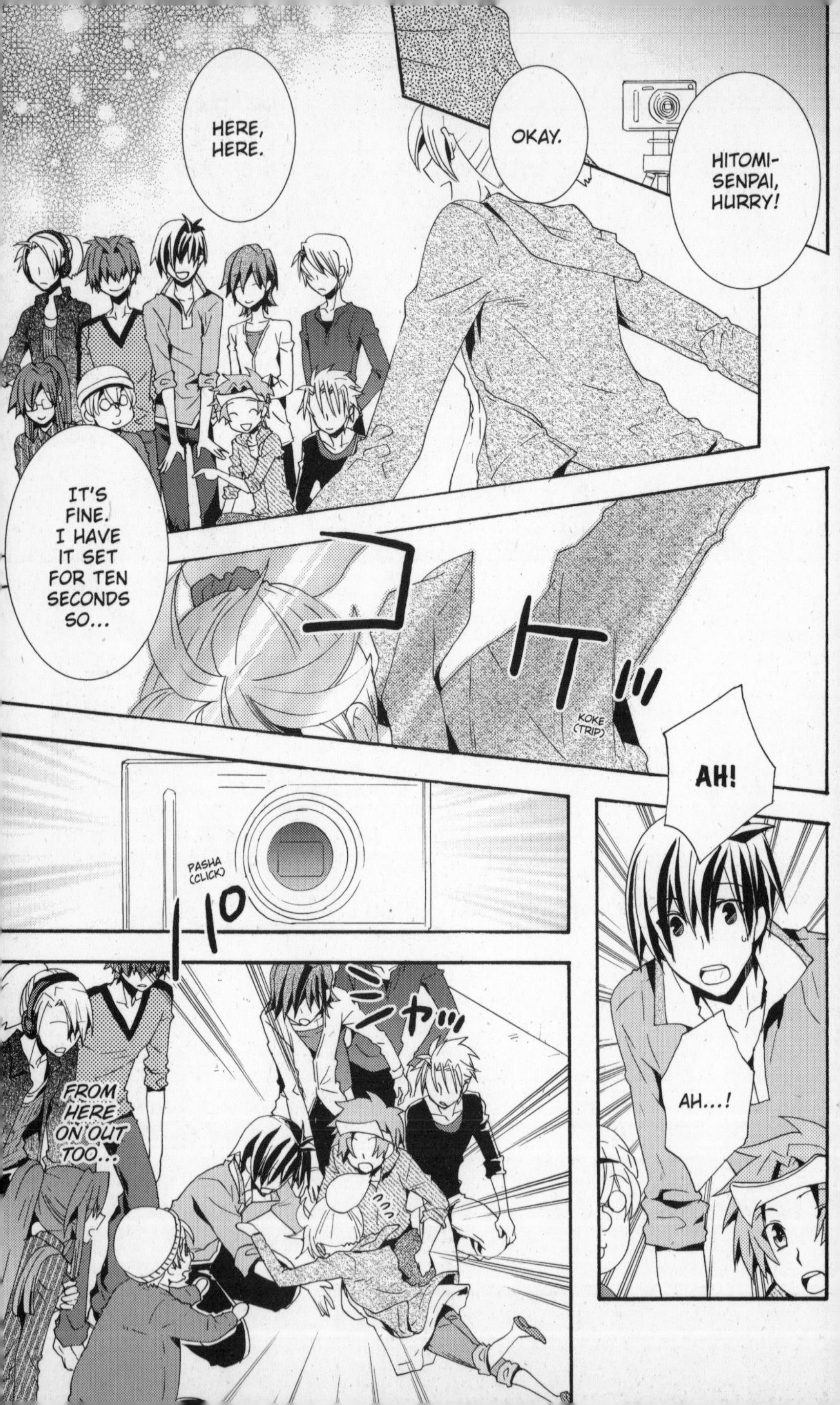
HITOMI-SENPAI, HURRY!
OKAY.
HERE, HERE.
IT'S FINE. I HAVE IT SET FOR TEN SECONDS SO...
KOKE (TRIP)
AH!
AH...!
PASHA (CLICK)
FROM HERE ON OUT TOO...

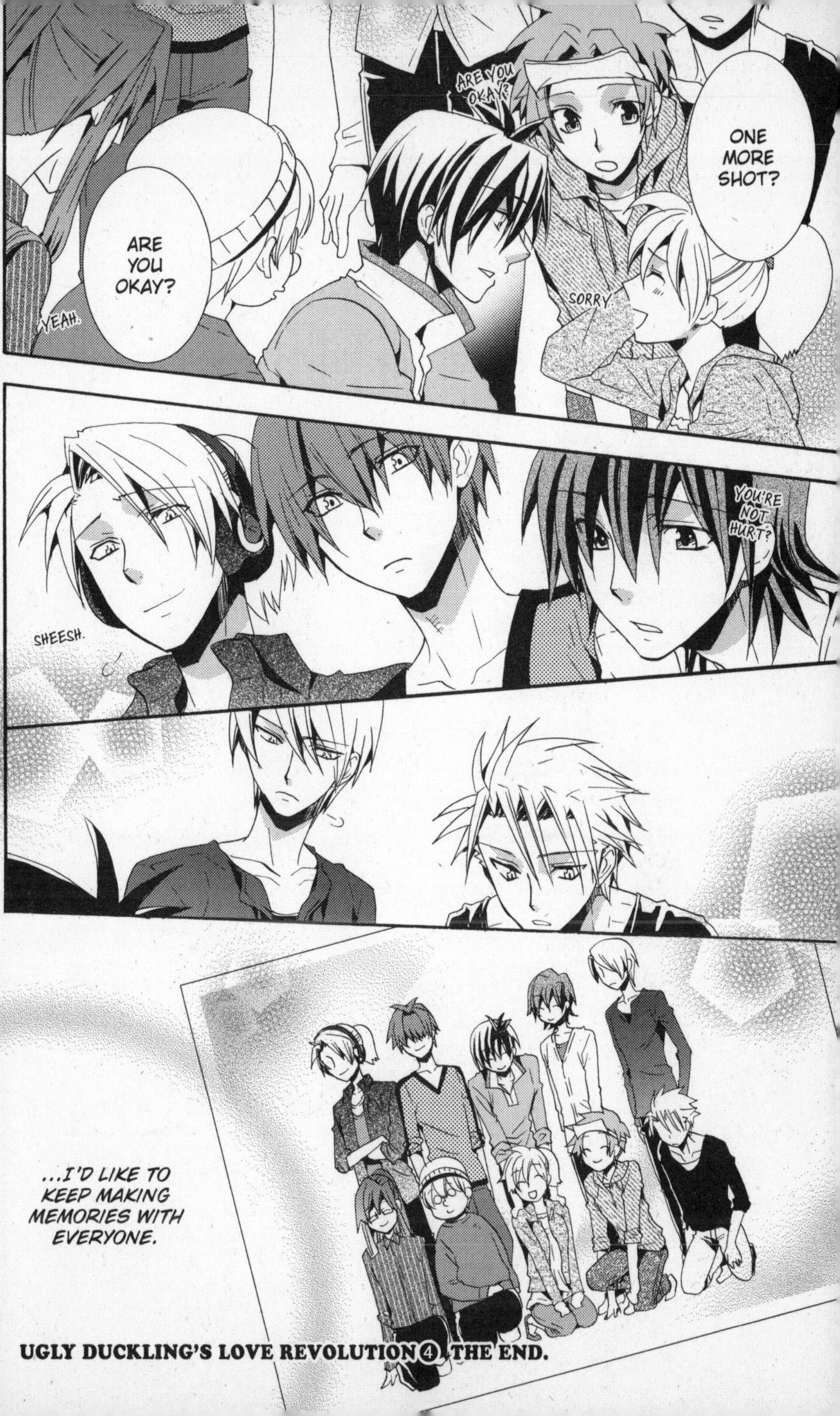
ONE MORE SHOT?
ARE YOU OKAY?
SORRY.
ARE YOU OKAY?
YEAH.
YOU'RE NOT HURT?
SHEESH.
...I'D LIKE TO KEEP MAKING MEMORIES WITH EVERYONE.
UGLY DUCKLING'S LOVE REVOLUTION 4 THE END.

AFTERWORD

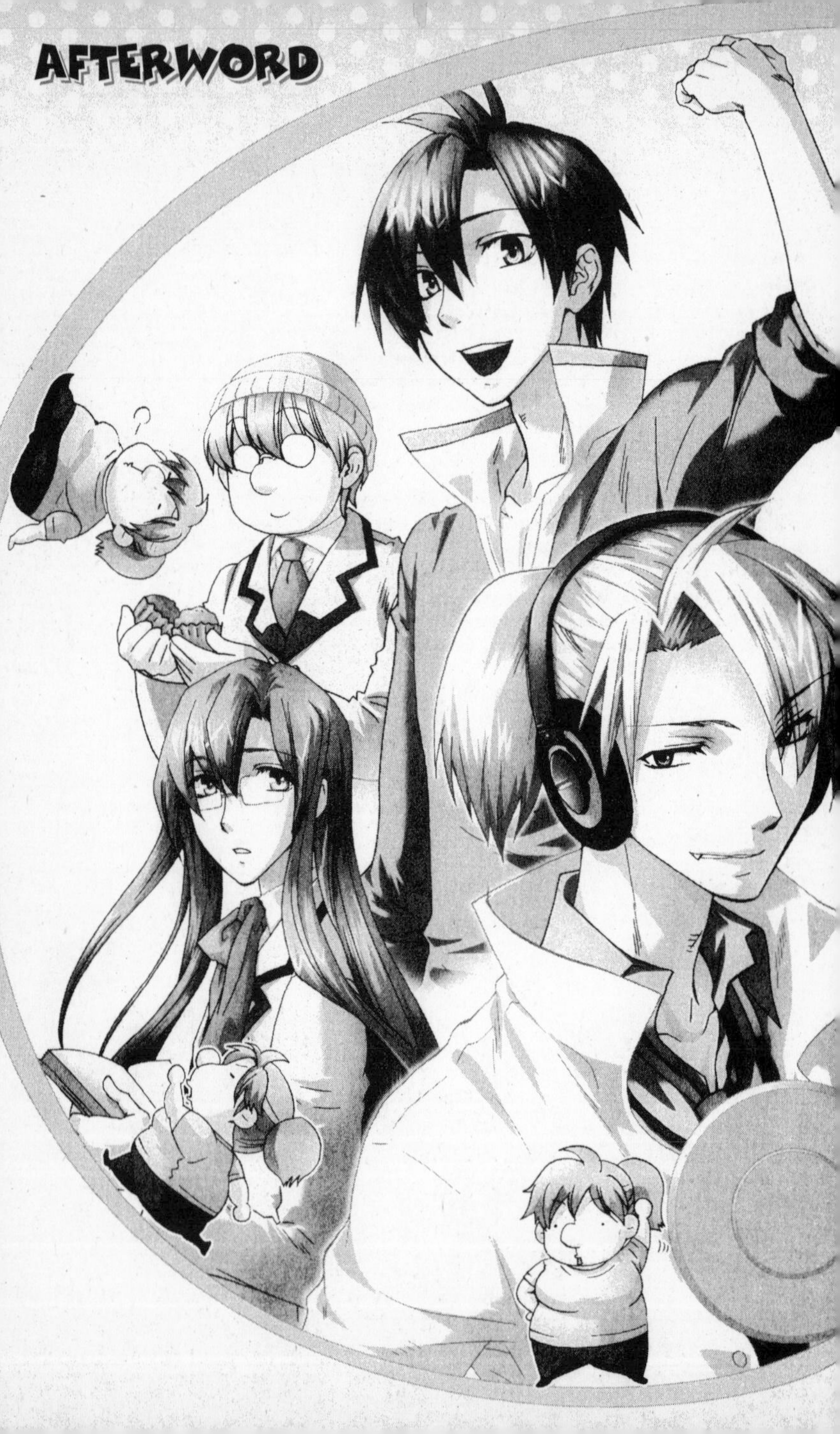

◆ Fujinari here with this final volume. I mentioned it before too, but time really did pass in a flash. I am deeply appreciative of these two and a half years.

◆ This was originally just supposed to be a three-part story, but luckily I have been able to continue the series for two and a half years. Only when I received word that the series was going to be extended did I realize the power of "LoveRevo!!" It has been a privilege to be part of this title.

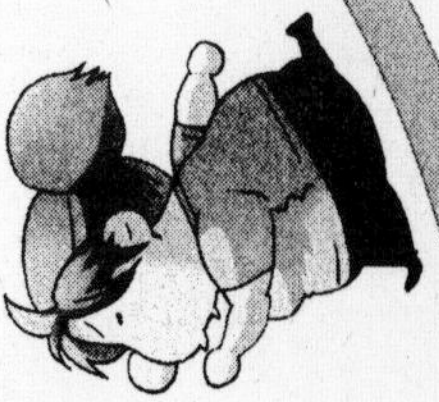

◆ I got into playing this game, and at first it was pretty hard, and I couldn't get anyone to lose weight. But once someone taught me some pointers, things went smoothly. There's a certain satisfaction when Hitomi-chan gradually loses weight, isn't there? Hitomi-chan's movements when she's exercising are so cute, I love it. I like the thin Hitomi-chan, but I might prefer the Hitomi-chan when she was less so because she is so cute. I had a lot of fun drawing her throughout.

◆ Speaking of Hitomi-chan, thank you for all the requests to see the thin Hitomi-chan! During the magazine serialization, I did not draw her this way even though I wanted to, so I'm glad I got the chance.

◆ I was only able to get this far with the help of many friends: the game developer, my editor, my friend S, and last but not least, my fantastic fans. Thank you so very much!

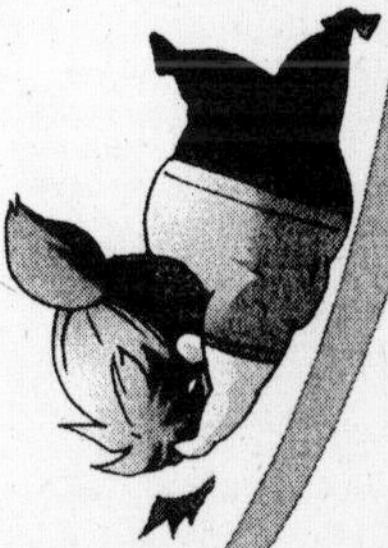

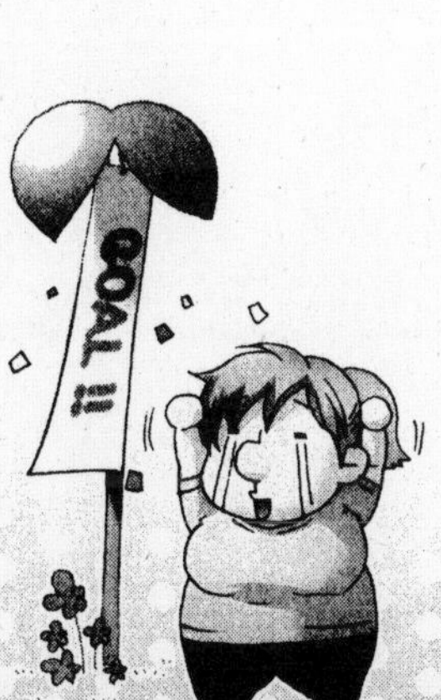
GOAL!!

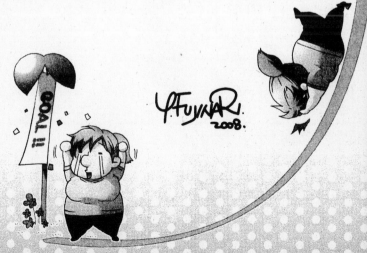

Y. FUJINARI. 2008.

TRANSLATION NOTES

Common Honorifics

No honorific: Indicates familiarity or closeness; if used without permission or reason, addressing someone in this manner would constitute an insult.

-san: The Japanese equivalent of Mr./Mrs./Miss. If a situation calls for politeness, this is the fail-safe honorific.

-sama: Conveys great respect; may also indicate that the social status of the speaker is lower than that of the addressee.

-kun: Used most often when referring to boys, this indicates affection or familiarity. Occasionally used by older men among their peers, but it may also be used by anyone referring to a person of lower standing.

-chan: An affectionate honorific indicating familiarity used mostly in reference to girls; also used in reference to cute persons or animals of either gender.

-senpai: A term used to address a more experienced coworker or upperclassman.

-sensei: A respectful term for teachers, artists, or high-level professionals.

THE GAME

Ugly Duckling's Love Revolution (*Otometeki Koi Kakumei Love Revo!!*)

Love Revo is a single-player dating sim game. The story takes place over a school year, during which the player decides on a variety of actions (each with a given "star" value) to take over the course of a one to three day block (diet, eat, study, go out, etc). Balancing eating (reduces stress levels) and dieting (increases stress levels) is the key to playing a successful game. There are several endings to this game: gaining love, gaining friendship, and/or dieting successfully or unsuccessfully (with different combinations among these endings).

PAGE 12 - *Shochuu*

Japanese liquor similar to vodka.

PAGE 34 - The Perseid Meteor Shower

A meteor shower that appears to fall from a point in the constellation Perseus.

PAGE 108 - *Kenzan*

Flower arranging tool that consists of many flower pins (usually made of metal) standing upright on a base. When flower stems are placed onto the pins, it allows the stalks to stand upright in a display bowl/dish and helps the plant get a regular flow of water. Also called needle point holders or metal frogs.

PAGE 132 - *Otaku*

Term used for hard-core enthusiasts of a particular subject. Here it refers to an interest in the anime *Ninnin-kun* (ninja boy).

PAGE 142 - *Kanpai*

Used as a toast at a celebration: "Cheers!"

Yakiniku

A grilled meat dish, often cooked right on the table at a restaurant.

PAGE 143 - *Mozuku*

Okinawan seaweed often eaten with a vinegar dip.

PAGE 160 - *Ikebana*

An minimalistic, artistic form of flower arranging that focuses on the careful appreciation of natural forms and the methods of arranging the plants.

Can't wait for the next volume? You don't have to!

Keep up with the latest chapters of some of your favorite manga every month online in the pages of **YEN PLUS**!

Visit us at www.yenplus.com for details!

THE BLOG THAT STARTED IT ALL...

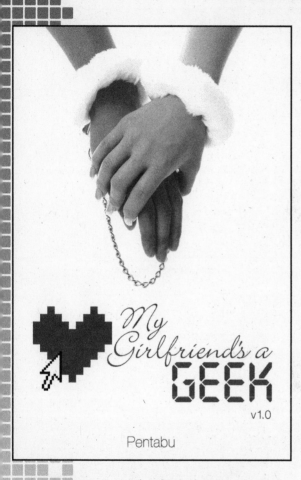

This blog is a record of battle as dictated by a man with a fujoshi girlfriend.

Okay, that was a lie. I'm not fighting at all.

The war is purely one-sided. Each day I am dragged farther and farther into the world of otaku.

I cannot be held responsible for any damages incurred by reading this blog and falling into the same predicament.

There is much otaku talk contained within, so please follow your directions carefully and do not exceed your recommended dosage.

NOW AVAILABLE FROM YEN PRESS!

Kieli sees ghosts.
Harvey cannot die.
He will throw
her world into
chaos...
...and become her
one true friend.

STORY BY **Yukako Kabei**
ART BY **Shiori Teshirogi**

KIELI

THE JOURNEY CONTINUES IN THE MANGA ADAPTATION OF THE HIT NOVEL SERIES
AVAILABLE NOW
SPICE & WOLF
MATURE M
Yen Press
Spice and Wolf © Isuna Hasekura/Keito Koume/ASCII MEDIA WORKS

ENJOY EVERYTHING.

YOU SHOULD COME PLAY WITH YOTSUBA TOO!

Join Yotsuba as she delights in the
things many of us take for granted in
this Eisner-nominated series.

VOLUMES 1-9
AVAILABLE NOW!

Hello! This is YOTSUBA!

Guess what? Guess what? Yotsuba and Daddy just moved here from waaaay over there!

And Yotsuba met these nice people next door and made new friends to play with!

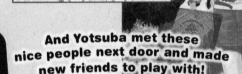

The pretty one took Yotsuba on a bike ride!
(Whoooa! There was a big hill!)

And Ena's a good drawer!
(Almost as good as Yotsuba!)

And their mom always gives Yotsuba ice cream!
(Yummy!)

And...
And...
OHHHH!

UGLY DUCKLING'S
LOVE REVOLUTION ❹

. . . .

YUUKI FUJINARI
GungHo Online Entertainment, Inc.

Translation: Kaori Inoue • Lettering: Lys Blakeslee

. . . .

Otometekikoikakumei★Loverevo!! Vol. 4 © 2008 Yuuki Fujinari © 2006, 2008
GungHo Online Entertainment, Inc. / Will. All rights reserved. First published in
Japan in 2008 by ENTERBRAIN, INC., Tokyo. English translation rights arranged
with ENTERBRAIN, INC. through Tuttle-Mori Agency, Inc., Tokyo.

Translation © 2011 by Hachette Book Group, Inc.

Yen Press
Hachette Book Group
237 Park Avenue, New York, NY 10017

www.HachetteBookGroup.com
www.YenPress.com

Yen Press is an imprint of Hachette Book Group, Inc. The Yen Press name and logo
are trademarks of Hachette Book Group, Inc.

First Yen Press Edition: August 2011

ISBN: 978-0-316-18759-6

10 9 8 7 6 5 4 3 2 1

BVG

Printed in the United States of America